DOMUS UNIVERSITATIS 1650

VERÖFFENTLICHUNGEN
DES INSTITUTS FÜR EUROPÄISCHE GESCHICHTE MAINZ
BAND 128
ABTEILUNG UNIVERSALGESCHICHTE
HERAUSGEGEBEN VON KARL OTMAR FREIHERR VON ARETIN

FRANZ STEINER VERLAG WIESBADEN GMBH
STUTTGART 1988

GERMANY'S INFORMAL EMPIRE IN EAST-CENTRAL EUROPE

GERMAN ECONOMIC POLICY
TOWARD YUGOSLAVIA AND RUMANIA,
1933–1939

BY
WILLIAM S. GRENZEBACH, JR.

FRANZ STEINER VERLAG WIESBADEN GMBH
STUTTGART 1988

CIP-Titelaufnahme der Deutschen Bibliothek

Grenzebach, William S.:
Germany's informal empire in East-central Europe: German
econom. policy toward Yugoslavia and Rumania, 1933-1939 /
by William S. Grenzebach jr. — Stuttgart: Steiner-Verl.
Wiesbaden 1988
   (Veröffentlichungen des Instituts für Europäische Geschichte Mainz;
   Bd. 128: Abteilung Universalgeschichte)
   ISBN 3-515-05005-1
   NE: Institut für Europäische Geschichte < Mainz > : Veröffentlichungen
   des Instituts . . .

In Loving Memory of My Parents
William S. Grenzebach, Sr.
and
Edla Edin Grenzebach

CONTENTS

VIII   Contents

Acknowledgements

In writing a work of this scope, one incurs a debt of gratitude to many people and institutions. Without the intellectual encouragement and moral support of the late Professor Geoffrey Barraclough this project would have never been conceived, let alone completed. Geoffrey Barraclough's patience was often sorely tried, but he remained unfailingly helpful. This study originated in his seminar on the Origins of World War II; his example of scholarship has been a goal for which to strive.

The research for this work could not have been undertaken without the support of Brandeis University during the years of 1971–72 and 1974–75. Special thanks go to Professor Eugene Black of the Brandeis Department of History, who actively intervened on my behalf.

Two German institutions deserve special recognition for their generous financial and moral support – the DAAD and the Institut für Europäische Geschichte (Mainz). Franz Eschbach (Bonn) of the American Referat and Professor Doktor Freiherr von Aretin, head of the Abteilung Universalgeschichte in Mainz, were especially helpful during my stay in Germany. Professor von Aretin has kindly accepted this work into the Institute's publications series.

Professor Dr. Hans-Jürgen Schröder (Justus Liebig University Giessen) was particularly generous with his time and his extensive knowledge of the German archives. He has maintained his interest in this work throughout its long genesis, for which I am very grateful. I also owe a debt of gratitutde to Dr. T. W. Mason (St. Peter's College, Oxford), who told me of the importance of the archives of the Gutehoffnungshütte and offered other suggestions which I have tried to incorporate.

Without my colleagues formerly at the Institute for European History, particularly Dr. Robert Schulmann (Einstein Project, Boston University) and Professor John Gillingham (University of Missouri), and the discussions that often lasted long into the night, many points covered in this work would not have received the attention given them here.

Special acknowledgment is due to the staffs of the Political Archives of the Auswärtiges Amt, in particular, Herr Dr. Gehling and Fr. Dr. Keipart; the Bundesarchiv Koblenz, Dr. Rust; Bundesarchiv/Militärarchiv, Freiburg im Breisgau, Oberstleutnant Forwick; Historisches Archiv – Gutehoffnungshütte, Herr Bodo Herzog; the Public Record Office, London; the National Archives, Washington, D. C.; and Miss Dorothy Barnett of the inter-library loan department of the Boston Public Library.

I am grateful to the late J. Herbert Hollomon, founding director of the Center for Technology and Policy, Boston University, and his colleagues, Professors George Heaton, K. Nagaraja Rao, and Robert Lund for their interest and encouragement at a crucial time in my career.

This work is dedicated to my parents. Unfortunately, they did not live to see this work in its present form. My interest in German history first arose out of lively dinner table discussion over the fate of the German labor movement. My parents, active trade unionists throughout their working lives, inspired in me a concern for the origins and consequences of the Great Depression which so wracked their generation. This work is a considerably reworked and edited version of a Ph. D. thesis presented to the Comparative History program, Brandeis University in May 1978. My thanks to Mr. Lee Fischer (Fine Print and Production, Cambridge, Mass.), for his editorial assistance in preparation of this present volume. Additional word processing and optical scanner services provided by Mr. Paul Saluzza (Connections Information Services, Cambridge, Mass.) considerably eased final preparation of the manuscript. Dr. Jeff Brenner (Image Analysis Laboratory, New England Medical Center) kindly provided technical assistance without which this book would have been considerably delayed. Finally, my former associate in the oil services industry, Mrs. Rosa Lee Bachtel, (Pearland, Texas) did yeoman's work in proof reading the manuscript at short notice.

Of course, all errors of fact or interpretation are solely mine.

William S. Grenzebach, Ph. D.
Center for Technology and Policy
Boston University
Boston, Massachusetts

Chapter I

GERMAN EXPANSIONISM AND THE POLITICAL STRUCTURE OF EAST-CENTRAL EUROPE BETWEEN THE WARS

1. Collapse of the Multinational Empires: The New Political Order

In the years between 1917 and 1919 Germany's goal of European hegemony contended with a Wilsonian system of independent nation-states for east-central Europe and its 100 million people.[1] German imperialism, victorious over a Russia prostrated by economic collapse and political revolution, sought to create a European colonial empire in the vast area between East Prussia and the Black Sea and form a network of states subservient to German economic and political demands. The treaties dictated to Rumania and the new Soviet government, which could serve as a foundation for the emerging German sphere of influence, required a German victory in the West to force Allied recognition of German hegemony in eastern Europe. German troops were transferred to the West after the war against Russia was won, but victory on the western front continued to be elusive as the German armies came close to collapse after the Allied counteroffensives in the later summer of 1918. Germany's western defeat made the eastern gains worthless. By November 1918 the three great multinational empires that had dominated east-central Europe were dead and new political forces emerged to take their place.

The political structure that emerged in eastern Europe after World War I was primarily imposed by the formerly oppressed nationalities — the Poles, Czechs, Rumanians, and Serbs, rather than by the Big Four in Paris. Only Wilsonian slogans of self-determination and the diplomatic sanctions of the Versailles Treaty followed. The Peace Conference, and subsequently the League of Nations, although influential in many controversial issues, could not change the emerging political structure without armed intervention to impose a settlement[2], while issues such as the western border of Soviet Russia would remain unsettled until well after the Peace Conference had adjourned. When the Franco-British and Franco-American security treaties fell through, the task of maintaining the new political order in

---

[1] Throughout Chapter I, I have relied on the authoritative studies of Macartney and Seton-Watson. C.A. MACARTNEY and A.W. PALMER, Independent Eastern Europe: A History, London 1962; Hugh SETON-WATSON, Eastern Europe Between the Wars 1918-1941, Cambridge 1942.

[2] Victor S. MAMATEY, The United States and East Central Europe, 1914-1918, Cambridge 1957, pp. 346-380.

east-central Europe fell to the states who had created it, with some support from France.

The restructuring of Europe's political map inevitably brought dissatisfaction from the losers in the settlement; their determination to redress the "wrongs" of the peace settlement became generally known as "revisionism". In varying degrees, Germany, Hungary, and Bulgaria each had a revisionist foreign policy during the interwar period. In the catalog of alleged oppressions suffered by these revisionist countries, it is difficult to separate real grievances from propaganda aimed at the United States and England. Further, both revisionist policy and propaganda were purposefully vague — to specify grievances might prejudice a future settlement.

The contradictions within revisionist policy are clear in the case of Hungary, whose pre-1914 borders had included provinces with subject nationality majorities.[3] Hungary lost three provinces after 1918 — approximately two-fifths of her former population and one-third of her territory — to Czechoslovakia, Rumania, and Yugoslavia. The problem arose in that some three million Hungarians were now included within these new borders, a fact skillfully exploited by Hungarian propaganda which maintained that Hungary was interested only in border rectifications that would "liberate" fellow Hungarians and form an ethnographically homogeneous nation. In reality, Hungarian propagandists mastered the rhetoric of Wilsonian self-determination to implement a policy of reconstituting Greater Hungary, as Hitler would later use the Sudeten question to disrupt and finally annex Czechoslovakia. Whatever the relative merits or defects of the Versailles settlement, the issues raised by the allegedly oppressive character of the settlement were a means to the goals of revisionist policy.

2. German Revisionism, 1919-29

It is significant that Germany remained virtually intact in interwar Europe[4]: German economic strength was based on industrial organization, which was not significantly disrupted by the loss of Alsace-Lorraine ore, Silesian and Saar coal, the merchant marine, or property and investments in foreign countries. Politically, the loss of Alsace-Lorraine, the Polish Corridor, and Posen, although not marginal,

---

[3] Neither recent American research nor the massive efforts of postwar Hungarian scholarship lend support to Macartney's sympathetic treatment of Hungarian policy: Endre GASTONY, Revisionist Hungarian Foreign Policy and the Third Reich's Advance to the East, 1933-1939, U. Ph.D. Dissertation, Univ. of Oregon 1970; C.A. MACARTNEY, Hungary and Her Successors: The Treaty of Trianon and Its Consequences, 1919-1937, London 1937; idem, October Fifteenth: A History of Modern Hungary, 1929-1945, London 1956; Thomas SAKMYSTER, Hungary and the Coming of the European Crisis, 1937-1938, U. Ph.D. Dissertation, Univ. of Indiana 1971; Betty Jo WINCHESTER, Hungarian Relations with Germany, 1936-1939, U. Ph.D. Dissertation, Univ. of Indiana 1970. An important new book on Hungarian-German relations in the late Weimar period is : Judit FEJES-SCHULMANN, Hungarian-German Relations, 1928-1932, (in Hungarian) Budapest 1981.

[4] Gerald L. WEINBERG, The Defeat of Germany in 1918 and the European Balance of Power, in: Central European History 2 (1969), pp. 248-260.

was even less disruptive than the economic losses. In east-central Europe, Germany emerged from the war with a relatively improved position in that Russia's collapse had eliminated the single Great Power capable of political and economic competition or, if necessary, a military balance: the new independent Polish state enhanced German military security by buffering one of the two Great Powers that had bordered on Germany[5], while the end of Austria-Hungary freed Germany from the constant opposition to the national aspirations of the subject peoples necessary under the alliance with the Habsburg Empire. Once domestic conditions had stabilized, Germany was better placed to regain its old standing in the markets of east-central Europe than Czech, Austrian, or Hungarian industry. The industrialization programs of Yugoslavia, Rumania, and Bulgaria, demanding the import of capital goods, meshed with the structure of German industry, while their industrialization policies and infant industry protection, a direct threat to Austrian and Czech textile exports and Hungarian food processing, were not a serious barrier to German capital goods, high technology products (chemicals, opticals, etc.), or consumer durables such as automobiles.[6]

Despite the harsh Versailles settlement, Germany had considerable room to maneuver, as shown by the long struggle over reparations. Germany pursued several tactics from 1919 to 1924 to minimize the burden of reparation payments,

---

[5] Both Gaines Post, Jr., and Harold von Riekhoff take seriously the Wilhelmstrasse and military concern over the security problems created by the cession of Posen and the Corridor. However, the neck of East Prussia stretching over Russian Poland was a liability before 1914. The loss in territory was hardly commensurate with the relative military weight of Czarist Russia versus post-1918 Poland. As long as Germany was disarmed and the western border demilitarized, the German General Staff took the Polish "threat" seriously; after 1936 this "threat" was treated with disdain. For a differing view, see Gaines POST, Jr., The Civil-Military Fabric of Weimar Foreign Policy, Princeton 1973, pp. 99-100; Harold von RIEKHOFF, German-Polish Relations, 1918-1933, Baltimore and London 1972, pp. 14, 20. Attitudes to the Polish threat at the top levels of the *Reichswehr* bordered on the paranoiac. Training of right wing patriotic organizations was conducted secretly in the east Prussian border regions: "The Minister-President of Prussia [Otto Braun] resented the anti-republican ideology of the Verbände in question. He contended that their behavior could be interpreted as treasonable." Edward REED, Wilhelm Groener and the SPD – January 1928 to May 1932, U. Ph. D., University of Penn. 1972, p. 75. In the German political spectrum fear of Polish "aggression" developed in direct proportion to the right wing designs upon Polish territory.

[6] The exports of Austrian, Czech, and Hungarian industry suffered a decline in Bulgaria, Rumania, and Yugoslavia throughout the interwar period. By comparison Germany registered impressive gains in 1925-1929 and 1934-1939. In spite of the economic nationalism, total trade between Danubian countries was well maintained during 1925-1929, but fell to 15.5% of the 1911-1913 average in 1935, according to Frederick Hertz. Antonin BASCH, The Danube Basin and the German Economic Sphere, New York 1943, pp. 28-29, 86-87, 187-195; Ivan T. BEREND and György RANKI, Hungary: A Century of Economic Development, New York 1974, pp. 102, 138, 145-146; idem, Economic Development in East-Central Europe in the 19th and 20th Centuries, New York 1974, pp. 178-179, 206-209, 296-297; Frederick HERTZ, The Economic Problem of the Danubian States: A Study in Economic Nationalism, New York 1970 [First ed., London 1947], pp. 79-84; Leo PASVOLSKY, Economic Nationalism of the Danubian States, New York 1928, pp. 536-537, 563-564, 566-569, 575; Zora PROCHAZKA, Foreign Trade and Economic Development of Czechoslovakia, 1919-1937, U. Ph.D., Radcliffe College 1960, p. 328; RIIA, The Balkan States, London 1936, pp. 31-32, 107.

going from payment by deliveries in kind to passive resistance during the French occupation of the Ruhr. The policy of passive resistance resulted in the 1923 hyperinflation. The ensuing economic chaos, with Anglo-American pressure on France, brought an interim settlement of the reparations problem under the Dawes Committee, whereby Germany agreed to pay reparations in cash in return for a loan sponsored by American and British bankers[7], while France allowed temporarily reduced payments but reserved its rights to its total capital claim. The Dawes Plan led to the Locarno Pact, which reflected the new compromise attitudes of the French and German governments. For Germany, Locarno meant renouncing any claims on Alsace-Lorraine, an acceptance of the status quo in the West. England and Italy guaranteed the Pact, pledging to intervene against either France or Germany if the treaty were violated.

Europe's stabilization after 1924 was a direct result of the political and economic compromises of the Dawes Plan and Locarno Pact. Gustav Stresemann's foreign policy was admittedly revisionist, but under his leadership Germany accepted the political and economic structure imposed by the Versailles Treaty. He recognized the great opportunities for German economic, and, eventually, political expansion within the imposed structure; his policy in 1927 of trade expansion through negotiation of most-favored-nation treaties with France, Yugoslavia, and Rumania was an outstanding success in promoting German exports.[8]

Whatever Stresemann's ultimate goals, a major objective of his foreign policy was restoring Germany's 1914 border in the East[9], prompting him to initiate the Pol-

---

[7] Recent research indicates how important United States foreign economic policy was for this compromise: "Without allies and incapable to force a French retreat alone, British politicians, greatly aided and sometimes led by the British members of the Reparation Commission, finally succeeded in arranging a study of the whole reparations problem. When this happened, the United States joined the investigation and from then on determined the outcome of reparations." Hermann-Josef RUPIEPER, Politics and Economics: The Cuno Government and Reparations, 1922-1923, U. Ph.D., Stanford Univ. 1974, p. 485. Other important recent works on the role of the United States in the European situation: Frank COSTIGLIOLA, The Politics of Financial Stabilization: American Reconstruction Policy in Europe 1924-1930, U.Ph.D. Dissertation, Cornell Univ. 1973; Werner LINK, Die Amerikanische Stabilisierungspolitik in Deutschland, 1921-1932, Düsseldorf 1970; William McNEIL, American Money and the German Economy: Economics and Politics on the Eve of the Great Depression, U.Ph.D., University of California – Berkeley, 1981; Robert Van METER, Jr., The United States and European Recovery, 1918-1923: A Study of Public Policy and Private Finance, U.Ph.D., Univ. of Wisconsin 1971).

[8] For example: As a consequence of the most-favored-nation treaty with France, German chemical exports to France increased from 561 million reichsmarks in 1927 to 934 million in 1929. John Palen POWELSON, French Exports and Commercial Policy, 1919-1949, U.Ph.D., Harvard Univ. 1949, p. 321.

[9] While Stresemann's reputation has survived better than any other German statesman of 1900-45, there is no scholarly consensus on his ultimate goals; Henry Bretton characterizes Stresemann as a "pacific revisionist" who was "dedicated to peaceful change rather than change by force . . .", while H. W. Gatzke refuses to speculate on whether Stresemann envisaged the actual use of force. Henry BRETTON, Stresemann and the Revision of Versailles: A Fight for Reason, Stanford 1953, pp. 13, 117; Hans W. GATZKE, Stresemann and the Rearmament of Germany, Baltimore 1954, p. 115.

ish-German trade war designed to erode Polish resistance to German demands.[10]
Stresemann's Polish policy and the attitude of German conservatives to Poland is
curious. While accepting the Corridor and the creation of Polish Silesia could have
brought about excellent economic and political relations between the two states (a
policy that Hitler would later pursue), Stresemann's policy seems economically and
politically self-defeating. The restoration of the 1914 borders in the East was a sentimental goal cherished particularly by the Junkers and military but was hardly
worth great political and economic sacrifices — *if* one's primary foreign policy goal
was peaceful political relations with neighboring countries and maximum economic
growth.[11]

Unlike Hungarian and Bulgarian revisionism in the 1920s, German efforts to
modify Versailles had some success — Germany was important enough to the
world economy that British and American statesmen diligently sought a basis for
agreement between Germany's grievances and France's demands. The economic
exhaustion that resulted from the 1923 inflation provided a foundation for a tentative acceptance of the Versailles order, but such acceptance by Germany's center
and right-wing political leaders, bankers, industrialists, and the camouflaged general staff was precarious indeed. Stresemann's policy of confrontation with Poland
presaged underlying political attitudes that would later crystallize into a program of
political expansion. Even granted that revising the Polish border was a modest project compared to Hitler's continental vision of expansion eastward, how did Stresemann and his supporters think such revision could be achieved short of war?[12] The
propaganda and economic war against Poland in the late twenties encouraged
revanchist sentiment and links Stresemann to Brüning's policy of eastward political
expansion.

3. *The Little Entente*

The Little Entente originated in a bilateral alliance between Czechoslovakia and
Yugoslavia (August 14, 1920) that was " . . . to operate in the event of an unpro-

---

[10] As early as February 1926, Stresemann realized that the tariff war with Poland was not
having the desired effect of weakening Poland. In spite of a threat to resign if trade negotiations were not reopened (November 1927), he was not able to achieve a satisfactory liquidation of the conflict before his death in October 1929. In spite of Harold von Riekhoff's careful
apportionment of German and Polish responsibility for the trade war — with the balance
against Germany — Stresemann certainly could have reached an agreement with Poland if
negotiations had been conducted in a less niggardly spirit. von RIEKHOFF, Relations, pp. 161-
193.

[11] "A revisionist war against Poland, he [Stresemann] clearly realized, could not be local-
ized and would become a general conflagration which would have destroyed the very foundation of his European policy. Stresemann's fault was not that of conducting a consciously
aggressive foreign policy but of failing to realize the futility and inherent dangers of insisting
on a revision of the German-Polish frontier." Ibid., p. 269.

[12] The "specific and limited objectives" of the Wilhelmstraße included: Danzig and the
Corridor, Upper Silesia and western Posen. (The latter was renounced by Stresemann in 1925
but later reinstated as a secondary objective). POST, Civil-Military Fabric, pp. 24-25.

voked attack by Hungary against either party or an attempted Hapsburg restoration."[13] On April 23, 1921, a similar treaty between Czechoslovakia and Rumania was signed and in June 1921 the circle was completed by a third treaty between Yugoslavia and Rumania, in this case also directed against Bulgaria. In each instance the treaty was supplemented by a military convention. In early 1933 a comprehensive agreement was signed by the three countries, transforming the alliance from a series of bilateral treaties into a multilateral pact, although this systemization of the Little Entente did not involve any new political obligations and only confirmed its anti-Hungarian thrust. The alliance was reinforced by the creation of a Permanent Council, proposals for preferential economic arrangements and regular periodic meetings between the foreign ministers and general staffs. The new alliance agreement included a proposal for an Economic Little Entente, designed to mitigate the danger to the alliance from the Great Depression by increasing Czech-Yugoslav and Czech-Rumanian trade. The modest success of these efforts in 1934-36 was quickly overshadowed by the German trade drive.[14] Three factors hampered Czech economic diplomacy: Czechoslovakia had a small national market compared to Germany; Czechoslovakia's traditional reliance upon textile exports and other consumer products threatened Rumanian and Yugoslav industrialization programs; and domestic pressure for increasing agricultural protection severely restricted Czech ability to compete with Germany's policy of bulk purchases.[15] The Little Entente's failure to develop a viable economic basis, either through unilateral Czech action or a combined Franco-Czech policy of bulk purchases of Yugoslav and Rumanian products, left the field open to the machinations of Hjalmar Schacht, former president of the Reichsbank (1924-1930) and later minister of economics and confidant of Hitler in the mid-1930s. (Schacht replaced Luther as Reichsbank president in 1933 and succeeded Schmidt as acting economics minister in mid 1934).

---

13 MACARTNEY/PALMER, Independent Eastern Europe, p. 253. In addition, the following works on the Little Entente, Czechoslovakia, Rumania and Yugoslavia have been consulted: Eliza CAMPUS, Mica Intelegere, Bucharest 1968; Ozer CARMI, La Grande-Bretagne et la Petite Entente, Geneva 1972; Jeno HORVATH, Die kleine Entente, Beitrag zur Geschichte der Diplomatie, Budapest/Leipzig n.d.; J.P. HOPTNER, Yugoslavia in Crisis, 1934-1941, New York 1962; Rudolf KISZLING, Die militärischen Vereinbarungen der kleinen Entente, 1929-1937, München 1959; Frank LITTLEFIELD, Yugoslav Relations with Germany and Italy and the Nationality Problem 1933-1941, U. Ph.D., New York Univ. 1973; Robert MACHRAY, The Little Entente, London 1929; idem, The Struggle for the Danube and the Little Entente, 1929-1938, London 1938; I.M. OPREA, Nicolae Titulescu's Diplomatic Activity, Bucharest 1968; PROCHAZKA, Foreign Trade; Günter REICHERT, Das Scheitern der kleinen Entente, 1933-1938, München 1971; Henry ROBERTS, Political Problems of an Agrarian State, New York 1951.

14 "Czechoslovak imports from Yugoslavia and Rumania rose from 407 kc (6.7% of total imports in 1933) to 942 kc (8.5% of total imports in 1937); Czechoslovak exports to those countries rose from 418 kc (7% of total exports in 1933) to 1250 kc (10.4% of total exports in 1937)." Godfrey BRIEFS, Shifting Patterns in Eastern Europe's Foreign Trade, 1928-1948, U. Ph.D., Harvard Univ. 1951, pp. 147-148, 149-150; also, PROCHAZKA, Foreign Trade, pp. 271-272, 289, 309-311.

15 BRIEFS, Shifting Patterns; PROCHAZKA, Foreign Trade.

Both Czechoslovakia and Rumania supported French attempts to create regional security pacts to defend the status quo (the Eastern and Danubian Pacts), but Yugoslavia under Stojadinovic adopted a more reserved attitude. The combined Polish-Yugoslav opposition doomed France's last and feeble effort before the diplomatic crisis of 1939 to transform her bilateral pacts into a general alliance system to contain German expansionism. France's bilateral treaties with Czechoslovakia and the Soviet Union, concluded after the Eastern and Danubian Pact initiatives had failed, did nothing to stabilize the Little Entente as a potential anti-German rallying point. On the contrary, Czechoslovakia's alliance with the Soviet Union created a rift within the alliance; Yugoslavia continued its policy of nonrecognition of the Soviet government and Titulescu's fall from power in Rumania in the late summer of 1936 can be directly attributed to unresolved tension between Rumania and Soviet Russia, particularly over Bessarabia. Never developing its potential as an anti-German barrier in southeastern Europe, the Little Entente became ever more restricted to its original purpose, defending the territorial status quo against Hungarian revisionism. Yugoslavia, followed by Rumania, let Berlin know that Czechoslovakia would not be supported in the event of a confrontation. For all practical purposes the Little Entente was destroyed as an effective alliance by the Munich Agreement's legal sanction of the dismemberment of Czechoslovakia. Neither Yugoslavia nor Rumania was obligated to oppose the Hungarian annexations of Czech territory sanctioned by the First Vienna Award; Czechoslovakia had "voluntarily" ceded its territory and the Vienna Award received the *de facto* endorsement of all the Munich powers, although only Germany and Italy actually acted as arbitrators. Insofar as Rumania and Yugoslavia had any political agreements or alliances upon which they could rely, their bilateral alliance undoubtedly ranked first. It remained a viable instrument against Hungary, although seriously weakened by factors relating to the Balkan Entente.

4. The Balkan Entente

The Balkan Entente was the last, and weakest, multilateral, anti-revisionist alliance to emerge before the diplomatic crisis of 1939.[16] This alliance stemmed from Greek and Turkish attempts to thwart an incipient rapprochement between Yugoslavia and Bulgaria in 1933, as they feared the emergence of a Great Slav State in the Balkans. To draw Bulgaria away from Yugoslavia, in May 1933 Turkey and Greece offered a mutual treaty guaranteeing the inviolability of existing borders. Their reasoning as to why Bulgaria would find this offer attractive is obscure and, in any case, Bulgaria rejected the idea out of hand. At this point Rumania's energetic Titu-

---

[16] Literature on the Balkan Entente is scanty. Theodore GESHKOFF, Balkan Union: A Road to Peace in Southeastern Europe, New York 1940; Robert KERNER/Harry HOWARD, The Balkan Conferences and the Balkan Entente, 1930-1935, Berkeley 1936; Christian POPISTEANU, Romania si Antania Balcanica, Bucharest 1971.

Iescu intervened with a plan to sign "mutual Treaties of Non-Aggression, the whole to be crowned by a grand multilateral Treaty of Mutual Guarantee."[17]

Nonaggression treaties were soon concluded between Rumania and Turkey (October 17) and Yugoslavia and Turkey (November 27). Bulgaria, while willing to sign a general nonaggression agreement, naturally refused to participate in the guarantee of borders imposed by Versailles. Turkey and Greece agreed to sign with the proviso that the guarantee not apply to aggression by non-Balkan states, thus protecting their respective flanks *vis-a-vis* the USSR and Italy. King Alexander's declared preference for a bilateral solution to Yugoslavia's relations with Bulgaria notwithstanding, he bowed to diplomatic pressure and agreed to participate. The stage was now set for agreement among the Balkan states. The "Balkan Pact", signed on February 9, 1934 by Greece, Rumania, Yugoslavia, and Turkey, mutually guaranteed existing borders and provided for mutual consultation in the event of any political action concerning another Balkan power. In effect, the agreement amounted to an alliance against Bulgaria, which, considering Bulgaria's military weakness and political isolation, was certainly superfluous.

Czechoslovakia's hopes that the Balkan Entente could be used for the wider purpose of creating a Balkan front against Great Power interference were dashed by explicit Turkish and Greek reservations. Even as an alliance against Bulgaria, the limited value of the Balkan Entente was considerably undercut by Yugoslavia's independent policy of rapprochement. The alliance played no significant role in the diplomacy of the 1930s and became a concern to the Wilhelmstraße only in 1939, after the British-Turk agreement was concluded. Berlin then began to pressure Yugoslavia and, particularly, Rumania to repudiate the Entente based on Turkey's allying with a non-Balkan power without consulting her allies. Even then, concern in Berlin that the Yugoslav-Turk or Rumanian-Turk connection would be maintained was not intense.

5. A Balance Sheet of Political Barriers to German Expansionism

A survey of the political constellations existing between the two wars leads to the conclusion that the French employed a poorly designed alliance system as a barrier to German expansionism. Only the Franco-Polish pact operated unconditionally against Germany, and it was weakened in the 1930s by Beck's collaboration policy. France's alliance with the Soviet Union was never followed up by a military agreement and the Soviet alliance with Czechoslovakia became effective only if France honored her commitments. The Little Entente and Balkan Entente were never more than alliances against Hungary and Bulgaria, the weak revisionist states.

The Versailles status quo was further complicated by strained relations among the war's beneficiaries: Czech-Polish relations, poisoned by the award of Teschen to Czechoslovakia, further deteriorated with Beck's policy of rapprochement with Germany and cordial relations with Hungary during the 1930s; Rumanian-Polish relations went from bad to worse after the Polish-Soviet Non-Aggression Pact was

---

[17] MACARTNEY/PALMER, Independent Eastern Europe, p. 318.

concluded in 1932, to such an extent that on the eve of World War II the British Foreign Office maintained that Rumania could not rely on Polish support if the German blow fell on Rumania rather than Poland.[18]

French policy fell between two stools — the League of Nations collective security system never really developed into a viable means of defending the status quo and France's own alliance system, developed on an ad hoc basis, was allowed to deteriorate during the Locarno era and the first years of the Great Depression. When France did attempt to repair the damage through the Danubian and Eastern Pacts and the bilateral alliances with Czechoslovakia and the Soviet Union, it was simply too little too late for southeastern Europe; both Yugoslavia and Rumania could have been written off after the financial crisis in 1931. Apart from the defects inherent in France's agreements with Czechoslovakia and the Soviet Union, these alliances did nothing to counter German influence in southeastern Europe. Hoping to draw Italy into an anti-German bloc, France equivocated with Yugoslavia, and while France tried harder with Rumania, French mediation could not resolve tensions between Bucharest and Moscow nor quiet Rumanian fears of granting a right-of-passage to Russian troops.

The failure to provide a sound economic foundation sealed the fate of French influence in eastern Europe. French trade with eastern Europe was low-key even during the 1920s boom, and during the Depression the French quota system, imperial preference for French colonial products, and agricultural protectionism made the French market increasingly difficult for Yugoslavia and Rumania to enter. Additional loans could provide no solution — neither country could pay for loans already made. To pay external debts, ensure domestic political stability, and buy in the world market, both Yugoslavia and Rumania needed markets in hard-currency countries. France could have consolidated her position in southeastern Europe with preferential quotas but the attitudes of economic Malthusianism, restrictionism, and retrenchment prevailing in France precluded a quota policy, as did domestic pressure for agriculture protection.[19]

---

[18] " . . . there is great doubt whether in fact Poland would support Roumania against Germany since the military conventions accompanying the Polish-Roumanian alliance between the two countries are only concerned with Russia." Chancery, British Embassy (Warsaw) to Halifax, March 21, 1939, PRO, F.O. 371/23840. Polish foreign policy also played a role in undermining the efforts of Titulescu to reach an accommodation with the Soviet Union: "Even as he was acting as an intermediary in Paris, rumors circulated that Titulescu had agreed to Soviet troop passage through Romania and to Soviet overflight of Romanian territory. These rumors, which may have had a solid basis in fact, were primarily the work of Miroslav Arciszewski, the ostracized Polish minister in Bucharest." Walter BACON, Nicolae Titulescu and Romanian Foreign Policy, 1933-1934, U.Ph.D., University of Denver 1975, p. 254-255.

[19] In spite of the deflationary policy pursued until the advent of the Popular Front (1936), France faced severe budgetary problems, a situation further excerbated by the flight of domestic capital. John HANNAFORD, French Interwar Monetary Problems, U.Ph.D., Harvard Univ. 1953, pp. 253-256, 270, 315-316, 347; Robert O. PAXTON, Vichy France: Old Guard and New Order, 1940-1944, New York 1972, p. 210; POWELSON, French Exports, pp. 22, 50, 140-141, 323, 341; Willard SHARPE, The Economic Problems of the Popular Front in France, 1936-1938, U.Ph.D., Harvard Univ. 1955.

Opposed only by this array of weak, ineffective alliances, Nazi Germany could politically exploit the potentially enormous consumptive power of its market.

6. The Foreign Policy of the Brüning Government

The Austro-German Custom Union Project

Within eight months of Stresemann's death in October 1929, German foreign policy was diverted from a moderate, accommodationist course to outright confrontation.[20] In retrospect, the ease with which this policy shift was carried through is astounding. Stresemann's political successor as foreign minister was Curtius, a member of the same political party and a personal friend and confidant. Yet Curtius was a sponsor of the Austro-German customs union project — a political venture that destroyed the modest political capital built up by Stresemann's moderation and the tentative political and economic rapprochement with France begun during the Locarno era.

Both the Anschluß and customs union project originated in the early days of the Weimar Republic but the customs union project became practical government policy only under the chancellorship of Heinrich Brüning during the summer of 1930. Brüning headed the first and longest presidential government in the late Weimar Republic ("presidential" because his government ruled without parliamentary majority and he was appointed by President Hindenburg under the emergency powers provision for the constitution). Brüning, determined upon a more vigorous struggle for revision, forced Stresemann's state secretary in the Wilhelmstraße, Carl von Schubert, to resign and appointed a mere counselor (*Ministerialrat*), Bernhard von Bülow, in his place. Bülow supported the political expansion policies of Brüning and Curtius and did, in fact, play a greater role in foreign policy formation between 1930 and 1932 than was customary for a state secretary. Most of the important instructions to embassies and legations during this period bear his name and were probably written by him.

Brüning and Bülow had certain conceptions, affecting foreign policy, of Germany's political goals:

---

[20] There is no comprehensive work on the foreign policy of the late Weimar presidential governments. I have found the work of Helbich to be the most insightful on Brüning's foreign policy. Edward W. BENNETT, Germany and the Diplomacy of the Financial Crisis, 1931, Cambridge/Mass., 1962; Fenton CAMPBELL, Jr., Czech-German Relations During the Weimar Republic, U.Ph.D. Dissertation, Yale Univ. 1967; Wolfgang J. HELBICH, Die Reparationen in der Ära Brüning, Berlin 1962; idem, "Between Stresemann and Hitler: The Foreign Policy of the Brüning Government", in: World Politics 12 (1959), pp. 24-44; Norman JOHNSON, The Austro-German Customs Union Project in German Diplomacy, U. Ph.D. Dissertation, Univ. of North Carolina, Chapel Hill 1974; POST, Civil-Military Fabric, pp. 265-303; F.G. STAMBROOK, "The German-Austrian Customs Union Project of 1931", in: Journal of Central European Affairs 21 (1961), pp. 15-44; Stanley SUVAL, The Anschluss Question in the Weimar Era, Baltimore 1974, pp. 146-165; von RIEKHOFF, Relations, pp. 327-379.

What should Germany do in view of the political situation of Europe?
Where do Germany's possibilities lie?
In the West there are no possibilities for Germany, except to maintain friendship with
France. Possibilities for Germany lie only in the East and Southeast. . . .
Today one must make policy with new means and new methods.[21]

The customs union project was not originally presented as a "revision" of the Versailles Treaty, thus allowing Germany to argue that it contradicted neither the Versailles prohibition against *Anschluß* nor Austria's obligations under the 1922 League of Nations loan. The *Zollunion* was an example of Brüning's conception of nonviolent "means" and "methods" for advancing Germany's political interests in east-central Europe. Germany's sponsorship of the customs union with Austria owed little to concern about the unstable Austrian economy or to alleged economic benefits for Germany; it was conceived by Bülow as a "forcing play" to extract political and economic concessions from France:

> The prerequisite for all these plans is that in the course of this year we succeed [in opening] negotiations on the most generous scale with the French. This desire is not so utopian as it first appears. Indeed, the French in general do not negotiate on a very generous scale. But if one is successful in subjecting them to pressure, then one can obtain something in spite of everything.[22]

Bülow believed that a disarmed Germany could coerce France, the most powerful military and financial European power, into accepting policies contrary to its best interests: "If in the next few months we undertake in Central Europe independent steps in the direction of an economic union, to use this catch-word which admits of so many explanations, then France would certainly be compelled to discuss similar projects with us, and in the general condition of economic distress it is likely that the tempo of such negotiations will be greatly accelerated." Bülow had in mind not only the customs union project but also French recognition in principle of Germany's right to military equality.

Added to the alleged benefits of the *Zollunion* in relation to Germany's demands that the economic and military restrictions of Versailles be revised, Bülow considered the economic union with Austria as a first step in a revolution of the political formation of east-central Europe that would eventually revise the border with Poland:

> The inclusion of Czechoslovakia in our economic system is completely harmonious with the long range foreign policy of the Reich as I view it. Once the Austro-German customs union has become a reality, I calculate that the pressure of economic necessity will force the entrance of Czechoslovakia within a few years in one form or another. I would see therein the beginning of a development that would be calculated to lead to a solution of vital political interests of the Reich, which scarcely seems solvable in any other way. I am thinking of the German-Polish boundary problem. If we succeed in linking Czechoslovakia with our economic bloc and if we shall have in the meantime closer economic relations with the Bal-

---

[21] Wolfgang RUGE/Wolfgang SCHUMANN, (ed.), "Die Reaktion des deutschen Imperialismus auf Briands Paneuropaplan 1930", in: Zeitschrift für Geschichtswissenschaft 20 (1972), p. 64. David Kaiser has recognized the critical nature of this turning point in German foreign policy: David E. KAISER, Economic Diplomacy and the Origins of the Second World War, Princeton 1980, p. 15-16.

[22] Bülow to Hoesch, January 23, 1931, cited in JOHNSON, Customs Union, p. 285.

tic States, then Poland with its weak economic organization will be encircled and exposed to all kinds of dangers. We shall have it in a pincer that, over short or long, can bring it closer to the idea of exchanging political concessions for obvious economic advantages.[23]

In the frontal diplomatic assault used by Brüning, Curtius, and Bülow to establish German hegemony in east-central Europe, the customs union project was the key to obtaining a wholesale revision of the Versailles Treaty.

France and Czechoslovakia reacted predictably to Germany's March 21, 1931, announcement of the customs union project; Germany's expressed shock at the violence of the French and Czech reaction can only be attributed to German obtuseness. "By suddenly confronting France with the customs union, Germany had dissipated what was left of the spirit of mutual trust created by Briand and Stresemann; had aborted a promising French project for extending financial aid to Germany; had scuttled Briand's bid for the presidency and had rekindled the French public's fear of *Anschluß* and hostility toward Germany. There could be no question that France would take whatever steps were necessary to destroy the customs union project."[24]

France exerted financial and political pressure from April to September 1931, finally obtaining the Hague Court's decision against the project in September. The financial panic that enveloped Austria, Germany, and east-central Europe, while fundamentally a result of the widespread Austro-German banking policy of borrowing short and lending long, was exacerbated by French financial pressure upon Austria. The customs union project thus caused the complete political isolation of Germany and materially contributed to the Central European financial crisis that struck at Germany's own economic and financial well-being.

The Preferential Treaties with Hungary and Rumania

The Brüning government's program of eastward expansion also involved the negotiation of preferential agricultural treaties.[25] During the European economic revival Germany's commercial policy toward southeastern Europe was oriented toward regaining her prewar market share in the imports of the successor states by a trade policy based upon the most-favored-nation treaty system, whereby a tariff concession offered to an individual trading partner was generalized to all countries enjoying most-favored-nation status with Germany. Preferential treatment for German exports was not a priority, nor did Germany offer special treatment of south-

---

[23] Bülow to Koch, April 15, 1931, ibid., pp. 410-411. The importance of this document for the characterization of German policy towards east-central Europe has been recognized by several important scholarly works: J. W. BRÜGEL, Tschechen und Deutsche, 1918-1938, München 1967, p. 222; CAMPBELL, Czech-German Relations, p. 199; POST, Civil-Military Fabric, p. 280.

[24] JOHNSON, Customs Union, p. 353.

[25] There is, as yet, no adequate scholarly treatment of the preference treaties. Background is provided by Hermann SCHURMANN, Grundzüge südosteuropäischer Außenwirtschaftspolitik, 1929-1934, Diss. rer. pol., Köln 1947. See as well the recent insightful analysis of KAISER, Economic Diplomacy, pp. 20-26.

eastern European exports to the German market. This policy succeeded in promoting exports to southeastern Europe, reestablishing the prewar pattern of a German export surplus in the area. The Danubian countries paid for these increased imports by increased exports to Germany, an export surplus in trade with western Europe, and, most importantly, by net imports of United States, French, and British capital.

This pattern was destroyed by the Depression. Primary product prices sharply declined, European agricultural importers, including Germany, increased protection of their domestic agricultural sectors, capital stopped flowing to the primary producing countries and a reverse flow to the creditor countries began. German exports suffered when the Danubian countries had no cash to pay for a German export surplus. In addition, the Danubian countries regarded German agricultural policy as particularly harsh, causing German exports to east-central Europe to decline more than did trade in general.[26]

Although Germany's preferential treaties with Hungary and Rumania, if realized, could have improved the position of German exports, the Brüning government emphasized their political grounds, as a complement to the customs union project and as diplomatic "successes" for domestic consumption. German business leadership was reluctantly persuaded to support the government on such bases, rather than economic grounds.[27] German business was apprehensive that breaking the most-favored-nation system with preferential grain duties for Hungary and

[26] The American representative in Warsaw commented that the Agricultural Conference of Eastern European Agrarian Countries could not help but be anti-German "inasmuch as the Congress was largely made possible by the increased German tariffs on agricultural goods." Weilich (Warsaw) to the secretary of state, September 6, 1930, NA, RG 59, 561. P 1/5.

[27] Both the *Reichsverband der deutschen Industrie* and *Deutsche Industrie- und Handelstag (DIHT)* supported the treaties on political grounds but feared their impact on German exports in third markets: "Der Reichsverband der deutschen Industrie hat den Abschluß von Präferenzverträgen von vornherein nicht befürwortet und sich nur infolge der von der Reichsregierung vorgetragenen politische Gesichtspunkte eine gewisse Zurückhaltung auferlegt." Reichsverband der deutschen Industrie to the RWM and AA, October 29,1931, BA, R 43 I/1206. A similar attitude was taken by the *DIHT*, i.e., that the most-favored-nation principle, the foundation of German foreign trade policy, should not be endangered by the preference treaty with Rumania, DIHT Rundschreiben, April 23, 1931, p. 3, BA R 7 VI/350/2. Kaiser, on the basis of other sources, notes the lack of enthusiasm on the part of German industry for the preference treaties: KAISER, Economic Diplomacy, p. 23. It is not possible to follow the complicated negotiations over reparations ending in the Lausanne Conference nor the futile discussions over "equality of rights" which eventually led to Hitler's torpedoing the Geneva Disarmament talks and walking out from the League of Nations. On both these issues Brüning was far more conciliatory than his sucessors Papen and Schleicher. In terms of the crisis of the agrarian countries of east-central Europe, both Germany and France advanced proposals for multilateral assistance (fonds commun) to the area. Germany resisted any scheme like the Tardieu Plan which implicitly favored Czech industry over German (if the Danube were treated as an economic entity with common tariffs German industry would have been put at a disadvantage). The notion of a fonds commun was favored by both the Germans and the French, but the idea came up most often in the context of a comprehensive settlement (i.e., cancellation) of reparations obligations and inter-allied war debts. The United States not only resisted Germany's preference treaties with Hungary and Rumania but regarded all proposals for a fonds commun as a device to shore up the French alliance system in eastern Europe. Similiarly the United States reasoned that if the Germans and French wished to aid the agricultural

Rumania would only worsen the situation of German exports elsewhere in the world. The late Weimar leadership of the *Reichsverband der deutschen Industrie* – Carl Duisberg, Paul Silverberg, and Ludwig Kastl – remained firmly committed to the principle of a nondiscriminatory trade policy and, until their ouster in the spring of 1933, their policy had the support of a majority of the business leadership. They considered the benefits of the Danubian market far too small to risk Germany's trade with western and northern Europe and the United States. However, the Depression, radically reducing German exports to those areas, also radically altered the attitude of Germany's business elite to the most-favored-nation system.

Negotiation of the preferential treaties proceeded without friction and treaties with Hungary and Rumania were initialed in the fall of 1931. Both treaties featured Germany's unilateral extension of preferential grain duties for the Hungarian and Rumanian exports, although Germany was not granted preferential tariffs for industrial products. The true economic value of the treaties was limited as Germany did not intend to alter its program of agricultural protectionism; nor were specific grain quotas allocated to the treaty partners or guaranteed entrance into the German market. During 1931 and 1932, Rumania and Hungary could expect no dramatic increase in grain exports, even with preferential tariff rates, in view of Germany's exchange control policy limiting payments for imports to a percentage of the country's 1931 exports.[28]

The preferential treaties acquired political significance in the Brüning government out of all proportion to their potential benefits because political prestige had suffered with the defeat of the customs union project. Diplomatic success was deemed necessary to quiet domestic political discontent. In the government's program for political expansion, the customs union project and the end of reparations had loomed large; the customs union had led to a diplomatic fiasco and reparations were ended not by German efforts but by President Hoover's moratorium declaration on war debt payments in June 1931. Able to claim no credit for ending repara-

---

nations of eastern Europe they could easily reduce their defense budgets and encourage the eastern European states to do the same. Great Britain concerned over the development of imperial preference and protection of the home market was reluctant to support French plans for a customs union among the Danubian countries. The best survey of these negotiations may be found in György RANKI, Economy and Foreign Policy: The Struggle of the Great Powers for Hegemony in the Danube Valley, 1919-1939, Boulder, Colorado 1983, pp. 96-134. The failure of all these quid pro quos eventually gave Hitler his great opportunity for an expansionist foreign economic and political policy. For detailed analyses of these negoiations see: Isaac ALTERAS, The Geneva Disarmament Conference: The German Case, U.Ph.D., City College of New York 1971, pp. 26-27, 56, 102; James MOORE, A History of the World Economic Conference: London 1933, U.Ph.D., State University of New York at Stony Brook 1972, pp. 10, 21-22, 200, 230; Ralph SMILEY, The Lausanne Conference, 1932: The Diplomacy of the End of Reparations, U.Ph.D., Rutgers University 1971, pp. 190, 200-201, 344, 348-349, 351; Michael SOPER, The Lausanne Conference 1932: A Political and Diplomatic History, U.Ph.D., University of Wisconsin 1971, pp. 26, 32, 243-244, 275, 285-286.

[28] Theoretically, exports of cereals could increase somewhat if the composition of Rumanian-Hungarian exports to Germany shifted in favor of grains at the expense of other products.

tions, Germany continued to have legal obligations concerning the reparations question until the Lausanne Conference in the summer of 1932, after the fall of Brüning. He had not succeeded with the customs union or reparations, and a third major goal eluded him as well — Germany's military equality of rights, which was not achieved until December 1932 under the Schleicher cabinet. The preferential treaties with Rumania and Hungary were the only hope for diplomatic success for the Brüning government.

But even this modest achievement was not to be: Germany could not ratify the treaties without voluntary and explicit acquiescence by her most-favored-nation partners in the abrogation of their treaty rights; because the preferential treaties concerned grains, Germany needed the consent of Canada, Argentina, Australia, and the United States, the overseas grain exporters. After difficult negotiations, Germany gained the consent of Canada, Argentina, and Australia, and her other most-favored-nation partners. The United States remained silent on the question throughout 1931 and for the first four months of 1932.[29] Considering this to imply America toleration, the Wilhelmstraße pressed Rumania to ratify the treaty, but strong French pressure and American ambiguity made Rumania hesitant to be the first to act. In May 1932 Secretary of State Stimson telegraphed to the American Embassy in Berlin America's refusal to countenance any lessening of its treaty rights.[30] Bound by its commercial treaty with the United States, the Brüning government could only acquiesce to the American dictate, and another foreign policy failure beset the already faltering regime.

---

[29] The preferential treaties were given serious consideration by the American government (State Department, Department of Agriculture) in the late summer and autumn of 1931. The treaties were opposed by the Bureau of Agricultural Economics on the grounds that the preferences would stimulate the production of cereals in the Balkans; the State Department was concerned over the violation of the most-favored-nation clause. However, the decision was made to "let the treaties ride for the present" (J. G. Rogers, assistant secretary), subject to several conditions – such as no opposition in Congress, etc. Sussdorf (Bucharest) to Castle (acting secretary of state), July 31, 1931, NA, RG 59, 662.7131/79; Memorandum on "Preferential Tariffs for Balkan Cereals", Office of Economic Advisor, October 16, 1931, 662.7131/38; J. G. Rogers, "Our Policy Towards Eastern European Tariff Agreements", October 22, 1931, 662.7131/48; Livesey to Feis, October 31, 1931, 662.7131/43. For background on German policy see: Holm SUNDHAUSSEN, Politisches und Wirtschaftliches Kalkül in den Auseinandersetzungen über die deutsch-rumänischen Präferenzvereinbarungen von 1931, in: Revue des Etudes Sud-Est Européennes 14 (1976), pp. 405-424; and idem, Die Weltwirtschaftskrise in Donau-Balkan-Raum und ihre Bedeutung für den Wandel der deutschen Außenpolitik unter Brüning, in: Wolfgang BENZ/Hermann GRAML (ed.), Aspekte deutscher Außenpolitik im 20. Jahrhundert: Aufsätze Hans Rothfels zum Gedächtnis, Stuttgart 1976, pp. 121-165.

[30] Stimson's decision was made in spite of high-level recognition that the treaties were " . . . part of the compromise required to permit a viable Government under Brüning and von Hindenburg . . ." (Livesey to Feis, October 31, 1931, see fn. 30) and against the advice of Ambassador Sacket who emphasized the political importance of the treaties. Stimson to Sackett, May 27, 1932, FRUS, 1932, Vol. II, Washington, D.C. 1947, pp. 346-347.

Brüning's Foreign Policy in Historical Perspective

Stresemann's policies were abandoned by Germany with apparent ease. Brüning's government relied upon support from the upper strata of the bureaucracy, military, and big business, and nowhere was there significant opposition to his adventures in foreign policy. The customs union and preference treaties were nothing less than attempts to achieve the wartime goal of *Mitteleuropa* on the cheap; the absence of substantial opposition indicates how shallow were the roots of Stresemann's compromise policy. Although temporarily submerged by defeat, inflation, and economic prosperity, the *Mitteleuropa* chimera reemerged full force after America's stock market crash. The Brüning government's foreign policy directly anticipates Hitler's expansionism, resting on the same unquestioned premise that German hegemony in east-central Europe was necessary, moral, and politically expedient.

It should be emphasized that both Hitler and Stresemann had a greater sense of political realities than did Brüning or Bülow; Stresemann, for example, had been well aware that raising the Austrian question in any form could lead only to the complete political isolation of Germany: "We find ourselves today face to face with a closed ring of *Anschluß* opponents, which stretches from Warsaw through the Little Entente and Rome to Paris and London. . . . It seems to me therefore, to be of the greatest importance to avoid everything in the *Anschluß* question which might provoke these states and strengthen their opposition to *Anschluß*."[31] Hitler drew the opposite conclusion from the same factors: a disarmed Germany in a multilateral organization such as the League of Nations could never dominate in east-central Europe; only an armed Germany that had greater economic, political, and military strength in bilateral relations with her neighbors could achieve anything in foreign affairs.

Brüning's government attempted political expansion via diplomatic means, which succeeded only in liquidating the positive achievements of the Stresemann era without creating the political, economic, or military bases for realizing its ambitious program in foreign affairs. Politically, Brüning paved the way for Hitler by encouraging expectations of diplomatic success that were unrealizable without war; Hitler knew full well that German hegemony in east-central Europe could be maintained only by military victory over France. Brüning, Curtius, and Bülow were guilty of self-deception amounting to unyeilding obtuseness concerning the political and military realities of interwar Europe.

Hitler and East-Central Europe[32]

Hitler had a tactical advantage over his diplomatic adversaries in his conception of history — to him wars were natural events in the struggle of nations for "living

---

[31] Stresemann to Loebe, August 21, 1925, cited in JOHNSON, Customs Union, p.58.
[32] Despite the extent of the literature on Nazi Germany's relations with east-central Europe, few studies are well grounded in the available archival sources; few treat 1933-39 as a unit; and fewer still are interested in German economic relations with these countries. Works

space"; war and the risk of war were inevitable consequences of state policy. He accepted the risk of war as a policy option from the very beginning, something that French and British politicians had to be driven to accept and then with great reluctance.

Another logical deduction from his Social Darwinist premises was Hitler's conception of expansion into Russia: Germany was overpopulated, needed living space, could not feed the present population; therefore, as a vigorous and superior race, the Germans necessarily had to appropriate the living space of inferior races to survive. But German goals in the East were unreachable while France threatened Germany's rear; therefore France had to be defeated before German living space could be secured in the East. Hitler knew that war with France could revive the allied

by Andreas Hillgruber, Klaus Meiss, and others [see below] either appeared too early to have made extensive use of the German archives and are based primarily upon the Nürnberg documents, or they concentrate on the period immediately preceding the war and the war itself. Outstanding exceptions to this generalization are the works of Hans-Jügen Schröder, Bernd-Jürgen Wendt, and the Hungarian team of Berend and Ranki. Except for the study by Wojciechowski, and Berend/Ranki, no works use both West German and East European archives fully. The literature from the socialist countries generally makes full use of neither the archival resources of that country nor of West Germany. Only Hungary has published extensively from the important archives and has permitted regular access by western scholars. The extensive literature on the *Volksdeutsche* question in eastern Europe sheds little light on the economic and political goals of Nazi Germany before the outbreak of war, with the important exception of the study by Ronald Smelser. Ivan T. BEREND/György RANKI, Magyarorszag a Fasiszta Nemetos "Elettereben" 1933-1939, Budapest 1960; György RANKI, Economy and Foreign Policy: The Struggle of the Great Powers For Hegemony in the Danube Valley, 1919-1939, Boulder, Colorado 1983; Judit FEJES-SCHULMANN, Hungarian-German Relations; idem, Alternativen der ungarischen Außenpolitik während der Weltwirtschaftskrise, Paper presented to the Mainz Symposium on Southeastern Europe, Institut für Europäische Geschichte, Mainz, December, 1979; Andreas HILLGRUBER, Hitler, König Carol und Marschall Antonescu. Die deutsch-rumänischen Beziehungen 1938-1944, Wiesbaden 1954, second edition 1965; Klaus MEISS, Die deutsch-jugoslawischen Beziehungen von Hitlers Regierungsantritt bis zum Ausbruch des Zweiten Weltkriegs, Diss. Phil. Göttingen 1955; Hans-Jürgen SCHRÖDER, Südosteuropa als 'Informal Empire': Das Beispiel Jugoslawiens, in: Jahrbücher für Geschichte Osteuropas 23 (1975); idem, Deutsche Südosteuropapolitik 1929-1936, in: Geschichte und Gesellschaft 2 (1976), pp. 5-32, 70-97; Ronald SMELSER, Volkstumspolitik and the Formation of Nazi Foreign Policy: The Sudeten Problem, 1933-1938, U.Ph.D., Univ. of Wisconsin 1970; Bernd-Jürgen WENDT, England und der deutsche 'Drang Nach Südosten'. Kapitalbeziehungen und Warenverkehr in Südosteuropa zwischen den Weltkriegen in: Imanuel GEISS/Bernd-Jürgen WENDT (eds.), Deutschland in der Weltpolitik des 19. und 20. Jahrhunderts, Düsseldorf 1973, pp. 483-512; Marian WOJCIECHOWSKI, Die polnisch-deutschen Beziehungen, 1933-1938, Leiden 1971. More recently younger scholars have turned their attention to economic diplomacy and German ambitions in east-central Europe. David Kaiser in the work cited previously provides a broad *tour d'horizon* of the interaction of German, French, and British foreign policy vis-a-vis east-central Europe. His work is, however, more insightful in the analysis of French and British policy than German. Philip Marguerat has focused upon German policy and the problem of Rumanian oil in the periode 1938-1940. While discerning in some respects Marguerat ignores the careful preparation which went on before 1938. KAISER, Economic Diplomacy; and Philipe MARGUERAT, Le IIIème Reich et le Pétrole Roumaine, 1938-1940: Contribution a l'étude de la pénétration économique allemande dans le Balkans a la veille et au début de la Seconde Guerre mondiale, Leiden 1977.

coalition, drawing Great Britain into war against Germany, but he hoped to secure British acquiescence by renouncing naval and colonial rivalry with England.

Hitler's fundamental political conceptions and strategic orientation were formulated before he took office in January 1933, as *Mein Kampf* and his second book testify[33], but these major sources and other public statements are mute on the 100 or so million people who occupied the space between Germany and Russia: "It [Hitler's program] dealt exclusively with the major powers and consequently never even mentioned how the war for living space was to be carried into Russia, considering there was no common Soviet-German border. In other words, the later operations against Czechoslovakia and Poland had received no consideration in the over-all plan despite the fact that they were the necessary first steps."[34]

Since the appearance of Jäckel's book, new documentation has been published concerning this lacuna. An alleged secret interview in 1932 by a Munich newspaper editor shows Hitler as a typical Pan-German nationalist regarding east-central Europe: "We must take the necessary measures to protect our people and historic influence in the East; the Baltic States, lying between Germany and Russia, must come under our influence, not that of the Soviets . . . once this East European area, called 'inter-Europe' by certain journalists, has become a German military protectorate, the destruction of this colossus with feet of clay – should it oppose German interests – will be a mere bagatelle."[35] From the context, Hitler would be referring to the total area between Germany and Russia, not merely to the Baltic States.

If solving the Soviet question required the domination of east-central Europe, what would be the prerequisites of such hegemony? In the supposed interview Hitler demanded *Anschluß* and annexation of the Sudetenland. "The Austrian *Anschluß* will present no difficulty." Hungary was Germany's "natural ally" because she was carved up by Versailles "just like Germany." Hitler already envisaged a regrouping of the German minorities in Transylvania (Rumania) and "at the mouth of the Save and Danube", perhaps at Belgrade, which "was and still is, Prince Eugen's fortress."[36] Both Yugoslavia and Czechoslovakia had to be broken up and an independent Croatia and Slovakia established under German aegis, " . . . if the Serbs and Bohemians do not come to their senses." Furthermore, "Bratislava and Zagreb are mere suburbs of Vienna. The people there must learn to speak German again and so acquire German respectability."

---

[33] Adolf HITLER, Mein Kampf, New York 1940, First German edition published in two volumes in 1925 and 1927. Gerhard L. WEINBERG, Hitlers Zweites Buch, Ein Dokument aus dem Jahre 1928, Stuttgart 1961.

[34] Eberhard JÄCKEL, Hitler's World View, Cambridge/Mass. 1981, pp. 41-42.

[35] Edouard CALIC (ed.), Secret Conversations with Hitler, New York 1971, p. 62. Subsequent citations are also from this page. Kaiser uses a long quotation from Rauschning which contains similiar revisionist racial imperialist themes. However, neither Hitler's harangue in Rauschning nor the Calic interview gives much insight into the actual policies which Hitler pursued until 1939. KAISER, Economic Diplomacy, p.63 citing Hermann RAUSCHNING, The Voice of Destruction, New York 1940, pp. 32-39.

[36] CALIC, ebd.

The first part of this monologue presumes that the French allies in east-central Europe would necessarily resist Germany's expansion and would thus have to be dismembered. "Revisionist" thinking is contained in the assumption that Bulgaria, Hungry, and Italy were Germany's natural allies and would be satisfied by Hitler's award of " . . . Dalmatia and the Balkan areas beyond . . ." to Italy, and Macedonia and an Aegean port to Bulgaria. "In short, Austria, Switzerland, Belgium, Yugoslavia and Czechoslovakia must disappear as states; Poland and Rumania must change their status. Both these countries are a biological reservoir of Jewry." A "special mission" was assigned to Finland and Bulgaria as anchor points in a "protective wall against Russian imperialism and the Slavs from Northern Norway to the Black Sea. . . ."

In this supposed 1932 interview Germany's interests were defined exclusively in terms of uniting all branches of the German nation into a greater German state, but Hitler departs from typical ultra-right or conservative expansionist views in omitting a harangue against Poland, that "mutilation in the East", which was not to be broken up but only have its "status changed". This does anticipate Hitler's policy of conciliation with Poland that led to the 1934 Non-Aggression Pact.

Once in power Hitler allowed neither the *Volksdeutsche* question nor hopes for a revisionist alliance to dominate his foreign policy, and he soon recognized that he could not rely on Mussolini to support the resurgence of Germany, particularly as Italy remained opposed to *Anschluß*. Hitler cleverly pacified the nationalist frenzy of both Nazis and conservatives by permitting the Austrian Nazi leader Habicht to first conduct a propaganda war from Bavarian soil against the Austrian state and later the putsch of July 1934 in which Dollfuß was assassinated. But Hitler carefully avoided staking government prestige on the success of *Anschluß*, thus defusing his overzealous followers on both sides of the border and avoiding a debacle like Brüning's customs union project.

Hitler soon made it clear that, regarding Yugoslavia, he would be bound neither by Pan-German prejudices (Prince Eugen's fortress)[37] nor sentimental regard for revisionist solidarity (Mussolini's expansionist appetites). In the summer of 1933 Germany offered to grant economic concessions to Yugoslavia, in this case a preferential plum quota, and in October Hitler ordered the suppression of the Croatian Exile press in Germany, telling Rosenberg and the APA to break off political contacts with the Croatian opposition. The commercial treaty of 1934 with Yugoslavia began a period of political and economic detente that culminated in Hitler's January 1938 offer to guarantee the status quo between Hungary and Yugoslavia. Before the outbreak of war Hitler consistently subordinated "her natural ally" Hungary to conciliate Yugoslavia and Rumania. If Prince Paul's government had survived the April 1941 putsch, it is highly unlikely that Hungary (or Italy or Bulgaria) would ever have been "satisfied" at the expense of Yugoslavia.

From merely recognizing Poland in his 1932 interview, Hitler went a long way

[37] For the recurrence of this theme: Hans-Ulrich WEHLER, 'Reichsfestung Belgrad', Nationalsozialistische 'Raumordnung' in Südosteuropa, in: Vierteljahrshefte für Zeitgeschichte 11 (1963), pp. 72-84.

after he came to power; shelving the explosive Corridor, Posen, and Silesian issues initiated Hitler's remarkable innovation in German foreign policy: detente with Poland. Hitler saw no useful purpose in struggling to restore the 1914 borders; his conception of expansion eastward put the issues of the Corridor and Silesia in second or third place. Knowing that his policy of conciliation with Poland was not popular among conservatives, Hitler still regarded it as a necessary sacrifice, and his shock at Polish recalcitrance in refusing his "generous offer" in 1939 was genuine, because in terms of the conservative demand that the 1914 borders be restored, his demands for integration of Danzig and an autobahn under German control through the corridor were moderate. Why Hitler's "moderation" failed is, of course, another question.

None of Hitler's pre-1933 statements or writings indicate clearly his foreign policy from 1933 to 1939 in east-central Europe, but once in office he inaugurated a policy of political conciliation toward Poland and Yugoslavia. Whatever his private views on the viability or desirability of maintaining these states, Hitler built up a circle of German-dominated states in east-central Europe by political support of the status quo and economic expansion.

CHAPTER II

THE IMPACT OF THE GREAT DEPRESSION

1. Economic Disaster and Political Detente with Yugoslavia

Following World War I, Germany was determined to regain its former economic position and to make inroads into the new provinces of Yugoslavia and the old Serbian state core. This, with German reparations obligations of deliveries in kind ("*Sachlieferungen*"), determined relations with Yugoslavia during the 1920s and until the Lausanne Conference in 1932. German trade policy was successful in that a most-favored-nation commercial treaty with Yugoslavia was signed in 1927; but Yugoslavia, unlike Rumania in 1927, carefully avoided any settlement of German prewar loans and limited itself to friendly negotiation on the loan question.[1]

Despite the Depression and its resulting frictions, Germany maintained more cordial relations with Yugoslavia than with Rumania, where growing animosity was increased by the failure of the preference treaties. The absence of serious recrimination between Yugoslavia and Germany is surprising considering the possible friction points between them: Germany's protectionist agricultural policy was as harmful to Yugoslavia as to the other states of east-central Europe; the termination of reparations deliveries decreed by the Lausanne Conference was a blow to the Yugoslav budget, which had relied upon the deliveries in kind to finance many capital projects.

Yugoslavia and Germany met precipitous capital withdrawals with similar policies of import restriction in the hope of creating the trade surplus necessary to obtain cash to service the capital flight and foreign bondholders. Germany's continuing export surplus during the Depression led to Yugoslav countermeasures against German imports and finally to freezing German claims in a special dinar account at the Yugoslav National Bank in Belgrade[2], thus denying Germany the cash needed to

---

[1] Negotiations on the prewar loans continued until the end of 1930. Yugoslavia, despite its disastrous economic situation, negotiated in good faith, but a tentative settlement reached in July 1930 was forestalled by German bondholders who repudiated the agreement. Given the economic conditions of the period, any settlement would have broken down: Von Hassell (Belgrade) to AA, December 11, 1930. PA, Gesandtschaft Belgrad, Fach 79, Po 19, Vorkriegsanleihen.

[2] Hagemann (RWM) to AA, May 26, 1932. PA, Sonderreferat Wirtschaft, Jugoslawien, Finanzwesen 16, Devisenangelegenheiten mit Deutschland, Bd. 2. Hagemann commented on the difficulty in arranging barter agreements with Yugoslavia to unfreeze German claims, but noting the financial weakness and nondiscriminatory character of Yugoslavia and its policy, advised against countermeasures.

meet its obligations.[3] Germany omitted Yugoslavia from its preference policy, which could have worsened relations, but the Germans promised to negotiate after the preference treaties with Rumania and Hungary were ratified.[4] (These treaties were met with opposition from the United States; as a result, they were never concluded.)

Exchange difficulties were, however, only a contributing factor to Germany's denunciation of the 1927 Commercial Treaty in September 1932.[5] The prime cause of the German denunciation was pressure from agricultural interests wanting to regain the freedom to impose new tariffs on eggs[6]: the egg tariff set in the 1927 commercial treaty had been generalized to all most-favored-nation treaty partners during the treaty's term.

Germany's determination to impose a supertariff on eggs foreshadowed the radical agricultural policy changes under Hugenberg and Darré. The traditional compromise between the East Elbian Junkers and the small peasantry of the West, begun in 1925 with tariffs on bread grains, was broken by the new tariffs and quotas imposed on feed grains; successful support of the outmoded rye culture of the East Elbe required increasingly comprehensive agricultural protection, including complete control of imports of eggs, dairy products, and cheap fats. Each new stage of protection worsened German relations with the agricultural countries of eastern Europe: cheap eggs were an important export commodity in Yugoslavia's trade with Germany, whose 20-mark tariff imposed in the spring of 1933 meant falling prices and a surplus on the Yugoslav domestic market.[7]

---

[3] Germany, although approving barters in principle, refused to approve Reich insurance for such transactions because of the doubtful state of Yugoslav finances: Flach (RWM) to AA, April 11, 1932, ibid. A second memorandum indicated that German firms were withdrawing from the Yugoslav market because no cash was available for payment.

[4] Unsigned and undated minute (between February 13, 1932, and November 6, 1932), BA, R 43, II/1457.

[5] Prince (Belgrade) to the secretary of state, September 19, 1932, NA, RG 59, 66OH.662/6. The treaty originally had only a two-year term but was tactically prolonged by both parties, according to Yugoslav Commerce Minister Mohorić. Enclosure 1, Mohorić Statement, *Politika*, September 14, 1932 (translation), ibid. The treaty ceased to be binding on March 6, 1933.

[6] By autumn 1930 German industry was considering support of a 30-mark egg tariff rise if German export interests would not suffer an "unerträgliche Belastung". Scherer (GHH staff economist) to Paul Reusch, Oberhausen, September 23, 1930: 'Stellungnahme und Schreiben von Reichsverband der deutschen Industrie, "Markierungszwang für ausländische Eier und Hopfen"', HA-GHH 40010124/2. In July 1932 Karl Ritter, head of the Economic Policy Department, told Fotić, Yugoslav Minister at Lausanne, that Germany wanted freedom on the egg tariff. Von Hassell (Bled) to AA, July 19, 1932, PA, Sonderreferat Wirtschaft, Jugoslawien, Finanzwesen 16, Bd. 2.

[7] Emil Kekich, Economic and Trade Notes, April 18, 1933, commercial attaché Belgrade, NA, RG 151. In July 1932 Fotić indicated to von Hassell that the egg tariff question was more important to Yugoslavia than any potential grain barter transaction. Von Hassell (Bled) to AA, July 19, 1932, op. cit. Fotić may have been anticipating the bad Yugoslav harvest of 1932 that produced no exportable wheat surplus, naturally decreasing Yugoslavia's interest in a grain preference treaty on the Hungarian-Rumanian model and increasing the importance of other exports, such as eggs. Morgan (Berlin) to the secretary of state, September 23, 1932, NA, RG

Although relations with Yugoslavia did remain more cordial than those of Germany and Rumania, the large German firms active in Rumania were relatively inactive in Yugoslavia and the efforts of German trade organizations to promote trade apparently foundered completely.[8]

Germany's and Yugoslavia's mutual tolerance cannot be attributed to any discernable economic accommodation; the absence of the trade war mentality characteristic of Germany's relations with Rumania and Poland can be explained only by the political rapprochement begun in the mid-1920s.[9] There was no particular German political stratagem responsible for this political detente in the midst of economic chaos; German foreign policy was merely drifting after the failure of the customs union with Austria and the preference treaties with Hungary and Rumania.

One cause of the detente was Yugoslav fear of Italian revisionism. Fascist Italy, by virulent propaganda encouraging Hungarian and Bulgarian revisionism and by subsidizing Utase Croatian terrorists, brought unremitting pressure against Yugoslavia and was the chief concern of Yugoslav foreign policy. Mussolini's campaign against Yugoslavia reached a fever pitch in 1932-33, leading French observers to conclude that Italian policy was premised upon eventual dismemberment of the Yugoslav state.[10] The real threat to Yugoslavia's continued existence, however, was equivocation in French foreign policy: Yugoslavia, the least favored of France's eastern allies, had merely a Friendship Treaty dating from 1927, not a military alliance, and France was accommodating Mussolini in his drive for Balkan domination to win Italian support against revisionist Germany. Yugoslavia, although never for-

*

59, 66OH.6231/37. In this situation the German attempt to make lifting of the egg tariff dependent upon the tariff-free export of 100,000 tons of wheat was doomed, even without the United States *diktat* on the preference question. On the grain offer, see: HPA 32, March 17, 1932, PA, Ha Pol, Handakten Wiehl, Präferenz, Bd. 1.

[8] Basson/Keiwarth (*Reichsverband des Deutschen Groß- und Überseehandels e.V. — Berlin*) [RDG] to AA, August 12, 1932, PA, Sonderreferat Wirtschaft, Jugoslawien, Finanzwesen 16, Bd. 2. This organization proposed to purchase Yugoslav fruit in order to release frozen claims estimated at 30 million marks.

[9] In 1927 Austen Chamberlain, British foreign minister, proposed Great Power mediation in the Italo-Yugoslav conflict. At that time Stresemann believed that Yugoslavia would "perhaps" welcome German participation. 'Ministerbesprechung: Italien/Südslawischer Streitfall', March 24, 1927, BA, R 43 II/1957. Later rumors of Yugoslav-German rapprochement made the Wilhelmstraße fearful that German intentions would be misunderstood and blocked a visit to Yugoslavia by the noted pan-German publicist Paul Rohrbach. Koepke to DG Belgrade, March 6, 1928, PA, Politische Abteilung II, Jugoslawien, Politische Beziehungen Jugoslawiens zu Deutschland, Bd 2. British Minister Kennard, commenting on increasing German influence in Belgrade, laid it at the door of "shortsighted" Italian policy. Köster (DG Belgrad) to AA, December 1, 1928, ibid. Whatever the reason, German diplomats were pleased at the progress of German influence in Yugoslavia. Busse (DG Belgrad) to AA, June 18, 1928, ibid. Memorandum by Köster on a conversation with Father Koroschetz, September 27, 1929, ibid.

[10] This was the opinion of the French ministers in both Belgrade and Rome. Naggiar (Belgrade) to Paul-Boncour (Paris), January 6, 1933, DDF, 1st Series, Vol. 2, pp. 370-371; Dampierre (Rome) to Paul-Boncour (Paris), January 15, 1933, ibid., p. 454.

mally abandoned either by France or by its allies in the Little Entente, was nonetheless in a very exposed position with regard to Italy.[11]

Yugoslavia naturally looked to Germany as the only Great Power whose support could be reasonably expected. Hitler and the Wilhelmstraße clearly understood the implications of Yugoslavia's fear of Italy and anger with France — Germany and Yugoslavia had a joint interest in preventing Italian domination of Austria and restoration of the Habsburgs.[12] King Alexander was not happy at the prospect of Hitler's coming to power[13], but he expressed his fears privately and without drawing closer to France. He and his ministers avoided identification with the League of Nations and the loyalty to France characteristic of Rumania's Titulescu. In 1933, when Nazi Germany signaled support for a united South Slav state by granting concessions for Yugoslav plums and silencing the Croatian emigrant press, the way was open for the commercial treaty of 1934.

The Yugoslav-German political detente during the Depression, although intangible, was very real — neither country allowed the recriminations and hostility, so easily created by an economic slump, to fester. There were no political obstacles in the way of economic rapprochement between Germany and Yugoslavia.

2. From Trade War to Economic Rapprochement, 1933-34

Mutual goodwill was not sufficient to prevent a brief trade war, an inevitable result of the economic logic behind the foreign trade policies of both Germany and Yugoslavia. In February 1932, Germany anticipated the formal expiration of the commercial treaty on March 6 by imposing comprehensive agricultural quotas, which Yugoslavia met with maximum tariffs on German goods. Immediately after the treaty expired, Germany imposed its *Obertarif* but rescinded it when faced with a trade war with Yugoslavia *and* Czechoslovakia: "Under these conditions we wish to avoid sharpening relations with Yugoslavia and possibly awakening the appearance that we are seeking economic conflict with the Little Entente as a whole, part-

---

[11] Prince commented in early 1933: "There can be no denying the fact that Yugoslavia has not a single neighbor which is friendly." Prince (Belgrade) to the secretary of state, NA, RG 59, February 20, 1933, 76OH.00/45.

[12] Memorandum by von Hassell, Belgrade, April 17, 1931, PA, Geheim, Politische Abteilung IIb, Jugoslawien, Politik 2, Bd. 1. Characteristically von Hassell reported King Alexander's agreement with this view in somewhat exaggerated form: "Jugoslawien müßte doch ein großes Deutschland als Nachbar gerade im Hinblick auf Italien sehr viel lieber sein, als ein schwaches Österreich. Dem stimmte der König restlos bei." This assessment would later prove to be the case, but in 1931 King Alexander was still hoping for increased French support, indicated by earlier segments of the interview.

[13] King Alexander spoke of his fear of the German right to the American minister in Belgrade. It is interesting to note that both before and after the Nazi *Machtergreifung* Alexander assumed a political rapprochement between the two "Fascisms" that, in terms of Balkan policy, existed only after the outbreak of war in 1939. Prince (Belgrade) to the secretary of state, NA, RG 59, August 3, 1932, 76OH.00/42; and Prince (Belgrade) to the secretary of state, March 28, 1933, ibid., 76OH.00/46.

icularly as we have repeatedly told Yugoslav representatives here that the amalga-
mation of the Little Entente in the economic area as well creates a new situation for
us and we must first await further developments."[14] Wiehl proposed a three-month
operating procedure allowing the maximum tariff on certain commodities and giving Germany complete tariff autonomy regarding the Yugoslav harvest. Although
more moderate than an outright tariff war, this proposal would have been certain
provocation under normal circumstances; the tariff war was to be limited but the
maximum tariff would be levied on some of Yugoslavia's most important agricultural exports (plums, poultry, and hides), and there would be no protection for
Yugoslavia after the harvest was in.[15]

But in 1933, conditions were far from normal and Belgrade accepted the German
proposals as a basis for discussion.[16] Pilja, Yugoslav state secretary in the Commerce Ministry, declared via the Yugoslav legation in Berlin that Yugoslavia "was
ready to take up negotiations at any time, so long as Germany gives up its ridicu-
lously high protective tariffs." Pilja particularly wanted the egg tariff reduced from
70 to 20 marks.[17] Under Hugenberg, however, the German drive toward supertar-
iffs was underway, despite Wilhelmstraße warnings of the consequences of such a
policy. In early May the Wilhelmstraße unsuccessfully opposed raising the egg tariff
from 70 to 100 marks, pointing to the "disastrous effects" of such an increase on
Germany's relations with the states of southeastern Europe.[18]

Pilja traveled to Berlin for economic talks in mid-May despite the provocation of
the increased egg tariff. After verbal sparring covering Germany's assertion that
while the Yugoslav maximal tariff was prohibitive, Germany's own was not, he outlined his proposals for a trade detente, insisting on a one-year renunciation of the
German supertariff on eggs, and further tariff concessions on eggs, plums, beans,
and carp. Pilja did agree to Germany's suggested three-month provisional agree-

[14] Wiehl to DG Belgrade, March 15, 1933, PA, Direktoren, Handakten Ritter, Ha Pol,
Jugoslawien, Bd. 2. The *Reichsverband des Deutschen Groß- und Überseehandels e.V. — Berlin*
[RDG] reported that the Yugoslav customs authorities imposed the maximum tariff without
transitional measures and German export firms who had shipped to Yugoslavia figuring price
and profit margin on the old tariff schedule had to pay either for the difference in tariff rates
or for the return of the products to Germany. Although hoping for some sort of transitional
period, the RDG was pessimistic considering the German agricultural policy. Basson/Kei-
warth (RDG) to RFM, March 13, 1933, BA, R 2/10220.

[15] Plums, poultry, and hides amounted to only 3.5 million marks in German imports from
Yugoslavia in 1932. Thus most of Yugoslavia's exports would have been exempt from the
maximum tariff.

[16] Dufour (DG Belgrad) to AA, March 22, 1933, PA, Ha Pol, Handakten Clodius, Jugoslawien, Bd. 1.

[17] Unsigned minute (interview with Yugoslav attaché Rachić), April 15, 1933, PA, Direktoren, Handakten Ritter, Ha Pol, Jugoslawien, Bd. 2.

[18] HPA (Interministerial), May 3, 1933 (21), and May 8, 1933 (23), PA, Ha Pol, Handakten Wiehl, Ha Pol Ausschuß. At this later meeting the decision to study possible agricultural
concessions to Hungary was recorded. Germany's economic relations were unique in that the
way for the 1934 commercial treaty was prepared by the informal diplomacy of Werner Daitz,
head of the Außenhandelsamt of the NDSAP. See the analysis of G. Ranki and I. Berend,
most recently in RANKI, Economy and Foreign Policy, pp.126-127.

ment, which would allow serious negotiations to begin after the world economic conference. Wiehl, although refusing concessions on eggs or carp, indicated tentative approval of a 3- to 4-million-mark corn purchase at 14% above the world market price, but only if " . . . German big business takes over the loss."[19] There were various other barter initiatives involving German industry, but none was very successful[20], and as this one was not mentioned again, it apparently did not excite much interest in business circles either. Pilja went home empty-handed.

Barren negotiations continued through the late spring and summer. In late May the German minister to Belgrade, Dufour von Feronce, received a letter specifying Yugoslav demands: Yugoslavia wanted "special facilities" for exports to Germany, including tariff preferences for wheat and corn and a general most-favored-nation treaty (no preferences requested on eggs, fish, or fruits) incorporating the wheat and corn preferences and an agreement on tourism.[21] A few days later Yugoslavia banned the export of oil seeds or oil seed products, a gesture Berlin found encouraging in that it opened the way for importing such commodities from Yugoslavia via a clearing agreement.[22] Germany was vitally interested in developing oil seed production in southeastern Europe because the fats import gap had proved impervious to the most radical agricultural protectionist measures.

Germany met Yugoslavia's demands with the offer of a simple most-favored-nation treaty premised upon acceptance of Germany's new superprotectionist agricultural policy.[23] Ulrich, a Wilhelmstraße official maintaining that Germany could not grant tariff concessions on eggs, poultry, fish, and fruits because of the domestic agricultural situation and the impending World Economic Conference, stated further that preferential treatment of Yugoslav grain was impossible because the Hungarian and Rumanian preferential treaties had not yet been ratified. Also, a tourist agreement would be negotiable only if Yugoslavia agreed to place supplemental orders with German industry equal to the spending of German tourists in Yugoslavia.[24]

---

[19] Memorandum by Wiehl, May 15, 1933, PA, Direktoren, Handakten Ritter, Ha Pol, Jugoslawien, Bd. 2.

[20] German business activity in Yugoslavia during this period was far less than in Rumania. Material on the barter transactions conducted can be found in: PA, Sonderreferat Wirtschaft, Jugoslawien, Handel 11 3A, Austauschgeschäfte, Bd. 1.

[21] Pilja to the AA, Belgrade, May 26, 1933, PA, Ha Pol, Handakten Clodius, Jugoslawien, Bd. 1. This was summarized in a telegram: Dufour (DG Belgrad) to AA, May 27, 1933, PA, Direktoren, Handakten Ritter, Ha Pol, Jugoslawien, Bd. 2.

[22] Hess (DG Belgrad) to Sarnow (RWM), June 4, 1933 and June 11, 1933, PA, Ha Pol, Handakten Clodius, Jugoslawien, Bd. 3. The latter dispatch noted that Pilja had opened negotiations on the question of promoting oil seeds production.

[23] Ulrich to DG Belgrad, June 15, 1933, PA, Direktoren, Handakten Ritter, Ha Pol, Jugoslawien, Bd. 2. The proposed treaty was for three months with a one-month denunciation period.

[24] The German government took the position that money spent by German tourists in Yugoslavia should be treated as German purchase of Yugoslav exports and compensated as such in the clearing. Eventually Yugoslavia was forced to accede to a variant of this idea; given the totality of German currency control, without Reich agreement there was no way tourists could legally spend cash in Yugoslavia.

Yugoslavia's surprisingly restrained reaction was to moderate its position and offer to exchange a four-month most-favored-nation treaty with a one-month denunciation period for German compromise on the plum tariff.[25] Initially, Germany spurned this offer. The German legation in Belgrade was advised that the Agricultural Ministry refused any tariff concessions on plums and Dufour was told to negotiate in a dilatory fashion.[26] Yugoslavia eventually accepted Germany's proposed four-month most-favored-nation treaty with denunciation possible after three months, to take effect one month after notification.[27] Thus, with no German concessions to Yugoslav agriculture, the tariff war ended.

There was a German policy reassessment after the fall of Hugenberg as agricultural and economics minister, which, despite the success with Yugoslavia, led to a limited break in agricultural tariff escalation and market isolation from foreign agricultural producers. Ironically, Walther Darré, Nazi Bauernführer, new agricultural minister and apostle of agricultural autarchy, although not sympathetic to German export interests, was more flexible than Hugenberg, the reputed representative of heavy industry, in implementing agricultural protection. Two weeks after Germany rejected any agricultural concessions and two days after Yugoslavia had accepted a treaty on this basis, the interministerial Economic Policy Committee reversed itself and declared Germany willing to conclude a one-year treaty containing tariff concessions on plums.[28]

As the earlier offer was also still good, Germany was ready to conclude either an immediate four-month treaty with the prospect of tariff concessions on plums after the denunciation of the Franco-German supplementary agreement or a one-year treaty having similar provisions. Under the four-month treaty the plum preferences would depend upon Yugoslavia's one-year guarantee of most-favored-nation treatment for German exports. If Yugosavia rejected both offers, Germany would raise tariffs on fresh and processed plums after the tariff truce, which had followed the collapse of the World Economic Conference, expired.[29] There was as yet no plan for implementing the concessions to Yugoslavia, but Berlin was prepared to compensate Yugoslavia for any difficulty in marketing fresh plums in Germany with increased marketing opportunities for dried plums. In other words, by one means or another, Germany would guarantee the current volume of plum imports from Yugoslavia.

Despite these concessions and a possible supertariff on plums if a one-year treaty

---

[25] Dufour (DG Belgrad) to AA, June 23, 1933, PA, Direktoren, Handakten Ritter, Ha Pol, Jugoslawien, Bd. 2. Dufour indicated that Yugoslavia was holding in abeyance its demands on grapes and apples but not dropping them.

[26] Ulrich to DG Belgrad, July 1933. (Written between June 29, 1933 and July 10, 1933.) ibid. The Yugoslav position was discussed at the HPA meetings on June 29, 1933 (30) and July 5, 1933 (31), PA, Ha Pol, Handakten Wiehl, Ha Pol Ausschuß.

[27] Dufour (DG Belgrad) to AA, PA, Direktoren, Handakten Ritter, Ha Pol, Jugoslawien, Bd. 2.

[28] HPA meeting, July 13, 1933 (32), PA, Ha Pol, Handakten Wiehl, Ha Pol Ausschuß.

[29] Ritter to DG Belgrad, July 13, 1933 and July 20, 1933, PA, Direktoren, Handakten Ritter, Ha Pol, Jugoslawien, Bd. 2.

were not concluded, Yugoslavia was reluctant.[30] The Wilhelmstraße insisted a one-year treaty was a prerequisite for a binding plum tariff at the old rate; the other alternative offered was a special plum quota at a preferential tariff rate for a four-month treaty.[31] Yugoslavia found this more acceptable and a provisional four-month most-favored-nation treaty became effective August 1, 1933.[32]

The exact character of German concessions on plums remained to be determined. Ritter had already indicated that there would be no "official" sanction of the guaranteed quota for plums; it would be a purely "private" transaction between the German canning industry (*Deutsche Obst- und Gemüse-Verwertungsindustrie*) and *Prizad*, the Yugoslav state trading organization.[33] The Wilhelmstraße hoped that this convenient fiction would conceal its violation of the most-favored-nation principle from the United States. Although the issue was small, Germany was not being overcautious; American opposition had already scuttled preference treaties with Hungary and Rumania, embarrassing the Brüning government. Moreover, Yugoslavia and the United States in 1932 ranked first and second in plum production and so competed on the world market.[34] German preference tariffs for Yugoslav plums, directly contradicting the most-favored-nation principle, thus threatened United States export interests.[35]

By the second week of August Bülow, state secretary in the Wilhelmstraße, gave the Yugoslav minister in Berlin a detailed outline of the proposed plum preference system.[36] There was to be an import subsidy, or rebate, system for plums, plum

[30] Dufour (DG Belgrad) to AA, July 21, 1933, PA, Ha Pol, Handakten Clodius, Jugoslawien, Bd. 2.

[31] Ritter to DG Belgrad, Jul 27, 1933, PA, Direktoren, Handakten Ritter, Ha Pol, Jugoslawien, Bd. 2. With prohibitive German tariffs of 30 marks per 100 kilos for fresh plums and 40 marks per 100 kilos for sacked plums, the offered preferential tariff rate of 10 marks per 100 kilos on sacked plums for a quota of 6,000 tons was attractive, although not legally binding on the German government. Yugoslav fears about apple and grape exports were allayed — no new tariff increases were being contemplated.

[32] Dufour (DG Belgrad) to AA, July 29, 1933, PA, Ha Pol, Handakten Clodius, Jugoslawien, Bd. 2. The official exchange of notes was published in *Reichsgesetzblatt*, II, 1933, p. 519.

[33] *Prizad* — "Privilegovano Izvonzo Aktionarsko Drusto" — was the state trading organization, functioning as a monopoly purchasing agent for agricultural products. It attempted to buy agricultural produce from the peasantry at high domestic prices and then sell abroad with the least possible loss. The policy, as practiced by Yugoslavia and other countries of southeastern Europe was a failure and a financial disaster.

[34] Memorandum of the Yugoslav Ministry for Commerce and Industry, Belgrade, July 1933, BA, R 7 VI/268/1. In 1932 Yugoslavia produced 850,000 tons of plums, the United States produced 700,000 tons. For France, the next leading producer, the figure is 200,000.

[35] This has been pointed out by Hans-Jürgen SCHRÖDER in his book, Deutschland und die Vereinigten Staaten, 1933-1939, Wiesbaden 1970, pp. 149, 274. Kaiser, while pointing out correctly that this period was the crucial turning point in the movement away from the most favored nation system to a policy of discrimination, fails to credit the Wilhemstraße for its initiative in the plum quota. Although a small thing in itself, this quota foreshadowed the future course of German foreign economic policy, and, in particular, put Germany on a collision course with the United States. KAISER, Economic Diplomacy, pp. 73-74. For a brief analysis of this episode see, RANKI, Economy and Foreign Policy, p. 129.

[36] Bülow (AA) to Balugdžić (Berlin), August 9, 1933, PA, Ha Pol, Handakten Clodius, Jugoslawien, Bd. 3.

sauce, and geese, whereby part of the German tariff fee would be returned to the Yugoslav National Bank to help bridge the gap between the world market price and the Yugoslav export price. In addition, Yugoslavia was granted a 20,000-ton quota for flax seed, one-half of which by weight could be used to export the soja beans that were also to be covered by substantial subsidies.

According to Dufour, the Yugoslav commerce minister intended to denounce the provisional August treaty despite the concessions, in order to improve his domestic political position, but Dufour continued to recommend a conciliatory attitude toward Lazarević, department chief in the Yugoslav Commerce Ministry, who was going to Berlin to negotiate.[37] The commerce minister was, in any event, forestalled by the Yugoslav foreign minister who told Dufour that peace in trade relations was in the interest of both countries and prolonging provisional agreement would make negotiation of a long-term treaty possible.

Berlin found the Yugoslav foreign minister's proposal of an 8,000-ton quota at the earlier tariff rate acceptable as a basis of negotiation.[38] Agreement was rapid and was formalized in an exchange of letters and a protocol signed by Köhler.[39] The terms included Germany's guarantee of a plum import quota of 8,000 tons at a tariff of 10 marks per 100 kilos (3 marks above the old rate)[40]; a loophole in the increased tariff was in a provision allowing, for the period of August 1933 to July 1934, tariff-free import of plums up to 65% of the requirements of individual factories manufacturing plum sauce. Provided the plums were made into sauce, individual canning factories could purchase Yugoslav plums tariff-free, giving the plums a clear edge in the German market. Bülow made it clear in a supplementary letter that the 65% quota was intended to give Yugoslavia a *minimum* quota of 3,000 tariff-free tons and it would be raised if insufficient.[41] Germany also conceded the same preferential carp tariff to Yugoslavia that had been accorded Hungary.[42]

Meiss correctly comments that this agreement " . . . did not have great significance for the total trade transactions . . ." between the two countries[43], but the preferential agreements with Yugoslavia and Hungary paved the way for the 1934 commercial treaties of February (Hungary) and May (Yugoslavia) and indicate the policy reorientation that was to culminate in Schacht's New Plan in September 1934.

[37] Dufour (DG Belgrad) to AA, August 23, 1933, ibid.
[38] Dufour (Belgrade) to AA, August 29, 1933, PA, Direktoren, Handakten Ritter, Ha Pol, Jugoslawien, Bd. 2; Ha Pol Ausschuß Meeting of August 29, 1933, PA, Ha Pol, Handakten Wiehl, Ha Pol Ausschuß.
[39] Bülow (AA) to Balugdžić (Berlin), September 14, 1933, PA, Ha Pol, Handakten Clodius, Jugoslawien, Bd. 2; Protocol signed by Dr. Fritz Köhler and Dr. Milan Lazarević, September 14, 1933, PA, Direktoren, Handakten Ritter, Ha Pol, Jugoslawien, Bd. 2.
[40] This covered all types of plums and plum products. Protocol, September 14, 1933, Paragraph 1.a.
[41] Bülow to Balugdžić, September 14, 1933, op. cit.
[42] Protocol, September 14, 1933, op. cit., Paragraph 2. Interestingly, Yugoslavia claimed, and Germany granted, this concession under the most-favored-nation principle. Of course, these preferences and quotas were not made available to Germany's other most-favored-nation treaty partners.
[43] MEISS, Beziehungen, p. 60.

America's refusal to countenance any deviation from the most-favored-nation principle had helped bring about the collapse of Brüning's preferential treaty policy with southeastern Europe. In the summer of 1933, with the special quota and tariff concessions to Hungary and Yugoslavia, Germany began to systematically bypass that principle.

Plums, carp, and soja beans are clearly small beer in European power politics. When, however, the great creditor powers — the United States, France and Great Britain — failed to implement any viable policy to deal with the agricultural catastrophe of east-central Europe, National Socialist Germany was presented with its great opportunity. Plums and carp in 1933 paved the way for petroleum, copper, and bauxite in 1939.

CHAPTER III

THE GERMAN-YUGOSLAV COMMERCIAL TREATY OF APRIL
1934

1. German Policy

The concessions to Yugoslavia and Hungary in the summer of 1933 evidence Germany's willingness to implement a discriminatory trade policy. By the end of 1933 Berlin decided to inaugurate a new trade policy in southeastern Europe and begin negotiating new trade treaties with Hungary and Yugoslavia. The key agricultural concessions that made these treaties possible were still justified on political rather than economic grounds, however. Reichsbank President Schacht had been advocating a discriminatory trade policy since December 1932, but it took the crisis of German raw materials supply to bring about the complete break with the nondiscriminatory trade characteristic of the New Plan (September 1934).

The existing treaties with Hungary and Yugoslavia had been a step toward a discriminatory policy even though neither the Economics Ministry nor Finance Ministry thought that economic benefits alone justified paying large subsidies to market agricultural products within Germany. Therefore, within German ministerial councils, the Wilhelmstraße's argument that the treaties would undermine the Little Entente was a crucial factor in the approval of the subsidy policy.

In December 1933 the Economic Policy Committee (HPA) opened negotiations with Hungary and Yugoslavia for new commercial treaties. The treaty with Hungary, containing secret sections based upon a previous informal understanding on the scope and method of trade discrimination, was signed in February 1934. Negotiations with Yugoslavia were more complicated as Yugoslavia would not reveal its intentions before the trade talks began.[1] It was mid-February 1934 before Ulrich,

---

[1] Stein to RWM, RFM and RMEL, March 3, 1934, PA, Direktoren, Handakten Ritter, Ha Pol, Jugoslawien, Bd. 2. As early as October 4, 1933, Hans Posse (State Secretary, Economics Ministry), advocated an "active commercial policy based on reciprocity" which should concentrate upon "markets ruled by German merchants, especially Southeastern Europe and Northern European states." Kaiser sees this position as a fore-shadowing of Schacht's *New Plan* of September, 1934. However, Posse was not able to carry the day with his boss, Kurt Schmitt (Economics Minister, former chief executive of the Allianz Insurance Company). While in his analysis of Posse's policy suggestions Kaiser emphasizes general macroeconomic problems — rising imports, declining exports, overvaluation of the Reichsmark — he later indicates that "although the original impetus behind German trade agreements with Southeastern European countries in 1934-1935 was largely political, trade under the Nazi regime increasingly had to serve pressing economic needs generated by Hitler's rearmament policies." KAISER, Economic Diplomacy, p. 130. Kaiser blurs the distinction between economic and pol-

acting for the Wilhelmstraße, told Balugdžić that Germany was ready to send a delegation to Belgrade.[2] Berlin was informed within a few days that Pilja had agreed to the German proposal.[3]

Hitler set the tone in an interview with Balugdžić[4], stressing that Germany harbored no hostility toward Yugoslavia and was ready to expand trade relations:

> We are ready to take Serbian products insofar as it is in our power to do so, but it is recognized that this is only possible within very circumscribed limits; furthermore, we can only bear the burden of imports if German goods are taken in return. We are ready, however, to seriously study the existing possibilities and towards this end a commission will go to Belgrade in the course of this month. The Serbian government should not doubt our good will.[5]

Hitler was interested in economic issues, although undoubtedly less well informed on the technical functioning of the clearing system and the details of economic negotiations than, for example, on military procurement and hardware. Pursuing a consistent economic policy in east-central Europe in interviews with east European diplomats between 1933 and 1939, he repeatedly emphasized the economic compatibility of industrial Germany and agricultural eastern Europe and German willingness to support their agricultural sectors. Hitler's declarations of German disinterest in "purely political" questions, and his avoidance of traditional diplomatic methods such as treaties of friendship, strengthened his emphasis on economics.[6]

German policy was frequently not as rigid as Hitler in his interviews. This is not to say that there was a Hitler and "Nazi policy" opposed by a Schacht/Wilhelmstraße bloc.[7] The reality was one of diplomatic technique: German negotiators could

---

itical motivation and fails to alert his reader to the fact that Germany continued to adhere to the most favored nation system until September, 1934 (except for the Hungarian and Yugoslav treaties). Clearly, these treaties do foreshadow the New Plan but it must be emphasized that their original justification was political. In a sense, then, they were a political anticipation of a policy which would later be worldwide in consequence. One of Schmitt's last acts as Economics Minister was to reaffirm his commitment to a non-discriminatory foreign economic policy. This is, of course, why Schmitt had to go, and why Schacht assumed the Ministry of Economics in addition to the Reichsbank presidency: see Reichswirtschaftsminister to Reichsbankdirektorium, June 4, 1934, BA, R 2/14214. For a differing interpretation: KAISER, ibid., p.74, citing Posse, T-120/5650/H003733 (Cabinet Meeting, October 4, 1933 in which Hitler was not present.) Ranki notes that in the meeting between Neurath, Schwerin von Krosigk, and Schacht on January 17, 1934 the new treaties were justified from the political point of view and that Neurath indicated subsidies from the Reich treasury only came into question for Yugoslavia and Hungary. RANKI, Economy and Foreign Policy, p. 135.

   [2] Memorandum by Ulrich, February 17, 1934, PA, Direktoren, Handakten Ritter, Ha Pol, Jugoslawien, Bd. 2.

   [3] Minute by Ulrich, February 23, 1934, ibid.

   [4] Memorandum by Neurath, March 9, 1934, DGFP, C, Vol. 2, pp. 557-558 (original in PA, Büro Reichsminister, Po 58, Jugoslawien, Bd. 3.)

   [5] Ibid.

   [6] In 1939 Ribbentrop's attempts to secure Hungarian and Yugoslavian adherence to the Anti-Comintern Pact marked the beginning of Germany's attempt to bring east-central Europe into some sort of formal relationship of political dependence. Ribbentrop's policy in the case of Yugoslavia was not strongly endorsed by Hitler, however.

   [7] There was tension, however, between the Hitler-Göring attitude toward Hungarian revisionism and that of the Wilhelmstraße.

point to Hitler's statements and then claim that Germany had gone much further than first intended.

In the 1934 treaty negotiations with Yugoslavia the financial latitude of the German negotiators was circumscribed by interministerial decision. Correspondence between Ritter and Sarnow (Economic Ministry) indicates that the 10 million marks set aside to market Yugoslav products was the extreme limit to which the Economics Ministry and Wilhelmstraße were able to carry their case with the Finance Ministry.[8] The particular mix of commodities that Germany undertook to import *was* negotiable, however.

Before the German delegation went to Belgrade, Ritter drafted a memorandum clearly expressing the concepts and motivations behind German policy. Germany intended to conclude an agreement with Yugoslavia on the Hungarian model, but noting that the Yugoslavs had not yet agreed to a discriminatory basis for the agreement, Ritter felt that the delegation should not bring up the possibility of preferences outside the most-favored-nation clause and simply explain that it was economically impossible for Germany to extend agricultural preferences to all most-favored-nation treaty partners. A discriminatory treaty would then appear as the only solution.[9] Ritter clearly expressed the political motivation of German policy. "The reason for this prospective compromise in the case of Yugoslavia is — apart from the purely economic wish for the increase in German exports — chiefly that we wish to attempt the creation of a secure economic foothold within the economic circle of the Little Entente as well."[10]

The Wilhelmstraße was concerned with the possible rapprochement of Italy and France over east-central Europe in opposition to Germany's new Austrian policy. Ritter, in speaking of the recently concluded commercial treaty with Hungary, was confident that Germany had succeeded in establishing a "political-economic position" in what had previously been an exclusively Italian sphere.[11] Germany's failure to secure a similar position in French-oriented Rumania despite continuing efforts led Ritter to conclude that "we must give up this effort as hopeless, at least so long as Rumanian foreign policy is led by Herr Titulescu."[12] Germany's second choice was Yugoslavia. "After this experience the attempt will be made to strengthen the permanent interest of Yugoslavia in the German market."[13]

Ritter instructed the delegation that in presenting Germany's new trade policy to hostile interests, particularly Italy, emphasis was to be on Germany's past willingness to participate in any general plan of economic rehabilitation of the Danubian countries. The grain preference treaties initiated by Germany had fallen through,

---

[8] Ritter to Sarnow (DG Belgrad), April 5, 1934, PA, Direktoren, Handakten Ritter, Ha Pol, Jugoslawien, Bd. 2.

[9] Memorandum by Ritter, March 12, 1934, ibid.

[10] Ibid.

[11] Ibid.

[12] Ibid.

[13] Ibid.

according to Ritter, because of Italian opposition[14], so, while willing to work with
the other Great Powers as shown by the Stresa and Lausanne conferences, Germany would continue to defend her position in the Danube against "one-sided and
politically influenced special actions of individual European Great Powers."[15]

After imparting this generous European tone to Germany's past record and the
Reich's new policy, Ritter went on to the more important theme of propaganda in
favor of Germany's reorganization of the agricultural sector. Germany was now in
a better position to grant agricultural concessions to Danubian countries because
"the secure organization of domestic production and market relations" and "controlled foreign imports" caused "fewer disadvantageous consequences for German
agriculture." Negotiations with Holland, Denmark, and Hungary showed that,
contrary to hostile opinion, Germany was not building up an autarchic agriculture
sector at the expense of neighboring agricultural countries. The satisfaction of these
countries with the German proposals, compared to the mistrust of previous years,
was proof that Germany could offer more than before.

Such propaganda, although an effective weapon of German expansionism after
the Hungarian and Yugoslavian treaties began to succeed, was belied by the actual
discrimination of German agricultural policy against east-central European grain
exporters. Not until the work creation and rearmament programs helped restore
1929 levels of production and employment were earlier consumption levels restored
by importing grain and other agricultural commodities; and even then Germany's
protectionist policy was so restrictive that large-scale grain imports from Rumania
were not resumed until after Germany's poor harvest in 1936.

Ritter and German propagandists were, however, correct in stressing import control and monopoly marketing that allowed Germany to guarantee bulk commodity
purchases at fixed prices, even if they were to be marketed in Germany at a loss or
dumped on the world market. Import control via quotas also meant that Germany
could eliminate the quotas of countries unamenable to German export demands and
allocating such quotas to other, more pliable, nations. The continued existence,
however, of interministerial conflict over agricultural concessions indicates that the
rear-guard resistance of Darré's Agricultural Ministry inhibited the expansion of
trade.

2. Treaty Negotiations at Belgrade

In mid-March 1934 Sarnow, head of the German negotiating team, set the tone
of the discussions in an interview with *Politika*, Yugoslavia's leading political journal, maintaining that existing trade relations should be extended as the geography,
former economic relations, and complementary nature of the two countries called

---

[14] Ibid. It is very peculiar that Ritter cites Italian opposition as the reason that the Brüning
preference program failed. It was America's refusal to allow any violation of the most-
favored-nation principle that doomed the treaties.

[15] Ibid.

for a long-term comprehensive treaty. He explained that the National Socialist agrarian program dictated caution in concluding trade agreements, "in the first instance we . . . must consider [the interests of] our own agricultural sector"[16], but "Germany . . . was no longer able to pursue a policy of autarchy." It was on the basis of German agriculture's insufficiency and Germany's need to increase industrial exports that compromises could be reached with Yugoslavia.

This friendly atmosphere did not preclude six weeks of hard bargaining before agreement was reached on the key points of the tourist agreement and the type and scope of German agricultural purchase guarantees. Contributing to the cordiality, Germany did not raise the issue of the prewar loans or request equivalent guarantees for German industrial exports.[17]

Tourist trade, the first sticking point in the negotiations, had ground to a halt when both countries had forbidden the "export" of currency or of foreign exchange, although businessmen and officials had probably been able to make special arrangements with their respective national banks. The problem was a pressing one for Yugoslavia, already unable to pay for Germany's export surplus in bilateral trade. A revival of tourism would mean importing additional German goods to pay for German tourist expenditures. The question could have been resolved by financing tourist trade with the frozen claims accumulated between 1931 and 1934[18], but Yugoslavia opposed any wholesale solution of the frozen claims issue until *after* bilateral trade had substantially increased.

When Sarnow first raised the question of a travel agreement, Berlin's inflexible position was one of requiring payment in free currency for supplemental German exports earmarked for tourist expenditure.[19] A long letter of instruction by Baer, an official of the Wilhelmstraße, indicates that sabotaging a possible tourist agreement was deliberate policy.[20] He noted that the Yugoslav National Bank continually failed to keep its agreements[21] and argued that such special agreements were ultimately paid for by normal exports channeled away from commodities.[22] If this were

---

[16] Min. Dir. Sarnow über die Handelsvertragsverhandlungen mit Südslawien, March 19, 1934, ibid.

[17] Before the German delegation departed, it was decided at an interministerial conference not to bring up prewar loans for substantive negotiation, but to seek a simple formula noting the agreement of both parties to future negotiations. Unsigned minute, March 9, 1934, BA, R 2/3614.

[18] German tourists would pay marks into a special account at the Reichsbank reserved for frozen claim liquidation, the Yugoslav National Bank would give the tourist the dinar equivalent when he arrived in Yugoslavia, and the German firm would receive its payment from the special account at the Reichsbank.

[19] Benzler to DG Belgrad, March 17, 1934, PA, Ha Pol, Handakten Clodius, Jugoslawien, Bd. 2.

[20] Baer to Sarnow (DG Belgrad), March 19, 1934, Sonderreferat Wirtschaft, Jugoslawien, Finanzwesen 16, Devisenangelegenheiten mit Deutschland, Bd. 2.

[21] According to Baer, the Yugoslav National Bank had reneged on its promise to permit the Reichsbank to buy certain commodities with frozen credits and its promise to support the exchange rate of the mark.

[22] Czechoslovakia was the only exception to this policy; the Czechs guaranteed a 5:4 ratio in foreign trade and payment for Germany's export surplus in free currency.

to be the case, the clearing purchases forfeited from Yugoslavia would have to be purchased elsewhere for foreign exchange.

Sarnow still believed that a tourist agreement would satisfy Yugoslav demands and promote German exports and argued that rejecting a tourist agreement on the basis of technical currency considerations was shortsighted. He saw German policy regarding Yugoslavia as a transfer question: "We are seeking opportunities to once again establish our active balance *vis-a-vis* Yugoslavia without, however, losing the possibility of transfer and allowing our actual balance to be frozen."[23] A tourist agreement could help implement an active trade balance with Yugoslavia if, for every German tourist who purchased dinar in Yugoslavia, the Yugoslav National Bank would receive a mark credit that could be used to purchase German commodities. "Through the promotion of German foreign travel to Yugoslavia we arrive at what the travel agreement should serve, supplemental opportunities for the German commodity creditor and at the same time an automatic widening of the opportunity for supplementary exports to Yugoslavia. The more we strive [for such exports], the more we can avoid the freezing [of commodity payment]."[24]

Sarnow carried his point in Berlin and a compromise travel agreement, the first important German compromise, was incorporated into the final version of the treaty.[25]

The type, the scope, and the price of agricultural commodities had to be negotiated. The German delegation had come prepared with two major concessions (40,000 tons of corn, and 20,000 tons of linseed) and a number of smaller ones.[26] The delegation was authorized to suggest (in passing) that Germany was willing to import Yugoslav raw materials. (Berlin of course would have leaped at the chance to buy Yugoslav copper, lead, and zinc.)

Yugoslavia's reaction to the German proposals was mixed and Pilja, head of the Yugoslav delegation, made it clear that any treaty would depend on agriculture, not raw materials: "Pilja sees no value in the guarantee and extension of raw material markets."[27] He presented a list of agricultural commodities different from those Germany had requested and in quantities far above the initial German program. Yugoslavia wanted to export 50,000 tons of wheat, the corn Germany had mentioned, and substantial quantities of eggs and plums. According to Sarnow, eggs and plums were in a "key position" as both were critically important in the "social structure of the old Serbian peasantry."[28] German offers for walnuts, beans, linseed, and horses, although welcome, were not as critical as wheat, eggs, and plums and could serve only to round out the package. Ritter promised to do what he could but

[23] Sarnow (Belgrad) to Ritter, March 26, 1934, Sonderreferat Wirtschaft, Jugoslawien, Finanzwesen 16, Devisenangelegenheiten mit Deutschland, Bd. 2.

[24] Ibid.

[25] Ritter told Sarnow 11 days later that the Reichsbank agreed to his proposal. Ritter to Sarnow, April 7, 1934, PA, Direktoren, Handakten Ritter, Ha Pol, Jugoslawien, Bd. 2.

[26] HPA, March 10, 1934, PA, Ha Pol, Handakten Wiehl, Ha Pol Ausschuß.

[27] Sarnow/Heeren (Belgrad) to AA, March 21, 1934, PA, Direktoren, Handakten Ritter, Ha Pol, Jugoslawien, Bd. 2.

[28] Ibid.

warned Sarnow that Germany would probably not go as far as Sarnow thought necessary.[29]

Two days later the Economic Policy Committee did agree to Sarnow's proposed concessions on wheat and plums and offered a new quota for lard but refused to extend the earlier egg offer and rejected any concession on cattle.[30] Finally, on April 1 Yugoslavia agreed to conclude a treaty on the Hungarian model *if* there were further concessions on plums and eggs.[31]

Yugoslavia's egg demands, although minor enough and certainly unimportant in terms of Germany's total trade, posed a problem for the German government. The Wilhelmstraße had to satisfy the competing demands of Yugoslavia and Turkey (the latter was also demanding increased German egg purchases) before signing a treaty, while reconciling the differing priorities of the Economics, Finance, and Agricultural Ministries at home. It was not going to be easy to reconcile the contradictions of German agricultural and fiscal policy with the demands of export promotion and political expansion.

German agricultural policy was based on the principle of "feeding the market." The low consumption levels still prevailing as a result of high unemployment meant that foreign eggs could come into the German market only to the extent that German agriculture could not supply the domestic market.[32] Germany had hitherto allocated quotas on a nondiscriminatory basis to other countries and had not used the quotas to channel trade from one country to another. So if Germany were to begin to discriminate in favor of an individual country, it would set off an inevitable chain reaction with other trading partners. Trying to improve her commercial position with several countries, Germany had already faced a clamor from hopeful beneficiaries of discriminatory trade policy when preferences had been granted to Hungary and when German latitude for appeasing such demands was not large. Low domestic consumption meant any substantial increase in agricultural imports would destroy Darré's careful policy of price stabilization and price supports; at the same time, dumping on the world market, storage, or subsidized sale in Germany ran counter to fiscal restraints jealously guarded by the Finance Ministry.

Into this already complicated situation entered a political factor. "The negotiations with Turkey naturally do not, at the moment, have nearly the political interest which we ascribe to the negotiations with Yugoslavia, nevertheless, we naturally want to come to an understanding with Turkey as well, because when looked at

---

[29] Ritter to Sarnow, March 22, 1934, ibid.

[30] The Economic Policy Committee agreed with Sarnow's proposal for a 50,000-ton wheat quota and offered a 30-mark preferential plum duty. Sarnow wanted an egg quota of 7,000 tons, but it was to remain at 1,800 tons. Originally, the first lard offer was to stand but was later raised to 4,000 tons. HPA, March 24, 1934, PA, Ha Pol, Handakten Wiehl, Ha Pol Ausschuß. Figures for the earlier offer are contained in the March 10 meeting, ibid.

[31] Sarnow (Belgrad) to AA, March 26, 1934 and April 1, 1934, ibid.

[32] The forced use of East Elbian rye as a feed grain was another constraint on consumption levels. If the intensive peasant agriculture had been permitted to use cheap overseas feed grains, poultry and egg production costs would have been lower and the market broadened. This factor kept German consumption levels low after almost full employment was achieved. This cut into Germany's potential as a market for trading partners.

from a purely economic point of view, Turkey offers at least the same, or perhaps even somewhat better prospects than Yugoslavia. Not only has Turkey made very valuable concessions to us for regular, continuing transactions in negotiations hitherto, but — as you know — particular large industrial firms play a special role in Turkey."[33] Ritter did not propose meeting Turkey's demands but he did not want to give them a flat no. Such a dilemma could be resolved only at the expense of a third party, in this case Ireland, whose egg quota would be divided between Yugoslavia and Turkey.[34]

German policy, Schacht's ambitions notwithstanding, was initially based upon *reallocation* rather than *expansion* of trade. Dividing the Irish quota between Yugoslavia and Turkey could not solve the problem because the Agricultural Ministry considered the inferior Turkish eggs unmarketable in Germany. They could only be dumped on the world market, which meant a Reich subsidy, bringing Ritter up against the Wilhelmstraße and Economics Ministry commitment to fiscal restraints. "You know from the previous consultation of department heads that Herr Posse and I said *vis-a-vis* the apprehensions of Reichsminister Graf Schwerin von Krosigk that financial subsidies only came into consideration for Hungary, and perhaps for Yugoslavia. If we now go to Herr von Krosigk in light of this declaration even for a small request . . . we would lose our credit with him in the future."[35] To circumvent this problem some half million marks had to be deducted from Sarnow's 10-million-mark subsidy fund for allocation to Turkey. Ritter assured Sarnow that Yugoslavia would be satisfied with further concessions on plums and processed eggs. His letter to Sarnow was the basis on which subsequent sections of the agreement were hammered out. There were further German concessions on plums, poultry, lumber, furs, and hides to round out the treaty package[36], but the crucial point of the negotiations was the egg concession in Ritter's letter of April 5.

3. The Commercial Treaty of May 1, 1934

Apart from the secret agricultural quotas guaranteeing Yugoslav commodities a German market, the published portions of the treaty were similar to other most-

[33] Ritter to Sarnow, April 5, 1934, PA, Direktoren, Handakten Ritter, Ha Pol, Jugoslawien, Bd. 1.

[34] Ritter proposed the Irish quota be primarily allocated to Yugoslavia, raising its quota from 1,800 tons to 3,300 tons, which almost met the Yugoslav demand for a 4,000-ton quota. Turkey would get the remainder of the old Irish quota, increasing its share from 370 tons to 870 tons. But if the egg quota did not appear to be crucial for the negotiations, Ritter advised Sarnow that the Irish quota would be divided in half between Yugoslavia and Turkey.

[35] Ritter to Sarnow, April 5, 1934, op. cit.

[36] Sarnow wanted Berlin to import fresh plums to be marketed in processed form as prunes or sauce. Berlin eventually agreed to increase the plum quota, but in stages; the first being from 8,000 to 11,000 tons. Also granted were secret tariff concessions on grapes and specific quotas of plums, and further tariff concessions on poultry, furs, hides, and lumber. Sarnow (Belgrad) to AA, April 8, 1934; Sarnow/Heeren (Belgrad) to AA, April 15, 1934; Ulrich to DG Belgrad, April 16, 1934, PA, Direktoren, Handakten Ritter, Ha Pol, Jugoslawien, Bd. 2; Ha Pol Ausschuß meeting April 18, 1934, PA, Handakten Wiehl, Ha Pol, Ha Pol Ausschuß; Ritter to DG Belgrad, April 19, 1934, PA, Ha Pol, Handakten Clodius, Jugoslawien, Bd. 2.

favored-nation treaties[37], and the tariff concessions granted Yugoslavia would be generalized to Germany's dwindling most-favored-nation treaty partners.[38] The treaty, far more extensive than Germany's 1927 treaty with Yugoslavia, regulated the rights of nationals to carry on business in the other country, shipping questions, and other technical points of international commercial law, as would Germany's 1935 treaty with Rumania. It established a binational Mixed Commission to govern trade relations between the two countries. These committees were to become a central feature of German trade relations under the Schacht system and the study of their annual or semiannual deliberations provides a key to German trade policy.

The treaty had a two-year term, but if not denounced six months before expiration, it could be automatically extended *ad infinitum*, thus providing a solid legal framework for developing bilateral trade relations.

Consisting of over 20 separate sections, the treaty included the published most-favored-nation treaty and a number of secret or confidential protocols, exchanges of notes, and agreements, which, particularly the Confidential Closing Protocol, contained the German purchase guarantees intended to double Yugoslav exports to Germany within one year. The original German offer for corn was marginally increased from 50,000 to 53,000 tons but the original linseed quota was reduced to 20,000 tons from 25,000 tons. The initial German program had not involved quotas for wheat (50,000 tons), lard (2,500 tons), tobacco (2,500 tons), or the eggs and plums discussed above. Additional lesser quotas, some for periods of less than one year, were allocated for horses, tomatoes, and apples. Such guaranteed purchases increased trade in specific commodities beyond the 1929 level and allowed particular branches of Yugoslav agriculture to reap enormous benefits from the changed pattern of German imports, as the following table, comparing 1929 with 1936, illustrates:[39]

	Metric Tons		Percentage change
	1929	1936	
Live animals (exclusive of horses)	193	6,949	+ 3,490
Meat & meat products	766	9,953	+ 1,190
Lead ore	2,245	21,796	+ 873
Flax and hemp	2,178	11,845	+ 440
Hides, skins & feathers	1,133	5,091	+ 350
Bauxite	67,891	217,542	+ 220
Fruit	9,526	22,486	+ 137
Copper	8,139	13,000	60

[37] MEISS, Beziehungen, p. 62.
[38] Ibid.
[39] William T. Chase (U.S. Consulate, Hamburg), 'Report on German Penetration of Yugoslavia', December 15, 1937, NA, RG 59, 660 H. 6217/3.

Until 1937, the losers in this policy were such traditional exports as eggs, wheat, and corn. The above comparisons do not contradict the decisive role played in the negotiations by German concessions on eggs, wheat, and corn but illustrate the relative decline in these traditional exports as a result of German agricultural policy and the Depression. Before the German grain crisis of 1937, the phenomenal increase in such products as live animals, meat, flax, hides, and fruits was a general characteristic of German trade policy in southeastern Europe. Berlin tried to circumvent the limitations of the Darré agricultural policy by promoting such commodities over traditional agricultural imports of grains, poultry, dairy products. Why Germany found it easier to absorb such commodities is not clear, but the policy existed.

Germany's guaranteed import of a specific volume of Yugoslav agricultural commodities meant the price of such products would be determined not by market forces but by government negotiation. The world prices for agricultural commodities had fallen below production costs for even the most efficient producers, a description none of the agricultural countries of east-central Europe could lay claim to. With agricultural world prices far below the Yugoslav cost of production, Yugoslavia had tried an export subsidy dumping program that proved a financial disaster; the urban population was too small to bear the costs. Yugoslav prices, however, were substantially lower than German internal prices. Theoretically, Yugoslav products could be charged a preferential tariff increasing their price to, but not beyond, that of competing overseas commodities, but in practice the problem of marketing Yugoslav commodities could not be so simply resolved. The pattern of German autarchy was necessarily uneven; not all sectors needed the degree of protection required, for instance, by the rye producers. For those commodities supplied in some measure from foreign producers and not subject to a heavy tariff, the world price for the commodity continued to play a determining role in the German market, and Germany tried to buy cheap when possible. If Germany chose to import Yugoslav commodities at rates higher than similar products on the world market, these commodities either had to be marketed at a loss within Germany, dumped on the world market, or further measures had to be taken to raise the internal German price to make the Yugoslav products competitive. This last course was not practical because of domestic political considerations — Berlin feared a hostile reaction to a further rise in food prices. Berlin's recognition that subsidies would be needed gave Sarnow his 10-million-mark fund when he went to Belgrade.

The subsidy question was complicated by German frozen claims. Sarnow commented that Germany hoped the subsidy program would "unfreeze" her credits in Yugoslavia and Hungary. The export subsidies for Hungary, according to the February 1934 treaty, would be financed from German claims frozen in Budapest, but Yugoslavia refused to go along with a similar scheme. While Yugoslavia did recognize, in the "Agreement over the Promotion of German-Yugoslav Commodity Traffic", that implementing the German purchase guarantees involved financial loss for Germany, Sarnow could not secure Yugoslav agreement to the Hungarian formula.[40] It was clear that Germany would foot the bill; the only question was how?

Yugoslavia wanted Germany to advance the subsidy funds in block to the appropriate Yugoslav authorities, who would then use the money to raise the domestic price level of those commodities to be exported to Germany. Under this proposal Germany would lose all control over the amounts of specific commodity subsidies. The compromise reached guaranteed Germany control via agreed subsidies in marks or by unit of volume for each specific commodity.[41] Eventually, almost all commodities were regulated by price, volume, and date of delivery with specific individual contracts between the state agricultural authorities of both countries. These contracts were a unique feature of German trade policy, indirectly assuring markets by discriminatory allocation of import quotas while contracts between the two governments guaranteed that the products would be marketed in Germany. No other industrial country was willing or able to provide such secure markets.

The confidential agreements also regulated the future of German exports to Yugoslavia. Traditionally, Germany had run a trade surplus with Yugoslavia and the *export* orientation of German foreign trade policy is clear in Berlin's obvious delight with Yugoslavia's acknowledgment of this tendency as the "natural" trade relationship between the two countries.[42] Berlin hoped that such a formal acknowledgment would act as an incentive to developing German exports. Later events would demonstrate how wrong these expectations were; Germany did not develop a trade surplus but ran a consistent deficit in trade with Yugoslavia. Schacht, learning from this experience, quickly became proficient at manipulating the Yugoslav export surplus to further German ends. Despite his skill, it is important to remember that the German trade drive was originally expected to develop in an entirely different manner.[43]

A second aspect of the article on German exports was Yugoslavia's promise to promote German exports: "The Royal Yugoslav Government will work towards a favorable development of imports from Germany. It will especially make efforts to ensure that through equal conditions German industry will be considered in the carrying out of large public projects and investments."[44] This provision, a simple nondiscriminatory declaration concerning the award of public contracts, is mentioned in the agreement probably because of Germany's wish to promote such exports. Despite preferential treatment of Yugoslavia, Germany had a cautious attitude toward specific mention of similar discriminatory treatment for German exports to Yugoslavia, for several reasons. Earlier, Germany had opposed the Tar-

---

[40] Unsigned memorandum, June 18, 1934, Appendix to Ulrich circular, June 21, 1934, PA, Ha Pol, Handakten Wiehl, Jugoslawien, Bd. 3.

[41] Supplement to 'Vereinbarung über die Förderung des deutsch-jugoslawischen Warenverkehrs', PA, Ha Pol, Handakten Wiehl, Jugoslawien, Bd. 3.

[42] The tone of the Ulrich circular (June 21, 1934) and appendices and the Propaganda Ministry Report make this delight evident.

[43] How Germany expected Yugoslavia to pay for this export surplus is not indicated anywhere.

[44] Article 4, 'Vereinbarung über die Förderung des deutsch-jugoslawischen Warenverkehrs', PA, Direktoren, Handakten Ritter, Ha Pol, Jugoslawien, Bd. 2.

dieu Plan with the argument that no major power vitally interested in the Danubian area should be excluded by a system of mutual preference; in other words, preferences should be granted to the agricultural countries of the Danube but not demanded in return. A German attempt to gain export preferences in 1934 would have weakened its diplomatic strategy against Italy and France. Also, Berlin believed that German industry would have no trouble competing in the Yugoslav market, making preferences unnecessary.[45] It was only later that it became clear that German exports needed preferential treatment to keep pace with German imports from Yugoslavia, and eventually Yugoslavia grudgingly agreed to a discriminatory quota system in order to liquidate its frozen credits in Berlin. German heavy industry was the chief beneficiary, receiving preference in state contracts for public works — a notable example being the Zenica rolling mill project built by Krupp.

The commercial treaty with Yugoslavia was concluded simultaneously with a clearing and payments agreement establishing the special clearing accounts in the respective national banks into which importers would pay for the exports of the other country, and exporters would be paid monthly from the payments accumulated.[46] These provisions were standard; the important fact is the agreement's existence. The commercial treaty could not function without a payments agreement establishing a legal means of settling debts between each country. To conclude the payments agreement simultaneously with the commercial treaty indicated that Yugoslavia was serious about implementing the treaty and that the government was united behind it. In Rumania the payments agreement followed the commercial treaty by several months, while the majority of the Rumanian cabinet, backed by the Rumanian National Bank, actively tried to sabotage the treaty after it was concluded.

With the treaty package Germany had a solid basis for a drive to dominate Danubian Europe. The Non-Aggression Pact with Poland and the commercial treaties with Hungary and Yugoslavia were crucial to Hitler's expansionist policy, a policy characterized in a perceptive contemporary observation: "German control over Yugoslavia would undo the present cooperation in Central Europe between the Little Entente states, solve the Anschluß and Hungarian problems, and force Italy not only out of Central Europe but also out of Trieste and the Adriatic. Furthermore, Germany, by reconciling Yugoslavia and Bulgaria, would gain control in the Bal-

---

[45] Unsigned memorandum, June 18, 1934, Supplement 1 to Ulrich despatch of June 21, 1934, op. cit.

[46] 'Abkommen über Zahlungen aus den deutsch-jugoslawischen Warenverkehr', PA, Direktoren, Handakten Ritter, Ha Pol, Jugoslawien, Bd. 2. One aspect of German trade policy which needs more research is the encouragement of industrial plants in which IG Farben played a key role: "In the 1930's, the influence of the Reich's demand for the cultivation of certain industrial plants made itself felt in Yugoslavia. In the Reich's sphere of economic planning, the Vojvodina was foreseen as the producer and exporter of hops, various oil seeds (especially sunflower seeds), soy beans, castor beans and certain types of fruit and poppy seeds." Prisca von BAGNELL, The Influence of National Socialism on the German Minority in Yugoslavia, U.Ph.D., Syracuse Univerisity 1977, p. 46.

kans, and over the Danube, since an isolated Czechoslovakia and Rumania would be unable to offer any noteworthy resistance."[47] Although Hitler would later conciliate Italy by renouncing any interest in the Adriatic, Germany's commercial policy in the Danube was directed as much at the Italian position in Austria and Hungary as at the French alliance system.

German official circles were enthusiastic about the new treaty with Yugoslavia, although the Reich Chancellery was subdued, characterizing the hope for a fresh increase in trade between the two countries as "justified" in view of the extensive advantages the treaty granted to Yugoslavia.[48] The press instructions of the Propaganda Ministry were more revealing of German intentions and aspirations: "[The Treaty] will create an open door for Germany in Yugoslavia . . . ['The open door treaty'] builds the foundation for the policy of the Reich government in the Danubian Region. It is not a treaty, however, which makes economic concessions to reach political ends. Seen from the economic perspective the treaty is fully balanced. A treaty, with which both partners can be satisfied, particularly as in the course of time further economic rapprochement between both the countries is thoroughly probable."[49] The treaty's importance was, however, to remain semi-confidential: "In light of the enormous importance of the treaty for German trade policy the Reich government attaches great importance to an unsensational treatment of the treaty before the German public."[50]

A circular by Ulrich, a Wilhelmstraße official, expressed enthusiasm similar to that of the Propaganda Ministry: the new treaty represented a fundamental remodeling of the relations between the two countries which had two objects in mind: first, to open the Yugoslav market to German penetration, and second, to build up an economic foothold in the Little Entente that could be used to drive a wedge between the alliance partners. Although the treaty had just been signed, Ulrich had already concluded that German agricultural concessions would make the German market indispensable to Yugoslavia, which in turn "places us in the position of being able, if required, to exert adequate pressure on Yugoslavia."[51]

Ulrich's circular illustrates the clear political purpose and strategic vision characterizing Nazi expansionist policy in southeastern Europe. "In reality, however, there was much more than this at stake, not only in the sense that both treaties [with Hungary and Yugolsavia] were the first successful vanguards of the German economic offensive, but also because they represented not just improved acts but the basis of a conscious economic policy conception as well."[52] Berlin was very con-

---

[47] "Germany and Italy. Struggle for Control over Yugoslavia", *Ceske Slova* (Belgrade), May 19, 1934. Translation in Benton (Belgrade) to the secretary of state, Ma 24, 1934, NA, RG 59, 660 H. 6231/54.

[48] 'Handelsvertrag mit Jugoslawien', May 16, 1934, PA, R 43 II/323.

[49] 'Der deutsch-jugoslawische Handelsvertrag', by Bertinger, May 4, 1934, 'Streng Vertraulich ', BA, ZSg 101/27.

[50] Ibid.

[51] Ulrich to DB Rom, June 21, 1934, DGFP, C, Vol. 3, 23 [copy in PA, Handakten Wiehl, Jugoslawien, Bd. 3].

[52] RANKI, Economy and Foreign Policy, p. 144.

cerned that France and Italy would join together to block Germany's ambitions in the Danubian valley. The commercial treaties with Hungary and Yugoslavia were designed to prevent this by creating German strongholds in the Italian and French camps. Yugoslavia was hostile to and openly suspicious of the French policy of wooing Mussolini; German fears that, because of French Minister Barthou's visit to Belgrade in June 1934, Yugoslavia was prepared to "blindly follow the French alliance policy for safeguarding the status quo", proved to be unfounded.[53] The murder of King Alexander (alongside Barthou) in Marseilles and the subsequent equivocation by the League of Nations on Italian complicity did nothing to endear French policy to the Yugoslav government. French maneuvers to draw Yugoslavia into the Danube Pact were not openly rejected but quietly sidetracked. Yugoslavia also responded with open hostility to Italian mobilization on the Brenner in the summer of 1934. Germany's strategy of economic penetration needed time before it would be effective, but the antagonism between Italy and Yugoslavia combined with the French equivocation provided an ideal climate for Germany's success.

[53] Heeren (Belgrad) to AA, June 27, 1934, DGFP, C, Vol. 3, 39.

CHAPTER IV

THE GERMAN EXPORT OFFENSIVE IN YUGOSLAVIA

1. 1934 - The Crisis Summer and the Difficulties of Agricultural Purchase

Before the new trade policy could be implemented, the Nazi Reich faced three crises, each of which reflected upon a different aspect of the regime's stabilization.

The slaughter of political dissidents, including Schleicher and Röhm, whose military pretensions and bombastic threats of a "brown revolution" could no longer be tolerated if Hitler were to consummate his alliance with the Army and heavy industry, was a diplomatic liability for the new Reich. The barbarity of the slaughter was of great propaganda value to Germany's enemies.

Hitler's encouragement of Habicht and the Austrian Nazis responsible for the assassination of Dollfuß allowed him to dissipate the adventurism of the Austrian Nazis and offered the possibility of Anschluß on the cheap, but it literally forced Italy into alignment with France.

In August 1934, after the other situations had subsided, the foreign exchange crisis reached its peak, primarily caused by the failure of Germany's exports to keep pace with domestic revival. Because Germany's domestic price level was substantially higher than that of competitors in the world market, increasing production necessitated an increase in domestic prices, however modest. German exports were further hampered by the boycott movement, the protectionism particularly affecting Germany's exports to western and northern Europe and the imperial protectionism of the European colonial powers. With exports lagging behind imports and without foreign exchange to pay the difference, the German economy threatened to break down because of shortages of such critical raw materials as copper.

Taking over as "acting" economics minister from Kurt Schmitt, who was forced to resign, Schacht began implementing the discriminatory trade policy he had outlined to Hitler and Paul Reusch (GHH) in December 1932. The new trade policy for Danubian Europe sailed into largely uncharted waters. Its experimental character is clear in the export surplus provision of the commercial treaty with Yugoslavia and German agricultural purchase guarantees in 1934-35. The success of German policy depended upon implementing these guarantees and, while Germany's willingness to conclude "long term purchase agreements" was a unique characteristic of Nazi trade policy, difficulties arose over the purchase of three key agricultural commodities — plums, lard, and wheat.

Before the treaty became effective, the Control Board for Milk Products and Fats protested to other ministries that Yugoslav lard could be imported only at a loss. "He [Hüberner, head of the Control Board] expressed this position to you as well as to Ministerial Counselor Müller [Agriculture] and Legation Secretary Schnurre [Wilhelmstraße] and pointed to the negative effects upon [domestic] price in the case of the immediate appearance of the import . . . of these commodities. It has been explained to him that for political reasons the import of lard from Yugoslavia must proceed."[1] After paying tariffs and fees, Yugoslav lard was seven marks per 100 kilos more expensive than American.[2] The Control Board and Agricultural Ministry demanded that other ministries take over the financial responsibility for storing the lard (the only option open). Germany depended upon imports for approximately half its annual fat consumption and, even optimistically, could reduce this figure only by reducing per capita consumption. Given the extraordinarily low consumption levels between 1931 and 1934, Darré had succeeded somewhat in increasing domestic production and decreasing imports, at least to the extent that the small amount of Yugoslav lard threatened his price stabilization program in the summer of 1934. Eventually, the Economics Ministry took over the cost of storing the lard.[3] By autumn, however, the shortage of fats, particularly in the Ruhr, was characterized by Clodius as a catastrophe. Under such conditions even the expensive animal fats of Yugoslavia could not be considered a burden on the German economy.[4] From "surplus" to shortage illustrates the margin of error allowable in the German agricultural planning program.

The plum purchase guarantee caused similar problems for the German processing industry. Importers patiently explained in a letter to the Finance Ministry that the transaction with Prizad for plum sauce and prunes was impossible under existing tariff regulations.[5] Prizad wanted purchases to go duty free but the importers, unsure of the legality of this, were anxious to have it resolved. They claimed that the new tariffs made it impossible to make a profit on sales.[6] Seidel (Finance Ministry) made it clear that only the plums and processed plums subject to the new duties

---

[1] Dr. Müller (RMEL) to Sarnow (RWM), May 18, 1934, PA, Ha Pol, Handakten Clodius, Jugoslawien, Bd. 3.

[2] As to why Germany did not simply give Yugoslavia a preferential tariff on lard as she had with plums, it must be remembered that the German tariff was not levied as a fiscal measure nor designed as a simple protectionist measure. It was an instrument of price policy. Duties were differential sums (*Unterschiedsbeträge*) between the German internal price and the world price. Reduced duties would have adversely affected the Darré price policy aimed at stabilizing domestic fat prices at a level to promote production and give peasants a "fair" price.

[3] Sarnow (RWM) to Müller (RMEL), June 29, 1934, op. cit.

[4] Germany could and did buy more expensive Danubian agricultural products but although not spending foreign exchange, the Agricultural and Economics Ministries continued to use the world price as the benchmark of profitability. The Agricultural Ministry preferred to buy cheaper and higher-quality products from Denmark, Holland, Argentina, and the United States rather than Danubian commodities, while in the interests of export promotion Schacht was willing to subsidize Danubian agriculture to some extent, although he, too, preferred to buy cheap where possible, if foreign exchange expenditure could be avoided.

[5] Einkaufsgesellschaft der deutschen Konserven Industrie to the RFM, June 26, 1934, op. cit.

[6] Ten tons of plums, valued at 2,500 to 3,000 marks, subject to an import duty of 6,000 marks, could be sold, at a maximum, only for 5,000 marks. The new duties were grossly prohibitive: 60 marks per 100 kilos for plum sauce, 30 marks per 100 kilos for fresh plums.

would receive the promised subsidies ("*Verlustausgleich*").[7] Germany interpreted the treaty provisions to mean that payment of the subsidy, in the form of a rebate paid into the Yugoslav National Bank account at the Reichsbank, would follow only after the duty was paid.[8] The relevant protocol stated that the Yugoslav government was "to pay" the subsidies, a formula causing considerable confusion among the German importers and Prizad.[9] Yugoslavia would never have signed the treaty if it had to assume financial responsibility for the subsidies rather than merely distribute them. Ultimately, the German consumer was to pay the cost no matter how the subsidies were technically administered, either through higher prices or taxes.[10]

A third problem arose over the price of the guaranteed purchase of 50,000 tons of wheat slated to be dumped on the world market. Germany had promised to buy the wheat at the internal Yugoslav wheat price [*auf der Grundlage der jugoslawischen Weizenpreise*].[11] Yugoslavia naturally enough assumed Germany would buy at the prevailing Yugoslav domestic price. The German Agricultural Ministry thought differently. "The commitment alluded to simply means that the good offices of German interests will be placed at the disposal for marketing the Yugoslav wheat on the world market."[12] In German terms, "on the basis of the Yugoslav wheat price" meant only that the Yugoslav domestic price would be considered in determining the subsidies. The price Germany paid was to be kept as low as possible[13] and negotiated between the two parties. Although prepared to pay substantially more than the world market price, Germany wanted to limit its liabilities as much as possible.

These difficulties in the new Yugoslav-German trade relationship involve an important aspect in the structure of German expansionism. Increased exports would not immediately compensate for the subsidies on Yugoslavia's agricultural products, making the Yugoslav treaty initially an added burden to German taxpayers that did nothing to alleviate Germany's raw materials shortages. Although the technical questions besetting the early purchase agreements would be largely resolved by experience, dissension over Danubian agricultural prices would become characteristic of German policy until the outbreak of war, propaganda about *Großraumwirtschaft* notwithstanding.[14] The Economics Ministry and Agricultural Ministry both

[7] Seidel (RFM) to Sarnow (RWM), June 30, 1934, op. cit.

[8] Sarnow (RWM) to Hess (DG Belgrad), July 3, 1934, ibid.

[9] Unsigned minute, August 20, 1934, BA, R 2/10220.

[10] For details on the resolution of this question, see: Sarnow to Hess (DG Belgrad), July 3, 1934, Hess (DG Belgrad) to Sarnow, August 30, 1934, PA, Ha Pol, Handakten Clodius, Jugoslawien, Bd. 3; Sarnow to Pilja, August 21, 1934, BA, R 2/10220.

[11] 'Vertrauliches Schlußprotokoll', PA, Geheim, Jugoslawien, Handel 13, Handelsvertragsverhältnisse zu Deutschland.

[12] Dr. Mortiz (RMEL) to Steinhardt (Die Gesellschaft fuer Getreidehandel), July 30, 1934, PA, Sonderreferat Wirtschaft, Jugoslawien, Handel 13, Handelsvertragsverhältnisse . . . zu Deutschland, Bd. 1.

[13] Ibid.

[14] As late as 1938-39 the RMEL put up a rearguard resistance to the implementation of certain agricultural purchase guarantees that jeopardized increased petroleum imports from Rumania: Walter (RMEL) to AA, December 24, 1938, PA, Ha Pol, IVb, Rumänien, Handel 13A, Handelsvertragsverhältnisse zu Deutschland (Regierungsausschüsse), Bd. 1.

continued to use the world market price as a standard of economic rationality and profitability. The Agricultural Ministry would have preferred to spend foreign exchange on cheaper, higher-quality products from overseas export countries (the United States, Australia) or develop clearing trade with equally competitive European countries such as Holland or Denmark.[15] The Economics Ministry, particularly under Schacht, was willing to subsidize Danubian agriculture within strict limits, but when possible wanted to buy more cheaply without spending foreign exchange. Schacht's discriminatory trade policy found its ideal arena in Latin America, where cheap producers were willing to engage in bilateral clearing trade.[16]

In each meeting of the Mixed Commissions, Germany and its trading partner had to decide how much in purchase agreements and subsidies was required to advance German exports and which commodities would have to be taken to get the agricultural products or raw materials Germany needed. The resulting patchwork compromises determined the volume and composition of Germany's trade.

2. The Problem of Yugoslav Export Surplus

Germany developed a passive trade balance with its Danubian trading partners during 1933-37. One interpretation has it that Schacht deliberately bought everything in sight to relieve Germany's raw materials deficit and to force exports on the Danubian countries. But was it Schacht's design to pass on some of the cost of German rearmament to southeastern Europe by not paying trade debts, or was trade passivity an unexpected product of economic forces and only later adapted to war-economy ends? In the spring of 1934, Ruhr steel barons were talking of "going under" unless the export picture improved.[17] German sources are virtually silent on the use of blocked credits as instruments of trade policy but blocked trade balances were intended from the start to provide export promotion.[18] Uneasy about the developing trade passivity, Germany tried to liquidate the trade deficit by promoting preferential purchases by Yugoslavia.

One explanation of the development and persistence of the German trade deficit is that from 1936 to 1937, during the slow revival of the world market, purchases of the industrial countries of Europe and North America began to exceed the value of purchases of industrial products by overseas raw materials and producers.[19] In other

[15] This emerges clearly from a long RMEL position paper critical of the RWM: Köhler (RMEL) to RWM, AA, September 28, 1935, PA, Ha Pol, Handakten Clodius, Rumänien Bd. 1.

[16] See, for example, two good studies on Germany's relations with Argentina and Brazil: Arnold EBEL, Die Diplomatischen Beziehungen des Dritten Reichs zu Argentinen 1933-1939, Geneva 1972; Stanley HILTON, Brazil and the Great Power Trade Rivalry in South America, 1934-1939, U.Ph.D., Univ. of Texas at Austin 1969.

[17] This was frankly stated by Finance Minister Schwerin von Krosigk in 1937.

[18] Von Krosigk feared that an exchange guarantee to one clearing partner would precipitate the same demand from each of Germany's Danubian trading partners.

[19] J.B. CONDLIFFE, International Trade, in: The Political Quarterly 1938, pp. 99-105.

words, the failure of the raw materials and agricultural countries to keep pace with the industrial revival was a general phenomenon not peculiar to German trade with southeastern Europe between 1934 and 1937. Actually Germany was more success-ful in maintaining an active trade balance than other major industrial powers. J.B. Condliffe blames part of this import deficit tendency on "the inability of manufac-turers to get the materials — particularly steel — that were being used for arma-ment production."[20] His observation, primarily concerned with 1936 to 1937, does not apply to German policy in 1934-35 and seems to exaggerate the importance of armaments production in western Europe or the United States in 1936 to 1938.

What did the the primary producers do with export revenues in 1936-37? Again according to Condliffe, they allowed large short-term balances to accumulate in the great financial centers; strong countries (South Africa and India) repaid part of the external debt while weaker countries began, resumed, or enlarged external debt ser-vice. Thus, revival of world trade was held back by the aftermath of the financial debacle of 1931.

This is relevant to Yugoslav-German trade relations in that Yugoslavia's short-term balance in Berlin was involuntary. It could not be used as a means of financial settlement or as a hedge against a new financial crisis, but only to purchase German commodities. Although it was certainly in Yugoslavia's interest to get a return for her exports to the Reich and despite Germany's traditionally strong position in the Yugoslav market, Yugoslav importers did not buy up the mark balances from exporters. This lack of demand for marks led in turn to depreciation of the mark exchange rate, which should have made German goods cheaper and thus more attractive to the Yugoslav market, but it did not. The German government was cooperating with semistate cartel organizations in a comprehensive discriminatory price policy intended to give German firms a decisive price advantage in areas of strong foreign competition, so that products subject to competition were subsidized while the prices on "safe" commodities were raised.[21] The clearing balance in Yugoslavia's favor remained, reaching approximately 14.6 million marks by March 1935.

The failure of Yugoslav demand for German products to keep pace with German monopoly agricultural purchases is understandable given the demographic problem of east-central Europe and the impact of the Depression. Eighty percent of Yugos-lavia's population consisted of an impoverished peasantry, a situation common in

[20] Ibid.
[21] Some evidence of a differential pricing policy was uncovered by William Chase, an American consular official. "It is noteworthy, however, that only in the cases of machine tools and of agricultural implements and tools did domestic prices apparently decline further between 1933 and 1936 (in comparison, of course, with 1929), whereas in every case cited, except machine tools and miscellaneous hardware, unit export prices apparently declined in most cases substantially farther. These changes in export prices would indicate that premiums were being paid to German exporters." W. T. Chase (U.S. Consulate, Hamburg), 'Report on German Penetration of Yugoslavia', pp. 22-23, December 15, 1937, NA, RG 59, 66OH.6217/3.

the Danube area.[22] Whole provinces were so severely overpopulated that additional inputs of labor on the dwarf plots only decreased production per head.[23] A significant section of the population engaged in subsistence agriculture was hardly likely to become an important consumer of German commodities.

The modest needs of Yugoslavia's rural population for simple consumer goods — cotton, nails, kerosene — were easily met by Czech, British, and other competitors having easy access to raw materials on the world market. German light industry, handicapped by raw materials restrictions favoring heavy industry, could not compete and in some cases was simply shut down. One new German light industry that did enjoy phenomenal growth in the domestic market and in trade with the Danubian countries was the synthetic textile industry, but *Zellwolle* and other synthetics were not really competitive with cotton and wool even when exchange depreciation allowed Germany to offer an equal or lower price.

German heavy industry, which had the largest relative share of the machine tool and machine building sector of any industrialized country[24], was amply represented by the big Ruhr firms in export promotion. Under normal circumstances Germany could have expected to supply a large proportion of the new capital requirements of northern and western Europe. But the Depression, its protectionism, the anti-German boycott, and worldwide industrial overcapacity dictated no new capital investments. Neither Yugoslavia nor any country in the Danube could function as an alternative market for high-quality capital and labor-intensive German exports. The traditional hallmarks of German business acumen — quality, price, credit, and superior marketing organization — had allowed Germany to expect easy domination of the Yugoslav market. But German exports could not catch up until Yugoslavia agreed to channel state contracts to German firms.

3. Discrimination and the Promotion of German Exports

Only six months after ratifying the commercial treaty, Yugoslavia began to realize that something was very wrong with the developing trade relationship. In early November 1934 Pilja, state secretary in the Commerce Ministry, complained to Hess, German trade attaché in Belgrade, that Yugoslav credits at the Reichsbank were rising dangerously: ". . . while on the other hand the apprehension exists that the Yugoslav credits will rise still further, particularly as the fruits transaction is not fully and the grain transaction only partially developed."[25] Pilja wanted to call an

[22] See the classic works: Jozo TOMASEVICH, Peasants, Politics, and Economic Change in Yugoslavia, Stanford/Cal. 1955; Doreen WARRINEER, The Economics of Peasant Farming, London 1939.

[23] Doreen WARRINEER, The Population Question in Eastern Europe, in: Slavonic Review 16 (1937-1938), pp. 628-637.

[24] H.C. HILLMAN, The Comparative Strength of the Great Powers, in: RIIA, Survey of International Affairs, 1939-1946, Vol. 1 — The World in 1939, pp. 446-450.

[25] Hess (DG Belgrad) to Sarnow (RWM), November 2, 1934, PA, Ha Pol, Handakten Clodius, Jugoslawien, Bd. 3.

early meeting of the Mixed Commission but Hess commented that "it lays solely in Yugoslavia's hands to stimulate German exports to the larger volume which occurred in the past and thereby all concerns would cease of themselves."[26] Hess hoped that if an atmosphere of goodwill was maintained in Belgrade, the problem could be worked out: "It is certainly believed here that ways and means can be found in common discussions so that we can reach [the goal of] the promotion of German exports to Yugoslavia."[27] He requested instructions as to whether to cooperate or allow the Yugoslavs to go it alone "breaking their heads on the issue."[28]

Simultaneously, Balugdžić, Yugoslav minister in Berlin, brought the question to Schacht's attention. Schacht agreed to meet with the president of the Yugoslav National Bank in Berlin and ordered the appropriate ministries to take part in the discussions. Sarnow, chairman of the Mixed Commission, indicated in reply to Hess's questions that every effort would be made to promote exports: "Under all circumstances the problem of the increased taking of German products by Yugoslavia will be raised."[29] Hess raised the possibility of increasing Yugoslav coal purchases from Germany that would reduce Yugoslavia's passive trade balance with England. "Herr Pilja responded to me that the Commerce Ministry was working on this at the moment, thoroughly analyzing Yugoslavia's trade balance with different countries. The goal of this effort was to achieve the best possible balancing of accounts and to transfer imports from countries with which Yugoslavia is passive to other countries. In the first position for transfer are imports hitherto from England."[30] Pilja refused to commit himself to methods or a timetable for obtaining this goal.

Although Yugoslavia was worried and Berlin was willing to discuss, nothing came of Pilja's proposals. In early 1935 he told Hess that going to Berlin would be pointless without prior consultations between the Yugoslav National Bank and the Reichsbank. Pilja wanted an increase in the wheat preference and further German concessions on plums, as well as liquidation of the clearing credits in Berlin.[31]

By mid-January the increasing Yugoslav credits at the Reichsbank were beginning to worry Berlin. Sarnow (Economics Ministry) outlined German plans and expectations in a long letter, emphasizing that the problem had to be solved through positive action and could not be regarded as seasonal in nature.[32] ". . . furthermore, in light of the domestic German raw materials situation import possibilities from Yugoslavia can be expanded without difficulty, the raising of German industrial exports, which alone can be a permanent and natural balance to the clearing debt, must be our main concern . . ."[33] Yugoslavia had to be convinced that this was a valid basis for discussion.

---

26 Ibid.
27 Ibid.
28 Ibid.
29 Sarnow (RWM) to Hess (DG Belgrad), November 10, 1934, ibid.
30 Hess (DG Belgrad) to Sarnow, November 16, 1934, ibid.
31 Ibid.
32 Sarnow to Hess (DG Belgrad), January 16, 1935, ibid.
33 Ibid.

The Economics Ministry had been encouraging German industry to bid for Yugoslav state contracts for supplying railway cars to the state railway, coking coal to a state steel mill and War Ministry, electrical lighting fixtures to the state railway and for constructing a cable car system, long distance cables, and silos. The most important of these was the proposed construction of a rolling mill at the state steel works at Zenica. Sarnow believed that this project, estimated at eight million marks, could lead to a "quick liquidation or at least diminution" of the clearing debt."[34]

This was Germany's answer to Yugoslav concern over the ever-increasing clearing debt. Germany's demands for the discriminatory award of Yugoslav state contracts and Yugoslav complaints about the clearing debt were the dominant issues at the first meeting of the Mixed Commission in Munich in March 1935.

4. The Protocol of March 1935

The negotiations that began in Munich on February 20, 1935, lasted little more than a week, indicating that the Yugoslav delegation came prepared to agree to a policy of preferential awards of state contracts to German firms. This was the first sign that the Schacht strategy was going to pay off. The period of greatest risk, when Germany was granting extensive trade concessions but not receiving important raw materials or increasing exports, was drawing to a close, albeit slowly.

The two delegations agreed that the clearing surplus in favor of Yugoslavia stood at 14.6 million marks, but Yugoslavia reserved the right to correct this figure. Projected German exports of five million marks were expected to shortly reduce the balance to the more acceptable level of nine million marks. The two central banks promised to speed up payments by debtors into the respective clearing accounts. Because neither central bank was in a position to regulate the movement of goods and payments in detail, the same articles provided for the joint consultation in exceptional cases. The second paragraph of the Protocol was a unique provision guaranteeing payment of exchange losses to the Yugoslav exporter when transactions were concluded in a third currency. Germany naturally tried to conduct trade exclusively in marks or dinars, making this provision only a formal victory for Yugoslavia.[35]

In the Protocol Yugoslavia explicitly agreed that payments difficulties should be solved "through the increase of German exports to Yugoslavia." "In order to prevent renewed blockage of payments traffic in the future, the Yugoslav Governmental Committee will propose to its government that Yugoslav purchases of commodities from Germany . . . be brought into corresponding relation with the level of German commodity purchases in Yugoslavia, but in no case to remain under the level of these commodities purchases."[36] If the current clearing surplus was not

[34] Ibid.
[35] Protokoll, paragraphs I.1, I.2, March 1, 1935, PA, Ha Pol, Handakten Wiehl, Jugoslawien, Bd. 3.
[36] Ibid., paragraph I.3.

liquidated, further measures to hold Yugoslav exports to Germany to the level of German exports to Yugoslavia could be considered. A year earlier German export surplus had been considered the "natural relationship" between the two countries; now it was treated as an abstract possibility.

Except for a guarantee on specific German commodities in return for German purchase guarantees on tobacco, the agreement did not include specific assurances for particular German exports but was rounded out by German concessions on Yugoslav agricultural commodities. This pattern, established in the original treaties with Yugoslavia and Hungary, would characterize each stage in the development of bilateral relations with Germany's various trading partners in the Danube.

German subsidies for Yugoslav tobacco were doubled per unit, to a limit of 500,000 marks. The subsidy was unusual in that payment was made contingent upon the implementation of Yugoslav promises to take German exports. Yugoslavia received, in addition, a 50% increase in the bean quota and a 100% increase in the egg and horse purchase guarantees. In a special exchange of letters, Sarnow promised German technical aid for the cultivation of oil seeds; in exchange, Germany naturally expected an "appropriate portion" of the crop would be exported to Germany via the clearing agreement.[37]

Although not a notable turning point in German-Yugoslav relations the Munich meeting did mark the moment when Yugoslavia, beginning to see the consequences of the bilateral clearing system, chose to plunge ahead with the relationship. Germany could see in the success of this Munich meeting an opening vista of political and economic breakthroughs. "In light of the declaration given by the Yugoslav delegation we have the impression that the Yugoslav Government actually is seriously committed to utilize all means at their disposal to increase German exports to Yugoslavia, and if necessary to newly regulate the entire import regime of the country from the perspective of preferential treatment of German imports. It is generally evident that the advantageous consequences of the commercial treaty for Yugoslavia has substantially increased the feeling for the significance of better relations with Germany, at least in the case of the Yugoslav personalities concerned with economic questions."[38]

Two months after the Munich Protocol, Germany would begin negotiating a new treaty with Rumania that would follow the Hungarian and Yugoslav model. In less than a year Germany had created one economic stronghold in the Little Entente and was well on the way to creating another. With both Yugoslavia and Rumania, German policy consciously underplayed such traditional diplomatic devices as "friendship" pacts. The Wilhelmstraße repeated often that Europe had too many pacts and that friendly bilateral relations based on strong economic ties were preferable. Both Hitler and the Wilhelmstraße meant their declarations of disinterest in the narrowly defined political issues such as border disputes and nationality

---

[37] Sarnow to Pilja, March 1, 1935, PA, Ha Pol, Handakten Clodius, Jugoslawien, Bd. 3. The oil seeds question was not settled by the Conference; Germany counted on agreement by the end of July 1935.

[38] Memorandum by Clodius, March 6, 1935, PA, Ha Pol, Handakten Wiehl, Jugoslawien, Bd. 3.

problems inherited from the Versailles settlement that went under the general rubric of "revisionism", but politics were not absent from German policy. The dissociation of German policy from the narrow political questions raised by Hungarian and Bulgarian revisionism was one of the primary strategies behind Hitler's expansionist policy toward east-central Europe. Dominating key agricultural sectors of Yugoslavia and, eventually, Rumania would allow Germany to exert "adequate pressure" on both countries to isolate Czechoslovakia, break up the Little Entente, and eliminate French influence in the Danube.

5. Problems in German Export Promotion

From 1935 to 1936 Germany had cause for concern in Yugoslavia's failure to increase its imports from Germany as promised. After the Munich negotiations German policy makers had been optimistic. Sarnow wrote to the German legation in Belgrade to encourage the *Reichsgruppe Industrie* to take advantage of the situation offered by the Munich Protocol. Sarnow noted that Pilja had complained that there were not enough representatives of German industry in Belgrade and, emphasizing the duty of "official agencies" to assist in penetrating the Yugoslav market, he instructed Hess, the German trade attaché, to act as go-between and seek new possibilities for German industry with the Yugoslav Commerce Ministry.[39]

More than a month later Hess could report only that Yugoslav authorities were still discussing *preparatory* measures to change the geographical structure of Yugoslav import trade.[40] Technical preparations for implementing import controls were ready but political resistance remained in the National Bank and Finance Ministry. Various import control schemes were being contemplated, and Hess thought it possible that, considering the Yugoslav payments and currency situation, such controls might also be imposed on German products. "The balancing of trade accounts with different countries is so important to him [Pilja] that he must reach it even at the cost of lessening the trade volume. In case of emergency, exports to Germany must be limited."[41] In a covering letter to this memorandum Hess relayed Pilja's doubts concerning the ability of the simplified system of import control to deliver as Pilja had promised at the Munich meeting.[42]

Two weeks later Hess reported that while the liberal scruples of the Finance Ministry stood in the way of introducing an import quota system, Pilja had promised to make the issue a question of confidence with the Cabinet.[43] This impasse continued throughout the spring and summer of 1935 while friction over tourist traffic, payment of freight, and Germany's lack of interest in a silo project made

---

[39] Sarnow to Hess (DG Belgrad), March 18, 1935, PA, Ha Pol, Handakten Clodius, Jugoslawien, Bd. 3.
[40] Memorandum by Hess, Belgrade, April 24, 1935, ibid.
[41] Ibid.
[42] Hess to Sarnow, April 26, 1935, ibid.
[43] Hess to Sarnow, May 7, 1935, ibid.

relations even worse.[44] Von Heeren, German minister in Belgrade, commented on the general rise in tension and noted that desire for trade with Germany was "considerably less than even three months ago."[45]

In late August, 1935, Pilja told Hess that he was concerned about the possible limitation of Yugoslav exports to Germany by an "ominous" import quota system against, not in favor of, German interests but indicated that no final policy decisions had yet been made, one way or another. Hess concluded that Yugoslavia was simply not prepared to make a decisive policy turn: "Until Yugoslavia is itself clear on what it wants and can do, it really is virtually impossible to come to any conclusion, no matter what stimulus is given from the German side."[46]

Such indecisiveness made Germany increasingly dissatisfied with the trade expansion policy toward Danubian Europe. Schacht's Economics Ministry was concerned enough with the problem of lagging exports to the Danube to propose ending the excess price payment system for agricultural commodities. Reinhardt, head of the Danubian desk of the Economics Ministry, detailed Berlin's complaints in a long letter of instructions to Hess[47], chief among them being that immediately after the Munich meeting neither the planned exchange projects nor the proposed restructure of Yugoslavia's imports had been realized. Given the existing pattern of trade and the level of demand for German goods on the Yugoslav side blocked credits in Berlin could be avoided.[48] The only possible solution was increasing German exports to Yugoslavia. "Here the goal of the expansion of German exports has been pursued unremittingly and energetically."[49] Reinhardt dealt summarily with Yugoslav claims that German industry was not paying sufficient attention to the Yugoslav market: "It has been clearly shown that German export efforts, in spite of many

[44] Germany wanted supplementary coal purchases in exchange for implementing the tourist accord. Hess to Sarnow, May 7, 1935, ibid.; Heeren to AA, May 8, 1935, PA, Ha Pol, Handakten Wiehl, Jugoslawien, Bd. 3. Yugoslavia did not consider the German offer to build grain silos adequate. Hess to Reinhardt, July 18, 1935, PA, Ha Pol, Handakten Clodius, Jugoslawien, Bd. 3. The refusal by German importers to pay freight costs on eggs and lard also caused friction. Sarnow to Pilja, July 18, 1935, ibid. It is also interesting to note that it was at this time the AO of the NSDAP began subsidizing the new pro-Nazi wing of the German minority in Yugoslavia, in spite of the opposition of the Wilhelmstraße and Viktor von Heeren. On July 28, 1935, a group of Nazi Volksdeutsche marched on Habag Haus, the seat of the moderate Kulturbund (German minority organization) and was dispersered by the police. Prisca von BAGNELL, The Influence of National Socialism on the German Minority in Yugoslavia, U.Ph.d., Syracuse University 1977, p. 116.

[45] Heeren (DG Belgrad) to AA, May 8, 1935, PA, Ha Pol, Handakten Wiehl, Jugoslawien, Bd. 3.

[46] Hess (DG Belgrad) to Clodius, August 29, 1935, PA, Ha Pol, Handakten Clodius, Jugoslawien, Bd. 3.

[47] Reinhardt (RWM) to Hess (DG Belgrad), September 5, 1935, ibid. The policy dispute over Danubian price policy is covered extensively.

[48] It is anomalous that Reinhardt did not even mention Stojadinović's decision in May 1935 to award 70 million dinar in state contracts to German firms. Stojadinović specifically requested that in light of this award Germany not reduce its imports from Yugoslavia. Heeren (DG Belgrad) to AA, May 18, 1935, PA, Sonderreferat, Finanzwesen 16, Jugoslawien, Devisenangelegenheiten mit Deutschland, Bd. 3.

[49] Ibid.

disappointments which German firms have experienced, have in no way become weaker but rather a number of difficulties and impediments in Yugoslavia have hindered greater results."[50]

In his complaints Reinhardt included the failure of Yugoslav public and private firms to pay their commercial debts promptly. Despite the blocked credits this was entirely possible; the Yugoslav clearing credit in Berlin (some tens of millions of marks) could not be used *until* Yugoslav merchants and state agencies paid into the dinar account to the Reichsbank in Belgrade. German firms could remain unpaid for months although millions of marks were on record at the clearing account at the Reichsbank. Reinhardt claimed that late payment of debts caused a marked increase in the risk of transactions, losses to German firms, and hindered the expansion of German exports. "Through the non-observance of fixed payment terms in contracts such insecurity will enter into transactions that an orderly basis of calculations will no longer be possible and the German businessman will lose his interest in the Yugoslav market."[51]

Reinhardt had various other grievances — Yugoslavia's taxes and other regulations limited profitability; Yugoslavia repeatedly did not make a final decision on contracts offered for bid, requiring German business representatives to travel several times to Yugoslavia for long and fruitless negotiations; Yugoslavia's too rigid enforcement of quality standards led to a *de facto* discrimination against German goods; and Yugoslavia's high protective tariffs and red tape for import permits were barriers to export expansion.[52]

Reinhardt cited the contracts for the Yugoslav State Railway and Zagreb municipal transit, where German firms were passed over in favor of the Czech firm *Wittokowitz*, stating that German industry's increasing skepticism about the potential of the Yugoslav market was entirely justified.[53] However, Reinhardt instructed Hess not to make a direct presentation of Germany's grievances, but use the letter of instructions to prepare for the projected autumn meeting of the Mixed Commission (which was not held until the following spring).

Hess's response to Reinhardt shows the calmer view of the legation in Belgrade. Hess complimented the Economics Ministry whose "energetic pressure" had led to a decided improvement in the Yugoslav market but acted as devil's advocate against Reinhardt's pessimistic analysis: existing contract agreements between German firms and the Yugoslav state totaled over five million marks and further agreements were not ruled out by conditions of political instability. Hess contradicted Reinhardt's assertion that public contracts had been lost to the Czechs. "In general, I, at least, have not had such experiences this year in interventions for public con-

[50] Ibid.

[51] Ibid.

[52] An official of the Reichswirtschaftskammer discounted high tariffs as a reason for exports to Yugoslavia failing to keep pace with imports from Yugoslavia. "Die Nachfrage ist zwar infolge der schlechten Wirtschaftslage der Landwirtschaft und der schwierigen Finanzlage der Regierung nicht sehr groß, Deutschland hat aber durchaus nicht den Anteil an der Einfuhr Jugoslawiens der ihm an sich zukommen müßte." Reichswirtschaftskammer to Außenhandelstelle für Baden und Pfalz, May 27, 1935, BA, R 7 VI/261/1.

[53] These contracts were for railway cars, railway car renovation, and patrol boats.

tracts."[54] He advised German firms to include sufficient interest in the sale price to protect against delayed payment.

Hess emphasized the legation's conviction that limiting Yugoslav exports was not a solution. Only expanding German exports, possibly through special barter trans- actions, could provide a permanent resolution to the problems of bilateral trade. The optimism of Hess and the criticisms of Reinhardt mirrored the dispute between the Economics Ministry and the Wilhelmstraße during September 1935. The impa- tient Economics Ministry resented the fiscal outlays for Danubian agricultural products when the beneficiary countries made no efforts to increase purchases of German goods. The Wilhelmstraße, successfully defending the policy, argued for more time to soften up the countries of southeastern Europe. Clodius, the Wil- helmstraße's authority on economic policy in southeastern Europe, maintained that, in the long run, current fiscal difficulties would be outweighed by economic and political advantages.[55]

Political consideration aside, the chief attraction of the treaties with the Danube countries was export promotion. In the initial stages of German expansion, when the treaties offered little in terms of raw materials supply, the persistence of the large clearing balance in Yugoslavia's favor was viewed with more alarm than the polemical literature of the time or subsequent scholarship would indicate. Germany pressed for a discriminatory quota system but the autumn meeting of the Mixed Commission was postponed and Yugoslav Minister President Stojadinović contin- ued to equivocate on implementing import controls.

Hess reported that Yugoslavia had decided to award the construction contract for an entire rolling mill at Zenica to a German firm (either Krupp or GHH)[56] but his report was premature, and German dissatisfaction grew so intense that Heeren presented German grievances directly to Stojadinović. Stressing disappointment over the patrol boat contracts and equivocation over the Zenica project, Heeren made the point that continuing the existing trade structure constituted a danger for trade relations. Stojadinović was conciliatory, thanked Germany for its assistance to the Yugoslav agricultural sector and replied that Yugoslavia was prepared, as before, to deepen trade relations with Germany. He maintained that there was no political motivation in Yugoslavia's award of contracts: "Quality and price alone are decisive."[57] Heeren concluded that Germany was still in the running for the Zenica project but that "strong pressure was being brought by the Czechoslovak

[54] Hess (DG Belgrad) to Clodius, September 10, 1935, PA, Ha Pol, Handakten Clodius, Jugoslawien, Bd. 3.

[55] 'Stellungnahme zu den Schreiben . . . betreffend Preisvereinbarungen mit dem Ausland', memorandum by Clodius, October 5, 1935, PA, Ha Pol, Handakten Clodius, Rumänien, Bd. 1.

[56] Hess (DG Belgrad) to Sarnow (RWM), October 11, 1935, PA, Ha Pol, Handakten Clo- dius, Jugoslawien, Bd. 3. However, when Heeren sounded out the Yugoslav government on the award of a patrol boat contract to Germany, he was politely rebuffed. Heeren (DG Bel- grad) to AA, October 24, 1935, PA, Ha Pol, Handakten Wiehl, Jugoslawien, Bd. 3.

[57] Heeren (DG Belgrad) to AA, November 23, 1935, PA, Ha Pol, Handakten Wiehl, Jugoslawien, Bd. 3.

side for Wittkowitz"[58] and suggested that agreeing to previously rebuffed requests for increased German hog purchases could be decisive in obtaining the Zenica project.[59]

The pattern set by the desultory negotiations of 1934-35 was characteristic of trading under the New Plan. As trade relations in the bilateral clearing system developed there were long periods with virtually no negotiations (while the Yugoslav credits pile up in Berlin), continual and bitter German complaints (over Yugoslavia's refusal to take more German products), and new German concession offers effective only upon the purchase of more German goods (Germany offered new agricultural concessions dependent upon Yugoslavia's increasing German imports).

Any German offer of new agricultural concessions meant inevitable internal conflict bringing the Agricultural Ministry into opposition with the Wilhelmstraße and the Economics Ministry. When the export considerations advanced by the Economics Ministry were not sufficient, as was the case when the Finance Ministry would become involved, the Wilhelmstraße could be relied upon to have "well-known political reasons" to overcome any rearguard resistance from the Agricultural and Finance Ministries. The Agricultural Ministry could only point to the contradiction between Schacht's fiscal conservatism, as evidenced by his decision in September 1935 to minimize subsidies, and his repeated requests for new agricultural concessions to promote exports.[60]

6. The Protocol of March 1936

By February, 1936, all parties agreed that an early meeting of the Mixed Commission was necessary. When the Yugoslav minister in Berlin asked the Wilhelmstraße to arrange for the increase of German imports of Yugoslav pork and poultry while admitting that he did not know the details of the new requests, the usually equable Ritter lost his temper: "I used the opportunity to point out in general to the Yugoslav Minister the unsatisfactory development of trade in the last two years. Yugoslavia has only itself to blame if restraints are introduced upon Yugoslav exports to Germany."[61] Yugoslavia adopted a conciliatory attitude, even showing willingness to negotiate the painful issue of prewar German loans[62], but Heeren cautioned Berlin that moving too quickly into the question of armaments could have unfortunate repercussions. "[The] tendency works toward award to Czechoslovakia for military-political reasons, in view of the contemporary political situa-

---

[58] Ibid.

[59] The RMEL was willing to cooperate with Heeren's suggestion but hedged with several qualifiers. Walter (RMEL) to AA, PA, Geheim, Abteilung II, Jugoslawien, Handel 13, Handelsbeziehungen . . . zu Deutschland.

[60] An example is Müller (RMEL) to Sarnow (RWM), January 8, 1936, PA, Ha Pol, Handakten Clodius, Jugoslawien, Bd. 3.

[61] Minute by Ritter, February 3, 1936, PA, Ha Pol, Handakten Wiehl, Jugoslawien, Bd. 3.

[62] Berliner Handels-Gesellschaft to RWM, February 6, 1935, PA, Ha Pol, Handakten Clodius, Jugoslawien, Bd. 3.

tion every [counter] effort can only be strengthened at dangerous cost."[63] The friendly tone in this meeting prompted plans for a ceremonial visit by Schacht to Belgrade.[64]

The Mixed Commission's second meeting at Zagreb in late March 1936 dealt chiefly with Yugoslavia's frozen claims in Berlin. Germany's clearing debt prior to the February, 1935, Munich meeting had stood at 14.6 million marks; by 1936 the figure had reached 30 million marks. Yugoslavia's reluctance to introduce a discriminatory trade policy favoring Germany was finally overcome, resulting in the promise: "to work with all means at their command to insure a structural reorientation [*Umlagerung*] of imports for the benefit of Germany. According to estimates of the Yugoslav Governmental Committee, German exports to Yugoslavia would permit an increase of 20 million [*Reichsmark*] yearly."[65] The Yugoslavs also promised to award the Zenica project, a contract worth 10 million marks, to German interests.

Germany refused to make any further commitments regarding Yugoslav commodities and rejected Yugoslavia's demands for higher prices. "Germany cannot permit higher prices than the world market price, or in the absence of such a price, [a higher price] than goods of similar quality which the Export Country sends to third countries or such commodities which Germany can import from third countries."[66] This negated Germany's promise in the Commercial Treaty of 1934 that the Yugoslav domestic price would become "the basis" of negotiation. In practice, however, Germany was forced by the internal logic of the trade drive to accommodate higher Danubian prices to some extent. Germany did agree to purchase wheat and corn at approximately the previous year's level and made additional concessions on eggs but reduced export rebates and relegated increased poultry purchases to the area of "further study".

The negotiators wanted to improve the functioning of the payments agreement and eliminate extreme fluctuations in the mark exchange rate. After 1934 Germany had single-mindedly pursued the idea that the National Bank should become the *de facto* owner of the mark balances and sell them at a fixed rate. The National Bank would be informed when a German debtor had paid into the appropriate account of the Reichsbank in Berlin and would then credit the account of the Yugoslav exporter in dinars. Limited versions of this practice did develop, but the National Bank chose to limit its liabilities by selling the mark at a discount that depended partially on the market (the demand for marks from Yugoslav importers) and allowed the exchange rate to fluctuate from month to month. Germany wanted to even out the fluctuations of the discounted mark and set a minimum under which it would not be sold but was unsuccessful in opposing Yugoslavia's new currency regulations introduced on January 15, 1936.[67]

[63] Heeren (DG Belgrad) to AA, PA, Ha Pol, Handakten Wiehl, Jugoslawien, Bd. 3. Heeren gleaned this information from Director Hermanns (GHH).

[64] Heeren (DG Belgrad) to Schacht, March 13, 1936, ibid. Heeren advised postponing the visit until after the successful conclusion of the Mixed Commission meetings.

[65] Protokoll, April 1, 1936, ibid.

[66] Protokoll, ibid.

[67] Protokoll, ibid., paragraphs I.2e-f.

In promising that coal exports would not be subject to restrictive regulation and that payment would not be demanded in foreign exchange, Germany undertook obligations with respect to its exports to Yugoslavia for the first time.[68] The German delegation also promised that Germany would not use its monopoly position in the Yugoslav market to raise prices or sell at a price low enough to disturb the Yugoslav domestic price level.[69] In return for substantial German commitments on tourist travel and provisions for Yugoslav students to study in Germany[70], Yugoslavia agreed to the creation of a German bank in Belgrade but opposed the German proposal to use the prewar capital claims to finance the bank.[71]

Clodius summed up the conclusions of the German delegation in a telegram to Berlin.[72] Yugoslavia had finally steeled itself to introduce discriminatory import controls. The projected doubling of German exports from 20 to 40 million marks, in securing approximately one-third of the Yugoslav import market for Germany, would supplant Italy as Yugoslavia's chief trading partner. "I have the impression that the Yugoslav Government seriously reckons with the success of this reorientation."[73] Clodius reported that Yugoslavia hoped to eventually increase exports to Germany to 60-90 million marks, although both sides agreed this should await "the increase in German exports in the hoped for volume and the expected repercussions on the [clearing] debt and exchange rate."[74] Germany's attempt to increase imports of bauxite and iron ore was rebuffed. Clodius commented that the Yugoslav delegation felt it was negotiating from a strong position because "Germany would not allow the negotiations to collapse on such questions for political reasons."[75]

Despite setbacks, Germany did achieve a breakthrough with Yugoslavia's agreement to trade discrimination. On March 23, 1936, the Yugoslav Finance Ministry imposed the first quota measures against Japanese imports, with a general import quota system following a week later. A country having an export surplus in trade with Yugoslavia faced losing the surplus if it did not increase purchases of Yugoslav goods. On June 11 approximately one-third of Yugoslavia's industrial imports were listed as subject to quotas.

7. Schacht's Visit to Belgrade, June 1936

Although Germany's fledgling imperium was beset with political and economic contradictions which required another meeting of the Mixed Commission in Dresden, Schacht's ceremonial visit to Belgrade in June, 1936, formalized Yugoslavia's

---

[68] Protokoll, ibid., paragraph I.3a.

[69] Protokoll, ibid., paragraph I.3b-c.

[70] Protokoll, ibid., paragraphs III.12 and IV.

[71] Protokoll, ibid., paragraph V; see also Unsigned and Untitled report on 'Vorkriegsanleihen', Zagreb, March 19, 1936, PA, Ha Pol, Handakten Clodius, Jugoslawien, Bd. 3.

[72] Clodius (DG Belgrad) (Zagreb) to AA, March 27, 1936, PA, Ha Pol, Handakten Wiehl, Jugoslawien, Bd. 3.

[73] Ibid.

[74] Ibid.

[75] Ibid.

status as a dependency in Germany's growing "informal empire" in east-central Europe.

German economic expansion was cresting during June 1936 while Schacht was touring southeastern European capitals.[76] His visit to Belgrade and Athens was necessary if German policy was to be seen as more than a reconstituted wartime alliance.[77] Wilson, the American minister in Belgrade, maintained that, despite Schacht's demurs, his visit was politically motivated. "It is my opinion that he [Schacht] is conducting an astute economic political policy designed to bury the states of Eastern and Southeastern Europe economically under German dominance and which will possibly eventuate in their political dependency."[78]

German documentation on Schacht's two visits is thin and phrased in terms characteristic of German propaganda. Schacht was given a very cordial welcome and made an excellent impression on various officials, including Prince Paul, Stojadinović, the commerce minister, and governor of the National Bank.[79] In conversations he outlined German policy in broad and familiar terms: Germany, unlike other industrial nations, was willing to assist Yugoslavia in its mining industry and would take the national interest of Yugoslavia into full consideration.[80] Wilson provides a résumé of one of Schacht's talks at the German legation:

> A peasant country, he said, can never make war. Therefore, it is necessary to industrialize it especially for war needs. The industrialization cannot be expected from foreign capital, because it is not obedient and works against the interests of the country. . . . [Schacht then cited the example of foreign petroleum companies in Rumania.] The industrialization can be effected only if producing goods are imported (machines and installations) from a country to which the domestic goods are exported, because in such a way the industries required for the National Defense will be in the hands of the State.[81]

These arguments were far more than mere propaganda given German willingness to deliver capital goods through the clearing mechanism. When Schacht raised the question of arms purchases as a means of liquidating Germany's debts, Stojadinović expressed the opinion "in decisive fashion" that "the political obstacles in this area would be set aside to a greater extent in the future."[82] Stojadinović also agreed to German investigation of iron deposits in Ljubljana. It seems probable that Schacht used the occasion to finalize negotiations, giving Krupp the important Zenica contract[83], as the Zenica ground-breaking ceremony followed his visit by about ten days.

[76] Schacht visited Belgrade (June 11/12), Athens (June 13/15) and Sofia (June 15/17).

[77] Bucharest was not included in Schacht's tour.

[78] Wilson (Belgrade) to the secretary of state, June 25, 1936, NA, RG 59.600 H. 6231/66.

[79] He was also given the use of a villa. Heeren to AA, June 6, 1936, PA, Ha Pol, IVb, Jugoslawien, Wirtschaftliche Beziehungen zu Deutschland, Bd. 1.

[80] Heeren (DG Belgrad) to AA, ibid. [DGPP, C. Vol. 5, 376].

[81] Enclosure 1 to dispatch, Wilson (Belgrade) to the secretary of state, June 18, 1936, op. cit.

[82] Heeren (DG Belgrad) to AA, June 16, 1936, DGFP, C, Vol. 5, 376, p. 631.

[83] Heeren (DG Belgrad) to AA, June 17, 1936, PA, Ha Pol, Jugoslawien, Industrie 6, Bergbau und Hüttenindustrie, Bd. 1. Stojadinović was also successful in pressuring French interests to build a copper smelter at the *Mines de Bor* so that Yugoslavia would no longer have to import refined copper. Kanzler (Bled) (in Koncept Heeren) to AA, August 9, 1936, ibid.

In discussions with the governor of the National Bank, Schacht raised the controversial issues of service on prewar German loans and increased access to Yugoslav raw materials. "It is certainly important for Yugoslavia that next to its agricultural production, its raw material production develops as well, as Germany especially in this area promises to be a permanent customer of Yugoslavia. He himself [Schacht] is ready to give every possible assistance, especially in the utilization of Yugoslav mineral resources, for example, in the form of the delivery of the mechanical equipment which could be paid later in the form of ore, etc."[84] This suggestion did not receive any systematic treatment by Yugoslavia. Schacht turned down the National Bank's request that Germany guarantee the mark exchange rate and placed the burden on Yugoslavia to liquidate its credits in Berlin by state orders. The creation of a German bank in Belgrade was touched upon, but no immediate decision was made.

Wilson recognized the importance of the conjuncture of Schacht's visit, the Zenica project, and the new quota regulations, and he attempted to alert both Stojadinović and Pilja to the dangers inherent in the bilateral commercial system. Both were well informed on the American trade program, but neither offered Wilson much hope of a policy change; Stojadinović conceded that "the American came closer to the ideal than did the bilateral agreements", but argued that the present policy was necessary because "the special geographic, economic, and even political situation of Yugoslavia"[85] Pilja denied that Yugoslavia's new quota regulations were intended to aid German interests and told Wilson that "if the United States wished to export American products to Yugoslavia it must make up its mind to import an approximate equivalent of Yugoslav products."[86] "Yugoslavia", he added, "could not continue to pay for American goods in foreign exchange, and therefore, had turned for the same articles to countries with which it had clearing agreements, and under present conditions it seemed Germany would be the first beneficiary."[87]

8. The Protocol of October 1936, Dresden

Yugoslavia's new discriminatory policy, the Schacht visit, and the Zenica project were all indications of a German breakthrough in Yugoslavia; it seemed as if Schacht's trade policy would finally substantially increase exports to Yugoslavia. But barely two months after Schacht left Belgrade, Yugoslavia introduced raw materials export controls discriminating against Germany.

The persistent crises afflicting trade relations between Germany and its clearing partners were an inevitable result of the bilateral exchange clearing system. The economies had originally interrelated through the interaction of each domestic

[84] Heeren (DG Belgrad) to AA, June 17, 1936, PA, Ha Pol, Wirtschaft 6, Wirtschaftliche Beziehungen Jugoslawiens zu Deutschland, Bd. 1.
[85] Wilson (Belgrade) to the secretary of state, June 25, 1936, op. cit.
[86] Ibid.
[87] Ibid.

market with the world market — the market system had determined the sum total of trade relations. With the introduction of bilateral clearing, every conflict developed into a crisis because the administered trade structure allowed only one test of the relative benefits accruing to each party: the threat to injure the other party by refusing to import goods at the existing level or by denying it critical exports. Bluffing was an essential tool in the repertoire of the trade negotiator. The September/October, 1936, crisis stemmed from Yugoslavia's determination to use rising prices on the world market to coerce Germany into further support of the Yugoslav agricultural sector by imposing quotas on key raw materials exports.

Initially all had seemed to be going well in the summer of 1936. After the ground-breaking ceremony at the Zenica project, Germany had agreed to purchase a trial shipment of Yugoslav beef and German exports were finally beginning to balance the clearing debt according to both Yugoslav and German statistics. This brief halcyon period ended abruptly on August 20 when the Yugoslav Finance Ministry ordered corn and wheat exports be limited to hard currency, not to clearing, countries. (A loophole was provided by a clause permitting grain in the hands of Prizad to be exported.) On August 27 the order was extended to copper, lead, zinc, and lumber. Yugoslavia was willing to sell to Germany when there was no other alternative, comments Meiss, but as soon as an opportunity arose to sell for strong currency the Yugoslavs "disregarded part of the treaty agreement and utilized their chance on the world market."[88]

Berlin was convinced that any systematic implementation of these decrees would seriously jeopardize trade relations between the two countries[89], an impression confirmed by telephone calls from Hess in Belgrade leaving no doubt that "the measures are directed at Germany because these raw materials, according to the Yugoslav viewpoint, are sold again [by Germany on the world market] for free currency."[90] In reprisal Germany immediately cancelled a special tariff concession for Yugoslav fruit and denounced an agreement regulating freight payments between the two countries. By mid-September there was further escalation: Yugoslavia limited hemp exported to all clearing countries to two-thirds of the September-December, 1935, level while exports to nonclearing countries were not subject to any restriction. Wool and raw hides came under a total export embargo. There were negotiations under way in Berlin over Yugoslav requests for increased German purchases of apples and grapes and strangely enough Germany did not break off discussions — agreement was actually reached in September. As Germany always gave with one hand and took with the other, on September 16 Benzler, a Wilhelmstraße official, telegraphed Belgrade that German currency authorities would no longer allocate currency certificates for a wide range of Yugoslav commodities.[91] Exempting corn and wheat, this regulation amounted to an embargo on a large percentage of Yugoslav agricultural exports to Germany in that, without

---

88 MEISS, Beziehungen, p. 137.
89 Unsigned minute, August 28, 1936, PA, Ha Pol, Handakten Clodius, Jugoslawien, Bd. 3.
90 Memorandum by Kalisch, September 1, 1936, ibid.
91 Benzler to DG Belgrad, September 16, 1936, PA, Ha Pol, Handakten Wiehl, Bd. 3.

currency allocations by the appropriate authorities, commodities simply could not be imported into Germany.

If maintained, these discriminatory measures would have ended Schacht's carefully nurtured trade expansion policy. However, they were not to be the first round of a trade war but a means by which Yugoslavia could drive a harder bargain with Germany. The strong anti-German, pro-French sentiment that existed in the National Bank and General Staff was repeatedly outmaneuvered by Stojadinović. Rising primary product prices on the world market allowed Yugoslavia to coerce Germany into purchasing more agricultural products. The Germans, while acquiescing, made their concessions contingent upon Yugoslav compliance with German raw materials needs. The temporary revival of the world market gave Yugoslavia a measure of economic freedom at a time, September, 1936, when Yugoslav purchases had reduced the clearing balance in Berlin. Dismissing the chance to break away from its entanglements with Germany, Yugoslavia, after some initial sparring and threats, settled down to an amiable compromise with Germany, trying merely to extract the best possible terms from an unquestioned trade relationship.

That there would be no trade war became clear at the beginning of negotiations in Dresden. Sarnow met Pilja with complaints about anti-German commentary in the semiofficial journal *Politika*, which had alleged that Germany was exploiting the clearing mechanism to gain economic hegemony in southeastern Europe. Pilja quickly denounced both the *Politika* articles and the general press campaign against German-Yugoslav relations current in western capitals. He emphasized that he had a "positive" attitude toward strengthening trade relations and blamed the National Bank for making it impossible to demonstrate this attitude in negotiations. He went on to ridicule Czechoslovakia's plans for an Economic Little Entente, stressing that such an alliance would be simply a political method of controlling revisionism in the Balkans.

> It is of course natural, that one continually attempts to improve economic relations between such political friends, insofar as it is possible. Germany can view the situation with complete composure. Czechoslovakia will never be in a position to even approach taking the export surpluses of Yugoslavia and Rumania, and it is just as unable to satisfy the industrial needs of both countries. The attempts to make an economic bloc out of the Little Entente will always be continued, but according to the situation of the relations will be condemned to total harmlessness.[92]

Neither Paris, Prague, nor Berlin viewed an Economic Little Entente as "harmless" or a "natural" development. The plan had been sporadically tried since 1933 to block German hegemony in east-central Europe. What is important is not Pilja's wild inaccuracy in characterization but the indication his remarks give that the policy never had much credibility in Yugoslavia. Berlin had no cause for alarm.

Pilja stressed Yugoslavia's solidarity with Germany on international financial questions. The devaluation of the French franc had finished off orthodox efforts to bring domestic prices in line with world prices by deflation. The countries of east-central Europe, except for Poland, continued to maintain fictitious exchange values

---

[92] Memorandum by Sarnow, Dresden, October 12, 1936, ibid.

for their currencies to prevent domestic prices from falling to the world market price level. France's devaluation, followed by Italy's and Czechoslovakia's, put pressure on Yugoslavia to do likewise; Pilja's declaration of solidarity with Schacht's antidevaluation policy pitted Germany and Yugoslavia against American, British, and French financial policy. Pilja maintained,

> Devaluation can only have meaning when it occurs in the context of general international action, the simultaneousness secures the prerequisites for a stability through devaluation at the proper level. Without such prerequisites devaluation is both stupid and immoral.[93]

Pilja's position was that Yugoslavia would devaluate only if forced to by circumstances — a position allowing Germany a key role. If the domestic price level in Czechoslovakia and Italy did not rise, Yugoslavia could hope for increased exports to those countries; if it did, Yugoslavia would be forced to fall back on the German market. He also stressed that Yugoslavia would have nothing to do with a devaluation policy that functioned to impose economic isolation on Germany:

> He [Pilja] thinks this policy is very silly. It could lead in his opinion to a consolidation of non-devaluating countries around Germany rather than to an isolation. The countries he designates are Yugoslavia, Poland, Austria and Hungary.[94]

With Pilja projecting the possibility of a regional continental economic bloc, *Großraumwirtschaft* takes on more substance than a pipe dream of Nazi ideologues. The peasant countries of Danubian Europe regarded the devaluation of the United States, Great Britain, and France with fear and distrust, even though devaluation decreased the burden of foreign debt service. The post-World War I inflation that had ravaged Germany and all the eastern European countries had created a domestic political sitation that made devaluation virtually impossible. These countries were locked into a situation where their domestic price levels were substantially higher than the prices prevailing on the world market. Yugoslavia's ties with France, already strained by the French devaluation, were further weakened by fears generated by the Spanish Civil War and the French Popular Front government — Yugoslavia sought rapprochement with Germany.

The eventual compromise benefited both of the trading partners. The *Times* characterized the negotiations as motivated by a spurt of "boundless concessions", which is an exaggeration, but Germany did give further concessions to Yugoslav agriculture.[95] Yugoslavia insisted on maintaining export controls on certain raw materials but Germany succeeded in having quota restrictions lifted on copper, zinc, and lead.

To resolve the persistent problem of Yugoslavia's export surplus, if Yugoslav credits at the Reichsbank continued to increase, there would have to be a meeting of the Mixed Commission, but if necessary, Yugoslavia could limit exports to Germany without consultation.[96] Quotas, equal to the substantial ones granted in the

---

[93] Ibid.
[94] Ibid.
[95] The Times (London), October 22, 1936.
[96] Protokoll, October 20, 1936, Dresden, PA, Ha Pol, Handakten Wiehl, Jugoslawien, Bd. 3, paragraph I.

spring, were part of the deal, together with large quotas for apples, poultry, and plums.[97] Tourist travel was dealt with by making available 500,000 marks a month, excluding business travel expenses.[98]

Germany promised not to deny currency allocations to Yugoslav agricultural products available at the same price and under similar conditions as products of other Danubian countries. This promise, although granting Yugoslavia most-favored-nation treatment, was of more formal than real significance although it allowed Yugoslavia to make further demands at a later date.[99] The patchwork quality of Germany's relations with each of its Danubian trading partners would give Yugoslavia ample opportunity for protests under such a clause.

The political events of 1936 and the meetings of the Mixed Commission combined to push Yugoslavia farther down the road of satellite status within Germany's "informal empire" in east-central Europe. With intimate knowledge of Germany's trade policy at a time of rising prices on the world market, Yugoslavia still tried to increase its exports to Germany and maintained its distance from France and the Little Entente.

9. Conclusion: Causes of the Yugoslav Rapprochement with Germany

After 1936, Yugoslav foreign trade policy pivoted on its trade relationship with Germany. With the trade balance stabilized after mid-1936, Yugoslavia's introduction of discriminatory quotas and demands for increased agricultural concessions indicates the step toward adaptation of the Yugoslav economy to German needs had been made. Yugoslavia did not appear particularly affected by Germany's reoccupation of the Rhineland during the Zagreb and Dresden meetings of the Mixed Commission, even though the isolation of east-central Europe from French military assistance was certainly implicit in the reoccupation. Yugoslavia seems to have used Germany's desire to maintain good relations as a lever to pry out more trade concessions, not the attitude of a naive, weak, or duped government as Yugoslavia has been portrayed. Germany had been insisting on the introduction of discriminatory quotas and the award of the Zenica project since 1935, with no evidence of extraordinary pressure. With two years of experience of the clearing, with world market prices rising, and with the French interested in purchasing Yugoslav grains, Yugoslavia worked to coerce Germany into further support of her agricultural sector. The tactic worked — entangling Yugoslavia deeper in the German net.

---

[97] Ibid., paragraph IV.10.
[98] Ibid., paragraph III.
[99] Ibid., paragraph IV.17.

CHAPTER V

THE GERMAN EXPORT OFFENSIVE IN RUMANIA, 1935-37

1. Negotiation of the Commercial Treaty of 1935

The Wilhelmstraße found Rumania's denunciation of the 1930 treaty irritating in that it then had to face monthly renewals or enter a treatyless state. Although Clodius saw a loss of legal protection as "a potentially serious blow" to German business in Rumania, Berlin at first refused to extend the treaty for longer than one-month periods or to extend the existing cattle quota. Berlin finally agreed to an extension until the end of March if the beef quota was set at 1/12 the yearly amount.[1]

Negotiations for the new treaty, beginning in late January and continuing until March, could not settle the outstanding issues. Manolescu-Strunga, Rumanian under-secretary of state in the Agricultural Ministry and later Commerce Minister, had agreed with Germany that the negotiations could be conducted in three parts: (1) a trade treaty would be negotiated quickly, so that it could be signed in two weeks when Manolescu returned from London[2]; (2) a payments agreement would be negotiated in Bucharest in late February, and the ratification of the trade treaty would depend upon this negotiation; and (3) Rumanian requests for long-term credit to the national railway, oil industry, agrarian cooperatives, and the state would be negotiated separately, as would the question of Germany's import of Rumanian oil. Manolescu agreed that only oil would have to be paid for in convertible currency. "As a condition for every *Devisen* payment Herr Schacht insisted that unity between Germany and Rumania concerning the level and means of payments to the German creditors be reached first. Further *Reichsbank* President Schacht has designated a satisfactory regulation to the question of the old delivery of materials debt [about 30 million marks] as the prerequisite for a long term delivery contract."[3]

---

[1] Koepke to Comnen, February 26, 1935, PA, Abteilung II, Wirtschaft, Rumänien, Handel 13, Handelsvertragsverhältnisse mit Deutschland, Bd. 12. Philipe Marguerat has boldly proclaimed his disinterest in the period before 1938: "C'est a partir de 1938 seulement que la Roumanie devient l'objet des convoitises allemandes et le theatre d'une lutte économique tantot sourde, tantot acharneé entre l'Angleterre et le Reich." MARGUERAT, Le III Reich, p. 11, p. 15. The analysis and documentation in this chapter and chapters VIII and IX demonstrates how seriously Germany prepared for the breakthroughs of 1938-1939, and how important even a relatively small amount of aviation fuel was to German rearmament efforts.

[2] Of Rumanian exports to Germany, 80% would be balanced by German exports to Rumania, while 20% was earmarked for debt payment.

[3] Memorandum by Clodius, February 4, 1935, op. cit.

That the trade treaty would be ready for Manolescu's signature when he returned from London was a forlorn hope. Negotiations dragged over the relatively small number of outstanding differences until the Rumanian delegation left Berlin early, declaring that it was not competent to deal with certain questions.[4]

The negotiations pivoted upon Rumania's demand for German quota guarantees on beef and pork, establishing a higher price for Rumanian beef than Germany was paying Ireland or Denmark. The various German ministries were unanimous that "the guarantee of secret rebates as guaranteed to Hungary is out of the question. Perhaps the possibility exists that these price differences can be balanced through the conclusion of special compensation transaction."[5] A quota guarantee for hogs was impossible, according to the Agricultural Ministry, because this concession had to be reserved for negotiations with Poland. Rumania initially refused to treat German and Czech imports equally with regard to currency and quota regulations but Clodius believed that this German demand would be granted if Germany compromised on the agricultural question. Although Rumania refused to discuss the 1929 railway credit and the German frozen claims of 30 million marks resulting from it until the trade agreement had been concluded, Clodius thought it possible that an agreement combining the question of frozen credits with long-term German investment in the Rumanian oil industry and Germany's import of Rumanian oil could be reached.[6]

The next round of intensive discussion began with Manolescu's accusation that Germany was not showing enough willingness to compromise.[7] He promised that if Germany would make new concessions, he would use his influence to arrive at a solution of the frozen railway credits. However, he told Schacht that settling the railway credit question should not be a part of the trade treaty negotiations. His criticisms on specific issues were:

1. *Petroleum*: Schacht had promised a portion would be paid in free currency, but he was only offering 3% (raised to 5%) payment.
2. *Eggs*: The quota of 600 railway cars was sufficient but the price of 37 marks per 100 kilos was too low.
3. *Fruits*: Germany's offer to maintain the previous year's level of 40 tons was ridiculous.
4. *Hogs*: There was no understanding whatsoever.
5. *Cattle*: Germany's offer to buy 6,000 head was sufficient but again the price was so low as to ensure that the quota would not be met.
6. *Lumber*: He would rather sell it for free currency than at the German price.

[4] This is perhaps explicable by Rumania's reluctance to conclude a treaty with Germany. Manolescu, the driving force behind the negotiations, was in England negotiating a payments agreement. Rumania was able to make the first payment to English bondholders only with support from two international oil firms: Shell (Astra Romana) and Standard Oil (Romana Americana). Pochhammer (DG Bukarest) to AA, February 19, 1935, and Pochhammer (DG Bukarest) February 28, 1935, PA, Abteilung II, Wirtschaft Rumänien L 12, Handelsbeziehungen zu England, Bd. 1.
[5] Memorandum by Clodius, February 16, 1935, Ibid.
[6] Ibid. The Germans also demanded a nondiscrimination clause in Rumania's tariff policy for commodities exported through Gdynia or Danzig. Rumania refused.
[7] Pochhammer (DG Bukarest) to AA, telegram 34, March 10, 1935, PA, Politische Abteilung II, Rumänien, Politik 2, Politische Beziehungen . . zu Deutschland, Bd. 2. The dispatch contained a fuller report, Pochhammer (DG Bukarest) to AA, March 10, 1935, ibid.

If Germany would raise the prices for eggs and the price and quota for beef and would give Rumania equal treatment with Hungary and Bulgaria on tariff questions, Manolescu offered: (1) to accept the German export list without revision; (2) the prospect of increasing German exports at the expense of other countries; and (3) all future Rumanian public contracts would go to Germany. If this compromise was not accepted, he threatened to advise his government to break off negotiations and trade relations in general.

Pochhammer, German chargé in Bucharest, pointed out that the fall of Manolescu, who was the only Rumanian minister friendly to Germany, could precipitate an anti-German reaction. Germany had put Manolescu in a very difficult position in the Rumanian Cabinet. On his last trip abroad, while given full power to negotiate with Germany but not with England, he had returned with a treaty with England while the negotiations with Germany were still hanging. "Titulescu especially has the perspective of forcing him [Manolescu] to resign. Herr Manolescu-Strunga therefore fights for his existence with our treaty."[8]

Germany emphasized through Ulrich that it had generously offered to increase Rumanian imports from 50 to 80 million marks while receiving only approximately a 10-million-mark increase in German exports to Rumania — 50 to around 60 million marks. Germany had also offered price and purchase guarantees for important groups of commodities. According to Ulrich, the only outstanding question in the commercial treaty was the price of Rumanian cattle, which Germany intended to settle in a manner satisfactory to Rumania. He pointed out that Rumania had not met German requests to raise German exports, to make railway credit deliveries, or settle the issue of transportation. "Delay in the negotiations is exclusively attributable to the fact that Rumania conducts negotiations without a standing delegation; it is always changing and consists partly of non-plenipotentiary negotiators."[9]

The Wilhelmstraße began backpedaling a few days later. Manolescu had said that the cattle question was the essential compromise for the conclusion of the treaty. Ritter telegraphed Bucharest that Germany was prepared to agree to Rumanian demands on this question *if* negotiations would be quickly concluded. It was out of the question to extend the old treaty beyond March.[10]

Manolescu, trying for a few more concessions, renewed his demand that Rumania receive the same price as Hungary for eggs.[11] Although irritated that the concession on cattle had not pacified Rumania, Clodius nevertheless replied that the price of eggs should not be allowed to prevent the conclusion of the treaty.[12]

The successful compromise on cattle prices was dependent upon IG Farben, whose interest in German expansion led it to agree to supply two marks per 50 kilos

[8] Pochhammer (DG Bukarest) to AA, dispatch, March 10, 1935, ibid.
[9] Ulrich to DG Bukarest, March 12, 1935, PA, Abteilung II, Wirtschaft, Rumänien, Handel 13, Handelsvertragsverhältnisse mit Deutschland, Bd. 12. Ulrich made it clear that petroleum, German investments in the petroleum industry, and deliveries under the railway credit were to be the subject of general negotiatons at a later date.
[10] Ritter to DG Bukarest, March 16, 1935, ibid.
[11] Pochhammer (DG Bukarest) to AA, telegram 36, March [?], 1935, ibid.
[12] Minute by Clodius, March 18, 1935, ibid. The Rumanians were offered 35 marks per 100 kilos; the Hungarians had been guaranteed 50 marks per 100 kilos.

of the price support needed to market Rumanian beef in Germany. (Rumania was demanding six marks per 50 kilos more than the cost of Irish or Danish beef.) The remaining four marks would be furnished by the German government from funds set aside for Hungary and Yugoslavia[13], but paid out through IG in order to avoid complications with other German trading partners. In this instance, at least, IG surpassed MWT in supporting German expansionist policy.[14] Manolescu and Pochhammer carried out the last round of serious negotiations, with emergency telephone calls to Berlin.

In an interview at his retreat at Ploesti[15], Manolescu expressed satisfaction with Germany's guarantee of an 80/60-million-mark trade ratio favoring Rumania even though this was only a 25% surplus and the new Rumanian foreign trade law required all surpluses to be 40%. He thought, however, that he would be able to push the treaty through the cabinet and parliament.[16] Actually, Germany's agreement to allow Rumania an export surplus involved an interesting sleight of hand. Germany had no intention of paying for this surplus with free currency — when it appeared that Manolescu was moving toward claims for convertible currency, Clodius made it clear that this would make the treaty impossible.[17] Manolescu was unhappy that the German compromise on cattle depended upon a one-to-one barter with IG Farben and, while accepting Clodius's formulation of the petroleum question, held out for equal treatment with Hungary with regard to egg prices.

Pochhammer, in a written reply, emphasized Germany's goodwill, demonstrated by its willingness to compromise on the ratio of imports to exports and cattle prices. However, although (as Schacht had said) Germany remained interested in Rumanian oil and investment in the Rumanian oil industry, this interest could not be advanced at the expense of Germany's currency reserves. Also, Schacht's proposed compromise regarding deliveries under the 1929 railway credit could not be construed as renunciation of German rights. A necessary element in the conclusion of the present trade negotiations was Rumania's general assurance that these obligations would be honored in the future.[18]

The final trade treaty was far more comprehensive than earlier postwar treaties. It was, like the Yugoslav treaty, formally based on the most-favored-nation principle, although the published sections did allow substantial legal rights to German business in Rumania. The key sections of the treaty, however, were the secret protocols containing German compromises with Rumanian agricultural demands. For

---

[13] Dr. Walter (RMEL) to RFM, Abteilung II, Wirtschaft, Rumänien, Handel 13, Handelsvertragsverhältnisse mit Deutschland, Bd. 12.

[14] IG Farben was, of course, a member of the MWT.

[15] Manolescu was recuperating from an illness.

[16] Pochhammer (DG Bukarest) to AA, March 17, 1935, PA, Abteilung II, Rumänien, Handel 13, Handelsvertragsverhältnisse mit Deutschland, Bd. 12. Manolescu wanted most of the projected 25% Rumanian surplus to be made available for orders by the Rumanian state, not tied exclusively to debt payments.

[17] Clodius to RWM, RMEL and RFM, March 18, 1935, ibid.

[18] Pochhammer (DG Bukarest) to Manolescu-Strunga, March 18, 1935, DGFP, C, Vol. 2, 543, pp. 1023-1024.

reasons of his own, Manolescu revealed the existence of these secret clauses to American diplomats less than a month after the treaty was signed.

"Here", the Minister said, "is our most extensive accord. You will see", and he ran through the pages, "how complete it is, how it is supplemented by half a dozen schedules dealing with particular plans of trade, with particular commodities, with particular tariff reductions. Here", and he pointed at a section near the end, "is the section which is secret. You will see the word 'Secret' noted at the top of this page. I cannot give you this section. Without it you would be unable to give your government a true picture of our new commercial relationship with Germany. It deals, to be frank, with certain special privileges accorded to Rumanian merchandise. Let us be frank. In most of the trade conventions concluded recently between European countries each accords to the other such privileges. They must be kept secret or other countries, under their interpretation of the most favored-nation treatment clauses of their treaties, would claim the same reductions. The primary object of the conventions would be defeated. I hope that we, in turn, shall be able to reach some satisfactory agreement as to the future treatment of American trade."[19]

There were two separate secret protocols, two agreements and accompanying appendices in the confidential sections of the treaty[20] designed to regulate the volume and structure of bilateral trade between the two countries. These secret clauses were intended to initiate a discriminatory trade system irreconcilable with trade relations conducted under the most-favored-nation principle.

The success of the treaty depended upon German concessions embodied in an agreement on commodities traffic and its appended secret protocol guaranteeing the import of specific amounts of Rumanian agricultural commodities at prices substantially above those prevailing on the world market. Germany was obligated to import (according to Appendix A of the protocol) soybeans, fruit, poultry, eggs, and other agricultural commodities totaling 29.7 million marks[21], while further guarantees for lumber, minerals, and chemicals added another 7.0 million marks.[22] German purchase guarantees of approximately 37 million marks amounted to approximately 80% of Rumania's exports to Germany in 1933, the worst year of the Depression for bilateral trade and over 50% of Rumania's sales to Germany in 1934, a year of modest recovery. Concessions on such a scale, especially as Rumania could not have expected to market the commodities elsewhere, were significant.

In the treaty with Yugoslavia, a German export surplus had been considered the "natural" economic relationship between the two countries, but the secret protocol to the Rumanian commodity agreement had Germany accepting a Rumanian export surplus, with German exports to Rumania set at 60% of Rumanian exports

[19] Wadsworth to the Secretary of State, April 19, 1935, NA, RG 59, 671.116/66.

[20] 'Geheimes Schlußprotokoll', 'Vereinbarung über den deutsch-rumänischen Warenverkehr', 'Zusatzvereinbarung über das Übernahmescheinverfahren . . .' 'Geheimes Protokoll zur Zustatzvereinbarung über das Übernahmescheinverfahren . . .', and, additionally, two tables: one spelling out Rumanian exports to Germany (Anlage 2) specifying Germany's agreement to purchase specific amounts of agricultural products, and one detailing Rumania's general assent to increase imports from Germany by specific percentages for specific goods. PA, Ha Pol, Handakten Wiehl, Rumänien, Bd. 1.

[21] 'Vereinbarung . . . zum Warenverkehr', ibid., p. 30. 'Geheimes Protokoll . . . zum Warenverkehr', ibid., p. 31, Anlage A, ibid., pp. 37-38.

[22] Anlage A, ibid., pp. 37-38.

(with the exception of petroleum) to Germany. Of the resulting 40% balance in Rumania's favor, 20% was to be used to pay for orders from the Rumanian state and the remainder to pay long-term Rumanian debts.[23] The secret protocols also included the barter of cattle for IG Farben products.[24]

Germany was to receive payment in goods for the deliveries made under the railway credit and guaranteed exports to Rumania of 80% of the value for Rumanian imports. An agreed-upon quota system based on exports of 50 million marks (*Anlage 3*)[25] differed from German purchase guarantees in not requiring Rumania to buy any specific German commodities and expressing only Rumania's intent to set up quotas for German commodities and purchase German products in certain fixed proportions. German commitments, on the other hand, involved binding contracts between monopoly marketing authorities in Germany and agricultural organizations in Rumania.[26]

The treaty assured special handling of German pharmaceutical exports and gave assurances to German pharmaceutical businesses already operating in Rumania.[27] Each country waived fees for citizens of the other residing within its borders[28] and a number of mutual tariff concessions were agreed upon.[29]

Absent from the treaty, however, was a payments agreement and an agreement on petroleum. Until joined with a functioning payments system, the treaty could not be effective. It remained in abeyance throughout the summer of 1935, while the German currency office retaliated against Rumanian export premiums promoting exports to free currency countries. Although the treaty could not function, the German government and business groups seemed content with the extent of their success. Schacht sent a telegram to Manolescu congratulating him on the conclusion of the treaty[30], followed a few days later by a letter proposing a solution to the differences on the petroleum question. After expressing his sympathy for Rumania's plight when its most important raw material was exploited by foreign capital, Schacht suggested that the Rumanian government take over the exploration and development of new petroleum fields. "Germany should open up fresh sources of oil for an oil company to be designated by the Rumanian government and she should be paid in oil and not in foreign exchange for the material supplied and for installation."[31] He mentioned that Constantinescu of the *Creditul Minier*, the largest oil company wholly under Rumanian control, had already been to Berlin for

---

[23] 'Geheimes Protokoll . . . Warenverkehr', ibid., Article 3. This could also be used for other purposes: expenses of Rumanian students, patients, and tourists in Germany.

[24] 'Geheimes Schlußprotokoll . . .', ibid., pp. 28-29.

[25] 'Geheimes Protokoll . . . Warenverkehr', ibid., and Anlage 3, ibid.

[26] The agreement between the *Reichstelle für Tiere und Tierische Erzeugnisse* and the *Union der Viehexport-Syndikate Rumäniens* is an example of such a contract, included as an appendix in RMEL to RFM, March 19, 1935, BA, R 2/18165.

[27] 'Geheimes Schlußprotokoll . . .', op. cit., p. 27.

[28] Ibid.

[29] Ibid., p. 28.

[30] Schacht to Manolescu-Strunga, telegram, March 27, 1935, PA, Abteilung II, Wirtschaft, Rumänien, Handel 13, Handelsvertragsverhältnisse mit Deutschland, Bd. 12.

[31] Schacht to Manolescu-Strunga, April 1, 1935, DGFP, C, Vol. 4, 6, p. 5.

private discussions on this question[32] and suggested a new German credit in proportion to the proposed scope of the oil fields extension, for which Rumania would agree to repay the old 30-million-mark credit and the new credit with oil from the new wells delivered through the clearing.

This idea appears to have originated with the *Gutehoffnungshütte* (GHH), one of the seven pillars of the Ruhr steel-coal industry. The conservative Finance Ministry was aware of the enthusiasm and ambition of the GHH and of Schacht's interest in the proposed project. "Particularly planned is the extension of Rumanian oil production, the construction of refineries, the delivery of tankers, pipe lines for gasoline and natural gas, et cetera, with a total value of around 100 million marks."[33] The Finance Ministry remained skeptical, evidenced by the tone of its memorandum and by its refusal to consider a government guarantee for the GHH project, which it considered vaguely defined.

Schacht received no response to his personal approach from the Rumanian government. The Rumanian domestic political scene was being swept by xenophobic propaganda and the treaty, originally scarcely commented upon, came under increasing attack. Clodius wrote a letter clarifying the attitude of the German government to the question of German investment in the Rumanian petroleum industry and emphasized that it had been Comnen who had originally maintained, in repeated discussions with the Wilhelmstraße and Schacht, that a long-term credit from German industry was an "essential prerequisite" for increasing trade between the two countries.[34] Both the Rumanian delegation, during the negotiations in Berlin, and Constantinescu, during his trip to Berlin, had suggested similar ideas. Germany had been led to believe that the Rumanian government stood behind these proposals. Clodius argued that Germany had done nothing more than "respond to Rumanian wishes by making available their cooperation and help in facilitating credit transactions." He responded to a newspaper campaign accusing Germany of planning long-term investment or participation in the Rumanian oil industry by stating that German industry and the German government intended to conclude only long-term "delivery contracts." The agreement, already in German draft form, was only the basis for "friendly economic cooperation" and was not, as the newspapers accused, "secret political-economic agreements with a political background", but a "normal businesslike transactions."[35]

The Wilhelmstraße, Schacht, and the big business interests became increasingly aware that the strong campaign against Germany endangered the realization of the treaty. Germany saw this campaign as closely tied to an increasing effort to draw Rumania into the new French political combination[36]; i.e., the Franco-Soviet and

[32] On the Constantinescu visit; ibid.

[33] Minute by Nasse, April [?], 1935, PA, R 2/30936.

[34] Clodius to Manolescu-Strunga, May 29, 1935, PA, Ha Pol, Handakten Clodius, Rumänien, Bd. 1.

[35] Ibid.

[36] See, for example, Pochhammer's report on the *Weg mit dem Fremden* movement: Pochhammer (DG Bukarest) to AA, April 4, 1935, PA, Abteilung II, Wirtschaft, Rumänien, Handel 13, Handelsvertragsverhältnisse mit Deutschland, Bd. 12. Pochhammer reported that there was only one hostile article in the initial press reaction to the treaty. In an interesting study of

Czech-Soviet alliances. The Office of Currency Management authorized an unlimited issuance of marks to purchase Rumanian oil until further notice[37], but Pochhammer reported from Bucharest that implementation of the commercial treaty was being frustrated on all fronts. Manolescu told Pochhammer that the present financial situation made impossible any effort to make materials deliveries under the railway credit. Pochhammer replied that unless German firms were granted import quotas for such important types of machinery, the treaty could hardly function. Manolescu also refused to raise the quota for automobile imports above the 1932 quota. His response, when Pochhammer pointed out that these decisions made illusory the quotas laid out in the treaty, was that these were fundamental decisions of Rumanian economic policy that could not be changed. According to Pochhammer, American automobile firms were laying out large sums in order to prevent the import of German cars.[38]

The situation was extremely unstable. At the end of May, little more than a month after the treaty had been ratified, the Office of Currency Management ordered that no currency be issued for commodities from Rumania for which Germany was paying a higher price than free currency countries. The imposition of a 45% *ad valorem* tariff on all Rumanian commodities followed as Germany's answer to Rumania's attempt to promote exports to free currency countries by paying a 44% premium to the exporter financed by imposing a 44% tariff on imports from clearing countries (in this case, Germany). Germany refused to accept a situation in which it paid full price in lei while free currency countries effectively received a 44% discount.[39]

Further negotiations began in Bucharest at the end of May. Pochhammer noted unprecedented geniality, as when Titulescu attended a breakfast and toasted the *Reichsführer* and King Carol received the German delegation; but no progress was

Titulescu's foreign policy in 1933-1934 Walter Bacon notes how severely the Rumanian foreign minister underestimated the xenophobic atmosphere back home: "Far from home, Titulescu did not appreciate the rise of extreme nationalism in Romania, although he shared with the movement's leaders a complete disgust with the corrupt regime. Titulescu's solution was democratic nationalism, as unreasonable in Carolist Romania as Codreanu's mysticism." Walter BACON, Nicolae Titulescu and Romanian Foreign Policy, 1933-1934, U.Ph.D. University of Denver 1975, p.136.

[37] Landwehr (RSDB) to the UB, March 29, 1935, BA, R 7 VI/353/3. This was peculiar as the question of petroleum had not yet been settled. Because German currency was not convertible, authorization to purchase meant nothing without the Rumanian exporter's willingness to accept payment in blocked currency.

[38] Pochhammer (DG Bukarest) to AA, April 16, 1935, PA, Abteilung II, Wirtschaft, Rumänien Handel 13, Handelsvertragsverhältnisse mit Deutschland, Bd. 12. An American commercial delegation was in Bucharest during this time; the Wadsworth report cited above received attention from the highest levels of the U.S. State Department. American concern was not limited to potential injury to American business in the Rumanian market but included the implications of the policy for the most-favored-nation principle on a global scale: see the memorandum by Wallace Murray, May 16, 1935, NA, RG 59, 671.116/72.

[39] Flad (RSDB) to UB, June 19 and June 29, 1935, BA, R 7 VI/353/3. The tariff was not applied to wool, manganese ore, and oil, which involved a bookkeeping measure whereby the German government "paid" the tariff to itself. This was clearly directed against Rumanian agricultural commodities.

made in the discussions. The surprising geniality was the product of the struggle between two tendencies to control Rumanian political and economic policy. The king and his circle, fearful of the increasing role played by Soviet Russia in the French alliance system and searching for flexibility, viewed the Polish-Yugoslav model of rapprochement with Germany sympathetically. Carol also wanted German support against Hungarian revisionism.[40] Meanwhile, a systematic press campaign against Germany was making progress difficult for German trade and influence. "This agitation may be explained by an unfortunate interview of the Commerce Minister in which he admitted the existence of secret treaties which also stimulated irritation in Paris and led to Laval's and Litvinov's agitated questions of Titulescu."[41] The press campaign was partially responsible for ending the negotiations with German industry on the question of the old deliveries under the 1929 credit.[42]

Creating a sympathetic press in Bucharest became the key to successfully negotiating the payments and related agreements in September. Despite the experience of World War I, the Germans were somewhat naive on the inner workings of the Rumanian political scene and had to be prompted by an agent of Manolescu, who talked to Bleimeyer, the representative of Ferrostaal in Bucharest.[43] Manolescu's agent accused the Germans of doing nothing to ensure a good press, which forced Manolescu to ask the king's intervention to prevent the cabinet from refusing to ratify the treaty. "When the Germans are not in the position to act, the necessary money should be given them in order to bring the newspapers round. It must, how-

---

[40] Pochhammer (DG Bukarest) to AA, May 26, 1935, PA, Abteilung II, Wirtschaft, Rumänien, Handel 13, Handelsvertragsverhältnisse mit Deutschland, Bd. 12.

[41] Ibid. The treaty was attacked in Filipescu's *Epoca*, the *Adeverul*, and, most importantly, in Rumania's leading newspaper, *Universul*.

[42] Minute by Clodius, May 30, 1935, PA, Ha Pol, Handakten Clodius, Rumänien, Bd. 1. Hitler's astuteness in not relying upon the Nazi party offices to make policy is made clear by a report from Schmidt of the NSDAP *Reichsleitung (Hauptschulungsamt)* of his impressions of Rumania after traveling there in early May. He recommended the use of the *Volksdeutsche* community to dominate the Rumanian economy. Any policy based on such nonsense would have been a disaster. Schmidt to Himmler, May 31, 1935, BA, NS 19/221. Walter Bacon repeats many of the old allegations based upon documentation presented at the Nürnberg trails concerning Nazi infiltration of the German minority in Rumania and German agents in Bucharest: "Although the Reich was aware of the value of a Nazi fifth column in Romania, the NSDAP cautioned Fabricius [leader of the Nazi oriented ethnic Germans] to cultivate a low profile, avoding clashes with Romanian authorities and any apparent dependence on the Reich. The instructions were not obeyed. Clashes with German minority youth followed and in June and July the Romanian police uncovered a plot of a Hitlerist group in Bessarabia allegedly aimed at preparing a German invasion of the Ukraine via Slovakia and Bessarabia. . . Hitler's Germany was naturally interested in the German minority, using it for both political purposes through Rosenberg's NSDAP foreign office (the APA) and espionage through the *Gestapo* directed from the Bucharest legation by the notorius Edith von Cohler." BACON, Nicolae Titulescu, p. 169-170. While such activities, no doubt, went on, the fundamental thrust of German policy was to use the trading mechanism to soften up the resistance of King Carol and the state bureaucracy. Furthermore, German business representatives and the MWT provided better intelligence than all the Nazi party officials, hangers-on, and ethnic Germans put together. See footnote 44.

[43] Ferrostaal was part of the GHH combine.

ever, happen immediately."[44] A draft German document was leaked to the Rumanian press in late June, which certainly did not improve the situation. Madegreau, the former finance minister, demanded a response from Manolescu, who vainly insisted that the document was only a German draft and not the basis of an agreement. Madegreau maintained that the draft had been discussed and Manolescu had been ready to accept it but had been prevented from doing so only by resistance from the Foreign Ministry and National Bank.[45]

The German counter-campaign was begun by Max Hahn of the MWT, who felt that the treaty was being undermined by opposition from the francophile finance minister, Antonescu[46], and Stoicescu, the director of the National Bank. "German counter-measures have forced the Rumanian government to negotiate. The negotiations are to begin this week in Berlin. It is absolutely necessary that the atmosphere is not once again totally poisoned through press maneuvers. In order to influence the Rumanian press towards a quiet or else friendly tone, a special action which would cost 50,000 Rm [*Reichsmark*] is needed."[47] It is not clear if the Wilhelmstraße agreed to this special action, but Hahn and the MWT were determined to go ahead in any case. It seems reasonable to assume that the successful September conclusions to the negotiations and the absence of the legation's concern over the press atmosphere were not entirely unrelated to the efforts of Hahn and the MWT to subvert the Rumanian press. Later German efforts would be concentrated on the *Universul*, the most influential Rumanian newspaper. In 1934, the Dresdner Bank had already begun cultivating business connections with the son-in-law of the owner and publisher of the *Universul*, Popescu. According to Hahn, summarizing the first German experiments in this area, time was needed to build up real influence. "In all actions it must be recognized that they are only effective for a certain period, which indicates that it is not expedient to conclude long term agreements whose success is not absolutely certain and can easily lead to the discrediting of the newspaper involved. Last year the action was carried out for four weeks, and had the effect that during that period of the negotiations in Berlin no attack of importance occurred and the problems under discussion were continually given favorable interpretation for us."[48] In 1936, Popescu was attacked for having received money from a "foreign power." Titulescu went so far as to send a telegram from Montreaux defending his "old comrade in arms" against these accusations.[49]

[44] Minute of Pöhlmann (RWM), June 14, 1935, PA, Ha Pol, IVb, Rumänien, Handel 13, Handelsvertragsverhältnisse . . . zu Deutschland, Bd. 1. This information was passed on from Herr Willy Leese, director of Ferrostaal.

[45] Pochhammer (DG Bukarest) to AA, June 26, 1935, PA, Abteilung II, Wirtschaft, Rumänien, Handel 13, Handelsvertragsverhältnisse mit Deutschland, Bd. 12. The indiscretion appeared in the newspaper *Presentul* on May 24. Pochhammer felt that the new treaty and Germany were "free game" (*Vogelfrei*) in the press.

[46] Antonescu became finance minister after Slavescu resigned in opposition to the new treaty.

[47] Dr. Hahn (Berlin) to Clodius, July 24, 1935, PA, Ha Pol, IVb, Rumänien, Handel 13, Handelsvertragsverhältnisse . . . zu Deutschland, Bd. 1.

[48] Unsigned minute, May [?], 1936, ibid.

[49] Fabricius (DG Bukarest) to AA, July 1, 1936, PA, Politische Abteilung II, Politik 2, Politische Beziehungen . . . zu Deutschland, Bd. 1.

The importance of this successful operation in the summer of 1935 and its repetition thereafter should not be underestimated. While the large sums flowing to the Rumanian right and Iron Guard from the various wings of the Nazi party bureaucracy have received considerable attention, the effective subversion of Rumania was not accomplished by the traditional fifth column of fascists and *Volksdeutsche*, but by the type of policy sponsored by the MWT and big business. Nazi Germany needed friends at the center of Rumanian political life, not just in the traditional right, which had little chance of coming to power, or in the Iron Guard, which had even less.

2. *The Payments Agreement of September 1935*

Rumania's will to resist German pressure quickly evaporated. By July 4, Tartarescu, the Rumanian minister president, told Heinburg, the German chargé, that the Rumanian government wished to overcome the "misunderstandings" on the economic questions as soon as possible.[50] By the middle of July, Heinburg reported that the weakness of the Rumanian position was demonstrated by the fact that, although Rumania had not imposed the import quota tax on German imports, Germany's countermeasures were already in force.[51] He saw this as a sign of Rumanian willingness to come to an understanding with Germany.[52] Although Rumania delayed sending a delegation to Berlin until August, the combination of its lack of bargaining power and the subsidized Rumanian press determined the outcome of the negotiations in Germany's favor.

Although Manolescu had been discredited, Costinescu, the temporary commerce minister, was optimistic at the end of August that an agreement with Germany was as good as concluded.[53] A few days later a seven-part agreement was signed in Berlin regulating the payments question, export premiums, and soybean cultivation. In the second exchange of letters, Leon, the general secretary of the Commerce Ministry, assured the German government that export premiums would be paid on goods exported to Germany as to any country.[54] The list of 25 Rumanian commodities included petroleum and those agricultural products of greatest interest to Germany.

[50] Heinburg (DG Bukarest) to AA, July 4, 1935, PA, Abteilung II, Wirtschaft, Rumänien, Handelsvertragsverhältnisse mit Deutschland, Handel 13, Bd. 12.

[51] These German measures did not affect those commodities in which Germny was most interested.

[52] Heinburg (DG Bukarest) to AA, July 17, 1935, PA, Abteilung II, Wirtschaft, Rumänien, Handel 12, Handelsbeziehungen zu England, Bd. 1. Further proof of Rumanian weakness was its complete commercial isolation resulting from its currency and quota measures. Germany, Switzerland, Holland, and Greece all countered Rumanian measures with discriminatory policies at the same time that Rumania was in the midst of difficult negotiations over debt service. As an added complication, the governor of the National Bank was rumored to have been involved in a currency manipulation scandal. Heinburg (DG Bukarest) to AA, July 26, 1935, ibid.

[53] Pochhammer (DG Bukarest) to AA, August 29, 1935, ibid.

[54] Leon to Wohlthat, second letter, September 7, 1935, PA, Abteilung II, Wirtschaft, Rumänien, Handel 13, Handelsvertragsverhältnisse mit Deutschland, Bd. 13.

The third letter guaranteed that the Rumanian government would not impose a 44% import tax on any goods that Germany exported to finance the import of soybeans under the special agreement signed in June, 1935.[55] In the fourth exchange of letters Rumania promised to abolish the 44% import tax against Germany on November 1, the same time it was to be ended against Poland, Austria, and Hungary. In return, Germany promised to provisionally lift the 40% import tax on Rumanian goods.[56] Rumania promised in the fifth letter to conduct a "sympathetic study" of German imports dispatched before June 10, 1935, but arriving in Rumania after that date, to see if the 44% import tax could be waived.[57] In the eighth letter Wohlthat, chairman of the German delegation, agreed that Germany would limit its import of petroleum and petroleum products to one quarter of its total imports from Rumania and that the increased oil imports would not adversely affect Germany's import of other commodities.[58]

These letters generally attempted to clarify the confused situation resulting from the summer confrontation, but Germany also granted further agricultural concessions, supplementary to those in the secret protocols of the March treaty. These concessions, although limited to the last quarter of 1935, were by no means insignificant and included 1.2 million marks for barley, 1.5 million marks for corn, 1.8 million marks for beans, 1 million marks for Transylvanian clover seed, 1.25 million marks for apples, and 1.5 million marks for feather bedding.[59] In return, Rumania promised that 70 million lei owed to IG Farben and the Akzeptbank woud be included in the next governmental budget.[60]

The agreements of September, 1935, were not a new departure in trade relations but the last act in the tedious process that began with the first trip of Manolescu-Strunga to Berlin slightly more than a year before. The disastrous summer of 1935 demonstrated to the Rumanian government that however little it desired the expansion of trade with Germany, only Germany could provide the desperately needed markets for Rumanian produce. Commercially, Rumania did not have a single friend in the world. No matter how much the francophile liberals might wish to sabotage the treaty with Germany, the failure of Rumanian policy to work out any sort of arrangement with its other trading partners meant that the Titulescu-inspired rearguard efforts against the treaty with Germany were doomed, particularly during late summer when the Rumanian Cabinet had to find some market for the harvest. The September agreements do mark the point at which the treaty developed enough momentum to function despite resistance from the National Bank.

---

[55] Leon to Wohlthat, third letter, September 7, 1935, ibid.
[56] Leon to Wohlthat, fourth letter (a); Wohlthat to Leon, fourth letter (b), September 7, 1935, both in ibid.
[57] Leon to Wohlthat, fifth letter, September 7, 1935, ibid.
[58] Wohlthat to Leon, eighth letter, September 7, 1935, ibid.
[59] Wohlthat to Leon, tenth letter, September 7, 1935, ibid.
[60] Leon/Wohlthat note, September 7, 1935, ibid.

3. German-Rumanian Commercial Relations, 1936-37

Rumania's bilateral relationship with Germany was less harmonious than that enjoyed by Yugoslavia. Rumania encountered the same problems as did Yugoslavia but dealt with them differently. The political orientations of the two governments help explain their differing reactions to German trade policy. Even before Stojadinović became predominant, Yugoslavia was reasonably united in its trade and political approach to Germany and its growing relationship with Germany did not seem to occasion the rifts within the ruling elite that emerged in Rumania. The Rumanian cabinet, which had negotiated the treaty only under strong pressure from King Carol and agricultural export interests, would not have been unduly upset if it had failed, an attitude that put the pro-German Commerce Ministry in a weak position *vis-a-vis* the francophile National Bank.

Yugoslavia wanted the clearing system with Germany to work to its benefit and tried to influence German trade policy in the biyearly meetings of the Mixed Commission through negotiation. Rumania, however, seemed content to let its clearing credits build up in Berlin while it manipulated the mark exchange rate in Bucharest. While Yugoslavia tried to impose negotiated quotas on German purchases of Yugoslav goods, Rumania tried to extort what it wanted by attacking the exchange value of the clearing mark.

Yugoslavia was extremely cautious in approaching the question of armaments before 1938, but Rumania raised the issue in September, 1936, at the first meeting of the Mixed Commission. Rumania's greater industrialization meant it was initially less interested than Yugoslavia in government purchase of German capital goods such as that exemplified by the Krupp construction of the Zenica rolling mill. An additional factor was the increased pressure Germany exerted after September, 1936, for purchase through the clearing. Under the Four Year Plan, Germany was determined to barter armaments for increased raw material imports.

When the poor German harvest in 1936 necessitated supplemental grain purchases from Yugoslavia in 1937, Schacht feared that the trade relationship arrived at through Mixed Commission meetings would be irrevocably damaged by the resultant Yugoslav resentment. Similar developments caused no such fears for the German-Rumanian relationship. The Rumanian-German Mixed Commission had met only once and could easily begin the trade relationship at what corresponded to a second stage in Germany's trade expansion into Yugoslavia. Germany was demanding that Yugoslavia acquiesce to the creation of even more clearing credits in Berlin, with no prospect that they would be liquidated. Rumania, on the other hand, could be satisfied with German proposals to expand certain Rumanian industrial establishments and related projects.

The different periods in the growth of German influence are important to the developing relations with both Yugoslavia and Rumania. German-Rumanian relations until the end of 1937 correspond to Germany's relations with Yugoslavia until January of that year. During this period Germany bought agricultural products through the clearing while manipulating the clearing credits in Berlin to force more Rumanian purchases of German goods. Until Rumania agreed to increase imports from Germany by throttling competitive exports from other countries, the future of the expanding trade relations was uncertain.

Compared to the similiar period in German-Yugoslav relations, the Wilhelms-straße made few formal complaints, although it was mentioned that Rumania was not carrying out the provisions of the treaty with regard to the payment of export premiums agreed to in September, 1935.[61] Rumania continued to protest against Germany's continued reexport of Rumanian agricultural products for free currency.[62]

The basis of the treaty was Germany's agreement to buy large amounts of Rumanian agricultural commodities while limiting oil purchases to approximately one-fourth of total imports from Rumania. The volume of oil purchased through the clearing was also to be limited to that exported to Germany in 1934. Germany fulfilled its purchase obligations under the treaty that increased mark credits in the Berlin account of the Rumanian National Bank. Previously, Rumania would run an import surplus from March to September, compensated in the second part of the year by the export of harvested grains. If the Germany-Rumania relationship were to conform to "normal" circumstances, Germany's exports to Rumania, spaced throughout the year, should have made inroads into the German clearing debt in the first quarter of 1936. This occurred in neither the Rumanian nor Yugoslav situations, however.

There was an inevitable panic selling of the mark by Rumanian exporters. Some American observers assumed this would make German exports competitive with those of other industrial countries, but the situation was somewhat more complicated. Because currency was never transferred, the falling mark value meant that the Rumanian exporter who had been paid in full in marks was forced to sell those marks at a substantial discount to Rumanian importers or to the National Bank and was thus receiving much less than the expected price *in lei.* This gave rise to the peculiar situation in which Germany may have been paying prices in marks over the world market price, but the Rumanian exporter lacking reserves to carry the marks without selling at a discount was not in fact receiving the higher prices *in lei.* This may well have stimulated German exports to Rumania, but the effect on Rumanian

---

[61] Pochhammer had already complained of Rumanian noncompliance in October and had proposed a special meeting of the Mixed Commission to settle the issue. Pochhammer (DG Bukarest) to AA, October 28, 1935, PA, Abteilung II, Wirtschaft, Rumänien, Handel 13, Handelsvertragsverhältnisse mit Deutschland, Bd. 13. Artur Konradi, head of AO sponsored National Socialist Party organization in Rumania and secretary of the Rumanian-German Chamber of Commerce (Bucharest), complained as late as January 1936 that the commercial treaty was not working as expected. Konradi (Rundschreiben), Rumänische-Deutsche Handelskammer, January 30, 1936, BA, R 7 VI/356/2.

[62] Pochhammer reported a conversation with Badulescu, state secretary in the Finance Ministry, which took place in a "herzliche" and "vertrauliche" atmosphere. However, Badulescu was critical of alleged dumping of Rumanian commodities on the world market. Nevertheless, a few days later a transit agreement sponsored by the Dresdner Bank was approved. In this case a portion of the free currency was transferred to the Rumanian National Bank. Pochhammer (DG Bukarest) to AA, November 13, 1935, PA, Ha Pol, Handakten Clodius, Rumänien, Bd. 1; Krause-Wickmann (DG Bukarest) to AA, November 19, 1935, PA, Sonderreferat Wirtschaft, Rumänien, Handel 13A, Regierungsausschüsse, Bd. 1.

exporters and the peasantry behind them was not conducive to furthering German influence. If the situation were not quickly remedied the resentment could easily react against Germany. To quiet domestic discontent, the National Bank began to pay exporters in lei before receiving the countervalue from Rumanian importers paying for German goods. In effect, the Rumanian state was holding Germany's liability.

The Wilhelmstraße and other agencies proposed that the Rumanian National Bank take over all the mark proceeds from exports and sell them only at the fixed parity. Rumania would thus be supporting the official German parity; until such time that the Rumanian market was interested in German products at the price asked or the Rumanian government manipulated its state contracts toward German industry in order to liquidate the credits accumulated in Berlin, the Rumanian National Bank would be extending interest-free credits to Germany. On this ground the battle was waged. The Rumanian National Bank, representing pro-French orthodox financial circles, fought against this proposal until the end of 1937 by encouraging the sale of marks on the Bucharest bourse at a discount rate. This hurt the Rumanian exporter but benefited the Rumanian buyers of German goods and discredited Germany's commercial reputation in the Rumanian market.

Germany retaliated by trying to convince the Rumanian government to guarantee the mark or, failing that, to increase government purchases in Germany to liquidate the credits. The Wilhelmstraße had gained experience from the Hungarian and Yugoslav skirmishes and had developed a tactic of wearing its opponent down. While Germany dramatically increased its share of Rumanian trade, Rumania was not receiving commensurate benefits. Germany was put in a strong bargaining position by its ability to temporarily risk 1% or 2% of its export market while Rumania faced loss of revenue for 20% of its exports, which it could ill afford. If the Rumanian exporter and the peasantry were not to go bankrupt, the Rumanian government had to provide some sort of interim compensation, which in turn would lead to inflation, given the scarcity of internal savings and the character of the Rumanian money market. The losses of the Rumanian exporter and peasant could be met only by expanding paper currency.

In October, 1935, Pochhammer reported that Badulescu, the state secretary in the Finance Ministry, had suggested a possible three-cornered clearing agreement that would use Rumania's mark credits to pay its external debt.[63] This proposal stood no chance in Berlin, which saw the credits as a lever to increase Germany's share of the Rumanian market, not a means to ease Rumania's relations with France, England, or the United States. Preliminary negotiations by the GHH, the German firm most seriously pursuing the Rumanian market after the treaty, had failed because of the monetary issue. Throughout the Depression, and before the treaty, the mark had been relatively stable at 40 to 42 lei. After the September, 1935, agreements were signed, the Rumanian National Bank set the parity at 48 lei per mark, and at 58 lei per mark in negotiating with the GHH, although it

---

[63] Pochhammer (DG Bukarest) to AA, November 13, 1935, PA, Ha Pol, Handakten Clodius, Rumänien, Bd. 1.

retreated to 50.8 lei per mark after the negotiations. This high parity hurt German export interests and was not acceptable. Pochhammer speculated that as the National Bank was not yet willing to pay the export premium on exports to Germany, it set a high parity in order to cheapen Rumanian exports to Germany.[64]

By January, 1936, the National Bank was refusing to absorb German marks or to accept a compromise proposal of the German Clearing Office[65], and dumped three million marks on the free market; the result was an immediate drop in the mark parity to an unstable fluctuation between 35 and 42 lei.[66] The National Bank would agree to underwrite the mark if some of the blocked account in Berlin were released for exchange. Without increased German exports, or some special compensation agreement, neither of which was very likely, this proposal would mean either reestablishing the convertibility of the mark or paying for Rumanian goods in convertible currency. Pochhammer was told that paying the export premiums on commodities sold to Germany was impossible because of the demand of other most-favored-nation trading partners for the same privilege. There was strong Rumanian sentiment for denouncing the clearing agreement of February 12[67], but, according to Pochhammer, the Rumanian government was in complete disarray while negotiating simultaneously with Austria, Hungary, Greece, and England.

The various ministries of the Rumanian government differed almost as much as did the Rumanian and German governments. But Pochhammer was optimistic. The growing Rumanian credits in Berlin and Rome, the strong growth of German exports and Rumania's decision to cut imports from other countries in favor of Germany all augured well for the future.[68] The two tendencies within the Rumanian government were represented by the Commerce Ministry and the National Bank. The Commerce Ministry wanted to slow the growth of credits in Berlin by decreasing Rumanian exports to Germany, while the National Bank tried, as outlined above, to encourage a fall in mark value.[69] Pochhammer was nevertheless convinced that Rumanian government agencies would increase German imports to liquidate the clearing credit in Berlin.

---

[64] Pochhammer (DG Bukarest) to AA, October 28, 1935, PA, Abteilung II, Wirtschaft, Rumänien Handel l3A, Regierungsausschüsse, Bd. 13.

[65] *Deutsche Verrechnungskasse*: an agency of the *Reichsbank*. In analyzing the export imbalance which resulted in short term, interest free capital exports from the Danubian countries to Germany, Ranki comments: "In this sense, the export limiting overvaluation of the mark previously applied toward Southeastern Europe, increased the absorbing capacity of the German market and increased the clearing debts." RANKI, Economy and Foreign Policy, p. 152. However, in view of the continuing efforts of the Rumanian authorities to attack the exchange value of the *Reichsmark* which did not result in the spontaenous increase in German exports to Rumania, the explanatory power of the overvalued Reichsmark argument seems somewhat limited.

[66] Pochhammer (DG Bukarest) to AA, January 13, 1936, PA, Abteilung II, Wirtschaft, Rumänien, Handel 13, Handelsvertragsverhältnisse mit Deutschland, Bd. 13.

[67] Pochhammer (DG Bukarest) to AA, January 16, 1936, ibid.

[68] Ibid.

[69] The Rumanian Commerce Ministry feared that a low parity for the mark would undercut further exports to Germany by making Rumanian products too expensive.

The situation remained at an impasse until the spring of 1936, when the Wilhelmstraße began to consider negotiations. Until then, Rumania tolerated its unwilling interest-free mark credit in the clearing and Germany allowed the mark parity to fall far below what it considered reasonable.

Apart from a special compensation agreement for Rumanian lard to help ease the continuing fats shortage in Germany[70], the first new initiative from Germany began with an interministerial meeting to establish guidelines for a campaign in the Rumanian press to secure a friendly atmosphere for the upcoming negotiations of the Mixed Commission.[71] Max Hahn maintained that money could not come directly from official or semiofficial German agencies to Rumanians because of the danger of indiscretions and that it was useless to subsidize small newspapers with large sums because such actions were easily exposed and cost more in terms of German prestige than they were worth.[72] He considered the best object for German efforts to be the *Universul*, the largest Rumanian daily, which, according to Hahn, was right-wing and anti-semitic. He advised short-term agreements covering only the negotiating period: a spread-out subsidy would have less effect on the course of the newspaper's policy and would allow a greater risk of exposure. The figure arrived at for 1936 was 60,000 marks to be furnished by the following agencies:

Werberat der Deutschen Wirtschaft	monthly	RM 1,500
Ausland-Pressebüro GMBH		
(under control of the		
Propaganda Ministry)	monthly	RM 1,500
Wilhelmstraße	monthly	RM 1,000
MWT	monthly	RM 1,000

However, these monthly subsidies were not enough to secure the *Universul* during the crucial first meeting of the Mixed Commission at Munich in September, 1936, and there was apprehension that the newspaper would waver in advocating closer economic relations with Germany. Manolescu-Strunga, the former commerce minister and sponsor of the 1935 treaty, asked Max Hahn to forward a letter to Clodius recommending direct contact with Titus Ionescu, the chief editor of *Universul*.[73] Whether because of the prompting of Manolescu or for some other reason, Heide of the Propaganda Ministry and Aschmann of the Wilhelmstraße decided that a special subsidy of 25,000 marks was needed to ensure the proper

---

[70] IG Farben, Volkswirtschaftliche Abteilung, Die Reichsmark in Rumänien, p. 23, August 5, 1940, BA, R 63/216.

[71] Hüberner (*Reichstelle für Öl und Fett*) to RWM, RSDB and AA, January 23, 1936. This was a one-to-one transaction totaling 600,000 marks and was declared to be of "ein besonders dringendes Interesse." PA, Sonderreferat Wirtschaft, Rumänien, Handel 11 3A, Austauschgeschäfte, Bd. 1.

[72] Unsigned minute, May [?], 1936, PA, Ha Pol, IVb, Rumänien, Handel 13, Handelsvertragsverhältnisse mit Deutschland, Bd. 1.

[73] Hahn to Clodius, August 8, 1936; Manolescu-Strunga to Clodius, July 23, 1936, PA, Ha Pol, IVb, Handakten Clodius, Rumänien, Bd. 1. Clodius met with Ionescu on August 24; a marginal note by Clodius characterized the meeting as "nicht besonders."

atmosphere for negotiating. They had not consulted the MWT, which prompted Max Hahn to make his disagreement clear. He disapproved of directly involving the Bucharest legation in transmitting the subsidy, claiming that such a policy would sabotage the program; the owner of the *Universul* did not know that the subsidies came from German government circles.[74] Within the interministerial meeting, Fabricius was personally endorsing a policy of government noninvolvement, and Hahn was outraged at the decision made by Heide and Aschmann behind his back. "I would have immediately said in this case that I withdraw from any kind of participation in this matter and would leave it to government bureaus to make their own press policy in Rumania."[75] He refused to budge from the April agreement, particularly with respect to the division of financial responsibility. Representatives of big business were not loath to express their objections to government policy when it violated their interests or commitments.

Hahn was successful in dividing financial responsibility. Heide had been overly ambitious in accumulating subsidies for use in Rumania, requesting 25,000 RM from the MWT and 12,000 RM from the Wilhelmstraße.[76] The eventual compromise collected 25,000 RM for *Universul* from the same four agencies that had participated in the April decision.[77]

Werberat der Deutschen Wirtschaft	7,500 RM
Propaganda Ministry	7,500 RM
MWT	5,000 RM
Wilhelmstraße	5,000 RM

After September and the successful negotiation of the first protocol at Munich, Germany would have sufficient influence with the Rumanian government to make secret subsidies to newspapers unnecessary.[78] Until then, however, the subversion of the Rumanian press, prompted by pro-German circles in Rumania and led by a political agency of German big business, was important to the growth of German influence. While the Propaganda Ministry, the APA, and other agencies undoubtedly spent money supporting the Iron Guard, Goga/Cuza and various other right-wing tendencies, the effective subversion of Rumania was carried out by the Wilhelmstraße and MWT.

With the venality of the Rumanian press creating a cordial atmosphere for German interests, Ritter laid down guidelines for the German negotiators, suggesting they go slowly until the end of summer. ". . . the pressure of export interests on the Rumanian government in the sense of establishment of satisfactory trade relations with Germany will be far stronger after the harvest than it is today."[79]

[74] Hahn to Heide (*Auslands-Pressebüro*), August 13, 1936, ibid.

[75] Ibid.

[76] Heide to Aschmann (AA) and Heide to Hahn, August 17, 1936, ibid.

[77] Clodius to Kalisch, August 27, 1936; Kalisch to Dienstmann, September 17, 1936, ibid.

[78] This tactic was utilized again in the autumn of 1938, and again after the outbreak of World War II.

[79] Ritter to DG Bukarest, May 27, 1936, PA, Ha Pol, Handakten Clodius, Rumänien, Bd. 1.

For both governments the important question was oil. Germany had promised to limit oil purchases to one-quarter of its total imports from Rumania, but the Reich Currency Management Office issued almost unlimited oil import authorizations.[80] This manipulation, shown in the table below, structured German trade toward the one product Rumania could sell on the world market for convertible currency while it did nothing to alleviate the Rumanian agrarian crisis.[81]

Value of Rumanian Exports to Germany

(in million lei)

	Total Exports	Value of Oil Exports	Percent of Total
January	271	204	75
February	156	85	54
March	180	67	37
April	283	180	64
May	268	223	83

Rumania retaliated against German industrial exports.[82]

Ritter simply brushed aside Rumanian complaints and the agreement of September, 1935, when issuing instructions to the German legation in Bucharest. He referred instead to the treaty of May, 1935, which he claimed had included an understood ratio of 1-to-3 between oil and other Rumanian exports. He told the legation to deal with complaints about Germany's increased petroleum purchases in early 1936 by persuading the Rumanians to forget it.[83]

This took care of the Rumanian position. However, Ritter had claims of his own. He complained of Rumania's refusal to support the mark at 44 lei per mark and its failure to pay the export premiums provided for in the September, 1935, agreement to assist in marketing Rumanian foodstuffs in Germany. He also maintained that it was simply not true that German importers paid more for Bulgarian, Yugoslav, and Hungarian agricultural products than Rumanian. Of course, prices differed because of the different quality of goods involved, but there were just as many cases where Rumanian goods were purchased at a higher price than the other Danube countries as vice-versa. He advised the legation to avoid discussing the price question in detail

[80] See discussion of September Agreements in Section II of this chapter.

[81] Pochhammer (DG Bukarest) to AA, July 9, 1936, PA, Ha Pol, Handakten Clodius, Rumänien, Bd. 1.

[82] The *Wirtschaftsgruppe Eisenschaffende Industrie* (WESI) reported the imposition of new quotas on unprocessed iron amounting to a reduction of 40%. Of the remaining 60%, 90% was allocated to Czechoslovakia, while only 10% remained for Germany. Baare (WESI) to AA, RWM, July 25, 1936, ibid.

[83] Ritter to DG Bukarest, May 27, 1936, ibid. "Ich bitte bei den mündlichen Verhandlungen bei dieser Gelegenheit nach Möglichkeit durchsetzen, daß über die Bezüge der früheren vergangenen Zeit nicht mehr gesprochen wird und vom Tage des Inkrafttretens der neuen Vereinbarung ab eine Rechnung beginnt."

as that could be negotiated only by the appropriate bureaus in Berlin. He did insist that Rumania pay the export premium, at least from September 1 to December 31, 1935. The Wilhelmstraße was willing to forego the export premium for oil, however, if it was paid for other imports during that period.

Rumania wanted to renegotiate the whole treaty, but Ritter believed that the outstanding points on the agenda had to be agreed upon first. He wanted to avoid having to incorporate a whole new series of Rumanian demands into a meeting of the Mixed Commission. The treaty had been an important victory for German policy in southeast Europe and any denunciation of it would make it more difficult to extract concessions from Rumania and to foster the influence of German relations with the other Balkan countries.

Only agricultural products, not oil, had been discussed in the negotiations for the protocol of September, 1936. The negotiations for the agricultural sections of the treaty were largely conducted, independently of the Wilhelmstraße and the Economics Ministry, by the various bureaus of the Agricultural Ministry responsible for the monopoly marketing of foreign agricultural products. These officials and the Rumanian representatives in Berlin had reached agreement on horses, animal fats, eggs, and beans, among other products, while the outstanding issues were hogs, poultry, and grain.[84] During the summer, Germany made important concessions to Rumanian demands and by mid-July the quotas for fruit, hides, and pelts had been agreed upon. By then, however, Rumanian demands had escalated.[85] It was the opinion of the legation in Bucharest, as summarized by Clodius, that if Rumania agreed to German demands, Germany should raise the lumber quota from 11 to 12 million marks; agree to a cattle quota of 16 to 18 million marks (it had stood at 12 million marks), while extending the period of the quota from December 31, 1936, to March 31, 1937; meet Rumanian demands for a poultry quota of 7 million marks; and raise the egg quota to 1,500 carloads.[86] Although Berlin did not always follow the advice given it by the legation, the Wilhelmstraße would support these concessions if the oil question could be resolved. Germany had already tried to mollify Rumania for its high-handed oil imports exceeding the agreement.

The question was that of the relationship between Rumanian oil exports and its other exports to Germany. Rumania wanted to bind Germany to a "normal" quota, with any oil over this amount to be paid for in free currency, raw materials, and/or semifinished goods that could be converted to currency.[87] Rumanian industry had suffered when imported raw materials had been drastically curtailed during depression-motivated attempts to balance imports and exports and in 1936, while Germany saw Rumania as a source of raw materials, Rumania wanted to obtain over-

[84] Unsigned memorandum of the Rumanian legation (Berlin): "Als Ergebnis der Besprechnung vom 25.5. [1936] bei Herrn Ministeriadirektor Walter bleiben folgende offen", ibid.

[85] Pochhammer (DG Bukarest) to AA, July 17, 1936, ibid. After the Germans accepted the Rumanian price, the Rumanians increased their quota demands. Similarly, higher quotas were requested for a higher grain quota (from 12 to 17 million marks). Pochhammer advised meeting Rumanian demands only if Rumania agreed to German proposals on petroleum, prices, and the mark exchange rate.

[86] Clodius to Wohlthat, et al., ibid.

[87] Pochhammer (DG Bukarest) to AA, March 11, 1936, ibid.

seas raw materials from Germany via transit trade. Needless to say, with Germany operating in a semicrisis state throughout the 1930s, Rumania had little chance of success. Germany also consistently refused to export semifinished goods, often containing large proportions of raw materials obtainable on the world market only for free currency, to clearing partners, except in exchange for oil, copper, or similar strategic raw materials. Rumania was encouraged to buy capital intensive goods or armaments instead, reflecting the dominance of heavy industry in German economic life and the role of armaments as the ongoing spark of German economic development.

Rumania proposed a 15 percent oil quota in exchange for overseas colonial goods. The German Clearing Office, an agency of the Reichsbank, in a critique of Rumania's draft, rejected alterations to the clearing agreement[88], arguing simply that Germany did not have the necessary free currency available. The Wilhelmstraße did agree to reserve 20 percent of the oil for the payment of loans, as long as the owners of the loans were Rumanian citizens[89], but Ritter insisted that 80 percent, not 60 percent, of the purchase price of the oil must be reckoned through the normal clearing agreement, while the remainder would be paid in goods having a convertible currency value, not in free currency. This proposal went over very well with the more aggressive section of heavy industry, such as the GHH, which were hoping for large-scale compensation agreements outside the normal clearing agreement.

Germany maintained that Rumania's refusal to pay the export premiums promised in the September, 1935, protocol was responsible for the high percentage of oil in Rumanian exports to Germany and that only if Rumania paid the premium (or changed its export subsidy policy) could price calculations be made to allow stable imports of Rumanian foodstuffs into Germany.[90]

Rumania had been complaining that oil exported to Germany through the clearing was reexported for currency. In this instance the suspicion was probably unfounded (Germany needed oil badly). Clodius told the legation that since Rumanian and German statistics agreed on the volume of oil legally brought into Germany for reexport by the oil companies, Germany could not be reexporting any substantial volume. This reasoning ignored the possibility of collusion between the German government and oil companies to falsify statistics in order to conceal the actual reexport of oil.[91] The National Bank responded by deciding that no oil could be exported from Rumania to Germany without the proper papers from the German customs authorities; before the oil left Rumanian harbors, the Rumanian exporter or oil company had to present German papers to guarantee that the oil would actually be consumed in Germany. This regulation was immediately protested by the German government and the petroleum companies. As a large propor-

[88] DVK to AA, May 20, 1936, PA, Ha Pol, IVb, Rumänien, Rohstoffe und Waren, Petroleum . . . , Bd. 1.

[89] Ritter to DG Bukarest, May 27, 1936, PA, Ha Pol, Handakten Clodius, Rumänien, Bd. 1.

[90] Clodius to DG Bukarest, June 3, 1936, ibid.

[91] Pochhammer (DG Bukarest) to AA, July 9, 1936, ibid.

tion of Rumanian oil was stored in the facilities of the major oil companies in the free port areas of Hamburg, Rotterdam, and Antwerp, rather than shipped directly to Germany by the Danube or by sea, it was often mixed or processed with oil from the United States, Indonesia, or the Soviet Union. Only when the final product was shipped to the German market did it come under control of the German customs authorities, and by then it could not be identified as specifically "Rumanian." Also, from shipment from Constantza to final processing through German customs took from six to nine months.

The National Bank, in the person of Stoicescu, was not impressed. Rumania had been informed by the Swedish and Norwegian customs authorities, among others, that Germany was exporting Rumanian petroleum to their markets. Because Rumania would receive free currency from these countries for its oil, and got only blocked marks from Germany, the regulation would have to stand. He insisted that the National Bank would accept only receipts from German customs showing that the tariff had actually been paid because customs documents merely stating that the oil would remain in the free harbor area were easily circumvented. The year before, corn, which was to be exported to Austria, and for which documents had been presented, found its way instead to Hungary, with the complicity of Austrian customs.[92] Pochhammer reported that the National Bank could not be swayed and no more help could be expected from the Commerce Ministry. Although oil was in short supply for German refineries, the National Bank refused to accept the documents of the Control Board for Petroleum.[93] It appears that the National Bank succeeded. One month later, Fabricus, the new German minister in Bucharest, complained that the National Bank refused to permit the export of petroleum totaling about eight million marks, even though German tariff receipts had been presented.[94]

Rumania continued to demand that any oil which Germany imported over and above 25% of its total imports from Rumania had to be paid for in free currency or in specific goods.[95] There appeared to be a move toward compromise with Germany at the end of August when the demand for free currency was replaced with a demand for raw materials having convertible currency value or products of special economic interest.[96] This was a euphemism for the type of credit/compensation

---

[92] Unsigned minute, 'Über die Besprechung vom 29. Juli 1936 bei der Nationalbank', in appendix to: Pochhammer (DG Bukarest) to AA, July 30, 1936, PA, Ha Pol, IVb, Rumänien, Rohstoffe und Waren, Petroleum . . . , Bd. 1.

[93] Pochhammer (DG Bukarest) to AA, July 30, 1936, ibid.

[94] Fabricius (DG Bukarest) to AA, August 28, 1936, PA, Ha Pol, Handakten Clodius, Rumänien, Bd. 1.

[95] Fabricius (DG Bukarest) to AA, August 26, 1936, ibid.

[96] Fabricius (DG Bukarest) to AA, August 28, 1936, ibid. However, Fabricius was still concerned enough over the 25% quota to point out at the beginning of September that given the structure of trade in the first six months of 1936, almost two-thirds of Rumanian oil would have to be paid for in free currency while in other countries Germany paid only 25% to 50% in free currency. It is, however, highly unlikely that Germany paid Rumania any convertible currency for petroleum.

deals that the GHH, supported by Schacht, had suggested in the spring of 1935, and so was a major concession.

The clearing agreement and the parity of the mark had to be negotiated. Rumania had been ready to scrap the existing clearing agreement as early as mid-January, 1936, but did not press the question. In May the National Bank had presented a comprehensive draft for revision of the whole clearing agreement.[97] The problem lay in that there was no independent sphere of finance in German-Rumanian relations. Germany had no capital to invest; any credits or investments had to be financed out of trade, which was difficult as long as Rumania was in effect extending interest, commodities, and goods credits to Germany. In revising the clearing agreement, the National Bank hoped to gain some leverage on Germany, but this defeated the provisions of the earlier agreement establishing a complicated system of separate accounts. Presumably the first system had been designed to give the National Bank some control over the use of the frozen marks, but it had led to a situation of frozen marks in every account, thus making it difficult to use the surpluses in accounts D-E for the actual import of goods from Germany that was limited to account A (goods). Germany accepted the proposals to simplify and limit payments into the special accounts as they could hardly harm German interests.[98]

Germany was pressing for a Rumanian guarantee of the mark parity at 44 lei per mark. In August the National Bank issued new regulations requiring the Rumanian exporter to sell his mark claims within three days of receiving notice that payment had been made into the Rumanian account in Berlin. This meant, in effect, a monopoly purchasing position for the National Bank, with parity set much lower than the Germans would have wished: 37.5 for buying, and 42 for selling.[99] Although the mark had already fallen below 37.5, the legation in Bucharest and the Reichsbank were not happy about an official setting of the mark below parity with a high selling price for the mark giving substantial windfall profits in lei to the National Bank. By the beginning of September, Germany had succeeded in having the new regulations withdrawn, again defeating the francophile National Bank.[100]

The Mixed Commission began negotiating in Munich on September 8 and signed the supplemental protocols on September 24. The negotiations were rapid and relatively frictionless, probably because of German concessions during the summer that had gone a long way toward meeting Rumanian demands. According to Wohlthat,

[97] DVK to AA, May 20, 1936, PA, Ha Pol, IVb, Rumänien, Rohstoffe und Waren, Petroleum, Bd. 1.

[98] Ritter to DG Bukarest, May 27, 1936, PA, Ha Pol, Handakten Clodius, Rumänien Bd. 1.

[99] Fabricius (DG Bukarest) to AA, August 8, 1936, ibid.

[100] The selling period of the mark was extended from three to eight days, not including the day of payment into the Berlin account; memorandum by Kalisch, September 4, 1936, ibid. Fabricius reported a conversation with the governor of the National Bank, Constantinescu, who explained that the 11% difference between the buying and selling price of the mark was a temporary measure designed to recoup losses of the summer. Fabricius (DG Bukarest) to AA, December 4, 1936, ibid.

Germany's chairman, the negotiations were substantially over by September 16.[101] For Germany, the most important aspect was an agreement that all oil exports over the 25% limit could be paid for through special supplementary compensation agreements and armaments. "It is planned to take payment for those German deliveries and long term investments, which are of especial economic value to Rumania, in petroleum. This is particularly applicable to the delivery of war material."[102] Germany threw in a bonus quota for 80,000 hogs and 7,000 oxen.

The petroleum question was approached gingerly in the final protocol, with mention made only of a special understanding necessary to import all oil above the 25% limit. Germany promised that the Control Boards would see to it that Rumanian products would be imported when Rumanian prices were comparable to prices for the same products from the other countries of southeastern Europe. Rumania agreed to extend quotas for German exports unexhausted in any particular period but insisted on the right to limit the expansion of German exports to Rumania to the rate of Rumanian exports to Germany.

There was a compromise on the payment of export premiums. The German proposals, which demanded payment only on goods other than petroleum, won Rumanian acceptance. However, the German request to lift the 12% import tax was rejected.[103] Although Germany maintained that large-scale credit and exchange agreements with German industry were impossible because Rumania had not paid firms such as MAN and IG Farben, Germany was not actually prepared to tie the repayment of these old debts to the new proposals. The threat had no serious intention behind it. As Germany was not able to get a Rumanian commitment to back the mark at parity, both sides finally agreed that if the Rumanian National Bank could not find a use for its mark credits, it could sell them on the open market for the best price it could get. This was the prevailing practice, anyway.

The most important aspects of the negotiations are glimpsed only in Wohlthat's letter of September 19, where he outlines the compromise on the 25% oil question. Hardly had Titulescu's chair at the Rumanian Foreign Ministry cooled when the government agreed to the purchase of German armaments. Of the two German firms especially committed to the Rumanian market, GHH and Otto Wolff[104], the

---

[101] Concluded were: a supplemental agreement to the payments agreement, a confidential protocol to the clearing, and a confidential protocol on the results of the negotiations.

[102] Wohlthat (DG Bukarest) to Benzler, September 19, 1936, PA, Ha Pol, IVb, Rumänien, Handel l3A, Regierungsausschüsse, Bd. 1.

[103] This was a late request of the legation in Bucharest. Fabricius (DG Bukarest) to AA, September 4, 1936, ibid.

[104] Titulescu's fate was sealed by the failure of the French to act in the Rhineland crisis in March, 1936: "The most important effect of the Rhineland crisis on Titulescu's position was the collapse of credibility of the French alliance. As soon as it became apparent that she would not act Titulescu began to criticize France. Bucharest wondered since the West would not defend itself, how would the West defend the French clients in the East. In London, Titulescu asked Paul-Boncour, 'but how then will France defend her distant allies? . . . She does not even defend herself?'" BACON, Nicolae Titulescu, p. 272. On July 21, 1936 Litvinov and Titulescu initialled an agreement which would have given explicit de jure recognition to Rumania's Dniester frontier. This agreement never came into effect because of Titulescu's fall. BACON,

Otto Wolff proposals were by far the more ambitious. Rudolf, representing Otto Wolff, proposed a 100-million-mark credit for a period of three or four years[105] to the Rumanian state in an attempt to cover virtually all of Rumania's needs from the iron and steel industry, the machine tool industry, auto, aircraft, electricity, etc. The repayment was to be in marks at a fixed parity or in Rumanian products (wheat, corn, petroleum, or ores). The Otto Wolff proposal was a bid for monopoly of the supply of German heavy industrial exports to Rumania and not only excited suspicion in Rumania but caused dissension within German heavy industry.

More useful in liquidating the German clearing debt was an agreement for a GHH project involving a credit arrangement with the Rumanian state-owned mine company, Rimma, and a subsidiary of GHH, Ferrostaal.[106] Interestingly, Ferrostaal would not conclude the negotiations for the credit without a Reich guarantee, a request that met with little sympathy in the German Finance Ministry, which was highly skeptical of Rimma's ability to fulfill its obligations despite its control of important Rumanian deposits of gold, silver, copper, and zinc. German firms had already suffered in dealings with the Rumanian state, as evidenced by the railway credit. However, the Finance Ministry swallowed its objections without the pressure from the Wilhelmstraße and military that would be brought to bear later. "Rumania was earlier closely tied to France and ordered arms there. The Rumanian National Bank is hostile to Germany. It is possible, however, that in Rumania as well, because of the closeness of the Bolshevik danger, revulsion against democracy in the French sense and turn towards an authoritarian state form will result. Beginnings in this direction are discerned in the dismissal of Titulescu."[107] Although formulated in somewhat naive conservative terms, this was the background for the Finance Ministry's agreement to underwrite the Rimma-Ferrostaal credit. "Above all, decisive for my decision were the trade policy considerations cited by you, that because of the significance of the Rumanian markets for the total German raw materials and food economy it appears suitable to remain in many-sided transactions, even in the case of possible sacrifices. In this connection there comes into play the significance of the treaty in terms of foreign policy and its impact upon later armament transactions at a point when it appears that a shift of the Rumanian conception of politics to one near our own point of view seems to be in preparation."[108]

ibid., p. 285. The firm Otto Wolff (Köln) was one of the most important iron and steel marketing companies in Germany. Otto Wolff did not have productive facilities of its own but held shares in major firms in the Ruhr steel industry. It had participated in the 1929 railway credit.

[105] Otto Wolff was willing to extend credit for ten years. A Wilhelmstraße official marked the 100 million mark figure with an exclamation point. Rudolph (Otto Wolff) to Minister Leon, September 16, 1936, PA, Ha Pol, IVb, Rumänien, Handel 11, Handelsbeziehungen zu Deutschland, Bd. 1.

[106] Ferrostaal (GHH subsidiary) unsuccessfully attempted to convince the Rumanians to permit the financing of at least part of the new deliveries to Rimma out of the frozen credits accruing from the 1929 railway credit.

[107] 'Garantie Ferrostaal', September [?], 1936, Handakten Nasse, BA, R 2/309936.

[108] Finance Ministry [von Krosigk (?)] to Schacht (RWM), September [?], 1936, ibid. These agreements naturally overshadowed Titulescu's efforts to improve Soviet-Rumanian relations including the re-establishment of direct railway connections, direct telegraphic com-

In the late 1930s the Finance Ministry was the agency directly responsible for the startling and dangerous growth in the German public debt. Although it would often try to block or impede guarantees in order to place some limits on the growth of the state's obligations[109], under Schacht's regime, the Finance Ministry would follow the lead of the "Wizard." The importance of the Rimma-Ferrostaal credit lay in the potential liquidation of Germany's passive balance with Rumania by expanding purchases of official and semiofficial Rumanian state agencies. The pattern had been set in Yugoslavia with the Krupp construction of the rolling mill at Zenica, which was almost an exact parallel to the Rimma-Ferrostaal deal. In both cases expanding German influence would have been impossible using normal business calculations. Without state organization of the German agricultural market and the monopoly purchases of Rumanian foodstuffs, expansion of trade simply could not have occurred. Similarly, the German trade debt was not liquidated by a spontaneous increase in demand for German products on the Rumanian market, despite the *de facto* devaluation of the mark and the shortage of free currency, but by the channeling (or expansion) of Rumanian state contracts to German firms. The Finance Ministry reflects Schacht's waning influence in its view of armaments sales as an aspect of the growth of German influence. After Schacht, armaments would become the basis for the further expansion of trade, as the only way Germany could finance increased imports of Rumanian grains and raw materials. Although the Four Year Plan had just been adopted by Hitler's fiat, there was considerable room for German expansion without resort to this expedient.

This first meeting of the Mixed Commission was important to the expansion of German influence. The decisions made at Munich, coming at the same time as the fall of Titulescu and a final abandonment of any arrangement with the Soviet Union for the right of passage to aid Czechoslovakia, put Rumania firmly on the road to satellite status within the growing German economic sphere in southeast Europe. Pressured by the frozen credits in Berlin and the new harvest, the Rumanian government agreed to adapt the Rumanian market to the structural defects of the German political economy: a fateful step. Since Germany could not provide the consumer goods, semifinished products, or raw materials that Rumania needed, the clearing debt could be liquidated only by Rumanian state purchases that coincidentally were in the interest of German heavy industry. Rumania's willingness to agree to purchase German armaments was, however, not a direct result of the growth of German economic influence. The more Germany armed and the more powerful the German state became, the greater the political tension in central and southeast Europe. Rumania, like Yugoslavia, was not the beneficiary of priority treatment in armaments by the French, the British, or the Czechs. In these circumstances the

---

munication, reciprocal press representation, and finally a new economic agreement which resulted in over 50 million lei in bilateral trade in 1937. BACON, Nicolae Titulescu, p. 245. Certainly, a coordinated effort by France, Czechoslovakia, and the Soviet Union would have had the potential to counterbalance the temptation of capitulation to the rising German colossus. It is no wonder, then, that Titulescu has become something of a national hero in Rumania.

[109] In the end, von Krosigk invariably capitulated.

turn to Germany for arms became an ever more attractive prospect. Similarly, for a Germany whose armaments stockpile greatly exceeded its reserves of free currency and gold, paying for purchases of Rumanian oil with war materiel served the dual purpose of allowing the import of oil without draining the dwindling supply of gold and free currency and of tying the Rumanian military to German sources. Rumania was in the unenviable position of being the single country that would sell petroleum, particularly aircraft fuel, to Germany through the clearing (apart from the Soviet Union) and the only petroleum producer that was not vulnerable to a sea blockade against Germany. These two factors determined the course of Rumania's history for the next decade.

CHAPTER VI

THE FOUR YEAR PLAN

1. The New Plan

In certain respects, the New Plan was a remarkable success. Statistics from 1934 to 1936 indicate that Germany restructured trade as Schacht had outlined in December 1932. Its import balances with the United States were reduced from 215 to 60 million marks and with various other countries from 820 to 174 million marks.[1] Exports to eastern Europe almost doubled, while imports rose only from 599 to 635 million marks; trade with Latin America showed an export jump from 235 to 417 million marks, while imports increased only from 338 to 442 million marks. The export drive toward eastern Europe and Latin America had achieved as much as Schacht could have expected over a short period.

Germany's declining export surplus with western Europe and Great Britain was less promising, however. Exports fell from 891 to 808 million marks, while the earned foreign exchange came under restrictions limiting the purchase of raw materials in third markets. Some western European countries had introduced clearing agreements while others, including Great Britain, forced Germany to use part of the foreign exchange earned in bilateral trade to pay creditors.

In 1934, Germany's domestic expansion and raw materials hoarding allowed a slight increase in imports — about 6% in value and 5% in quantity. However, the continuing Depression in the gold bloc countries that were important markets for Germany, and a new wave of currency depreciations, led simultaneously to an export decline of 15% in value and 11% in quantity.[2]

The New Plan did not prevent a further trade deficit of 177 million marks in the first half of 1935, but German exports rallied with an export surplus of 288 million marks in the second half of the year, giving an active balance of 111 million marks for the year. By 1936, improved world economic conditions allowed German

---

[1] I have used Frank Child's convenient summary: Frank C. CHILD, The Theory and Practice of Exchange Control in Germany: A Study of Monopolistic Exploitation in International Markets, Den Haag 1958, pp. 203-204. Eastern Europe includes Bulgaria, Estonia, Greece, Hungary, Latvia, Lithuania, Rumania, Turkey, and Yugoslavia. Latin America includes Argentina, Brazil, Chile, Colombia, Mexico, Venezuela, and Uruguay. "Overseas countries" includes Africa, Asia (except Turkey), the East Indies, Australia, and New Zealand.

[2] Yuan Chao WANG, German Foreign Exchange Control, 1931-1936, U.Ph.D., Harvard 1937.

exports to increase enough that, despite slightly increased imports, Germany had an improved trade balance of 440 million marks.[3]

The New Plan affected the structure of Germany's foreign trade by allowing imports of finished goods to decline in both value and volume from 1932 to 1936. In 1931, finished goods had comprised 18.2% of total imports; by 1936, the figure was down to 12.5%. The value of imported foodstuffs declined 6.7%, from 1067 million marks in 1934 to 991 million in 1935, but the rising world prices meant volume fell more than value; the volume of food imports in 1935, compared to 1934, was down by 12%. During 1936, steadily increasing world market prices occasioned a further 2.5% decrease in volume although value increased slightly.[4]

The New Plan restructured imports to favor raw materials. By maintaining the 1932 levels of quantity and value, raw materials increased their share in total imports from 51.0% in 1931 to 61.6% in 1936. Agricultural autarchy and development of domestic raw materials resources increased the percentage of exported finished goods from 75.1% in 1930 to 82.8% in 1932, while the export of foodstuffs decreased from 4.0% to 1.5%, and raw materials from 20.3% to 15.0%.[5]

Despite Schacht's creation of an export surplus and stimulus to German exports in certain areas, the New Plan did not solve Germany's chronic foreign exchange difficulties. There was endless controversy during 1935 and 1936 between the conflicting priorities of food imports and industrial raw materials for the allocation of foreign exchange. By late 1935, Agricultural Minister Darré's "battle for production" had clearly failed to make Germany self-sufficient at a time when rising world food prices would necessitate allocating more foreign exchange to obtain the same amount of imported food. Increased employment brought increased purchasing power, created demand for basic foodstuffs, and caused a fat shortage in the Ruhr.

Although Schacht's program of work creation and rearmament had raised Germany's total industrial production from 61.5 in 1933 (base year 1928 = 100) to 107.8 in 1936, producers' and capital goods had risen disproportionately from 53.7 and 44.9 to 112.9 and 116.6, respectively, while consumer goods, lagging behind, went from 80.1 to a mere 95.6.[6] This disproportionate development of the capital investment sector created increased demands for raw materials such as copper, lead, zinc, rubber, which generally had to be paid for in foreign exchange. By discrimi-

---

[3] Ibid.

[4] Ibid., pp. 227-228.

[5] Ibid.

[6] Leon AGRANAT, Price Control in Germany, U.Ph.D., New School for Social Research 1954, Chapter 5, p. 28, citing: Reichs-Kredit-Gesellschaft, Germany's Economic Situation at the Turn of 1937/1938, Berlin 1939, p. 5. Kaiser points to the precipitous decline of exports as percentage of GNP [from 22.5% in 1933, to 16.2% in 1937, and only 13.1% in 1938 (first six months)] as evidence of the general domestic recovery being caused "almost exclusively" by "increased government expenditures and domestic consumption." KAISER, Economic Diplomacy, p.139. He also downplays the success of the trade drive noting that in 1936 the nine successor states of eastern Europe only supplied 13.8% of German imports compared to 5.9% in 1928. While it is surely correct to emphasize that the relative expansion of trade in eastern Europe was caused (in a static comparison sense) by the decline of German trade with other countries, the use of GNP statistics and static comparisons fails to take account of the impor-

nating against raw materials for consumer industries, Germany was able to substantially increase imports of metals and ores, as figures from 1937 demonstrate:

1937 Imported Quantities as Percentages of 1929[7]

Iron Ore	122
Manganese Ore	142
Other Ores	153
Iron and Steel (raw)	121
Copper (raw)	100

Still, the demand for such commodities outstripped the ability of exports to balance them. Whether to allocate foreign exchange for foodstuffs or raw materials brought Schacht and Darré into conflict in August 1935, while friction increased within the German government throughout 1935 and well into 1936. This conflict forms the immediate background to the foreign exchange crisis of 1936 and Hitler's promulgation of the second Four Year Plan.

2. The Foreign Exchange Crisis and the Food Question[8]

In May, 1935, Schacht, realizing that Germany would again face severe foreign exchange difficulties, had submitted a memorandum to Hitler calling for the reorganization of the agricultural sector, rigid price control, strict control over Nazi

tance of the trade that was left over so to speak, after the Great Depression. Neither individual firms nor the German government looked at the declining percentage of trade in GNP as a source of comfort. Rather, the retention and expansion, if possible, of markets in eastern Europe and Latin America was *sine qua non* of Nazi foreign economic policy. This was a broad economic platform on which Hitler, Schacht, and even Paul Reusch could stand. The best recent survey of the German foreign trade position is Hans-Erich VOLKMANN, Außenhandel und Aufrüstung in Deutschland 1933 bis 1939, in: Friedrich FORSTMEIER and Hans-Erich VOLKMANN (eds.), Wirtschaft und Rüstung am Vorabend des Zweiten Weltkrieges, Düsseldorf 1975, pp. 81-132.

[7] League of Nations, World Economic Survey, Seventh Year, 1937/1938, Geneva 1938, p. 128.

[8] The remainder of this chapter has drawn heavily on the work of Dietmar Petzina and Arthur Schweitzer. Among the works consulted are: Leon AGRANAT, Price Control in Germany; Wolfgang BIRKENFELD, Der synthetische Treibstoff, 1933-1945, Göttingen 1964; Bernice A. CARROLL, Design for Total War: Arms and Economics in the Third Reich, The Hague 1968; Dietrich EICHHOLTZ, Geschichte der deutschen Kriegswirtschaft, Bd. I, 1939-1941, Berlin 1969; René ERBE, Die nationalsozialistische Wirtschaftspolitik 1933-1939 im Lichte der modernen Theorie, Zürich 1958; Wolfram FISCHER, Deutsche Wirtschaftspolitik 1918-1945, Opladen 1968; Johann Sebastian GREER, Der Markt der geschlossenen Nachfrage: eine morphologische Studie über die Eisenkontingentierung in Deutschland, Berlin 1961; Jörg-

party finances, and stretching out the pace of rearmament expenditures.[9] Hitler simply ignored it. In October, 1935, Darré requested foreign exchange beyond that already budgeted, and Schacht rejected the proposal. Göring was appointed as mediator, but an interministerial meeting on October 15, 1935, reached no decision and Hitler stepped in three days later. He rejected the War Ministry's proposal for food rationing and authorized reducing the national grain reserve by 700,000 tons (to 1.3 million tons) for livestock feeding. He also affirmed Schacht's final responsibility for foreign exchange allocation by placing the agricultural control boards under the authority of the Economics Ministry.[10]

Hitler's mediation was soon overshadowed by events. In January, 1936, Schacht complained that Germany was receiving far less raw material from clearing agreements (in this case with Argentina) than was available, because the Agricultural Ministry insisted upon food imports. He claimed that agricultural imports had risen by some 102 million marks in the second half of 1935, while imports of industrial raw materials had fallen by 124 million. Schacht wanted to alter a compensation deal with Argentina and set up binding annual quotas for the allocation of foreign exchange to Darré's ministry. Hitler avoided making a definite decision, but he did approve Schacht's mandatory quota plan, albeit in milder form:

> Hitler thus reformulated Schacht's idea when he decided that the Minister of Agriculture should present to him each December 10th an agricultural plan that would detail the previous and expected outputs as well as import requirements for agricultural products. Darré agreed to collaborate with Schacht for the purpose of arriving at a mutually acceptable import plan prior to presenting the future agricultural plan to Hitler.[11]

Hitler's compromise was again short-lived; in early 1936, Darré first demanded the right to buy 850,000 tons of grain abroad, then doubled his demand when he received no answer from Schacht. In addition, foreign exchange was being drained to cover the fats deficit, from 21.6 million marks (second quarter, 1935) to 42.2

Johannes JÄGER, Die wirtschaftliche Abhängigkeit des Dritten Reiches vom Ausland dargestellt am Beispiel der Stahlindustrie, Berlin 1969; Burton H. KLEIN, Germany's Economic Preparations for War, Cambridge/Mass. 1959; Gerhard KROLL, Von der Weltwirtschaftkrise zur Staatskonjunktur, Berlin 1958; Samuel LURIE, Private Investment in a Controlled Economy: Germany, 1933-1939 , New York 1947; Gerhard MEINCK, Hitler und die deutsche Aufrüstung, 1933-1937, Wiesbaden 1959; Alan S. MILWARD, The German Economy at War, London 1965; R. J. OVERY, Transportation and Rearmament in the Third Reich, in: The Historical Journal XVI (1973), pp. 389-409; Dietmar PETZINA, Autarkiepolitik im Dritten Reich, Stuttgart 1968; idem, Die deutsche Wirtschaft in der Zwischenkriegszeit, Wiesbaden 1977; idem, I.G. Farben und nationalsozialstische Autarkiepolitik, in: Tradition (1968); Kenyon POOLE, German Financial Policies, 1932-1939, Cambridge/Mass. 1939; Arthur SCHWEITZER, Big Business in the Third Reich, Bloomington/Ind. 1964; idem, The Foreign Exchange Crisis of 1936, in: Zeitschrift für die gesamte Staatswissenschaft 118 (1962), pp. 243-277; Georg THOMAS, Geschichte der deutschen Wehr- und Rüstungswirtschaft (1918-1943/45), edited by Wolfgang BIRKENFELD, Boppard/Rhein 1966; Wilhelm TREUE, Gummi in Deutschland, Munich 1955.

[9] 'Financing of Armament', memorandum from Schacht to Hitler, May 3, 1935. ND, 1168-PS, NCA, Vol. VII, pp. 827-830.

[10] PETZINA, Autarkiepolitik, pp. 32-33; SCHWEITZER, Foreign Exchange Crisis, pp. 243-244.

[11] SCHWEITZER, Foreign Exchange Crisis, p. 254.

million marks (second quarter, 1936). "Adding to this the 36.4 million marks for the requested imports of feeding grain, it became clear that satisfaction of the agricultural demands would mean an end to the armaments boom."[12]

Schacht initially agreed in part to Darré's request and allocated approximately 10 million marks to the Agricultural Ministry, but by the end of March he countered with a demand for a complete investigation of the whole situation. He proposed a complete overhaul of German agricultural policy, amounting to the reintroduction of capitalism in the agricultural sector. Hitler again intervened to approve some 60 million marks for food imports and the food question merged into the general debate on foreign trade policy that dominated ministerial councils from April to September 1936.

3. The Petroleum Question

A secondary issue in the 1936 foreign trade policy debate was the buildup of a synthetic gasoline capacity. Both the Army and Air Force demanded rapid autarchic construction of Germany's hydrogenation plant. Schacht, while not opposed in principle to constructing some synthetic gasoline plants, questioned whether it would be economical to rapidly expand capacity when it was far cheaper to import petroleum. Throughout 1935, the War Ministry unsuccessfully maneuvered to become the responsible authority for synthetic gasoline. In the spring of 1936, open conflict between Schacht and Blomberg on this issue prompted Hitler and Göring to intervene. Immediate resolution was necessary because both Soviet Russia and Rumania, suppliers of about 50% of Germany's petroleum imports (via clearing) threatened to cut off supplies if not paid in hard currency. The War Ministry demanded "a uniform and planned steering of the entire German petroleum industry."[13]

4. The Rohstoff- und Devisen Stab

The food and gasoline crises caused Hitler, on April 4, 1936, to create a "Raw Materials and Currency Staff" under Göring's authority.[14] Göring, previously appointed to mediate between Schacht and Darré, had been approached by Schacht in March, 1936, to act as a "shield" against the unpopular economic measures of rationing, tight fiscal control of the Nazi party, and reorganization of the agricultural sector. Göring had no intention of allowing himself to be so used.

At the first meeting of the Ministerial Commission, it became clear that Göring intended to take over economic policy, initially by gaining control of foreign

[12] Ibid., p. 255.
[13] Ibid., NCA, Vol. 3, pp. 871-873. (Original in: BA-Mi., Wi/IF 5.433); PETZINA, Autarkiepolitik, pp. 36-39.
[14] THOMAS, Wehr- und Rüstungswirtschaft, p. 111.

exchange allocation. Behind the ensuing Schacht-Göring personal rivalry were fundamental differences over economic policy. Schacht emphasized the need to limit the pace of the armaments boom with strict economic controls; his economic outlook was dominated by the concept of "economy" defined in terms of prevailing world prices and, although prepared to support *Ersatz* production to a limited extent, he regarded a functioning world economy as a far superior alternative. Göring, on the other hand, emphasized almost exclusively the need to rearm; any halt in the tempo of rearmament would be neither contemplated nor tolerated. Göring simply ignored Schacht's argument that synthetic production of raw materials would eventually increase the price of Germany's exports and thus further increase the difficulty of obtaining foreign exchange. For Göring, at least in theory, dependence upon foreign trade was in itself a danger; it could play only a subsidiary role in Germany's economic life.[15]

In the struggle between Schacht-Darré and Schacht-Göring, the key was the attitude of the armed forces, particularly War Minister General Blomberg. Blomberg wanted the armed forces budget increased from some 10 to 13.6 billion marks, the outfitting of a 36-division army by October, 1936, and a completed *Luftwaffe* by April, 1937. Estimates of implementing such a program ran to twice the raw materials used in 1935 and Blomberg would not acquiesce to Schacht's financial restraints. In return for a guarantee that the armed forces would have priority in foreign currency allocation and that the three armed services' raw materials procurement offices would remain independent from fiscal or raw materials control, Blomberg supported Göring's claim to authority over the allocation of foreign exchange. The traditional alliance between the Army and big business had broken for the first time since 1918. Blomberg also refrained from holding Göring to a pledge of strict fiscal control over the Nazi party, thus foiling Schacht's attempt to force the party to submit to the financial requirements of rearmaments.

With demands from the War Ministry for an increased rearmament tempo, the foreign exchange crisis in the summer of 1936 required a fundamental policy decision in one direction or another. By midsummer, munitions plants were operating at only 70% of capacity because of raw materials shortages, but Hitler and Göring refused to cut food imports estimated at approximately 852 million marks for the second half of 1936, up 100% from estimates made in 1934. To bridge the raw materials and food gap, Göring ordered the forced sale of all foreign bonds in German hands, over Schacht's vigorous opposition. This first of several special actions netted some 500 million marks for equal division between raw materials and food imports. In mid-August, Schacht pressed for a resolution of the economic situation but was put off by Göring's postponement of ministerial meetings until after September 1st.

---

[15] In practice, of course, Göring was forced to recognize Germany's dependence on foreign trade. This led to increased reliance upon Germany's clearing partners, particularly in southeastern Europe.

5. Hitler's Memorandum

In August, 1936, when the Army High Command demanded "bold and immediate decisions" to remedy the "unbearable" shortage of raw materials[16], Hitler was
prepared. In mid-August, Carl Krauch of IG Farben had sent him a series of memo-
randa, prepared by IG experts, on the feasibility and scope of synthetic production
of gasoline, rubber, and textiles.[17] When Schacht spoke in a semipublic forum to
Gauleiter and other officials, attempting to mobilize support within the Nazi party
for his policies to immediately resolve the exchange crisis, Hitler produced the Four
Year Plan Memorandum.

The fundamental premise of the memorandum, and of Hitler's political outlook,
was the ultimate necessity of a war against Bolshevism. This was of course phrased
in terms of the defensive posture of Germany as the "focal point of the Western
world in the face of the Bolshevist attacks."[18] Because of Germany's political and
geographic position, only the Reich was capable of defending western civilization
against bolshevization. This was the "untenable" situation, the "catastrophe", the
impending "annihilation of the German people" that had to be the basis of German
policy: "In the face of the necessity of defense against this danger, all other considerations must recede into the background as being completely irrelevant." The
"extent and pace of the military development of our resources cannot be too large
or too rapid." Using no names, Hitler clearly had Schacht in mind when he labeled
"any arguments" on these points a "capital error." Developing the *Wehrmacht* into
the most powerful army in the world was the decisive goal of Germany policy. The
economic and financial position of the nation was to serve its political interest, not
vice-versa: ". . . finance and economy, economic leaders and theories must all
exclusively serve this struggle for self-assertion in which our people are engaged."

Hitler's economic analysis recapitulated well-known ideas: Germany was overpopulated and could not feed herself; the drop in unemployment, although welcome, put further strain on the food supply by increasing purchasing power. "It is
therefore, in spite of our difficult food situation, the highest commandment of our
economic policy to see to it that, by incorporating all Germans into the economic
process, the precondition for normal consumption is created." The unity of the

---

16 SCHWEITZER, Foreign Exchange Crisis, p. 267.

17 EICHHOLTZ, Geschichte der deutschen Kriegswirtschaft, Vol. I, pp. 42-43; SCHWEITZER,
Foreign Exchange Crisis, p. 276.

18 I have used the English translation in the DGFP series, C, and subsequent citations are
from this source. The German original is Wilhelm TREUE, Hitlers Denkschrift zum Vierjah-
resplans 1936, in: Vierteljahrshefte für Zeitgeschichte 3 (1955), p. 204, and following. Kaiser
notes that Hitler never explained in his memorandum how food was to be obtained without
foreign exchange. "Nevertheless, [Hitler] made it clear that imports would have to be
increased to ease shortages, and the solution Göring adopted during the next few months in
fact required relatively little foreign exchange. Although agreeing immediately to import much
larger quatities of foodstuffs, particularly cereals, he attempted to secure as much as possible
from countries with which Germany maintained clearings, especially Argentina and the agricultural countries of Southeastern Europe. KAISER, Economic Policy, p. 154. In general, the
subsequent discussion in chapters VII and IX does much to reinforce Kaiser's point.

armaments program with the Nazi domestic program of full employment could not be formulated with greater clarity. Domestic production could supply articles of general use but Hitler recognized that Germany had already reached the limit of growth in agricultural production. He was also aware that for certain raw materials it was simply impossible to manufacture *Ersatz* or find suitable substitutes but refused to be discouraged:

> It is, however, wholly pointless to keep on noting these facts, i.e., stating that we lack food-stuffs or raw materials; what is decisive is to take those measures which can bring about a final solution for the future and a temporary easing for the transitional period.
> (6) The final solution lies in extending the living space of our people and/or the sources of its raw materials and foodstuffs. It is the task of the political leadership one day to solve this problem.
> (7) The temporary easing can only be brought about within the framework of our present economy.

"Temporary" measures were the import of raw materials and foodstuffs. Hitler, however, doubted that increased German exports could balance this need as any marked increase was "hardly likely" given the "unprecedentedly severe" competition that German exports had to face in the world market. German exports had in fact declined less than the international average, but the great increase in imported foodstuffs meant another solution had to be found.

Foreign exchange earmarked for raw materials could not be used to purchase foodstuffs "without inflicting a heavy and perhaps even fatal blow on the rest of the German economy. . . . *But above all it is utterly impossible to do this at the expense of national rearmament.*" Hitler flatly rejected the arguments for stockpiling raw materials as this would deprive the army of ammunition it would need in the first months of war. Furthermore, stockpiling foreign exchange was useless, because war conditions could cause depreciation at any time; and even if gold were hoarded, there was no guarantee that raw materials would be available for purchase: "During the World War Germany still possessed very large assets in foreign exchange in a great many countries. It was not, however, possible for our cunning economic policy to bring to Germany, in exchange for them, fuel, rubber, copper, or tin in any sufficient quantity."

Hitler proposed to assure peacetime food supplies and "above all those means for the conduct of a war." This was to be Hitler's program for "the final solution of our vital needs." Foreign exchange was to be allocated for those goods obtainable only by import. German synthetic fuel production was to be increased and brought to completion within 18 months. As synthetic rubber was equally important, Hitler at this point directly threatened big business: if private industry was not interested, then private industry could be dispensed with. Orthodox objections to the high cost of synthetic production were irrelevant: it was better to produce synthetic tires that could be used than to talk of theoretically cheaper tires, for which no foreign exchange was available, and which therefore could not be used at all:

> If we are in any case compelled to build up a large scale domestic economy on the lines of autarchy — which we are — for lamenting and harping on our foreign exchange plight will in any case not solve the problem — then the price of raw materials individually considered no longer plays a decisive part.

The fourth point of the autarchy program was expanding German iron ore production, substituting German ore of low iron content for richer imports. "Nevertheless, if we still have the possibility of importing cheap ores, well and good. But the future of the national economy, and above all, of the conduct of war, must not be dependent on this." A fifth point forbade distilling alcohol from potatoes; every inch of land had to be used for the cultivation of foodstuffs or fibrous products. The seventh point called for national self-sufficiency in industrial greases through synthetic production. Hitler also recommended exploiting domestic ore resources to the utmost and increasing efforts to find adequate substitutes for light metals in armaments production. He concluded by proclaiming his intention to make Germany completely independent of foreign trade in "all those spheres where it is feasible", saving German foreign exchange, not only for the most important raw materials, but for food. As a stopgap measure, he proposed liquidating German credits held abroad to cover immediate import needs, while imposing two new laws to strengthen the government's hand in the economic sphere: one provided the death penalty for economic sabotage, and the other made the "whole Jewry" collectively responsible for economic sabotage. His goals were military:

I. The German army must be operational within four years.
II. The German economy must be fit for war within four years.

Hitler's new economic policy was "adopted" without vote or discussion at an interministerial meeting held on September 4, 1936.[19] Blomberg had had the opportunity to intervene before the meeting but had kept silent. Schacht was clearly defeated; his resignation as Economics Minister the following year was merely the working out of this decision.

6. Schacht, Hitler, and the Origins of Großraumwirtschaft

Schacht had dominated German economic policy by his success in finding new financial means for the work creation and rearmament programs and the success of the New Plan in creating an export surplus, stimulating exports, and securing raw materials. Once industrial production returned to near normal levels and unemployment was within manageable limits, he became superfluous to Hitler and Göring. The old "wizard" had succeeded too well. The policies that had brought Germany out of the depths of Depression could be adapted to ends other than those Schacht had envisaged.

Between 1933 and 1936, the struggle against unemployment, the attempt to restore production, and the promotion of rearmament provided a broad common platform upon which big business, the general staff, and Nazi leadership could cooperate. But when the unemployed were back at work, the factories producing at or above 1929 levels, and rearmament was a reality, the question became one of the direction of German policy: what should the Reich do with its new economic and

---

[19] 'Minutes of *Ministerrat* of 4 September 1936', ND, EC-416, NCA, Vol. VII, pp. 471-473.

political power? The issue became crucial when the foreign exchange crisis of 1936 made it clear that the tempo of the armaments boom could not be maintained by the same policies that had created it.

No one within Germany's political or economic elite regarded German domination of Danubian Europe as utopian or politically dangerous. Indeed, there was virtual unanimity on the need for political and economic expansion eastward and on the desirability of isolating Czechoslovakia. Meanwhile, conservatives in the army, bureaucracy, and business had hopes that Poland eventually would be forced to make extensive border rectifications in Germany's favor. Politically, Hitler's foreign policy was virtually unchallenged.

Disagreement did arise over the ultimate consequences of Germany's rise to power in east-central Europe. Hitler believed war was necessary because neither France nor the Soviet Union would permit the German Reich to go from strength to strength in consolidating an east European political and economic sphere with no attempt to stop it. He was acutely pessimistic over the relative strength of Germany *vis-a-vis* the other great powers in the years after 1943 and was aware of the pressures towards rearmament in Great Britain and France. Given his belief that war was an inevitable result of the struggle of peoples, Hitler's goal of making Germany ready for war in four years reflected both his desire to end the struggle as quickly as possible and his estimate of the developing constellation of anti-German forces in France, the Soviet Union, and perhaps in Great Britain. Hitler's judgment that the armaments' pace could not slacken rested upon his belief that Germany could not achieve her goals in east-central Europe without violent resistance from France, the Soviet Union, or both.

Accepting the necessity for an increased tempo in rearmament and given the failure of the New Plan to keep pace with the demands for strategic raw materials, how could the gap in the balance of payments be bridged? Hitler's answer for a "temporary, transitional" period was a synthetic raw materials sector. He simply did not believe that an export offensive in the world market could garner the foreign exchange necessary to import crucial raw materials. He regarded as even more unrealistic Schacht's idea that colonies could help the raw materials crisis in the immediate future. Also, Hitler wanted to use the colonial question as a bargaining point in a general settlement with Great Britain. Refusing to look overseas for the solution to the German raw material dilemma, Hitler looked eastward to Russia. The Four Year Plan was not motivated by any ideological preference for autarchy nor by visions of a nationally self-sufficient German economy; it was Hitler's firm belief that Germany's economic problems could be solved only on a continental scale, a belief supported by an important section of German industry and not merely by propagandists of *Großraumwirtschaft*.

Insofar as there was a coherent opposition to Hitler's political and economic policies, it stemmed from a coalition of Schacht and Colonel Thomas (Wi Rü-Amt)[20],

---

[20] Thomas supported unreservedly the armed forces' demands for a synthetic petroleum sector. However, he did not think that such a marked increase in investment was reconcilable with an accelerated armaments boom. THOMAS, Wehr- und Rüstungswirtschaft, pp. 111-113.

both of whom believed in slowing the armaments boom, rearming in depth rather than breadth, and the introduction of strict rationing for the civilian population. Paradoxically, Schacht apparently somewhat shared Hitler's pessimism over the feasibility of an export offensive. Schacht's objection to the autarchic program remained. The higher production costs of synthetic raw materials would inevitably have an inflationary impact on the general price structure, thus making it even more difficult for German exports in the world market. Also, given the full utilization of both capital and labor, increased state outlays for *Ersatz* industry could result only in a scramble for labor and materials, generating further inflationary pressures. He was also concerned that increased state outlays could not be covered by taxation or borrowing, which would lead to a dangerous expansion of the volume of currency and an increase in the rate of circulation. Although he considered southeastern Europe important for the long-term solution to Germany's raw materials problem, Schacht looked to overseas colonies, and not to the steppes of Russia, for the greater share of Germany's future imports.[21]

With the exception of Colonel Thomas, whose pessimistic views on Germany's long-term strength *vis-a-vis* the other great powers were considered virtually unpatriotic, neither Schacht nor the leaders of heavy industry faced the basic question Hitler always had in mind: what would be the political and military consequences of German domination of east-central Europe? These conservatives, as Brüning and Bülow before them, seemed to be possessed of the most striking naïveté when it was a question of foreign political reactions to Germany's "legitimate" interests. Although neither Schacht nor the Ruhr industrialists had access to the Four Year Plan Memorandum, the general thrust of Hitler's ideas was hardly unknown to them. Thus, Hitler's gaining of an effective monopoly over economic policy "with only the assistance of one group of the Generals and one group of capitalists"[22] indicates the political bankruptcy of Schacht and his supporters in heavy industry and the army. It was impossible to endorse a program of economic and political expansion toward east-central Europe and deny Hitler the means to carry it forward. If, as Colonel Thomas warned, such expansion would eventually involve Germany in a world conflict not limited to France and the Soviet Union but involving Great Britain and the United States, reconsideration of such an expansionist course was obviously of vital interest to German industry. There is no indication that the conservative industrialists, generals, or bureaucrats ever underwent such a process of political rethinking.

Schacht's fall and the breakup of the political solidarity of big business was a defeat of the traditional economic premises shared by him and the interest group he

---

[21] Schacht's championship of colonies to supply Germany's raw materials shortages was of long standing. Hjalmar SCHACHT, New Colonial Policy, Berlin 1926; idem, Why Germany Requires Colonies, Berlin 1936; idem, Germany's Colonial Demands, in: Foreign Affairs 15 (1937), pp. 222-234. During interrogation in the immediate aftermath of World War II, Schacht admitted that he had attempted to divert Hitler's attention from expansion in the East to an active colonial policy from 1931 onward. 'Schacht Testimony', Nürnberg, October 13, 1945, ND, 3727-PS, NCA, Vol. 5, pp. 478-480.

[22] SCHWEITZER, Foreign Exchange Crisis, p. 276.

championed. The objective realities of the German economy, not Hitler, undermined the political influence and the economic ideology of the heavy industry
power bloc. The demands of the armed forces, the agricultural sector, and heavy
industry were irreconcilable. Either there had to be a redefinition of interests or a
redefinition of economic terms and since no group was willing to alter how it conceived its interests, traditional financial and economic doctrine could no longer
serve the needs of German expansionism.

It was Schacht who had given the decisive impulse in this direction in the financial program for rearmament and in the New Plan. Normally, there is a simple
means of allocating resources between alternative options: the purchaser can choose
from the domestic or world market that commodity that satisfies his needs in terms
of price and quality; the consumer can purchase in the cheapest market, regardless
of the state of the trade balance between his country and the country where the
purchase is made.[23] Germany's orientation to the markets of Danubian Europe,
where the domestic cost of production was substantially higher than world market
prices, required a departure from the liberal economic principle which demanded
purchase in the cheapest market. In trade negotiations Schacht had attempted to
use the world market price as a benchmark of economic rationality to bring down
the price of Danubian products to or near this level, with an obvious purpose. As
Germany could not arbitrarily raise the prices of her exports, if it became necessary
to pay higher prices for Danubian products, Germany's terms of trade would seriously deteriorate. Despite Schacht's efforts, trade with Danubian countries did
bring higher import prices, and the partial abrogation of the liberal economic price
criterion: the world market price.[24]

[23] League of Nations, World Economic Survey, Fifth Year, 1935/1936, Geneva 1936, pp.
212-213. "The free trade by which individuals bought in the most specialised and therefore
cheapest markets and investors lent abroad without more than ordinary commercial risks has
increasingly given place to national autarchic systems. Where this development has gone fur-
thest, the individual investor and trader have given way to Government officials manipulating
discriminatory tariffs, quotas, subsidies and exchange rates in a fierce struggle to obtain essential raw materials. Raw materials are abundant, but acceptable means of payment are scarce,
since, while all desire to sell, none desire to buy more abroad than the barest minimum that is
necessary to maintain economic activity at home. The basic reason for the institution of such
restrictions in almost every case was the desire to maintain currencies (and national price-sys-
tems) at what was proved a high and even artificial level."

[24] This is apparent in the debate of the RWM, RMEL, and AA in the autumn of 1935 over
paying Überpreise for Rumanian cattle. Schacht's RWM clearly was willing to risk the whole
treaty structure with Rumania over the issue of reducing Rumanian cattle prices to a level near
the world market price. Clodius Stellungnahme, October 5, 1935, PA, Ha Pol, Handakten
Clodius, Rumänien, Bd. 1. Kaiser points out correctly that Schacht was "generally opposed to
paying generous prices for Southeastern European agriculutural products". KAISER, Economic
Policy, p. 77-78. In this case, the RWM spoke for Schacht's viewpoint. Clodius spoke for the
Wilhelmstraße which was the balance wheel of German foreign economic policy making. He
emphasized the long term political and economic benefits which the treaty with Rumania
provided in spite of short term losses such as the cattle deal.

Insofar as Schacht abandoned the world price system for imports and insulated the German price system from outside influences through exchange control, he had implicitly introduced the revolutionary economic foreign policy, *Großraumwirtschaft*, and opened the door to synthetic production of raw materials at home. The trading practices of the New Plan and the theory of *Großraumwirtschaft* overturned normal economic calculations. Trading under the New Plan meant government bureaucrats, representing countries with widely divergent price levels, made the decisions that moved commodities across borders. "Bargaining" replaced the market. In the "tie-in purchase", common under the repressed German domestic inflation, traders trying to evade price controls would sell a desired product only if the customer purchased some other product that he did not want.[25] In the same way, in trading under bilateral clearing, Germany was forced to take many commodities, wanted neither then or not at all, to gain a foothold in the market for its exports or to obtain wanted raw materials. Eventually, Germany's trading partner had to adjust its economy to the products Germany was willing (or able) to import. This mutual adjustment of both economies, at a price level above the prevailing world market, complemented the weaknesses of each economy, allowing products that would not otherwise have been exported to find a foreign market.

Trading under the New Plan, in substituting export promotion, securing strategic raw materials, and maintaining trade relationships for the price concept, gave Hitler a panoply of trade devices that could be used to achieve raw materials independence. Although the Four Year Plan concentrated almost exclusively upon creating domestic synthetic raw materials, the increased tempo of the rearmament economy put ever-increasing pressure on Germany's trading partners to supply needed raw materials. The adoption of the Four Year Plan was a turning away from export promotion to raw materials independence, but during the time required to bring synthetic raw materials into production, Germany had to fall back upon the clearing partners where the natural product was available. The corollary of Hitler's expectation of war within four to seven years (1940-43) was the view that east-central Europe was the single blockade-proof source of raw materials for the German war machine; thus his appointed task of "extending the living space of our people and/or the sources of our raw materials and foodstuffs" increasingly demanded total subordination of the national economies of east-central Europe to the needs of the rearmament economy.

7. *The Four Year Plan and Foreign Trade, 1936-39*

The improved world economy confounded the pessimistic forecasts of German economic experts. Instead of an export deficit in 1936, Germany registered an export surplus of approximately 440 million marks. But rising raw material and food prices caused the terms of trade to move against the Reich's favor. "In 1936,

---

[25] AGRANAT, Price Control, chapter 14, pp. 12-13.

compared with 1935, exports increased in value by 11.7% and in volume by 5.4%; the value of imports increased by 1.49% but the volume fell by 8.2%. Thus Germany had to give a 5% greater quantity of exports for 8% less imports."[26] The improved world market, which raised the prices of raw materials, caused Germany's terms of trade to deteriorate even though exports increased during 1936 and 1937. Contrary to expectations, German exports did surprisingly well in those two years. While the total volume of world trade had been rising since mid-1932, the sterling value of world trade had been expanding quarter by quarter since the beginning of 1934.[27] The volume of world trade in 1936 remained 14% below 1929 levels, but in 1937 it rose rapidly, reaching its 1927 level by the fourth quarter of that year.[28] While the 1937 volume of trade in food and manufactures remained below 1929 levels by 7% and 14% respectively, the volume of traded raw materials increased 11.5% above 1929, largely the result of rearmament and speculative demand.

During 1937, German imports and exports both rose rapidly. The rise in imports was largely the result of larger purchases of foodstuffs, but there was some increase in the import of raw materials for consumption goods and a marked increase in the imports of metals and ores obviously destined for rearmament and production drives.[29] Even so, Schacht, along with some Ruhr industrialists and various officials, worried that Germany was falling behind in export promotion. For example, the value of world trade had grown by 25% in the first quarter of 1937 over the average for the same period in 1936, but German exports had increased by only 13%. Under pressure from several directions, Göring authorized the formation of an export committee chaired by Ernst Poengsen (*Vereinigte Stahlwerke*) to increase finished exports of the iron and steel industry by some 500,000 tons per month in order to secure needed foreign exchange. German heavy industry was not able, however, to fulfill the demands of such an export program and the huge investment requirements of the Four Year Plan. By midsummer 1937, Göring intervened to secure the needed iron and steel for the Four Year Plan and so nullified the new export program. German exports, despite the strains imposed by the huge new investment program, did increase by 23% while imports rose by 30%. While the increase in exports was shared by almost all manufactured goods except textiles, the export of motor vehicles enjoyed a 79% increase from 1936 to 1937.[30] But, even with an active balance of 443 million marks, Germany still had only one-half of the foreign exchange needed for imports. The remainder came from a foreign exchange amnesty campaign, launched at the beginning of 1937, that netted a substantial sum of illegal foreign currency in private hands, virtually the last liquid reserves of the German nation. The synthetic industry contributed only an estimated 150 million marks to the saving of foreign exchange.

---

[26] League of Nations, World Economic Survey, Sixth Year, 1936/37, Geneva 1937, p. 38.
[27] Ibid., p. 121.
[28] League of Nations, World Economic Survey, Seventh Year, 1937/38, Geneva 1938, p. 118.
[29] Ibid., p. 128.
[30] Ibid.

The economic recession beginning in the late summer of 1937 in the United States caused a sharp decline in the volume and value of world trade from the last quarter of 1937 to mid-1938. Between 1937 and 1938, U.S. imports fell by some 35%, a figure surpassed only by Mexico.[31] Falling American imports accounted for almost one-third of the total decline in world imports and approximately one-half of the total decline in raw materials imports between 1937 and 1938: ". . . if allowance could be made for the indirect depressing effects of the American recession on the demand of other countries for imports, the influence of economic decline and recovery upon world trade would be correspondingly greater."[32]

The world economic recession had a profound impact on Germany's export markets and thus on the vulnerable trade balance. Experts at the Economics Ministry projected a modest 5% expansion in export trade but a foreign exchange shortfall of some 400 million marks. Declining prices for raw materials and foodstuffs led the Economics Ministry to revise its estimate of the hard-currency shortfall downward from 400 to 168-180 million marks[33], but even this modest optimism proved to be wrong. The raw materials demands of the rearmament economy and synthetic raw materials projects exceeded expectations, requiring Germany, alone of all the industrial countries, to increase the volume of imports between 1937 and 1938. "The quantity of oil seeds imported rose by 19%, of copper by 35%, of raw iron (including scrap) by 131%, of petrol by 28%, and of gas oil by 23% between 1937 and 1938."[34] Falling demand in foreign markets caused German exports to fall by some 610 million marks, or by 10% compared to 1937. Germany once again faced a severe balance of trade deficit, totaling about 192 million marks for 1938 in visible trade alone. The passive balance continued into the first quarter of 1939, albeit somewhat diminished.

The *Anschluß* brought Germany some 440 million marks in gold and foreign exchange.[35] After deducting some 145 million marks for Austria's import needs, German authorities allocated approximately 60% of the remaining 295 million for the planned deficit and 40% for a special raw materials purchase fund. In the spring of 1939, the reserves of the Czech National Bank gave Germany a similar windfall of about 189 million marks.[36]

Despite a new attempt at supplemental export promotion in October 1938 and the 1939 revival of the world economy, exports threatened to decline well into 1939; export orders were 40% lower in the last quarter of 1938 than in the same period of 1937. The gap in Germany's balance of payments was not materially les-

---

[31] League of Nations, World Economic Survey, Eighth Year, 1938/39, Geneva 1939, p. 168.

[32] Ibid.

[33] The Economic Intelligence Service (League of Nations) estimated that the ratio between prices paid for imports and those received for exports moved some 12% in Germany's favor. ibid., p. 33.

[34] Ibid., p. 171.

[35] PETZINA, Autarkiepolitik, pp. 112-113.

[36] Ibid.

sened by the increasing production of synthetic raw materials. The Four Year Plan had only limited successes in foreign trade policy, new production did not decisively assist in maintaining a trade balance, and no new methods of resolving foreign exchange shortfall were developed. Germany was able to pay for the increased quantity of imported raw materials in 1938 and the first nine months of 1939 because new sources of foreign exchange became available — Germany's import balance was covered by Austrian and Czech reserves, not increased exports.

The little that the Four Year Plan did to remedy the persistent German import surplus is understandable considering that it was designed to service an armaments drive unrestricted by import realities. The limited production of synthetics during the initial years of the Plan was not, however, the result of foreign raw materials shortages but of production delays caused by the short supply of skilled labor and a heavy industry overburdened with orders. Germany's economic planners could do little about declining German exports given the prevailing world economic trends; in 1938 it was not a uniquely German problem. Although the Four Year Plan did not develop a comprehensive approach to the foreign trade sector, Germany's foreign trade continued to supply the population with food and the productive apparatus with needed raw materials.

8. The Decision-Making Process in Foreign Economic Policy

The Four Year Plan brought with it a parallel bureaucracy to the official ministries and created a jungle of overlapping authorities. Göring, as plenipotentiary of the Plan, assembled a staff from the Prussian State Ministry, the *Luftwaffe*, Wilhelm Keppler's raw materials staff, and IG Farben.[37] Dietmar Petzina observed that the directives of the Plan were seldom enforced with a "firm hand", there was a lack of "leadership and command", and coordination often misfunctioned. Hans Kehrl, a self-styled former "crisis manager" of the Third Reich, gives a colorful description of Göring as an economic administrator:

> [Göring] possessed neither economic thought of his own nor a too frequent or too fundamental desire to become engrossed in economic questions. . . . He was not as good a negotiator or discussion leader as Goebbels, for example. Thereby he lacked not only the patience, but the ability as well, to think fundamentally, and [lacked] naturally, as well, the extensive knowledge of economic and political circumstances and relationships that one must know in order to make correct decisions. Göring was a highly talented dilettante, in whose essence light-heartedness and optimism, unconcern and impatience, were pre-pro-

[37] For example: Erich Neumann, ministerial director, Prussian State Ministry, (later state secretary of the Plan); Colonel Loeb Luftwaffe, (later the first Administrator of the *Rohstoff- und Devisen Stab* and the Plan); both Paul Pleiger (later head of the *Reichswerke Hermann Göring*) and Hans Kehrl (head of the synthetic textile plan, later top administrator in the RWM) were recruited from Wilhelm Keppler's raw materials staff; Carl Krauch (later Plenipotentiary for the Chemical Sector), a brilliant chemist, director of the *Braunkohle und Benzin A.G.*, member of the *Vorstand* of IG Farben.

grammed. As a consequence of his temperament he was interested in isolated phenomena and individual decisions, not the context. He wanted results and successes, and quick.[38]

Göring's inadequate administration was only part of the problem. The Four Year Plan was merely the sum of the industrial plans for synthetic production — fuel, rubber, cloth, etc., and although it had ample financing to implement these plans and authority to impose directives on the whole economy, neither the investment nor finished goods industries were brought within its compass. With each individual military service procuring arms to meet its own objectives and the several "plans" of the Four Year Plan all going full throttle, there was simply no way that any given economic or military objective could be met within a specified period of time. Excess means of payment competed for scarce factors of production.

Göring did not set up any special administrative bureau to supervise foreign trade negotiations. The Economic Policy Department of the Wilhelmstraße, consulting with concerned ministries and the Four Year Plan, continued to shoulder the major responsibility for trade negotiations. Göring did intervene occasionally in trade policy, usually during a crisis such as the grain shortage in early 1937. This division of responsibility and erratic supervision meant that crucial economic problems often ended up in the hands of the Economics Ministry or Control Boards. For example, critical decisions concerning German trade policy and Rumanian petroleum were initiated by the Control Board for Mineral Oil and a division of the Economics Ministry. Burdened with the consequences of policy decisions at the highest levels, these agencies had to find means of meeting the increased petroleum demands of the Luftwaffe and other services, and turned to the Wilhelmstraße to increase petroleum imports from Rumania. The Four Year Plan was informed of the new policy discussions but rarely contributed anything of substance to the decision-making process. Other demands for foreign trade to supply strategic raw materials were approached in similar piecemeal fashion. A shortage in a given commodity created pressure on the appropriate bureau of the Economics Ministry or on the Control Board, which then turned the problem over to the Wilhelmstraße for increased imports from suppliers of that commodity. Inevitably, with commodities such as petroleum primarily available from only one or two clearing partners without an outlay of foreign exchange, the supply of this commodity became a question of the bilateral relations between Germany and the supplier. Germany's foreign trade policy with regard to petroleum was essentially the bilateral relationship with Rumania and, to a lesser extent, Russia. Consequently, the foreign economic policy of Four Year Plan amounted to increased pressure upon Germany's trading partners, particularly in southeastern Europe, to expand exports of key raw materials.

Accidental circumstances also affected the role of the Plan in foreign trade policy, as evidenced by the contrast between German decisions regarding Rumania and Yugoslavia. The co-option of Helmuth Wohlthat from the Economics Ministry into the Four Year Plan as Göring's troubleshooter for foreign trade resulted in a unified policy toward Rumania and petroleum for the simple reason that Wohlthat

---

[38] Hans KEHRL, Krisenmanager in Dritten Reich: 6 Jahre Frieden — 6 Jahre Krieg, Düsseldorf 1974, p. 71.

had been chairman of the German delegation to the Mixed Commission for several years and had maintained excellent relations with his former colleagues in the Economics Ministry and the Wilhelmstraße after his resignation from that post. Despite his expert knowledge of the Rumanian situation and petroleum, Wohlthat's frequent trips as Germany's chief economic negotiator prevented him from determining the course of German policy toward Rumania. The implementation of the famous Wohlthat Treaty was thus not a province of the Four Year Plan but was assigned to a specially created bureau in the Economics Ministry.

Despite Wohlthat's other duties, there developed a relatively clear line on policy making and authority toward Rumania, while German policy toward Yugoslavia presents the familiar Nazi picture of competing authorities and interest groups. One major conflict, between Franz Neuhausen as Belgrade representative of the Four Year Plan and the official bureaucracy, resulted simply from Göring's friendship with Neuhausen, a German citizen living in Belgrade, an *alter Kämpfer* representing certain German businesses there. In 1934 Neuhausen was appointed head of the minuscule Nazi party in Yugoslavia.[39] In the fall of 1936, Göring gave him the honorary title of "Consul General" and appointed him Four Year Plan representative for Yugoslavia. Although undoubtedly amply funded by the Plan (or by IG Farben), Neuhausen had no standing whatsoever in the Belgrade legation and so set up his own bureau without Wilhelmstraße support. He nobly rose above this handicap to act like an officially accredited minister and played an important role in German policy until his arrest in 1943.

Between September 1936 and January 1937, Schacht ceased to be a determining factor in economic decision making. After him, German foreign trade policy lacked strong administrative supervision or a coherent guiding economic principle. While invoked to justify the trade drive to the southeast, the history of German policy in both Yugoslavia and Rumania indicates that the policy of *Großraumwirtschaft* was little more than the total of bilateral trade relationships with individual countries. For example, except for enlarging the Vienna harbor facilities after the Anschluß, no attempt was made to expand either Germany's rolling stock or river transport — both necessary to implement the *Großraumwirtschaft* strategy in case of war. Administrative chaos, executive incompetence, and personal favoritism were all characteristic of the Four Year Plan foreign economic policy. Nevertheless, the German juggernaut rolled on from success to success.

---

[39] The *Auslandsorganisation* (AO) of the NSDAP was headed by Ernest Bohle. Bohle was later appointed to a special state secretaryship in the AA for AO Affairs. Although Bohle and the AO played a significant role in economic policy with regard to Spain, he had no influence over Neuhausen in Yugoslavia. Neuhausen's authority stemmed directly from Göring. The role of the AO and its representative in Spain is covered in Glen T. HARPER, German Economic Policy during the Spanish Civil War, 1936-1939, U.Ph.D., Duke Univ. 1963.

9. A Foreign Economic Policy for a Blitzkrieg Strategy?

During the late 1930's and into the 1940's, popular press and scholarly analysis of German economic and war policy posited an overwhelming National Socialist commitment to a war economy in peacetime. Indeed, the spectacular successes of the German war effort in the first three years of the war seemed to have no other reasonable explanation than the commitment of Hitler and his close advisors to a war, and a concomitant war mobilization in peace-time to achieve the requisite foreign policy and military success which flowed from such a principled commitment. In wartime, the British Ministry of Economic Warfare (MEW), which relied on such a naive analysis of the German economy, soon found the realities of wartime struggle grossly out of synchronization with this scenario: "Whereas MEW was predicting economic collapse and chaos by the end of 1941, overall German war production actually more than tripled from the beginning of 1942 until the summer of 1944. This achievement seemed at first almost incredible in view of the Allied intensification of strategic bombing during this period from an average monthly delivery of under 6000 tons to 131,000 tons, more than a twenty-fold increase."[40] In the light of this spectacular performance, the reassessment of the German economy and war effort began with the Strategic Bombing Surveys sponsored by the United States government in the immediate post war period. On the basis of this massive governmental effort a new school of revisionist scholarship on the nature of the German economy before the outbreak of war in 1939 and the subsequent war effort arose which is associated with the work of the economists Burton Klein and Alan Milward.[41]

In the view of Klein and Milward, the German economy in the period before 1939 was a remarkably "peace-like" war economy. If, indeed, the National Socialist leadership under Hitler was intent upon totally mobilizing the Germany economy for war, Klein argued that the requisite economic evidence for such an arms build-up was simply lacking: not only was there "no pronounced concentration of investment in those activities associated with economic preparations for war" [as defined by Klein], but the statistical evidence shows that the "enormous diversion of resources from the civilian to the war sector of the economy did not occur."[42] Accordingly, "investment in armament plants and Germany's basic industries" was "a surprisingly small part of total investment."[43] Following up on Klein's work, Alan Milward posited a strategic orientation which could explain the relatively modest investments in armaments compared to the spectacular success of Germany in the initial wartime engagements. The *Blitzkrieg* strategy, in Milward's eyes

---

[40] Mark LORELL, The Politics of Economic Debate: Anglo-American Perceptions of Germany's Economic Preparations for War, 1937-1939, U.Ph.D., University of Washington 1976, p. 4. United States Strategic Bombing Survey, Overall Economic Effects Division, Washington/D.C., October 1945, p. 1, 163, 186, 286.

[41] Burton H. KLEIN, Germany's Economic Preparations for War, Cambridge/Mass. 1959; Alan MILWARD, The German Economy at War, London 1965.

[42] KLEIN, Preparations, p. 15, 16.

[43] Ibid., p. 15.

involved not just a military component of mechanized warfare and coordinated use of the air arm with infantry and tank units but an economic strategy which gave the Germany economy remarkable flexibility through creating a large body of "armaments in width" to strike a series of lightning blows at adversaries without committing resources to a long term total war economy which implied "armaments in depth." The *Blitzkrieg* economic strategy also had the added benefit of welding the German population to the war effort by means of maintaining civilian consumption: "The *Blitzkrieg* was a system of waging war without reducing civilian consumer standards. The aim was to accumulate more armaments than the potential victim, to be in a situation of greater preparedness than the opponent. But to be so prepared was to be prepared for a short war only. Germany relied on a greater volume of armaments than her opponent at a particular point in time. At such a time, a military strategy linked to this fragile, but effective, economic sub-structure would destroy the opponent. The *Blitzkrieg* was an economic concept, not a merely military one."[44]

The concept of a *Blitzkrieg* economic strategy has held sway over scholarly opinion in the last twenty years because of the seeming reconciliation of the contradictions of National Socialist domestic and foreign policy. While not questioning the aggressive character of Nazi foreign policy before 1939, Klein and Milward provide a clever explanation of how Hitler was able to reconcile his domestic goals for a *Volksgemeinschaft* with a strategy of aggression abroad. Recently, R.J. Overy has systematically challenged the entire concept of an economic *Blitzkrieg* strategy.[45] In direct opposition to the revisionists, Overy argues that Hitler's war economic plans were not limited but large in scale. The war which Hitler was preparing for was to break out in 1943, not 1939. The large armaments production failed to appear, not because of an alleged *Blitzkrieg* strategy, but because Hitler's foreign policy was out of step with his economic preparations.[46] The constraints caused by the mismatch between war economic preparations and the invasion of Poland was further exacerbated by the poor planning, structural restrictions within German industry, and inadequate coordination associated with Göring's stewardship over the German economy. Overy contrasts Hitler's aims and intentions with the results of the policy, which were meager by comparison. Thus, Overy does not challenge revisionist analysis of the GNP statistics on the ratio of armaments expenditures to the national income or the ratio of armaments expenditures to overall government expenditures in the pre-war period. Overy's main aim is to reassess the crucial period of Hitler's greatest success, 1939-1941.

In analysing the period of the Four Year Plan (1936-1939), Overy contends that all Hitler's statements point to a long war, not a series of *Blitzkrieg* wars. Indeed, the massive investments of the Four Year Plan, including the synthetic oil and rub-

---

[44] Alan MILWARD, Could Sweden Have Stopped the Second World War?, in: Scandanianvian Economic History Review XV (1967), p. 135.

[45] R. J. OVERY, Hitler's War and the German Economy: A Reinterpretation, in: Economic History Review, series 2, 35 (1982), pp. 272-291.

[46] Ibid., p. 273.

ber plants, the exploitation of low grade iron ore (the *Reichswerke Hermann Göring*), the huge naval build-up, only make sense in a longer term perspective than can be contained in a *Blitzkrieg* concept: "If it is argued that Hitler's intention had been a limited war fought in 1939 together with the safeguarding of domestic living standards, such preparations did not make sense. But that is not what Hitler intended. Hitler wanted a healthy and expanding economy so that he could convert it to the giant task of European and Asian conquest."[47] Overy, as Klein and Milward before him, is forced to confront the seeming contradiction between the apparently limitless scope of Hitler's political policy with the actual performance of the German economy. In contrast to the revisionists, Overy contends that the scholarly disarry over German policy and goals is largely a confusion caused by the *Führer*'s own lack of understanding between means and ends in the allocation of economic resources for policy goals. According to Overy, Hitler only had the vaguest notion of how an economy operated and actually believed that the war economic preparations, the *Autobahn*, the Volkswagen project, and massive building program were reconcilable. "These many ambitions betrayed Hitler's inability to see the economy as a whole, to grasp that cars and tanks could not be produced at the same time, that fortifications vied for resources with the rebuilding of Berlin. It is this inability that has been mistaken for a positive desire to restrict military production in favor of the civilian sector."[48]

Overy's critique of the revisionist view of economic strategy paradoxically leads him to argue that Hitler did not expect a European war to break out in the summer of 1939. As evidence, Overy notes that Hitler sent his planning staff chief on leave on August 18, 1939 and comments that Hitler had some reason to believe that the West would yield after the pact with Stalin was achieved. However, Overy concludes that Hitler did not shrink from launching the war against Poland: ". . . not because he had any *Blitzkrieg* economic plan prepared, but for the quite different reason that he believed, in the long run, that the economic and moral resources of the *Reich*, when stretchted to their utmost, would prove greater than those available to the Allies."[49] War in 1939, then, was the consequence of the first stage of Hitler's expansionist foreign policy: the creation of a Fortress *Mitteleuropa* comprising Germany, Austria, Czechoslovakia, and parts of Poland, which was to be girdled by huge fortifications. This core was to be the basis for an autrachic economy centered upon east-central Europe. In Overy's view Hitler believed that this stage would be achieved through diplomatic maneuver such as the Munich Agreement and the pact with the Soviet Union. When the strategy misfired leading to war with England and France as well as Poland, Hitler did not back down for a variety of reasons: "Hence the reasons which Hitler himself gave for the attack on Poland; that he was growing old and could afford to wait no longer to create the new German empire; and that what counted in foreign policy was will. Lacking the will to restrain Hitler

---

[47] Ibid., p. 274.
[48] Ibid., p. 275.
[49] Ibid., p. 276.

before 1939, the western nations had forfeited their claim to the status of great powers and would not fight."[50]

The contradiction between Hitler's immediate goals and the commitments to long term large scale economic projects caused the war economy to perform in particularly unsatisfactory and erratic fashion during the period 1939-1941. The restructuring of the economy symbolized by the Four Year Plan was barely half completed when war came. Rather than signalling a commitment to the maintainence of civilian consumption levels, the inadequate performance of the economy in the production of armaments was caused by the interaction between Göring's gross inadequacy as an economic administrator, the uncertainty of the leaders of big industry as to what Hitler actually wanted, the commitment of the armed forces to high quality production based upon skilled labor rather than mass production methods, and the continuance of prestige projects in the face of world war. The sheer scale of the Nazi armament effort dwarfed all other powers, with the possible exception of the Soviet Union. Perhaps, Overy argues, Hitler did not get value for his money, but to contrast the "limited moblization" of Germany before 1941 with the "total moblization" of the Allies is "historically misleading." In every category, the Germany economy in the summer of 1939 was poised for an even greater armaments effort: the Navy's Z plan which Hitler gave priority over all other programs in early 1939 had just begun when war broke out. In 1938, Hitler had demanded a fivefold increase in the strength of the *Luftwaffe* (from 20,000 aircraft in peace, or 30-40,000 aircraft in war). The *Luftwaffe*, less ambitious than Hitler, planned, in its last peacetime prognosis, the expansion of production to 14,000 aircraft per year, some three times the 1938 output: "All this suggests that Hitler wanted a huge increase in the proportion of the economy devoted to military purposes, even if war had not broken out in 1939."[51]

The very scale of the Nazi projects for self-sufficiency — the hydrogenation plant at Brüx (250 million marks), the *Reichswerke Hermann Göring* (400 million marks financed 93% from state sources) — militates against the *Blitzkrieg* thesis and also explains, as well, why Hitler did not get more armaments production in the first years of the war. The very scope of these projects diverted resources away from the production of armaments, threw the war economy in confusion, and in retrospect, explains the paradox of "large scale planning and expenditure and the poor return in the shape of finished armaments. Hitler's intention had been to create this necessary industrial substructure before developing the superstructure of armaments production."[52]

Contrary to the *Blitzkrieg* thesis, military expenditure increased with suprising uniformity across the board with the greatest percentage increases in monetary terms between 1939-1941. Civilian industries such as car production, construction, and consumer goods were increasingly throttled and diverted to military uses. While Hitler entertained the idea on occasion of running down the arms economy,

[50] Ibid., p. 277.
[51] Ibid., p. 281.
[52] Ibid., p. 282.

the actual fact is that he never did so in the face of the increasing array of enemies with which Germany was confronted. Ultimately, the failure of the German economy to perform, what Overy terms "the era of incompetence", resulted in the sacking of Göring as head of the economic effort, his replacement by Speer, and the utilization of big business executives in a policy of economic rationalization of the war effort.[53]

Todt, Speer, and Milch did not revolutionize production by a massive redirection of resources but by using existing resources in a more rational way. "The aircraft industry in 1942 produced 40 per cent more aircraft than in 1941 with only 5 per cent more labor and substantially less aluminum. What produced the low level of mobilization was not a lack of resources but the problem of coping with a premature war in an economy lacking effective central control, dominated by military requirements, and guided by an impulsive strategist whose understanding of the economy was deliberately obscured."[54]

Overy's provocative critique of the revisionist theory of *Blitzkrieg* strategy has manifold implications for the interpretation of German foreign policy in the period before the outbreak of war. Although Overy relies primarily on evidence from published memoirs and his own work on German military production in the period 1939-1941, recent archival work on German foreign economic policy in the period 1933-1939 provides some interesting confirmation of the long term objectives of German economic policy in east-central Europe and the nature of German foreign policy objectives in 1939. Whereas Milward in his limited research on German foreign economic policy in east-central Europe analyzes the Schacht policy of the "New Plan" as largely reactive and reflecting the weaknesses of the German economy, Overy sees the period before 1939 as reflecting the first stage in a coordinated and conscious strategy to build a *Fortress Mitteleuropa* in east-central Europe. As early as 1931 and 1932, important German industrialists and banking leaders such as Schacht and Wilmowsky proposed a reorientation of German foreign economic policy away from high income markets in the West towards the agrarian countries of southeastern Europe.[55] On the one hand, these efforts were formalized in the

---

[53] Ibid., p. 287.

[54] Ibid., p. 289.

[55] The *Mitteleuropäische Wirtschaftstag* was founded in Vienna by Austrian business interests with the support of academics. During the year 1931, a German group was formed under the leadership of Ruhr industry and the MWT was effectively transformed into an arm of German heavy industry. In November, 1932, Thilo von Wilmowsky, (Krupp's brother-in-law, chariman of the Krupp Aufsichtsrat), Max Hahn (business manager of the MWT), and Martin Sogemeier (Syndic of the *Zweckverband Nordeutscher Wirtschaftsvertretungen*) completed a trip to Yugoslavia and Rumania which resulted in a memorandum on trade policy which was presented to the Wilhelmstraße. This twenty-one page document advocated a policy of aggressive trade expansion towards Danubian Europe in the aftermath of the failure of the Tardieu Plan and concluded that: "Mit diesem Ergebnis ist der deutschen Wirtschaft eine große Chance geboten, die jetzt vorhandene Lücke durch eigene Initiative und konstruktive Vorschläge auf dem Gebiete der Wirtschaftspolitik auszuführen." Wilmowsky, Hahn, Sogemeier, 'Bericht über eine Reise nach Rumänien und Yugoslawien', Berlin, November 10, 1932; also a minute by Busse, November 10, 1932, PA, Abteilung Wirtschaft, Rumänien,

efforts of the *Mitteleuropäische Wirtschaftage* to influence late Weimar policy towards an active commercial policy, one the other, Schacht sought to influence Hitler in the direction of a "reasonable" economic policy which would reconcile the big business with the expansionist foreign policy of Hitler.[56] These efforts produced a remarkable consensus between Hitler, Schacht, big business, the armed forces, and the upper bureaucracy on a program which combined repression of organized labor at home with expansion abroad.

After 1933, Germany pursued a policy of aggressive commerical expansion abroad, particularly in east-central Europe and Latin America, which resulted in the doubling of German trade with these areas and the achievement of Germany as the world's number one importer by 1938. This remarkable success has been obscured by the reliance of economists and historians on the declining percentage of foreign trade in total GNP, a statistical truth which is overshadowed by the relative growth of the German economy in the period 1933-1939. This, in turn, made Germany's relative contribution to world trade grow faster than the countries which remained in the doldrums of the Depression. As for the long term German aims, as early as 1935 Schacht proposed the creation of a joint German-Rumanian petroleum sector which was intended to simultaneously build up large exports for German industry, secure a source of oil for Germany which did not require the expenditure of foreign exchange, and finally, create a rival to the great international oil companies which

Wirtschaftsbeziehungen zu Deutschland, Bd. 1. There is as yet no comprehensive scholarly work on the MWT, the most important big business pressure group in the promotion of an economic *Drang nach Osten*. In the view of the key role which this organization played in the expansion policy of the 1930's, Henry Turner's curious remark that "nothing in the voluminous industrial documentation supports [Sohn-Rethel's] story or the significance Sohn-Rethel attributes to the MWT" is perplexing. The documentation from the Wilhelmstraße archives gives ample evidence of the critical role which the MWT played in trade policy issues. Turner refers to Sohn-Rethel's claim that Carl Bosch of the IG Farben accepted a MWT plan for agricultural cartels and import quotas "calculated to impose 'imperialistic' designs on southeastern Europe" in December, 1932 . Henry A. TURNER, German Big Business and the Rise of Hitler, New York 1985, p. 466. Alfred SOHN-RETHEL, Ökonomie und Klassenstruktur des deutschen Faschismus, Frankfurt 1973, p. 94. Although Turner is correct in noting that Carl Bosch remained a defender of the most-favored-nation system and an opponent of discriminatory trade until December, 1932, it is also true that IG Farben, as a corporation, was one of the most vigorous proponents of the economic offensive in Danubian Europe and one of the first corporations to engage in barter trade, even before the 1935 trade treaty was negoiated with Rumania; see William S. GRENZEBACH, Germany's Informal Empire in East-Central Europe: German Economic Policy Towards Yugoslavia and Rumania, 1933-1939, U.Ph.D., Brandeis University 1978, chapter 7, pp. 208-238. IG Farben even used funds garnered from barter trade to subsidize right wing forces within Rumania as early as 1933. For IG's barter proposals: IG Farben (Zentralfinanzverwaltung) to Neurath, September 21, 1933, PA, Sonderreferat Wirtschaft, Rumänien, Handel 13, Handelsvertragsverhältnisse Deutschland zu Rumänien, Bd. 1.

[56] Schacht to Reusch, March 18, 1932, Nachla Reusch, HA-GHH, 40101290/3; Schacht to Reusch with Enclosure (the Einfuhrmonopol Memorandum), December 20, 1932. Although Turner is as familiar with the GHH archives as any living historian, he nowhere mentions the discriminatory impact of Schacht's proposals.

would, Schacht alleged, help both German and Rumanian national interests.[57] After
the fall of Schacht as Economics Minister in 1937, Göring and the Four Year Plan
increasingly relied on southeastern Europe as a reservoir of foodstuffs and raw
materials for the expansion of German power. The resultant increase in grain
imports from the Danubian countries before the *Anschluß* and Sudenten crises
pushed Germany over the previous trade expansion in the 1920's except in the case
of Rumania.[58]

Increasingly, both German business interests represented by the MWT and the
Göring/Four Year Plan combine sought to anchor German interests in the raw
materials sectors of the Danubian countries. In Yugoslavia Max Hahn, the manag-
ing director of the MWT, obtained concessions for antimony which he characterized as achieving "the antimony monoply for Germany in Europe."[59] Both Hahn
and Göring's representative in Yugoslavia, Neuhausen, waged economic war
against the interests of American oil companies, particularly, Standard Oil (New
Jersey) in order to dominate future oil concessions in Yugoslavia.[60] In Rumania the
Wolhthat Treaty projected a structural revolution in the Rumanian economy which
would involve total reorientation of the German economy to serve the needs of
German expansionism.[61] In terms of Overy's critique of the concept of the *Blitzkrieg* strategy, it is clear from the research in this work that Hitler, Schacht, and
Göring aimed at a long term structural revolution in the political economy of
Europe which presumed a political revolution of equal magnitude. While Alice Teichova has shown in her detailed study of the Czechoslovak case that there was no
"economic Munich before the political Munich", (that is, neither France nor England voluntarily sacrificed exisiting economic interests to Germany), the aims of
German foreign economic policy required nothing less than an "economic Munich."[62] In the eyes of German policy makers, the surrender of the West at Munich
meant precisely that German interests would prevail and that German political and
trade interests would be accorded special privileges, including the creation by the
Danubian states of German proprietary rights in the raw materials sector, directly
contrary to the interests of France, England, and the United States.[63] This policy
was one to which Poland refused to capitulate and which Chamberlain eventually
refused to countenance. Acquiescence in German trade hegemony in the Danube
was one thing, knuckling under to unilateral border changes and transfer of proprietary rights was quite another.

[57] Schacht to Manolescu-Strunga, telegram, March 27, 1935, PA, Abteilung II, Wirtschaft,
Rumänien, Handel 13, Handelsvertragsverhältnisse mit Deutschland, Bd. 12; Schacht to Manolescu-Strunga, April 1, 1935, DGFP, vol. 4, No.6, p. 5.
[58] See Chapters VII and IX below.
[59] Max Hahn (MWT-Berlin) to Clodius (AA), October 30, 1936, PA, Ha Pol, IVa, Jugoslawien, Industrie 6, Bergbau, Bd. 1. See chapter VII below.
[60] See Chapter VIII below.
[61] See Chapter X below.
[62] Alice TEICHOVA, An Economic Background to Munich, 1918-1938, London 1974; idem,
review of RANKI, Economy and Foreign Policy, in: American Historical Review 89 (1984), p.
1105.
[63] See chapters VIII, X, XI below.

The resource contraints on German policy also fit in with Overy's critique. In spite of German trade hegemony, actual successes in the penetration of the raw materials sector of southeastern Europe prior to the war were limited, suggesting that German policy required a longer period of time to achieve the desired dominance of the raw materials sectors. In the case of Rumania, the projected structural revolution embodied in the Wohlthat Treaty obviously required years to complete, not the months left to German policy in 1939.[64] Similarly, in both Yugoslavia and Rumania prior to the outbreak of war the overwhelming German presence still was not sufficient to break the proprietary rights of the international firms which dealt in raw materials: both Yugoslav and Rumanian governments were bound by treaty-like compacts with the international firms which required payment in strong currencies, not in the *Reichsmark*. In contrast to the recent work of Marguerat, Milward and Jones emphasize the relative weakness of the German position in Rumania. The fact that Germany had not yet achieved all of its goals in the spring of 1939 was hardly a source of comfort in Belgrade or Bucharest, let alone Paris or London. The question was precisely the nature of the long term goals: if proprietary rights within the the Danubian countries eluded the Nazi regime, this was a cause for increasing pressure upon the Danubian governments to create such sectors through special government measures. The Wohlthat Treaty was not regarded as an isolated special case, but the model for the future economic relations with the whole of east-central Europe.

As effective as the argument against the short war economic strategy is, Overy fails to provide a convincing synthesis of the existing historical literature. In terms of the Four Year Plan period during the years 1936-1939, Overy attempts to link Colonel Thomas' long range economic planning for "armaments in depth" with Hitler's large scale investment projects under the Four Year Plan. In fact, both Thomas and Schacht agreed that the pace of rearmament needed to be slowed in order to avoid overheating the economy and creating inflationary pressures.[65] The Four Year Plan was Hitler's answer to the Schacht-Thomas demand for retrenchment. If Hitler had accepted Schacht's demands for rationalization, he would have been forced to abandon super-protection of the agricultural sector, bring the Nazi party under the fiscal control of the ministries controlled or sympathetic to Schacht, and revise downwards the War Ministry's own plans for expansion of the German army. This kind of political and economic about-face would have contradicted the entire line of policy which Hitler had hitherto pursued.[66] The demand to slow down the pace of rearmament would have forced Hitler to replace Blomberg as War Minister in favor of a more moderate general. In the face of the foreign exchange crisis of the summer of 1936, Hitler choose the opposite tack and used the armed forces

---

[64] See chapters VIII and X below.

[65] See CARROLL, Design for Total War, for a discussion of Thomas' views. Thomas' critique of Hitler's policies can be summed up in his sarcastic remark in November, 1939: "We shall never defeat England with radio sets, vacuum cleaners, and kitchen utensils." Speech to the *Reichsgruppe Industrie*, November, 1939, THOMAS, Wehr- und Rüstungswirtschaft, p. 501.

[66] See the discussion above, section 6.

demand for an immediate and thorough resolution of the crisis to change the course of economic policy.

Overy's portrayal of Hitler as an economic ignoramous certainly continues an historical tradition begun by Alan Bullock, but hardly does justice to the capacity of this untutored man to master a wide range of reports prepared by IG Farben and synthesize this background material into the justly famous Four Year Plan Memorandum. The policies of the Four Year Plan not only reflected Hitler's inability to see that fortifications and the re-building of Berlin vied for economic resources but, as well, Hitler's political and social role as the spokesman of the rearmament effort. The demands which the separate branches of the armed forces made on the economy were never rationalized until the reforms of Todt and Speer in 1941 and 1942. This was part of an institutional structure which Hitler tolerated and the separate military services encouraged.

The ultimate effect of the piling up of separate demands upon the economy without priorities or ranking of projects was the scramble for labor and raw materials, where each separate Four Year plan administrator, each army, navy, or *Luftwaffe* procurement officer, and each contractor for the building projects vied with each other for Germany's resources.[67] The outcome of this Darwinian struggle could never be predicted in advance. Consequently, the results of the investments made in the Four Year Plan and rearmament drive seem unimpressive as Overy contends. This was less a consequence of Hitler's economic ignorance than the institutional structure of National Socialist Germany.

Secondly, Overy never challenges the use of national income statistics which led the revisionists to question the scale of German rearmament efforts. Klein describes the prewar German effort as "quite modest", meaning that in the context of the Cold War the German commitment of ten to fifteen percent of GNP for armaments seemed not excessive. "Klein's work might be put into better perspective if it is viewed not only as a scholarly evaluation of Germany's economic preparation for war but also as a Cold War plea for and justification of increased United States defense spending on conventional forces at levels most prewar economists would have considered appalling, if not economically disastrous."[68]

---

[67] In a full employment economy financial means were of little use in achieving a particular production goal. Consequently, the various procurement officers of the individual services and the project managers of the Four Year Plan stole workers from each other's projects: "In the summer of 1939, for example, the Navy began to poach building workers from the *Luftwaffe* on July 10 Thomas asked the Ministry of Labour to treat both sets of requirements as top priority . . . W. Stab [Thomas' war economic staff] found many cases of industrialists obtaining a 'control' number for the allocation of machinery for arms production and then using the machinery for other purposes . . . Todt had exactly the same experience with the civilian conscription of building workers. The examples could be multiplied indefinitely." Timothy W. MASON, National Socialist Policies Toward the German Working Classes, 1925-1939, D.Phil., St. Anthony's College, Oxford University 1971, p. 588. Unfortunately, Mason's path-breaking doctoral dissertation is not available in English; see, MASON, Sozialpolitik im Dritten Reich: Arbeiterklasse und Volksgemeinschaft, Opladen 1978.

[68] Mark LORRELL, The Politics of Economic Debate: Anglo-American Perceptions of Germany's Prepartions For War, 1937-1939, U.Ph.D., University of Washington 1976, p. 55.

In the context of the 1950's and 1960's United States spending on defense, where some 85 percent of government expenditures on goods and services went to defense and space (1960-1965), and the defense industry consumed 9 % of the net national product and employed 10 % of the work force, the German pre-war efforts do not appear outrageous.[69] Yet these comparisons with the post war period do not provide much insight into the dynamics of German policy because of the different historical nature of the two periods. The simple statistical inference on percentage of GNP devoted to armaments expenditure is inadequate to character-ize the aims and structure of German pre-war policy.

More appropriate is the comparison of German expenditures with the other Great Powers in the 1930's and with German pre-World War I policy. In terms of both pre-war and post-war estimates on percentage of national income spent on military projects, there is a remarkable convergence of opinion which belies the revisionist claim that most prewar observors concluded that Germany had a total war economy in peace:

Table 1   Pre-War Estimates of Military Expenditures as a Percent of National In-come

	1913 — 1914	1937[70]	1937[71]	1938[72]
Germany	3.8	14.8	15	20
France	5	9.3	11	9.1
Great Britain	3.8	5.04	6.6	6.5
USA	1	1.42	1.4	1.6

The postwar scholarship of Klein, Carroll, and Hillmann all center around the figure of 15 to 17 percent of GNP in 1938 for the German effort: 15 per cent

Although many of these statistics in the subsequent tables have long been published, I am indebted to Lorrel's work for pointing out the broad range of the pre-war discussion on Ger-many's rearmament and the similiarity in statistical conclusions of some of the more insightful pre-war economists with post-war scholarship.

[69] Ibid.; see also the exhaustively documented work by Jacques Gansler, former U.S. undersecretary of Defense: Jacques GANSLER, The Defense Industry, Cambridge/Mass. 1981.

[70] Alfred KÄHLER and Hans SPEIER, (eds.),War in Our Time, New York 1939. The 1913-1914 figures are from the same source. The basic statistical difference between the pre-war figures and those of the post-war lies in the use of national income by the former versus GNP by the later. National income will always be lower than GNP for the simple reason that certain taxes and transfer payments are excluded while GNP only considers gross capital formation not deducting depreciation as in national income.

[71] William T. STONE, Economic Consequences of Rearmament, in: Foreign Policy Reports (New York) XIV (October 1, 1938), p. 160.

[72] Economic Bulletin (London), January, 1939, p. 17.

(Klein), 17.2 (Carroll), 16.6 (Hillman).[73] The post war reevaluation of the other powers expenditures also falls within the range of the prewar estimates. Hillmann estimated military expenditures as per cent of "net available product" for the other great powers:
England: 7.9 percent; France: 7.9 percent; USA: 1.5 percent.[74]

The concern of prewar economists with the level of German expenditures is certainly understandable in view of the fact that Hitler was outspending the Wilhelmine state by a factor of four to one in terms of percentage of GNP. Contrary to Klein, this was not a modest effort. In terms of gross money expenditures, in dollars ·or local currency, the following tables tell a similiar story: a large German effort directed at catching up with the other powers, which was not underestimated by many prewar scholars (nor exaggerated into the total war economy thesis argued by some Marxists and liberals):

Table 2[75]   National Defense Expenditures (Millions of Dollars)

	1933	1934	1935	1936	1937	1938
Germany	299.5	381.5	2600.0	3600.0	4000.0	4400.0
Great Britain	455.5	480.6	595.6	846.9	1263.1	1693.3
France	678.8	582.7	623.8	834.4	909.2	1092.1
USA	540.3	710.0	911.7	964.9	992.1	1065.7

Table 3[76]   Military Expenditures (Millions of Local Currency)

	1934	1935	1936	1937	1938
Great Britain (pounds)	99.1	122.3	172.3	251.0	390.8
France (francs)	10802.7	10982.6	8276.6	9522.5	11186.5
USA (dollars)	803.1	806.4	932.6	1032.9	1131.5

[73] KLEIN, Preparations, p. 19; CARROLL, Design for Total War, p. 184; H. C. HILLMANN, The Comparative Strength of the Great Powers, in: Survey of International Affairs: The World in March 1939, Arnold TOYNBEE (ed.), London 1952, p. 456.

[74] HILLMANN, ibid., p.. 456.

[75] STONE, Economic Consequences, p. 159.

[76] England: League of Nations, Armaments Yearbook, 1939-1940, Geneva 1940, p. 74-75; France, ibid., p.161-162; USA, ibid., p. 366.

Table 4[77]   Military Expenditures (Millions of Dollars)

	1934	1935	1936	1937
England	490.1	602.8	845.6	1,254.1
France	712.9	751.4	701.7	729.5
USA	803.1	806.4	932.6	1,131.5
Germany (Economic Bulletin)	500.0	2,500.0	3,500.0	5,500.0
Germany (Foreign Policy Ass'n)	381.5	2,600.0	3,600.0	4,400.0
Germany (Carroll)	2,400.0	2,400.0	4,320.0	6,880.0

Even using the lowest possible figures for Germany and the best available estimates for the other powers, the extent of the German commitment cannot be mistaken. "German expenditures shoot up dramatically after 1935 and are consistently maintained at a level substantially in excess of the expenditure levels achieved by the other three powers. German military expenditures from 1935 to 1938 were indeed enormous in that they were two or three times England's size and some seven times those of France... After 1935 or 1936, Germany was spending significantly more, perhaps three or four times more, on the military than England, France, or the United States. For Germany, this represented a considerably larger percentage of national income than for the other aforementioned countries."[78]

Even if we could demonstrate that in some abstract way Hitler could have mobilized more of the GNP for armaments production before 1939 as the revisionist argument implies, this would do little to explain the origins of the Second World

---

[77] The French figures are roughly constant in dollars because of the declining value of the franc in terms of dollars (French devaluation and inflation). Carroll's estimates were converted into dollars at par value for comparison with Stone. The French effort, of course, has to been seen in a longer perspective. Both quantitatively and qualitatively the French armed forces matched up very well to the German adversary, with the exception of the air arm. In 1940, with the backing of the British Expeditionary Force, the British Navy, and British Air Force, the French forces were roughly equivalent to their German adversary. In many categories of weapons, such as tanks, the French possessed an absolute technological edge. Command and tactical deficiencies not material or technological inferiority doomed the Allied effort. Jeffrey Clarke provides a detailed comparison of the French and German armored forces on a weapon by weapon basis: Jeffrey CLARKE, Military Technology in Republican France: The Evolution of the French Armored Force, 1917-1940, U.Ph.D., Duke University 1969.

[78] LORRELL, Politics of Economic Debate, p. 58, 61.

War or its immediate outbreak in the summer of 1939. Thus, neither the revisionists nor Overy deal adequately with the domestic origins of German expansionism which T.W. Mason has so persuasively argued.[79] In fact, Mason has characterized Hitler's economic views and economic policy in terms very similiar to Overy (a point which is passed over by Overy): "Hitler in particular could not be persuaded that he could not have everything all at once. He insisted, for instance, that the West Wall be completed in six months, and that Speer press ahead with the rebuilding of Germany's city centers at the same time; in February 1939 Speer was given a large number of immigrant workers and in October he was allowed to purchase 8 million *Reichsmark* worth of building materials, in order that he could hoard them and be in a position to restart construction work in Berlin the moment the war ended." Again, Overy misses the mark when he attributes the *Blitzkrieg* economic thesis as defined by Klein and Milward to Mason: "Germany, under National Socialism, was setting out to conquer the world, without changing the life-patterns of the greater part of the working population. The main reason for such contradictory ambitions lay not in those positive, forward looking components of Hitler's *Blitzkrieg* strategy, but in the anxiety which held the political leadership back from imposing additional sacrifices on the mass of people."[80]

In Mason's view, the Reich faced a many-faceted crisis in the years 1938-1939, whose resolution pushed Germany towards a war of plunder. The forced pace of the rearmament drive combined with the huge investments in Four Year Plan, West Wall, and *Autobahn* created a situation where the German economy was facing shortages of finance, labor, and a vulnerable balance of trade. The sacking of Schacht and his close associates at the *Reichsbank* in January, 1939, was but a further indication that Hitler would not permit the lack of financial means to inhibit the expansionist course of German policy. Yet, the New Finance Plan of March, 1939, which used tax credit certificates for the payment of armaments expenditures, could provide only a very short term solution to the rising tide of government debt.

In contrast to the view of Klein, contemporary economists did not believe that the central isssue "was whether or not large scale deficits would lead to inflation and financial ruin." The problem in 1938-39 was not "the total debt itself" according to George Katona, but "the rapid rate of increase and the fact that the monthly deficit of 600 million *Reichsmark* was incurred in face of sharply rising tax receipts."[81] Mason points out that, in view of this situation, Posse, state secetrary in

[79] MASON, National Socialist Policies. Also: idem, Innere Krise und Angriffskrieg , 1938/1939, in: Friedrich FORSTMEIER and Hans-Erich VOLKMANN, (ed.), Wirtschaft und Rüstung am Vorabend des Zweiten Weltkrieges, Düsseldorf 1975, pp. 158-188; idem, Labour in the Third Reich, in: Past and Present 33 (1966); idem, Some Orgins of the Second World War, in: Past and Present 29 (1964).

[80] MASON, National Socialist Policies, p. 589.

[81] George KATONA, Why Germany is Still A Threat, in: Barrons (New York) XVIII (October 24, 1938), p. 8. Ironically, Katona's estimates on German governmental debt are almost identical with Klein's conservative post war estimates: Katona: 22.5 billion RM (to August, 1938); Klein: 25.1 billion RM (to end 1938); KLEIN, Preparations, p. 8. Katona was a German emigré economist who taught at the New School for Social Research (New York).

the RWM, was already contemplating debt repudiation in the spring of 1939.[82] Before the outbreak of war, no new initiatives were taken to rememdy the financial situation, and even after September, 1939, draconian financial measures were avoided. The commitment of public funds to a program of expansion caused national income to increase faster than industrial production, a permanent shortage of foreign currency, *Exportmüdigkeit* (inablity of German firms to compete on the world market because of home demand), and acute shortages of labor and raw materials.[83]

In the agricultural sector, Hitler's policies led to an increased flight from the land and a chronic shortage of agriculutural wage laborers. Mason estimated that some 500,000 workers had left the land between June, 1933, and June, 1938.[84] This resulted in a 16 percent drop in the agricultural labor forces, which the small peasant farmer could not make up with family labor. When the war against Poland was launched, school children were drafted to bring in the harvest. In the industrial sector, the labor shortage was equally acute by May, 1938. From the middle of 1938, there was an ever increasing tide of complaints over missed deadlines, unfulfilled export contracts, construction projects abandoned in mid completion. Carl Krauch complained that the shortage of labor endangered the completion of the synthetic petroleum industry, while the *Luftwaffe* bemoaned the shortage of aircraft engineers estimated at 2,600.[85] In the Ruhr, exports of coal were curtailed because of the shortage of 30,000 coal miners.

The regime faced the choice of either rationalizing production or the massive introduction of women into the labor force. For ideological and political reasons neither option was selected. This refusal to make hard choices led, in Mason's view, to a crisis of the whole ruling system.[86] Rising hourly and weekly wages were pumping at least 200 million more marks per week into the the hands of consumers by the spring of 1939. In order to curtail consumer industries and use the labor force and plant space for the rearmament effort, the German government had to confront the freezing of this enormous purchasing power in the hands of consumers. The obvious methods were increased taxes or sytematic wage and salary cuts.[87] Again, Hitler did not force these measures because of the fear of domestic discontent. In the face of this fear of political opposition and the full employment economy, the German government also encountered increasing demoralization,

---

[82] MASON, Innere Krise, p. 160; idem, National Socialist Policies, p. 586, p. 605, citing Posse's Memorandum of March 1939, BA-MA, Wi IF 5, file 420/3.

[83] MASON, Innere Krise, p. 164.

[84] MASON, Innere Krise, p.166; idem, National Socialist Policies, p. 593-594.

[85] MASON, Innere Krise, p. 168.

[86] MASON, Innere Krise, p. 169.

[87] MASON, National Socialist Policies, p. 601. During a meeting of the Reich Defense Council in the autumn of 1938, Göring defended his refusal to restrict the consumer goods industry by remarking that wages were so high that any increase in the output of consumer goods would be bound to cause inflation because too much purchasing power would be chasing too few goods. Mason notes that Göring said nothing about cutting wages.

unrest, slackness, and discontent within the labor force. The increaed use of police terror methods from 1936 onwards did little to resolve the crisis.[88]

In view of the acute tensions within the domestic political economy, Mason argues that the range of foreign policy maneuver of the regime was quite small. The "inner victory" sought by Hitler to prevent a recurrence of the November 1918 revolution was successful insofar as the left wing parties and trade unions had been crushed by police terror, but the confidence of Hitler in the enthusiasm of the working class for a war of expansion was undermined by continual problems which the regime faced in the labor market.[89] Even after the war broke out, measures needed to bring the labor market in line with the needs of the war economy had not been completed by December, 1939: an increased war income tax on wages, a halt to wage increases, an end to all remaining labor protection legislation, an across the board cut of 10 % in wages, and the ending of vacations.

Even worse, in order to increase morale on the home front, the wives of soldiers were given increased benefits which resulted in a further loss of 450,000 working women from the labor market at a time when the labor shortage was even more acute than in the spring of 1939.[90] In this situation there was, in Mason's view, neither a tactical sovereignty nor a calculated policy of risk, but rather a situation which was simply out of control.[91] The munitions supply was barely enough to cover the short Polish campaign. By October 8, 1939, there were only enough munitions left to cover the needs of one third of the army's divisions for four weeks, not to speak of shortages for the *Luftwaffe* and motorized transport.[92]

In this crisis situation, Hitler's original intention to prepare for a war which was to break out in 1943 was impossible to carry through. Only expansion abroad, including war, offered the opportunity to justify increased oppression at home, which in turn would enable the regime to carry out the armaments program and solve the economic crisis.[93] The unrestrained expansionist policy at home circumscribed the diplomatic maneuverability of the regime, amd pushed Hitler ever closer to the brink, to resort to war as a means of ameliorating the unresolved contradictions of the domestic political economy. Thus, Polish workers and war prisoners would help solve the German agriculutural labor shortage, and Polish agriculture assisted in remedying the import deficits of the German economy.[94]

The rearmament efforts and Four Year Plan produced not a total war economy nor a *Blitzkrieg* economy, but a plunder economy in which Germany would either gain world power and conquer, or perish in the effort: "As was the case with the economy as a whole, the armaments drive was superimposed upon a non-military supply and demand structure, which in every respect was as large in absolute terms

---

[88] MASON, Innere Krise, p. 176; idem, National Socialist Policies, p. 602.
[89] MASON, Innere Krise, p. 175; idem, National Socialist Policies, p. 597.
[90] MASON, National Socialist Policies, p. 622.
[91] MASON, Innere Krise, p. 181; idem, National Socialist Policies, p. 583.
[92] MASON, Innere Krise, p. 181.
[93] Ibid.
[94] MASON, National Socialist Policies, p. 624-625, 627-628.

as it had been in the later 1920's. In the labour market — as in the capital market, in the allocation of foreign exchange, the production of consumer gooods, the size of industrial undertakings, etc. — the guiding principle of the government's policies was addition to resources, not diversion of them. By 1939, if not before, economic stategy had driven society and the economy into a cul-de-sac, at the end of which lay either crisis and collapse, or the decision in favour of a break-out by means of armed force."[95]

Mason admits that the unresolved contradictions of German political economy only provided the context of Hitler's decision for war and do not explain the long term origins of the Second World War.[96] In terms of Germany's foreign economic policy, as exemplified in the case studies of Rumania and Yugoslavia, the Nazi regime provided a means of satisfying the export demands of German industry with the political demands for the reassertion of German power. The greater the German power, however, the greater the political tensions in eastern Europe. Chamberlain's forlorn hope that Hitler could be diverted into peaceful economic expansion towards the southeast and be preoccupied with empire building in eastern Europe for a generation foundered on the scope of German aims in the area. In response to the occupation of Prague and the Wohlthat Treaty, Chamberlain began to realize both the extent of German ambition and the methods which Hitler would use to realize his objectives.[97] As David Kaiser has recently pointed out, Chamberlain did not object so much to Germany's dominance in eastern Europe as he did to how she carried out her policy of hegemony.[98]

Yet, if the German government would not be bound by a contract or agreement, what hope could there be for the maintenance of peace in the area or the preservation of British economic interests? German aims in Yugoslavia and Rumania before the war reveal quite clearly that Chamberlain's tardy realization of the radical character of German policy was anything but off the mark. Only capitulation by the Polish government could have insured peace in 1939. The ultimate price would not have been mere border rectifications, the *Autobahn*, and return of Danzig to Germany, but the despatch of Wohlthat to Warsaw with a new draft economic treaty

[95] MASON, National Socialist Policies, p. 642. Other scholars who have emphasized the inherent instablity of Nazi economic policy and the tendencies toward "conquer or perish" economic policies: Wolfgang SAUER, Die Mobilmachung der Gewalt, in: Karl Dietrich BRACHER et. al. (eds.), Die Nationalsozialistische Machtergreifung, Cologne 1960, p. 744 ff.; Gustav STOLPER et. al., The German Economy: 1870 to the Present, New York 1967, pp. 134-146; Edward L. HOMZE, Foreign Labor in Nazi Germany, Princeton 1967, pp. 10-11, 299-301, 304 ff.

[96] MASON, Innere Krise, p. 182.

[97] "Chamberlain wrote privately on March 26 that should Germany successfully impose upon Bucharest 'a new commerical agreeement which in effect puts Roumania at her mercy', Britain would have no option but to present Germany with an ultimatum. 'We are not strong enough ourselves and we cannot command sufficient strength elsewhere to present Germany with an overwhelming force. Our ultimatum would therefore mean war and I would never be responsible for presenting it.'" KAISER, Economic Diplomacy, p. 301, citing the Chamberlain papers, Manchester University Library, March 26, 1939.

[98] Ibid. p. 302.

which would have demanded total subordinance of the Polish economy to German needs. The moderation of Hitler's political demands against Poland, for which Chamberlain had some sympathy, concealed a broader purpose to which the Polish government refused to acquiesce. The decision for war, then, lay in the hands of those who had the courage and fortitude to resist German aggression, because Hitler's crisis diplomacy left the German government with no way to exit gracefully from a situation once the ultimatums had been presented. "Hitler knew only two possibilities; Germany would either be a world power or would cease to exist. This unfoundedness of goals after 1939 increased German order over the Danube Basin so much that it multiplied the internal and international forces working against it. This conception developed *Großraumwirtschaft* in such a way that it deprived the goals of the slightest rationality, bringing to the surface their only significant feature: the nemesis of National-Socialist rule."[99]

[99] RANKI, Economy and Foreign Policy, p. 193.

CHAPTER VII

THE FOUR YEAR PLAN AND GERMAN BUSINESS IN YUGOSLAVIA: COMPETITION AND CONFLICT WITHIN THE "INFORMAL EMPIRE", 1937-38

1. Introduction

The German trade drive in southeastern Europe has been traditionally characterized as a prelude to the New Order in Europe. Varying interpretations assign different priorities to political and economic factors as the motivating force but there is unanimity on the imperialist character of German expansionism. The search for evidence of German "fifth column" activity, subversion, support of *Volksdeutsche* and native fascist movements, has tended to ignore the methods by which Germany furthered its aims within the conservative ruling classes of southeastern Europe. The image of a rampant Nazi juggernaut blindly distributing largess to fascist sects and stirring up *Volksdeutsche* discontent is hardly applicable to southeastern Europe. Even in the Czechoslovakian instance, Ronald Smelser has demonstrated Hitler's lack of interest in the Sudeten German movement until it could be integrated into his larger strategy.

From 1937 to the outbreak of war in 1939, Yugoslavia was a laboratory for the techniques and interests that would later characterize the Nazi New Order in Europe. In early 1937, German influence was so firmly established in Yugoslavia that Hitler and Göring could afford to permit two competing foreign policies in Belgrade, one administered by the Wilhelmstraße in consultation with other ministries, the other conducted by Franz Neuhausen[1], head of the *Auslandsorganisation* of the NSDAP in Yugoslavia and the personal Belgrade representative of Göring as head of the Four Year Plan. The byzantine intrigue and disparate tendencies of the National Socialist state were exported to foreign territory in this unresolved con-

---

[1] To date, there has been no extensive research into the important role that Neuhausen played in Yugoslav-German relations. Kaiser noted that "Göring personally supervised new grain purchases from Eastern Europe. He had always taken a lively political interest in the area; in 1934-1935 he designated Franz Neuhausen [sic] as his personal representative in Belgrade." KAISER, Economic Diplomacy, p. 155. Also Von Bagnell has commented on the lack of documentation concerning Neuhausen: "It is also known that the German Consul General Neuhausen in Belgrade, who was Göring's delegate and responsible for the Four Year Plan for Yugoslavia, often held confidential meetings with influential German politicians and played a much more important role in the economic sphere than did von Heeren. Yet no records of such meetings have ever been discovered. The possiblity exists, therefore, that when such conversations took place among the representatives of the German minority and the Reich, such transactions were also executed." BAGNELL, Influence, p.31.

tradiction of German political economy — a contradiction which would later be one of the basic elements of the New Order in Europe. "The war of each against everyone" (Jodl's characterization) for raw materials and manpower was character- istic of the rearmament economy. To ensure good political relations with the Reich, Yugoslavia tolerated the informal activities of Neuhausen, allowing him and the *Mitteleuropäischer Wirtschaftstag* (MWT) to scramble for Yugoslav raw materials. Germany's political and economic influence was so great in Yugoslavia before the war that Hitler and Göring were confident that such activities would not disturb good relations, giving virtual *carte blanche* to state and party agencies.

German influence can be defined by both trade dominance and Yugoslavia's poli- tical neutrality. Relations between them, however, require a new framework for analysis. Neither the traditional primacy of foreign affairs, emphasizing the ration- ality of the foreign office and the priority of political considerations in policy mak- ing, nor Eckart Kehr's primacy of domestic politics, stressing the social and economic pressure of domestic economic interests in forming foreign policy, are entirely satisfactory, either together or separately. For this period of Yugoslav-Ger- man relations, to consider diplomatic and trade relations as existing between two *sovereign* states, even allowing for the influence of domestic economic pressure groups, distorts analysis of the history of German policy.

German expansionism was so ubiquitous and German self-confidence so bound- less, that the best framework for analysis is the concept of "informal empire", where an imperial power secures its interests by cultivating a native political elite without resorting to direct administrative measures. Gustav Schlotterer, a high- ranking Economics Ministry bureaucrat, later aptly characterized this policy in reference to Rumania. "We do not wish to rule in Rumania, only to assert and secure our interests."[2] In the halcyon days before the outbreak of war, such goals involved a scramble by all and sundry for control of Yugoslav raw material resources and contracts with the Yugoslav state.

2. *Neuhausen versus Max Hahn and the Mitteleuropäischer Wirtschaftstag*

Franz Neuhausen, the head of the foreign organization of the Nazi Party in Yugoslavia since 1933, was made the Belgrade representative of the Four Year Plan in autumn, 1936, primarily because of his personal friendship with Göring. Very little documentation of his activities has survived, but inferences can be drawn from his conflict with official agencies and German business. Neuhausen was intimately involved in the TU escapade but agile enough to escape the consequences.[3] If the

---

[2] 'Bericht über die Sitzung an RWim betr. Rumänien am 12. Oktober, 1940', by Breyhan, October 14, 1940, BA, R 2/30703.

[3] "Neuhausen kennt die hiesigen Verhältnisse sehr gut und Mißgriffe wie die 'T.U.' sind von ihm nicht zu befürchten." Heeren (DG Belgrad) to Ritter, March 5, 1937, PA, Ha Pol, IVa, Jugoslawien, Handel l3A, Regierungsausschüsse, Bd. 1. At this time Heeren returned 40,000 dinars in subsidies intended for the radical elements in the *Volksdeutsche* community. From this point on Claus (VDA) "arranged the illegal financial deals between the VDA and the Nazi organzisations of the German minority." BAGNELL, Influence, p. 128.

TU had been successful, Neuhausen would have been in a position similar to that of Johannes Bernhardt in Spain and J. A. Kulenkampf in Brazil, Nazi businessmen heading monopoly trading organizations. Bernhardt and Kulenkampf both made substantial fortunes from their activities and played an important role in forming German policy.[4] Whether or not Neuhausen consciously imitated these two, he did hope to subordinate the economic activities of the German legation and German big business to the administration of his office. By cultivating Stojadinović and through his personal friendship with Göring, Neuhausen found it easy to bypass Heeren's German legation, but this informal diplomacy could not give him policy control over big business, which was primarily represented by the director of the MWT, Max Hahn. Neuhausen fought long and hard to remove Hahn from the scene and become the exclusive representative of German efforts to control of Yugoslav raw materials.

The Economics Ministry's immediate suspicions about Neuhausen's activities did not prevent Heeren from trying to live with the situation; he was, after all, a diplomat.[5] Heeren was informed of Neuhausen's appointment to the Mixed Commission in mid-February, 1937, but the disunity of the German government did not allow the German legation in Belgrade to inform the Yugoslav government.[6] Such official confusion did not prevent Neuhausen from acting as an official representative of the Reich and he certainly told Stojadinović of his appointment. Heeren did not try to circumscribe Neuhausen until Neuhausen attacked Max Hahn and War Minister Blomberg became involved.

If Neuhausen were to become the exclusive representative of Nazi economic policy in Yugoslavia, he had to prevent Hahn from playing an active role in Yugoslavia. As director of the MWT, the most important pressure group favoring an active trade policy in southeastern Europe, Hahn was certain to overlap Neuhausen's activities. In Rumania, the MWT had been instrumental in creating a favorable press climate for Germany by subsidizing Popescu, the editor of Rumania's leading newspaper *Universul,* and the MWT in Yugoslavia was actively creating a German-owned raw material sector. As the Four Year Plan representative, Neuhausen resented Hahn's presence in areas clearly belonging to the Four Year Plan.

By early May, 1937, Neuhausen was ready. At an Economics Ministry meeting, he questioned the propriety of Max Hahn remaining active in German-Yugoslav trade relations while functioning as a reserve officer in the *Abwehr* (counterintelligence) department of the War Ministry. Neuhausen expressed concern that the foreign press might discover Hahn's role in the *Abwehr* and use the information to embarrass the Yugoslav government. War Minister Blomberg reacted sharply to

---

[4] On Kulenkampf and the trade organization *Sociedade Internacional de Comercio,* see Stanley E. HILTON, Brazil and the Great Power Rivalry in South America, 1934-1939, U.Ph.D., Univ. of Texas at Austin 1969, pp. 175-199.

[5] Dr. Spitta (RWM) immediately complained that too many agencies were representing German political and economic interests in Belgrade. Spitta (DG Belgrad) to Ritter, January 11, 1937, PA, Ha Pol, Handakten Wiehl, Jugoslawien, Bd. 3.

[6] Clodius to Heeren (DG Belgrad), February 18, 1937, PA, Ha Pol, Jugoslawien, Handel l3A, Regierungsausschüsse, Bd. 1.

Neuhausen's ploy. "The choice of Dr. Hahn is therefore based upon the most careful considerations. The economic-political relations between Germany and southeastern Europe are being extended more and more to the armaments-political area, so that there is nothing unusual to be seen from abroad in that Dr. Hahn is directly associated with agencies of the War Ministry."[7] To Neurath, Blomberg characterized Neuhausen's opinions as neither "admissible" nor "factual" and made it clear that any information leak in Belgrade concerning Hahn would be attributed to Neuhausen. It was Neuhausen's "duty" to make sure that measures to defend the Fatherland were not "betrayed." A week later, Neurath wrote Neuhausen giving unequivocal support to Blomberg, even repeating Blomberg's letter to him and ending on the same ominous note. "I request, therefore, that this [Hahn's position at the War Ministry] be kept strictly confidential in the course of your further activity in the area of economic relations between Yugoslavia and Germany."[8]

In August, Blomberg was again compelled to defend Hahn against Neuhausen. "The accusation which General Consul Neuhausen levels at Dr. Hahn, that in the activity of Dr. Hahn the common good for Germany stands in contradiction to the self-interest of the person, is not proved by anything and is in my view not correct."[9] Between the first and second letters, Blomberg asked General von Faber du Faur, military attaché in Belgrade, for his opinion of Neuhausen's activities. Based on Faber's observations, Blomberg urged that Neuhausen be put under the authority of the legation so that the divided responsibility in Belgrade could be clarified.

In a minute attached to Blomberg's letter, Faber outlined the situation in Belgrade. Admitting that he saw Neuhausen only infrequently, Faber characterized his relations with him as "correct" but not as having "the closest and best understanding." He said that in fact he did not know in detail what Neuhausen was doing in Belgrade. State Secretary Neumann of the Four Year Plan had defined Neuhausen's role as merely supportive, but Neuhausen claimed responsibility for the whole area of economic relations between the two countries. No one in Belgrade knew whether or not Neuhausen was subordinate to the legation, but for his part, he would unhesitatingly recommend such subordination. Faber ended by endorsing Hahn, maintaining that the military could not do better than maintain its trust in him. "General von Faber confirmed that Dr. Hahn is an extraordinarily well informed and well established personality, and that the *Abwehr* could not find a better confidant for Yugoslavia."[10]

Army and War Ministry pressure forced the Wilhelmstraße into action and in late August, the Wilhelmstraße State Secretary, Mackensen, brought the whole matter to the attention of State Secretary Neumann of the Four Year Plan. Neumann readily conceded the War Ministry's and Wilhelmstraße's criticism of Neuhausen, but pointed out that when in Berlin the man enjoyed "unmediated and direct contact

---

[7] Blomberg (RKM) to Neurath, May 19, 1937, ibid.

[8] Neurath to Blomberg (RKM), May 26, 1937, copy of letter to Neuhausen enclosed, ibid.

[9] Blomberg (RKM) to Neurath, August 5, 1938, ibid.

[10] Minute, August 4, 1937, summarizing a telephone conversation with General Faber du Faur, ibid.

with Minister President Göring." Under such circumstances Neumann was unsure of what Neuhausen's responsibilities were and skeptical that he could be controlled.

He has been entrusted with special tasks in Yugoslavia from him [Göring] in his capacity as Reich Air Minister. In the economic area his special assignment arose in that he was to liquidate the collapsed *Technische Aufbauunion* of *Gauleiter* Koch, and to salvage what remained to be salvaged. Whether in conjunction with this or along with continuing and even newer economic relations in Yugoslavia he initiated or promoted, *Staatsrat* Neumann does not know, but he does not exclude the possibility. Minister President Göring very often gives orders directly without the participation of the concerned agencies under him; therefore even he — *Staatsrat* Neumann — cannot fully perceive how the responsibilities of Herr Neuhausen practically will appear.[11]

Neumann and Mackensen were convinced that the situation demanded immediate action but neither believed there was much chance that Göring would take a written position on the matter. The best they could do was propose that Neurath personally ask Göring during the Nürnberg Party Rally in September. Routine and order, the finest traditions of Prussian civil service, bowed before Göring's administrative vagaries and private empire building.[12]

In September, the Wilhelmstraße tried a new ploy and disciplined Neuhausen through the *Auslandsorganisation* of the Nazi Party. Although able to prevail on the AO to recall Neuhausen for consultations, subsequent developments would show the Wilhelmstraße that Neuhausen remained outside its control.[13]

Although the combined pressure of the military, business, and the Wilhelmstraße could not bring Neuhausen to heel, Hahn's support from the military and MWT prevented Neuhausen from controlling German development of Yugoslav raw materials. Neuhausen was not able to undercut Hahn in the raw materials sector until the question of petroleum leases arose in 1939, but even then the dual policy and structure remained. The official legation in Belgrade represented the authority of the Wilhelmstraße and other ministries while Neuhausen represented the Four Year Plan, the Air Ministry and other branches of the Göring empire. For Göring, there was no contradiction between building a National Socialist *Großraumwirtschaft* and building his own private empire. The emerging structure of the Nazi *Großraumwirtschaft* was less a result of planning than of a struggle by forces within the German establishment and was largely determined by a free-for-all between the various branches of German industry, banks, and party-state-personal combines similar to Göring's, all in search of market shares, raw materials, and, eventually, capital penetration. Neuhausen played a key role in this Darwinian struggle, sometimes representing Göring's personal interests (the Reich Air Ministry and *Reichsverband der deutschen Luftfahrtindustrie*) and sometimes representing Reich policy (the Four Year Plan), but always with his eye on the main chance for personal aggrandizement.[14]

[11] Memorandum by Mackensen, August 23, 1937, ibid.

[12] Ibid.

[13] See, in particular, Neuhausen's important role in the struggle for oil leases during 1939: Chapter VIII.

[14] In 1943, Neuhausen had the singular distinction among Nazi proconsuls abroad of being removed from office and jailed for corruption, incompetence, and malfeasance. Even Göring's influence did not prevent Neuhausen from being jailed for a time.

3. *Max Hahn, the MWT, and the Struggle for Raw Materials Independence*

Initially, the MWT concentrated almost exclusively on trade expansion. In the doldrums of the Depression it consistently advocated active trade expansion in southeastern Europe, and with the growing success of this policy it began to expand its activities. Along with helping organize and finance a campaign in Rumania to subvert the press, the MWT, in cooperation with IG Farben, was a prime sponsor of soja bean cultivation in Rumania, Bulgaria, and Yugoslavia. Yugoslavia became the most important field of MWT activity after 1936, as it attempted to create a German-owned raw materials sector, concentrating on ores. Although it seems curious that the MWT should choose ore and Yugoslavia rather than petroleum and Rumania, creation of a German sector in Rumanian petroleum, despite interest during the 1930s, became a matter of practical policy only in 1939 as a part of the Wohlthat Treaty.

The search for a toehold in the Yugoslav raw materials sector required chasing down even the most unpromising leads. The *Abwehr*, military counterintelligence, once asked the Economics Ministry to explore the possibility of using an obscure Russian colonel, a relative of Prince Paul, as mediator in securing copper, manganese, and antimony. In another case the Wilhelmstraße requested the legation in Belgrade to investigate the possibilities of a White Russian adventurer, one Fürst Awaloff Bermont, who had made broad claims of his influence over Prince Paul.[15] This avid pursuit of shady characters was part of a larger quest for *Vertrauensmänner*, confidants who could provide Germany with the expertise and contacts necessary to penetrate the raw materials sector. The efforts of the MWT were not as absurd as they first appear. Max Hahn did find trustworthy agents and eventually established several ore companies.

The MWT, the Economics Ministry, and the Wilhelmstraße had a common goal in circumventing Anglo-French domination of the raw materials sector, either by organizing a German purchasing firm to secure the output of the smaller Yugoslav producers or by directly investing German capital and purchasing small Yugoslav mines. Kisoveć, a Yugoslav lawyer who became an important German agent, maintained that Germany could expect great success if an ore purchasing firm were organized.

> As the sale of ores is not yet organized in Yugoslavia and the individual mines have no real ties, a joint stock company could immediately acquire large amounts of ores and have a considerably large turnover. It is self-evident that in the course of such business activity instances would quickly arise where it would pay to lease the appropriate mines or even to acquire them by means of purchase.[16]

Almost immediately Max Hahn and the MWT adopted this, together with a project to gain control of the antimony deposits. The owner of the French owned Lissa fields, one Giroux, was interested in selling. The English firm of Cookson had

---

[15] Heeren (DG Belgrad) to AA, January 25, 1937, PA, Ha Pol, Kriegsgerät, Jugoslawien, Bd. 1.

[16] Dr. V. Kisoveć to DG Belgrad, October 13, 1936; enclosure in Reinhardt (RWM) to AA, November 25, 1936, PA, Ha Pol, IVa, Jugoslawien, Industrie 6, Bergbau, Bd. 1.

caught wind of Hahn's negotiations and were trying to prevent a sale to German interests, and a rival French group had also come forward with an offer. Simultaneously, the powerful *Mines de Bor* group was threatening a successful securing of the antimony deposits at Krupanja by a German group. "This incident demonstrates as well the intensity with which foreign capital falls upon the few ore concessions which remain free in Yugoslavia."[17]

The Krupanja deposits had a distinct advantage in being richer but Hahn favored concentrating German efforts on the Lissa concession because it was already being exploited, however primitively. The terms of sale of the Lissa deposits were an added attraction; the Giroux interests had already reduced the price to 22 million dinars, hoping for a quick sale. Hahn decided that acquiring the Lissa mine had numerous advantages, including immediately available production of two tons per day. Excess production after modernization could be exported for free currency to purchase the Kostajnik-Zajaca fields. Acquiring the Lissa mine would also be a breakthrough in Germany's struggle for raw materials independence. "Kostajnik-Zajaca and Lissa in German hands constitutes the antimony monopoly in Europe."[18]

Despite Hahn's authority and enthusiasm, Heeren, German minister in Belgrade, was not prepared to give blanket endorsement to the MWT projects. He did not believe that formation of a German ore trading company was a necessary prerequisite to influencing smaller Yugoslav mines to export to Germany and, further, the plan did not provide for the reorganization of the smaller mines necessary to compensate for their poor marketing organizations. Although he thought the plan needed further detailed work, Heeren did recommend pursuing the project along purely private lines.[19]

Heeren's lack of enthusiasm did not deter either Kisovec or Hahn. They repeated their earlier arguments.[20] Kisovec even warned that failing to take prompt action could lead to the exclusion of German interests from the project. Berlin was interested in the Hahn-Kisovec project but the practical difficulties involved in mobilizing the required capital, and concern about a possible Yugoslav political reaction led to the cautious approach recommended by Heeren. By the late summer, however, the Reich government had approved Hahn's plan, without allowing, of course, any actual capital transfer from Germany to Yugoslavia via the export of foreign exchange. Germany's passive trade balance with Yugoslavia excluded any possibility of using a commodity export surplus to finance capital expenditure

---

[17] Max Hahn (Berlin) to Clodius, October 30, 1936, ibid.

[18] Ibid.

[19] Heeren (DG Belgrad) to AA, January 8, 1937, ibid. The legation was particularly concerned about assuaging Yugoslav sensibilities in the aftermath of the TU affair. Minute by Hess, March 12, 1937, PA, Gesandtschaft Belgrad, Fach 81, G 2, Wirtschaftliches Geheim, Bd. 3.

[20] Kisovec to Hess, January 28, 1937, ibid.

within Yugoslavia, posing a dilemma resolved only by the timely intervention of IG Farben.[21]

The fertile minds at IG had an ingenious plan: IG would export 450,000 marks in chemicals and pharmaceuticals to be marketed in France by the CMC firm. CMC in turn would liquidate its debt to IG by making arrangements with the IG subsidiary, *Juganil*, so that the dinar equivalent of 450,000 marks would be paid into the dinar account of the *Reichsbank* in Belgrade. This complicated procedure assured Hahn the capital necessary to purchase the Lissa antimony deposits. A problem arose when the earlier fears of the German legation that Yugoslavia would react hostilely to this maneuver proved entirely accurate.[22] Germany was diverting goods for cash or credit to third markets when Germany's clearing debt to Yugoslavia ran into millions of marks and the German government would have acted horrified at any suggestion that Germany use such transactions to pay its arrears. Resistance by the Yugoslav National Bank was apparently unsuccessful and Hahn and the MWT apparently did acquire the Lissa deposits.

In comparison to American, English, and French ownership or domination of the world's raw material production, the Hahn antimony project — all 450,000 marks of it — was tiny. Ignoring for the moment the extent of the western interests outside Europe, how many hundreds of such projects would be necessary before Germany reached parity with American, French, and English interests even in Danubian Europe? However, the situation in 1937 was not absurd, but grim. Nazi Germany, controlling no foreign raw materials resources and having little cash to pay for such commodities, was nevertheless determined to use its economic and political power to create a secure German-owned raw materials sector in Danubian Europe. The often proclaimed ultimate goal of parity with the western powers was necessarily consigned to the distant future, but it was on the agenda.

The Hahn antimony project reflected the contradiction between the extent of German ambition and the meager economic resources available for mobilization. By 1937, despite the successes of the Schacht trade expansion program in Latin America and southeastern Europe, the German foreign exchange reserves were dangerously depleted. The pace of the rearmament economy constantly outstripped the import of raw materials from these areas. The Four Year Plan was designed to make up the shortfall in the raw materials that Schacht's trade policy had failed to provide, but the experiences of 1936-38 showed that even the New Plan/Four Year Plan combination was inadequate to meet Germany's raw materials needs. Germany had no capital to export. Domestic capital formation consequent upon the Four Year Plan was overcommitted and the rearmament economy strain on heavy industry made it highly unlikely that Germany could achieve an export surplus sufficient to finance large-scale capital investments in Danubian Europe. The method used in

---

[21] Ibid. Although observers have characterized the MWT as a tool of IG (IG was the single most active firm in its support), the MWT's support was far more broadbased. Both the soja bean and Yugoslav ore projects would have been all but impossible without IG's backing.

[22] Minute by Hess, March 12, 1937, and unsigned memorandum, September 3, 1937, PA, Gesandtschaft Belgrad, Fach 81, G 2, Wirtschaftliches Geheim, Bd. 3.

the Hahn project — export to third markets — could not be a general tactic to mobilize capital. Even so, German business and the German government were determined to create a raw materials base in Danubian Europe. The structural inadequacies of the economy predisposed them to consider creating the German raw materials sector by forced appropriation of French, British, and American interests, by swapping stock of German companies with state-owned enterprises in southeastern Europe, by direct expropriation during occupation of southeastern Europe, or by indirect expropriation through political pressure, forcing a client state to put up the funds for a German project. This latter method more properly belongs to the period following the outbreak of war and the institution of the New Order, but the roots of the policy can be seen in the Hahn/MWT projects in prewar Yugoslavia.

4. Armaments

Although Yugoslavia was the "model" for German relations with other states in east-central Europe, German progress in selling armaments to Yugoslavia lagged behind successes elsewhere.[23] The reason lay with the Yugoslav officer corps. The General Staff offered no opposition to Stojadinović's political and economic accommodation with Germany, but drew the line at purchasing German military hardware. Stojadinović was sincere when, in June, 1936, he told Schacht that he would work for purchase of armaments from Germany, but he had to contend with powerful opposition from a francophile General Staff having no desire to equip its forces with both Czech and German weapons. The purchase of arms would also symbolize a political rapprochement with Germany, which the General Staff opposed for the traditional reasons of loyalty and affection for France.[24]

Apparently there was an abrupt change of heart in Yugoslavia during February, 1937. Hess, the German trade attaché, was taken by surprise by the interest of Yugoslav War Minister General Marić in German antiaircraft and antitank artillery. The general indicated that if credit were extended, the Yugoslav market would open up to Germany, and he appeared interested in German assistance in creating a domestic armaments industry. Whether it was German disinterest or Yugoslav coyness that made this initial feeler come to naught is not clear.

[23] German armament sales to revisionist Hungary and Bulgaria were political liabilities without a successful policy in former allied countries. The first breakthrough for Germany came in Greece, followed by Rumania in 1937. Yugoslavia lagged behind significantly. Early attempts to sell naval hardware were not successful. Heeren (DG Belgrad) to AA, October 24, 1935 and November 23, 1935, PA, Ha Pol, Handakten Wiehl, Jugoslawien, Bd. 3. Heeren warned against pressuring Yugoslavia to award a contract to Krupp in March 1936. Heeren (DG Belgrad) to AA, March 10, 1936, ibid.

[24] The Yugoslav General Staff supported Stojadinović's policy because of its estimate of Yugoslav military weakness and the unlikelihood of support from England and France. There was, however, a deep-seated animus toward Germany in the officer corps, probably reflecting the sentiment of the Serb population, which eventually led to the March 1941 *coup d'état* and brought about Hitler's decision to invade.

There were subsequent concrete discussions conducted by Neuhausen concerning aircraft, not artillery, but coordination between Neuhausen and the legation was so poor that Heeren learned of a proposed aircraft transaction only when Stojadinović told him of his discussions with Neuhausen.[25] "[Stojadinović] is ready to order the new Dornier 17 bomber series in spite of an attractive offer of England and France, as long as Yugoslavia is assured access to the future improvements in this type. A military commission will in the near future address this question to Colonel General [Göring]."[26] Stojadinović also was interested in fighters, supplemental aircraft motors, two submarines, and a destroyer. The OKM was more than willing to assist the Yugoslavs in this naval rearmament program.[27]

These preliminary steps would bear bitter fruit for Yugoslavia in 1938-39. As the war scares increased the general political anxiety, and the British armaments outlay in 1938 intensified the arms race, the scramble for weapons had a great impact on the states of east-central Europe. Yugoslavia could not avoid the general pressures dictating reliance upon France and Czechoslovakia *or* a turn to Germany, and the Munich capitulation made the possibility — or desirability — of obtaining arms from the Czechs virtually out of the question. The French had written off her southeastern European allies and the Yugoslavs had no hope from that quarter. During the first nine moths of 1939 Germany successfully used the lure of modern weapons to secure access to the vital raw materials — bauxite, copper, zinc, lead — previously unobtainable because of French and British capital control.

5. *The Dubrovnik Protocol, October, 1937*

After Yugoslavia agreed to German demands to increase grain exports, Germany's first quarter modest export surplus (approximately 16.6 million dinars) became a second quarter trade deficit of approximately 199 million dinars. The unpaid German commodity debt represented by the Yugoslav account at the *Reichsbank* increased by more than 12 million marks. Under these circumstances Yugoslavia avoided agreeing to a meeting of the Mixed Commission despite considerable German pressure.[28] Yugoslav motives are unclear here, but it appears that Yugoslavia wanted to avoid any further escalation in German demands. Yugoslav policy makers may also have hoped that the rising prices for primary products on the world market, characteristic of the spring of 1937, would be sustained. If so, they were cruelly disappointed by the collapse of the world cereals market in the second half of 1937.

[25] Minute by Hess (Belgrad), February 26, 1937, PA, Ha Pol, Handel mit Kriegsgerät, Jugoslawien, Bd. 1.
[26] Heeren (DG Belgrad) to AA, July 1, 1937, ibid.
[27] OKW to AA, July 24, 1937, ibid. The OKW noted that Krupp had already submitted tenders for the submarines in August 1936.
[28] Sarnow characterized a postponement of the Mixed Commission as "unacceptable." Pilja, however, refused to meet before mid-July. Sarnow to Pilja, March 31, 1937 and Pilja to Sarnow, April 20, 1937, both in PA, Ha Pol, IVa, Jugoslawien, Handel l3A, Regierungsausschüsse, Bd. 1.

Although Germany insisted that after July 1 it was no longer legally bound to extend the commodities agreement of the previous meeting of the Mixed Commission, there was no retaliation against Yugoslav intransigence. When the commodities agreements were extended to September 30, 1937, the annual grain quota was increased and the "other goods" quota reduced by 5%. It appears that Yugoslavia agreed to these changes out of fear of losing part of the German grain market to Hungary. In this interim period (July to October, 1937) Yugoslav dissatisfaction with the precipitous increase in Germany's clearing debt was reflected in a series of harassing tactics initiated by the National Bank against German interests. By this point, such tactics had virtually become a ritual at each meeting of the Mixed Commission. New exchange regulations introduced by the National Bank caused a sharp drop in lumber exports to Germany and severely circumscribed the use of clearing checks in bilateral trade.

The major impasse in the negotiations of the Mixed Commission, which finally began in Dubrovnik in October, was the Yugoslav demand for strict quota limitations on the structure of German imports from Yugoslavia. In the face of Germany's staggering trade debt, the German delegation quickly conceded a principle that they had always fought against before: import of Yugoslav products into Germany would follow the export of German goods to Yugoslavia. Strict observance of this principle would have made the German tactic of purchase without payment impossible. Obviously, the German government hoped to concede the principle in the abstract while negating it in practice. The Yugoslavs were not particularly mollified by this quick German concession. On the contrary, Sarnow reported "stiff resistance" to German proposals all along the line.

The key item to be negotiated was a new plan regulating imports and exports to replace the temporary expedients made necessary by the unplanned German grain purchases. The work of the preceding two meetings of the Mixed Commission, which had tried to balance trade between the two countries, had been destroyed by Germany's supplemental grain purchases. Although Yugoslavia acquiesced to German demands, the German delegation arrived in Dubrovnik with extensive demands. In return for the concession that German imports from Yugoslavia should not exceed Germany's ability to pay (German exports to Yugoslavia to precede imports from Yugoslavia), Germany wanted its exports to be guaranteed "full developmental possibilities" in the future. Furthermore, Germany wished to alter the existing quota structure in favor of industrial raw materials — antimony, copper, zinc, and lead. In other words, the German delegation came to Dubrovnik with demands nullifying earlier German concessions regarding the structure of imports from Yugoslavia. The most bitter pill of all for the Yugoslavs was, however, Sarnow's insistence that the supplemental grain purchase in the spring of 1937 be excluded from the new grains quota of 150,000 tons. In this way Germany's formal commitment to achieve a trade balance by promoting German exports to Yugoslavia would take effect only with respect to commodities exported under the new protocol, i.e., the Yugoslav government was still left without specific assurances regarding the clearing debt created by the German grain crisis.

Yugoslavia was in no mood to satisfy Germany's expectations without resistance.

The Yugoslav delegation led by Pilja came to the negotiations with proposals for quantity quotas for German exports designed to precisely balance trade and proposals to limit German purchases of both raw materials and certain agricultural products. Sarnow reported that "as regards these Yugoslav demands we were successful in pressing [our viewpoints] all along the line, but only after long and difficult struggles."[29] In exchange for the German promise to promote payment by exports, Yugoslavia reaffirmed the principle that German products would not be subject to quantitative quota regulations. More significantly, the German delegation achieved a substantial modification in the quota system for Yugoslav exports to Germany. The quota agreement adopted in March, 1937, in order to secure Yugoslavia's agreement to German grain demands had favored the export of Yugoslav agricultural products over raw materials. Germany was determined to revise the agreement in favor of industrial raw materials.[30]

Quotas on Yugoslav Exports to Germany

	Dubrovnik Protocol	March Agreement
Agricultural Products	50% (1/2 for grains, and all other) (1/2 for animal products)	25.5% grains & all other 22.5% animal products
Lumber Products under the authority of the German Economics Ministry	11% 39%	40%
To cover the debt of the Yugoslav National Bank at the Reichsbank	—	10%

A separate lumber quota meant that the possibility of importing raw materials was increased from 35% to 50% of total imports from Yugoslavia. Also, the Dubrovnik Protocol did not designate a raw materials quota as such but covered only those goods that were the responsibility of the German Economics Ministry. In

[29] Memorandum by Sarnow, October 4, 1937, PA, Ha Pol, Handakten Clodius, Jugoslawien, Bd. 3.
[30] 'Protokoll über das Ergebnis der 4. gemeinsamen Tagung . . . in Dubrovnik', September 29, 1937, PA, Ha Pol, Handakten Wiehl, Jugoslawien, Bd. 3, paragraph 2(a). For a brief summary of the negoiations see: KAISER, Economic Diplomacy, p.157.

other words, this quota was completely at the disposal of the German government to do with it as it pleased. Yugoslavia's attempt to alter the composition of exports to Germany in what it regarded as a more favorable direction had been thwarted. This aspect of the Dubrovnik Protocol was given particular stress by Sarnow. "In view of the increasing significance of the ore imports which belong to the industrial raw materials group it is especially important that they can be increased from around 20% to 39% [of total imports] according to new transactional regulations."[31]

Germany also achieved satisfactory results in the areas of grain export guarantees and armaments. In addition to the 150,000 tons of grain already delivered by Yugoslavia in 1937, Germany was given a further commitment for another 100,000 tons. For the first time, armaments sales were formally approved by the Mixed Commission, to the obvious satisfaction of the German chairman. "Thereby the desired special regulation of war material transactions desired by us is laid down in treaty form. We have informed the Yugoslavs that we have first in view importing supplemental grain in exchange for war material."[32]

After the Protocol was substantially negotiated, Sarnow met privately with Pilja and expressed his concern over closer economic ties between members of the Little Entente, particularly the possibility that Yugoslavia would grant preferences to Czech industrial products. Pilja responded by pointing out that while he was in Dubrovnik negotiating with the Germans, he had sent a subordinate to the Little Entente economic discussions. According to his point of view, "there could be no question of Yugoslavia granting industrial preferences to another country. Both domestic and trade policy considerations forbid it "[33] He not only gave his personal assurances that such a development simply could not occur but brought up his conversations with Czech Foreign Minister Hodža in which he had asserted that Yugoslavia would have nothing to do with such plans. "He [Pilja] emphasized in this connection that if he wanted something from Germany, then according to his experience it was better to work something out with Germany alone."[34] Pilja also volunteered assurances that the normalization of Italian-Yugoslav relations would not lead to Italy's regaining first place among Yugoslavia's trading partners. "Italy had nothing more to offer."[35] According to Pilja, Yugoslavia's industrialization made the traditional import of Italian textiles superfluous.

The Dubrovnik negotiations were an important step in the consolidation of the German position in Yugoslavia. While pressure was being exerted on Yugoslavia from industrial nations interested in the Yugoslav market, Göring gambled and won. The marked stimulation of German trade passivity by means of the supplemental grain purchases was only a harbinger of what the future would hold. While the German government conceded the priority of German payment through exports

[31] Memorandum by Sarnow, October 4, 1937, Abschrift zu W III SE 7865.
[32] Ibid.
[33] Sarnow minute, October 4, 1937, Abschrift zu W III SE 7851, ibid.
[34] Ibid.
[35] Ibid.

over German import needs, it was far more significant that the Dubrovnik Protocol virtually nullified the quota system that Yugoslavia had imposed as the price for supplemental grain shipments in the spring of 1937.

Symbolic of the consolidation of German influence was the opening of the rolling mill at Zenica built by a Krupp consortium in the fall of 1937, soon after the conclusion of the Dubrovnik negotiations. Among those attending the opening ceremony were Prime Minister Stojadinović, five cabinet ministers, and a representative of Krupp. Although in his remarks Stojadinović did not lay specific emphasis on Yugoslavia's special relationship with Germany, he did make it clear that the Zenica project was an integral part of his policy of disengagement from French tutelage. "The Zenica rolling mill will not only serve the economic progress of the country but national defense as well. The political horizon in Yugoslavia has, however, happily improved through the policy of understanding with Bulgaria and Italy. An understanding with Hungary is also in prospect."[36] Stojadinović's comment that no one would have believed in 1936 that such a great project could be finished so quickly held a significance which could not have been lost on perceptive observers. The conjunction of German-Yugoslav cooperation on large-scale industrial projects, Stojadinović's policy of "understanding" with former revisionist enemies, and German predominance in the Yugoslav market would be difficult to characterize in any way as accidental.

It is scarcely surprising that Stojadinović wished to downplay the opening of the Zenica plant by not inviting official German representatives. Acknowledged or not, German political and economic influence were already the dominant factors affecting Yugoslavia's history. The Dubrovnik negotiations concluded the purely bilateral phase of economic relations. Subsequent developments would be increasingly determined by the European political crisis and the consequent fears of, and preparations for, war. This atmosphere was as much a cause for the success of German expansionism in Yugoslavia as it was a consequence of the growth of German imperialism itself. Germany's policy of agricultural concessions of 1934-36 had never been intended as altruism. Berlin expected to collect its debts and did so with a vengeance.

[36] Janson (DG Belgrad) to AA, October 6, 1937, PA, Ha Pol, IVa, Jugoslawien, Industrie 6, Bergbau, Bd. 1.

CHAPTER VIII

YUGOSLAVIA, ARMAMENTS, AND WORLD WAR

1. Introduction

In the world crisis of 1939, Yugoslavia remained a spectator to the approaching catastrophe. The prudent Yugoslav withdrawal from the French alliance system, unaffected by the fall of Stojadinović in February, 1939, ensured that Yugoslavia would not be caught up in any foolish gestures that Berlin could interpret as "encirclement", as King Carol's acceptance of the Anglo-French guarantee had been interpreted in April, 1939. The oppressive crisis atmosphere did contribute to Yugoslavia's eventual capitulation to German raw materials demands, but there was to be no Balkan crisis leading to world war. Despite Franz Neuhausen's high-handed tactics in Belgrade, the Yugoslav government remained composed, showing no desire to exaggerate the character of German demands. The development of Yugoslav-German relations does not speak directly to the diplomatic causes of the outbreak of war in 1939, but a study of German policy toward Yugoslavia helps answer an equally significant question: what kind of Europe did Nazi Germany intend to create? Germany's relations with Yugoslavia in 1939, of all the countries in eastern Europe, were probably the most "correct", making a study of German policy in Yugoslavia a laboratory for the study of German expansionism. Understanding the structural characteristics of German policy should explain why it succeeded in Yugoslavia but failed in Poland. The story of German policy in Yugoslavia in 1939 is the story of the Nazi *Großraumwirtschaft*, the economic counterpart of Hitler's New Order.

2. German Armaments Sales in 1938

The 100-million-mark armaments credit of 1939 originated with the German Air Ministry, which was concerned that Stojadinović, influenced by pro-English advisors, had decided to place orders with England for 100 Blenheim bombers. The Wilhelmstraße believed the story and asked the German legation if a personal representative of Göering should be sent to Belgrade.[1] Schönebeck, German air attaché in Belgrade, reported that the actual transaction involved only two Blenheim bombers

---

[1] Bismarck to DG Belgrad, July 17, 1938, PA, Gesandtschaft Belgrad, Fach 81, G. 2, Wirtschaftliches Geheim, Bd. 3. As a consequence of the annexation of Austria, tensions between the Yugoslav government and the increasingly Nazified German minority began to increase

and twelve Hurricane fighters.[2] Heeren advised against sending a special envoy, arguing that German sales efforts required a solid foundation that could be achieved only by changing the traditional orientation of the Yugoslav army. The Yugoslav General Staff was concerned both with the quality of competing weapons systems and with potential military/political problems that could result from purchase in case of a European war. On this basis the Army remained suspicious of awarding contracts to Germany. English weapons were chosen not because of personal factors such as Prince Paul's connection to the English royal family but because of the conviction that no other aircraft industry could surpass the British in workmanship. Only if Germany could convince the Yugoslav military of the superiority of German arms would there be a secure basis for arms sales. Heeren recommended that the whole question be put off until the autumn when the leading political personalities would be back in Belgrade.[3]

Although this episode had no direct results, it is significant in what it reveals of the nature of German policy making. Normally, the Economic Policy Department of the Wilhelmstraße closely supervised any armaments sales, but in this instance the Wilhelmstraße learned of British competition only indirectly, via the Air Ministry, while the Air Ministry and Heeren specifically referred to the efforts of Franz Neuhausen to sell military aircraft. Neuhausen operated independently of the German legation in Belgrade and rarely consulted the Wilhelmstraße. It seems that the Wilhelmstraße was put in the picture only because of the flap over British competition.

The situation became even more confused when the next round of negotiations over armaments began in October, 1938. While Neuhausen pressed on with his campaign for the German aircraft industry, Freiherr von Lupin (*AKG Reichsgruppe Industrie*) and General Faber du Faur (military attaché, Belgrade) began discussing a large armaments package with the Yugoslav government. Another strand in the net of German influence was being woven by Max Hahn of the MWT in his struggle against Standard Oil (USA) for oil concessions in northern Yugoslavia. Eventually, all these elements would be neatly brought together in the Belgrade Armaments Credit Protocol of July, 1939. The process by which these disparate tendencies were woven into a unified whole is by no means as clear as its final product.

In broad outline, there were three conflicting groups within German policy: Neuhausen and the aircraft industry, the *Reichsgruppe Industrie* and Ruhr industry (backed by the Wilhelmstraße and Economics Ministry), and Max Hahn and the MWT — with each group tending to pursue its own special goal and ready to poach on each other's sphere of influence. Clear divisions between questions and

---

sharply. Stojadinović, so pro-German in foreign policy, ordered harsh measures to control what were perceived as subversive activities including imprisonment of *Volksdeutsche* activists, house searches, and fines. In spite of these actions, the German government guided the *Volksdeutsche* movement into supporting the Stojadinović ticket in the December, 1938, election. Out of some 300,000 minority votes cast for Stojadinović, Von Bagnell estimates that 120,000 were cast by Germans: BAGNELL, Influence, pp. 30, 32, 133, 136, 143.

[2] Schönebeck to Heeren, July 20, 1938, ibid.

[3] Heeren in draft, Feine (DG Belgrad — Denski Grad bei Bled) to AA, July 24, 1938, ibid.

issues do not exist in this struggle to dominate policy making. For example: although Neuhausen was primarily concerned with the sale of aircraft during the spring and summer of 1938, the *Reichsgruppe Industrie* contended that he had earlier taken responsibility for the negotiation of a heavy artillery contract for the Berlin Suhler Waffen company: "In this connection Herr General Consul Neuhausen was given certain assurances from responsible Yugoslav government agencies."[4] Despite informal Yugoslav promises, the contracts were eventually awarded to the Czech firm Škoda. There were further disappointments in the autumn when Stojadinović told Neuhausen that other heavy artillery contracts were to be awarded to Breda, an Italian firm. Dissatisfied with Neuhausen's ineffective maneuvering, in the summer of 1938 Faber du Faur and a representative of Berlin Suhler Waffen began to sound out the Yugoslav government after the dismissal of General Marić, the Yugoslav war minister known for his close association with Škoda.

For unknown reasons, Faber du Faur sent his report on the heavy artillery negotiations to the German Air Ministry, just when the Air Ministry, hearing of the English competition discussed above, pressed Neuhausen and the Wilhelmstraße to intervene. Faber du Faur's report was sidetracked around the Air Ministry from late July to the beginning of September, when the *Reichsgruppe Industrie* asked the Air Ministry about the results of his discussions. Stymied by the Air Ministry's obstruction, the *Reichsgruppe Industrie* prepared the necessary tenders for the Yugoslav War Ministry at Faber du Faur's direct request. Learning of this, Neuhausen went directly to Göring at the Nürnberg Party Rally to secure a verbal agreement that he would be the sole negotiator of armaments sales to Yugoslavia. Neuhausen then proceeded to lay down the law to the *Reichsgruppe Industrie*. "He [Neuhausen] informed us that he had discussed the matter personally with the Field Marshal and will negotiate with Minister President Stojadinović after his return to Yugoslavia. Neither we nor the firms are to undertake anything in this matter at his [Göring's] order until the discussions with Stojadinović take place."[5] The *Reichsgruppe Industrie* remarked that good relations with high personages was not a sufficient qualification for these negotiations as more needed to be done in order to secure the contracts for Germany. Göring did not expressly bar the *Reichsgruppe Industrie* from the Yugoslav market, but he continued to give Neuhausen informal support and acknowledged the demands of the aircraft industry for the lion's share of sales to Yugoslavia. The *Reichsgruppe Industrie* ignored Neuhausen's admonitions and pressed on with their sales campaign.

Freiherr von Lupin, the functionary in charge of armaments sales at the *Reichsgruppe Industrie*, arrived in Belgrade during the second week of October for talks with the Yugoslav War Ministry. General Nedić, war minister, explained that Škoda was originally awarded the artillery contract because the Yugoslav Army considered Czech weapons to be superior to German. However, signing the contracts had been delayed because Škoda refused to allow long-term credit, offering

---

[4] Reichsgruppe Industrie to Koch (Wi Rü-Amt), Schottky (RWM), Bergmann (Vierjahresplan), and Clodius (AA), October 7, 1938, PA, Ha Pol, Handel mit Kriegsgerät, Jugoslawien, Bd. 1.

[5] Ibid.

only five years instead of the six to eight years Yugoslavia asked. Nedić indicated that Yugoslavia was now seriously considering purchasing the German 2Omm cannon, particularly as Škoda would not commit itself to new orders in the aftermath of the Munich Agreement.

In a separate interview with General Hadiž-Ilić, the artillery technical expert in the War Ministry, Lupin found the ground even more fertile for Germany. Hadiž-Ilić said that tenders for the heavy artillery contract were still being taken but if Germany were interested, the offer must reach Belgrade "as soon as possible." "He [Hadiž-Ilić] requests that the delivery period date be as short as possible and if feasible direct delivery out of stocks."[6] Lupin assured him of delivery within twelve months (Göring's personal pledge) and that payment could be made through clearing.

Apart from Lupin's visit to Belgrade and efforts by Max Hahn of the MWT to secure oil leases for Germany, the period after Munich marked a pause in the expansion of German influence. Why the positive prospects suggested by Lupin's visit were not followed up remains a mystery. But however quiescent Germany was in the area of armaments, the German Agricultural Ministry and other agencies were active. The German currency authorities allocated 20% more payment permits for the last quarter of 1938 than for the same period in 1937.[7] German purchases from Prizad, the Yugoslav state company, were 83% above quotas agreed upon at the Mixed Commission meeting in October (17.6 million versus 9.6 million marks).[8]

Yugoslav demands for increased German purchases were being unexpectedly fulfilled, but the German purchase orgy predictably resulted in accumulated mark balances to Yugoslavia's credit in Berlin and renewed downward pressure on the clearing mark exchange rate. Because of German reluctance to take increased agricultural products, in October, 1938, there were no provisions made for a special push of German exports or the award of new state contracts and/or armaments sales to pay for the supplementary German purchases. By December, 1938, the Yugoslav government was once again worried about the increase in Germany's clearing debt: "Pilja expressed his concern over the increase in the clearing debt to over 30 million *Reichsmark*. A few days ago the National Bank notified Ministerial Director Spitta that the exchange rate guarantee reserve has declined from eight million *Reichsmark* to two million and proposed the use of Sudeten credits for the exchange rate guarantee. . . . Pilja fears that it could come to a temporary limitation of Yugoslav exports to Germany."[9] By early January, 1939, the German currency authorities imposed a drastic 35% cut in currency allocation for Yugoslav imports during the first quarter of 1939.[10] Germany increasingly saw large-scale armament

6   Second minute by von Lupin (interview with Hadiž-Ilić), October 14, 1938, ibid.
7   Bergmann (RWM) to UB, October 3, 1938, BA, R 7, XIV /240.
8   'Vertraulicher Sonderdienst' Nr.8, January 18, 1939, BA, R 7, VI 265/2; also 'Germany-Yugoslavia: Clearing Difficulties', Food (Defense Plans) Department, Board of Trade, February 2, 1939, PRO, F.O. 371/23874.
9   Heeren (DG Belgrad) to AA, December 10, 1938, PA, Ha Pol, Handakten Clodius, Jugoslawien, Bd. 3.
10   Bergmann (RWM) to UB, January 3, 1939, BA, R 7, XIV /240.

sales as both the medium-term solution for Germany's chronic passive trade balance and as the lever to open up Yugoslavia's mineral resources to unlimited German domination.

The open competition between the informal legation of Neuhausen and official government agencies, between Neuhausen and Max Hahn, and between the aircraft industry and Ruhr heavy industry to dominate policy, for contracts, and for control of Yugoslav raw materials, may be interpreted as an indication of the inefficiency and disorganization of German imperialism. But so overwhelming were the successes of German policy in Danubian Europe that few, if any, contemporary observers noted the disparate organizational tendencies within German activity in Yugoslavia. Such conflicts reflected only the domestic political economy of Germany, and while such chaotic tendencies certainly contributed to Germany's eventual defeat in World War II, they cannot be used as evidence to minimize the aggressive character of German expansionism. That an analogy can be made between Germany's domestic political economy and her policy in Yugoslavia indicates how strong German influence was. In Rumania, where German influence was much weaker, there was notable cooperation between official government bureaus, the Four Year Plan, and party agencies. German policy was disciplined in Rumania by the urgent need for petroleum; no Yugoslav commodity was as directly important to the German war machine as Rumanian petroleum.

Germany's reasons for not pursuing the sale of armaments in the last months of 1938 are obscure, particularly considering the large trade imbalance and the need to limit Yugoslav imports in the first quarter of 1939. Subsequent negotiations seem to indicate that the German government was consciously stalling in order to reap the highest possible dividend in raw materials from Yugoslavia. Interdepartmental frictions may have also played a role in Germany's failure to follow up on Nedić's offer. Ribbentrop's admission that the Wilhelmstraße had earlier agreed to delegate its exclusive responsibility for foreign affairs lends weight to this interpretation.

3. The 200-Million-Mark Credit: The Yugoslav Initiative

In early January, 1939, the Yugoslav government told both the German and British legations that tenders for 120 motorized antiaircraft batteries were being accepted by the War Ministry. Yugoslavia insisted upon a ten-year credit and told the representatives of both countries that the tenders had to be received quickly.[11] The British were given until January 21, leading Germany to interpret its January 9 deadline as an unfriendly gesture. Ross, an official of the Foreign Office, characterized the Yugoslav offer as "probably useless."[12] Yugoslavia was using a tactic upon

---

[11] Yugoslav Army and Navy Ministry to General Faber du Faur, January 2, 1939, PA, Ha Pol, Handel mit Kriegsgerät Jugoslawien, Bd. 1. Campbell (Belgrade) to Viscount Halifax, January 3, 1939, PRO, F.0. 371/23879.

[12] Feine (DG Belgrad) to AA, January 3, 1939, PA, Ha Pol, Handel mit Kriegsgerät, Jugoslawien, Bd. 1. Ross minute, January 6, 1939, PRO F.0. 371/23879. Ross noted that the

which King Carol based his whole foreign policy: approach the western powers and
Germany simultaneously, claim to both that the country is under enormous pressure from the other side, and hope that Germany or England's fear of "capitulation" to the other would make one of them improve its offer. At the first sign that
Germany was displeased, the Yugoslav government postponed its "deadline" until a
Krupp representative arrived in Belgrade (January 21).[13] Neuhausen, who had been
obviously bypassed in this new Yugoslav initiative, was made responsible by Göring
for the credit side of the negotiations.[14]

Before negotiations for the antiaircraft artillery got under way, Yugoslavia made
two overtures to Schönebeck, the German air attaché, which determined Yugoslav-German relations for the rest of the year. On January 30, 1939, both Prince
Paul of Yugoslavia and King Carol of Rumania requested large-scale armament
sales from the respective German air attachés assigned to their capitals. In Belgrade,
Prince Paul asked for a long-term 200-million-mark credit for 200 bombers, 100
fighters, 70 howitzers, and 120 antiaircraft artillery. Nothing could show more
clearly the bad times that had befallen the Wilhelmstraße than the fact that it did
not receive Schönebeck's first report and was not aware of the credit request until
after February 11, the date of the second interview. Although Heeren knew of the
Yugoslav initiative, he had simply assumed that Schönebeck's reports to the Air
Ministry were being passed on: "I did not consider it necessary for me to report on
the matter unless I had proposals to make with regard to the political exploitation
of the armaments transaction. There was, however, in my opinion no question of
this in view of our export interests and the instability of the situation here after the
fall of Stojadinović. The Yugoslavs had never discussed the matter with me."[15]
Heeren's acceptance of Schönebeck's independent activities is not surprising
considering that he had been expressly ordered to leave the issue of oil leases to
Neuhausen.[16]

British firms could hardly prepare tenders by January 21 and were in no position to offer ten-
year credit. A separate minute by Nicholls states "that as regards Greece we should certainly
not wish that country to suffer as a result of fulfilling Yugoslav requirements." Ibid. David
Kaiser points out that the Yugoslavs had sought 12 Blenheim bombers in 1937 but were actually only able to secure two: "An arms priority list drawn up within the Foreign Office in
May, 1937, to help allocate arms exports reflected this order of priorities: it stressed defense
of the Mediterranean and the Suez Canal. The first twenty countries on the list, in order, were
Egypt, Afghanistan, Belgium, Portugal, Turkey, Saudi Arabia, Yugoslavia, Greece, Argentina,
the Netherlands, Finland, Estonia, Latvia, Lithuania, Poland, Rumania, China, Iran, Yemen,
Brazil, and Chile... Thus, Yugoslavia could not receive ten Blenheim bombers because of a
previous allocation of planes to Turkey. Eastern European states without an Adriatic coastline
had much less chance of purchasing late-model British arms." KAISER, Economic Diplomacy,
p. 181-182. Yugoslavia had actually slipped in priority from 1937 to 1939.

[13] Feine (DG Belgrad) to AA, January 21, 1939, PA, Ha Pol, Handel mit Kriegsgerät,
Jugoslawien, Bd. 1.

[14] Moraht to DG Belgrad, January 16, 1939, and Dr. Schlotterer (RWM) to Moraht (AA),
January 17, 1939, ibid.

[15] Heeren (DG Belgrad) to AA, February 17, 1939, DGFP, D, Vol. 6, p. 397; PA, Ha Pol,
Handakten Wiehl, Jugoslawien, Bd. 3

[16] Wiehl to DG Belgrad, November 28, 1938, PA, Ha Pol, IVa, Jugoslawien, Rohstoffe
und Waren, Petroleum, Bd. 1.

Germany's struggle to obtain control over Yugoslav raw materials is also the story of a struggle within the German government over policy and between industrial groups for market shares. Ribbentrop and Weizsäcker saw an opportunity to reassert Wilhelmstraße control over Yugoslav policy when the Economics and Finance Ministries sharply disagreed with Neuhausen and the Four Year Plan about the possible economic benefits of the proposed armaments credit. Ribbentrop intervened in favor of a smaller credit with the proviso that it be used as leverage to secure major political concessions from Yugoslavia: withdrawal from the League of Nations and adherence to the Anti-Comintern Pact. Ribbentrop's intervention proved decisive for the specific course of the negotiations and the specific form of the armaments protocol but was of little lasting significance. Neither Hitler nor Göring seemed interested in this political *quid pro quo*. Both were more concerned with access to Yugoslav raw materials.

The dissension within the German government over the armaments credit began with the Krupp firm's application for government insurance to cover the transaction. Krupp alleged that its foreign obligations had increased so much since 1937 that it could not take the risk alone. Given German credit offers to both Turkey and Bulgaria, Krupp officials did not believe that Yugoslavia would accept anything less than a ten-year credit. The Wilhelmstraße's representative at the second meeting about the credit was skeptical of the project's economic justification. "I, myself, am of the opinion that the transaction offered on the terms which the Krupp firm has outlined is not feasible; based on the premise that no political interest is present which justifies the implementation of the transaction under all circumstances. The Finance Ministry, the Economics Ministry and representatives of the banks are of the same opinion. From the presentation of Herr von Lupin it is also clear that the Krupp firm will only take up the contract if it really is in [Germany's] political interest and the conditions presented [by the firm] are fulfilled."[17] The interministerial council made approval of the credit and Reich guarantee dependent upon the Wilhelmstraße considering the project to be politically important.

The Wilhelmstraße was not, however, able to come to an immediate decision. Wiehl, head of the Economic Policy Department, noted that the interministerial committee would agree only to a six-year credit, an 85% Reich guarantee, and price subsidies if the Wilhelmstraße declared a "political" interest in the project.[18] He commented that the transaction, supported by both Neuhausen and General von Faber du Faur, would be Germany's first inroad into the Yugoslav armaments market. Two days later, Neuhausen told Wiehl that Germany had competition for the Yugoslav market; Italy had offered a 500-million-lira credit. Neuhausen also revealed to the Wilhelmstraße (for the first time) that the Yugoslav government was interested not only in Krupp antiaircraft artillery but in a further 100 million marks for military aircraft and air materiel. Wiehl's summary judgment did nothing to resolve the interministerial quandary. "The transaction is desired for political rea-

---

[17] Tagesbericht by Busse, February 8, 1939, PA, Ha Pol, Handakten Wiehl, Jugoslawien, Bd. 3.
[18] Memorandum by Wiehl, February 9, 1939, ibid.

sons; however, political interest does not go so far as to justify an economic loss."[19]

Between the second and third meetings on the credit, Neuhausen was working informally on Göring, Funk, and Brinkmann (state secretary, Economics Ministry), and, armed with their support, he completely dominated the official bureaucratic apparatus. Brushing off an earlier conservative commitment to a six-year credit, he simply announced that Göring had decided in favor of the ten-year credit. He further claimed that a division of a 200-million-mark credit between heavy industry (80 million) and the aircraft industry (120 million) had Göring's approval. The payoff was raw materials.

> We would attach importance to the import to Germany of supplemental amounts of ores, wheat, and, hopefully, oil as well. We have had the luck to obtain large oil concessions. Drilling will begin early this year, and we may hope that by fall they will be in production.[20]

Arlt (Economics Ministry) echoed the importance of Yugoslav raw materials in observing that Yugoslav production of antimony (80-100 tons per month) was sufficient for Germany's needs. The Economics Ministry had already obtained options on chrome, lead, and zinc mines that were independent of British or French influence. Reinhardt, a key official of the Economics Ministry, saw the credit as a positive contribution to the solution of Germany's passive trade balance. "Our need for Yugoslav goods is so great that it could only do us good if the payments soon came on the credit to 20 million *Reichsmark* annually."[21] Only Nasse of the Finance Ministry opposed Neuhausen. The conservative officials of Finance were fighting a losing battle against the spiraling Reich debt and wanted to limit the Reich's obligations to the normal 70% guarantee with perhaps a supplemental guarantee to the banks for the remaining 30%.

Orthodox financial views were not likely to prevail in 1939. Gustav Schlotterer, a high Economics Ministry official, told his colleagues that both Reich Minister Funk and State Secretary Brinkman were determined that the transaction would not break down over the financial question. Other dissenting views were heard from the air industry representative, Killinger, who insisted that Krupp could not represent the air industry in the consortium. The aircraft industry did, however, support Krupp's demand for a 100% Reich guarantee. At the end of the meeting, industry representatives and their government supporters repeated their demands for further Reich support. "Because the Yugoslavian transaction is practically a governmental transaction in the private sphere and Krupp, therefore, has no influence of essential conditions, the firm cannot take over a great risk in this transaction."[22] Only the representatives of the Finance Ministry, Soltau and Niemetz, continued to oppose Krupp and Neuhausen.[23] Rearguard opposition from the Finance Ministry would

---

[19] Memorandum by Wiehl, February 11, 1939, ibid.

[20] Minute by Nagel, 'Zu R.T. 584 Konsortialgeschäft Krupp/Jugoslawien', February 13, 1939, PA, Ha Pol, Handel mit Kriegsgerät, Jugoslawien, Bd. 1.

[21] Ibid.

[22] Ibid.

[23] Krupp to RWM, February 1, 1939, enclosure in *Deutsche Revisions- und Treuhands AG* to Busse (AA), February 14, 1939, ibid.

complicate the negotiations until the Belgrade Armaments Protocol was signed in July, 1939.[24]

Characteristically, it was not until this point, after Neuhausen had entered in intrigue with Göring and Funk over the heads of the concerned ministries, that Ribbentrop decided in favor of the transaction. He did, however, decide to use his authority as foreign minister to limit the credit to 100 million marks. Prince Paul's original request had been for 200 million marks; Krupp had estimated the antiaircraft transaction at 100 million marks. In the discussion over the Krupp consortial guarantee, the second 100 million for military aircraft was simply tacked on by Neuhausen. Ribbentrop's decision, in Weizsäcker's words, resulted in a "lively struggle over his [Ribbentrop's jurisdiction] on all sides."[25] Neuhausen committed the one breach of hierarchy and authority that could get him in trouble: he openly speculated that Ribbentrop would see Hitler and force a ministerial crisis over the Yugoslav question. Director Wiehl called both Neuhausen and Busse on the carpet, lecturing both on the unseemly character of such speculation.[26] The end result of the interministerial conflict and Neuhausen's intrigues was a partial victory for Ribbentrop. The transaction was to be formally limited to 100 million marks and there would be an attempt to tie the deal to political concessions.

> He [Ribbentrop] considers that to sign for the whole amount of 200 million *Reichmark* desired by the Yugoslav Government would be defensible only if in addition to the transactions being desirable on the whole from the economic standpoint (which is the case in the opinion of the Ministry of Economics . . .) its specific terms can also be called advantageous; but this can be judged only from the subsequent course of the negotiations. The Foreign Minister intends moreover to make political capital out of the transaction and, before concluding it, to await the further attitude of the Yugoslav government toward the invitation to join the Anti-Comintern Pact.[27]

Although formally the transaction was conducted between the German firms and the Yugoslav government, Wiehl instructed Heeren to reassert the authority of the legation by a démarche to the Yugoslav government to the effect that all communications to the German government had to go through the legation, i.e., the Wilhelmstraße was formally repudiating Neuhausen's activity. Heeren faithfully carried out his instructions and told Neuhausen that he was not authorized to negotiate any final agreement with Yugoslavia.[28] Neuhausen promised to abide by decisions made in Berlin, but the subsequent negotiations indicate that he continued to see himself as an independent agent, a direct representative of the Four Year Plan and the highest authority on economic policy.

---

[24] Finance Minister von Krosigk capitulated on February 16: "Er [von Krosigk] sich weiterhin bereit erklärt, notfalls bis zu einer 100%igen Garantie zu gehen, wenn davon die Durchführung der als politisch bedeutsam bezeichneten Geschäfte abhängen sollte." Unsigned minute, 'Kreditverhandlungen — Jugoslawien', February 16, 1939, BA, R 2/16476.

[25] Weizsäcker to Heeren (DG Belgrad), February 22, 1939, DGFP, D, Vol. 6, p. 400.

[26] Memorandum by Wiehl, February 18, 1939, PA, Ha Pol, Handel mit Kriegsgerät Jugoslawien, Bd. 1.

[27] Wiehl to DG Belgrad, February 27, 1939, DGFP, D, Vol. 6, p. 408.

[28] Heeren (DG Belgrad) to AA, March 2, 1939, PA, Ha Pol, Handel mit Kriegsgerät Jugoslawien, Bd. 1.

Göring himself had unique conceptions as to how relations with Yugoslavia should develop. Wiehl learned from Schönebeck that Göring intended to meet with Prince Paul after his visit to Italy on April 18. "In this connection he [Göring] wishes to carry on conversations with Prince Paul, which he had had earlier, on the political rapprochement of Yugoslavia with Germany. With this in view the Field Marshal considers it advisable to carry on the negotiations over the armaments transaction in a dilatory fashion."[29] As a military man, Schönebeck, like his Bucharest counterpart Gerstenberg, was more interested in obtaining the concrete benefits of a military cooperation agreement than adherence to the vague provisions of the Anti-Comintern Pact.[30]

4. Prince Paul's State Visit to Berlin

Prince Paul's visit had to be successful before Germany would implement the armaments credit, but it was not intended that Prince Paul and Hitler negotiate the issue. Paul's visit was the most important of the visits by east European statesmen to Berlin in the summer of 1939, before the diplomatic crisis in late August. Germany intended to demonstrate that it was acting in a responsible and calm fashion in exercising its new dominance, and in his talks with Prince Paul and the Bulgarian prime minister, Hitler used his considerable diplomatic talents to assure them of Germany's peaceful goals and quiet any fears they may have had about ultimate German intentions toward their countries. Thus, these visits, and Paul's in particular, were significant in the consolidation of Germany's sphere of influence in east-central Europe before the outbreak of war. It is hardly conceivable that the Mixed Commission negotiations over the credit that were going on in Cologne would have been successful had Paul's visit gone badly.

Preceded by an organized press and radio campaign emphasizing the close association of Yugoslavia and Germany in cultural and economic areas, Prince Paul's visit began on June 1 and ended five days later. Paul arrived in Berlin accompanied by Yugoslav and German journalists.

> Berlin was elaborately decorated with Yugoslav colors and the royal arms, and an immense, but somewhat apathetic crowd, provided with red, white and blue flags, lined the streets between the Lehrter station and the Bellevue palace. . . . The crowd was composed of all classes of people, for in addition to appeals by the Minister of Propaganda for a display of popular enthusiasm and of flags, schools, factories and shops had been closed by official order to make certain that the populace would be present in sufficient numbers to provide an impressive demonstration of German friendliness toward Yugoslavia and its ruler. Chan-

---

[29] Memorandum by Wiehl, February 27, 1939, PA, Ha Pol, Handakten Wiehl, Jugoslawien, Bd. 3.

[30] The question of the Anti-Comintern Pact was not raised in German-Rumanian relations. Although Air Attaché Gerstenberg did not oppose the Wohlthat Treaty, he did regard some sort of military cooperation as more valuable. David Kaiser gives a brief summary of the negotiations but without exploring the Neuhausen-Ribbentrop rivalry or the tensions between the military preference for alliance versus Ribbentrop's Anti-Comintern Pact hobby horse. KAISER, Economic Diplomacy, p. 267.

cellor Hitler, accompanied by high functionaries of State, party, and military forces, received the visitors at the station and drove with them to their residence.[31]

At a formal dinner, Hitler toasted the Yugoslav-German border as one established for all time. His toast was given front page coverage in Belgrade, accompanied by "obviously government inspired editorials in both *Politika* and *Vreme*" that tried "to emphasize the good political relations existing between the two countries and the importance of their cultural and economic ties."[32] The second, third, and fourth days of Paul's visit involved various ceremonial functions — a three-hour military parade, laying a wreath at the tomb of Frederick the Great, an excursion to a *Luftwaffe* base conducted by Göring, and two official balls. On the last day, Hitler and Prince Paul conferred in the presence of their foreign ministers. That evening, after visiting Göring's Karinhall, Paul and Cincar-Marković left for Belgrade.

Only a brief memorandum documenting Paul's interview with Hitler exists, but the basic outlines of Hitler's conciliatory policy emerges even more clearly than in his talks with Cincar-Marković.[33] Hitler again raised the Anti-Comintern Pact in respect to Germany's alliance with Italy and not in the context of German-Yugoslav relations. He explained the importance of Germany's alliance with Italy and the identical nature of their interests. Yugoslavia had to make a gesture to reassure Italy, not Germany. "It now appeared of importance to the Italian Government that Yugoslavia should make some gesture to demonstrate unmistakably her policy of friendship towards the Axis." Ribbentrop suggested at this point that leaving the League of Nations would be such a gesture. Prince Paul remained noncommittal on this issue. "Yugoslavia had already considerably disassociated herself from the League of Nations, and he was not altogether disinclined to withdraw at the proper moment." Hitler repeated that it was important that Yugoslavia have a clearly defined attitude toward the Axis, assuring Paul that such a clarification would "consolidate Yugoslavia's internal position at a stroke." No longer would Croat and Slovene separatists have hope of Axis support. Furthermore, "Italy would have no interest in supporting Greater Hungarian tendencies." On the need to have an accommodating attitude toward Italy, Hitler chided Paul because "it was impossible to predict what impulsive step the Duce might not one day take." Taking these admonitions with good grace, Paul repeated his earlier assurances of the continuing Yugoslav friendship toward Italy and Germany. Apparently satisfied, Hitler then went on to the larger questions of European diplomacy. In a separate conversation, Ribbentrop asked about Yugoslav withdrawal from the Balkan Entente based upon Turkey's negotiation of a political agreement with England. Cincar-Marković did not respond directly, only repeating his earlier observation that adherence to the Anti-Comintern Pact would be extremely unpopular in Yugoslavia.

Although the armaments credit was mentioned only in the Cincar-Marković/ Ribbentrop conversation, it cannot be concluded that the arms question was of secondary importance. Germany's dilatoriness throughout the late winter and early

[31] Kirk (Berlin) to the secretary of state, June 26, 1939, NA, RG 59, 760 H.62/113.

[32] Lane (Belgrade) to the secretary of state, June 4, 1939, NA, RG 59, 760 H.62/113.

[33] Memorandum by Ribbentrop, June 7, 1939, DGFP, D, Vol. 6, 474, pp. 635-638. Quotations to note 34 are from this document.

spring, the elaborate preparations for Paul's visit, and Hitler's cautious handling of Paul and Cincar-Marković were all part of a carefully considered policy. Hitler was well aware that German political and economic influence could be increased by means other than frontal assault: assuring Yugoslavia of German support against Hungary, transferring responsibility to Italy for urging Yugoslavia to adhere to the Anti-Comintern Pact and to leave the League of Nations, and refraining from recriminations on the nationality question were all part of a political strategy to secure Yugoslavia's acceptance of the armaments credit that, in turn, would guarantee Germany unrestricted access to Yugoslav raw materials. Given the tense situation along the German-Yugoslav border and the presence of pro-German elements among both Croats and Slovenes, Hitler's studied restraint in avoiding the *Volksdeutsche* grievances indicates that German policy here was motivated by economic considerations rather than pan-German dogma.

That Germany was successful is demonstrated by Prince Paul's subsequent reactions recorded in a confidential interview with Fortier, the American military attaché in Belgrade. "It is evident that Hitler handled Prince Paul well on his visit to Berlin. The ultimatum, fist-pounding procedure was avoided on this trip. It was more the voice of a siren without, of course, neglecting the background of marching troops and endless rumbling of artillery and tanks. All set under a sky darkened by aviation."[34] Prince Paul was impressed with Germany's military strength and anxiously asked Fortier for his evaluation of the French armed forces. Paul regarded the Yugoslav air force as "woefully weak." Although a man of sufficient strength of character not to be overawed by Hitler, Paul did return to Belgrade with an impression of Hitler that helped weaken his will to resist German economic demands. "He [Prince Paul] says that Hitler is a man of force and yet a dreamer, an executive and a genius at making decisions. He was told that Hitler could make better military decisions than could his generals. Hitler had received him most cordially and he had enjoyed his conversation."[35] Hitler's diplomatic skills, which allowed Germany to conclude a favorable armaments agreement, were invaluable to Germany's continued political and economic expansion in Yugoslavia.

5. Oil Concessions: Key to the Cologne Armaments Protocol

The Wilhelmstraße delayed the armaments transaction on economic grounds (the elimination of American competition for oil leases in Yugoslavia) but, when finally signed, the armaments credit protocol of July, 1939, would give Germany a virtual monopoly in the exploration and exploitation of Yugoslav petroleum reserves. The ultimate goal of German foreign policy in east-central Europe was to obtain ownership of its trading partners' respective raw materials resources, control over their banking systems, and penetration of their basic industries. These three elements

---

[34] Fortier to Arthur R. Bliss Lane (U.S. minister — Belgrade), Belgrade, June 17, 1939, NA, RG 165, Military Attaché Report ·7-V-777.
[35] Ibid.

formed the "structural guarantees" with which Nazi Germany sought to supplement trade hegemony. Berlin felt, no doubt correctly, that German influence would never be secure until French, British, and American capital were supplanted by German.

Max Hahn had first raised the question of American competition in the Yugoslav market to the Wilhelmstraße in late 1938. With the aid of Pašić, son of the former minister president of Yugoslavia, Hahn had tried to secure petroleum bases for German interests in the Zagreb basin.[36] A few weeks after this attempt the Standard Oil Company (New Jersey) began negotiating with the Yugoslav government for a concession which completely encircled the Pašić leases and made the Pašić-Hahn area useless. By November, 1938, there was a draft agreement between Standard Oil and the Yugoslav government for a 50-year concession, but Stojadinović made a personal telephone call to Göring about the Pašić leases and the competition from Standard Oil. Wiehl, of the Wilhelmstraße, decided that Stojadinović was not aware of the draft agreement with Standard Oil. Wiehl did not underestimate the importance of the petroleum leases for Germany. "It is absolutely necessary for German interest to prevent the Standard Oil contract from being approved by the Yugoslav Ministerial Council. This contract, the way it is now formulated, comprises 7000 square kilometers which must be knocked out in order to make the Pašić concession valuable for German acquisition."[37] Wiehl advised a direct appeal to Stojadinović to stop the Standard Oil competition and a concerted effort by the German government to convince business to take an intensive interest in the Yugoslav market as did Standard Oil. He believed that Standard Oil was interested in obtaining oil exploration rights in Yugoslavia only to prevent competition from securing them and had no intention of exploiting its concessions for many years to come.[38] This was the official German position that would be presented to the Yugoslav government during the next eight months.

Heeren drew up a full report on the struggle for petroleum leases in Yugoslavia. Oil concessions were being sought in three major areas; the Pannoian Basin, along the border with Hungarian oil-producing areas and on the Yugoslav-Albanian border. Major concessions throughout Yugoslavia were held by the Yugoslav firm Pannoia and the Croatian Savings Bank. Although Franz Neuhausen and Wilhelm Keppler (state secretary, Wilhelmstraße) were in contact with Berlin representatives of Pannoia, Standard Oil had already acquired four major leases and was in the process of obtaining more. Under the terms of its contract, Standard Oil guaran-

---

[36] Hahn originally sought the support of the GHH combine for this project, but was rejected.

[37] Memorandum by Wiehl, November 26, 1938, PA, Ha Pol, Handakten Wiehl, Jugoslawien, Bd. 3.

[38] Wiehl telegraphed the above to the German legation in Belgrade a few days earlier. Wiehl to DG Belgrad, November 23, 1938, Ibid. Clodius noted that *Ministerialdirektor* Gramsch (RWM) had been informed on the question as well. Representatives of the German firm Itag (*Internationale Tiefbohrkommanditgesellschaft*) were also active in Yugoslavia at this time. They were, however, engaged entirely independently of the Hahn-Pašić project. Dr. Franke (RWM) to AA, November 14, 1938, PA, Ha Pol, IVa, Jugoslawien, Rohstoffe und Waren, Petroleum, Bd. 1.

teed Yugoslavia 12-13% of the profits and was required to make an initial investment of some 2.5 million dollars. Heeren could not say whether the Yugoslav
General Staff was directly supporting Standard Oil, but "the Standard Oil Company possesses excellent connections to the Yugoslav War Ministry."[39] He advised
against competing against Standard Oil because of the unfavorable geographic conditions and stiff Yugoslav conditions for exploration rights. He did not know
whether Standard Oil was trying to obtain a monopoly in Yugoslavia, but they certainly held the lion's share of Yugoslavia's most valuable lease rights.

Neuhausen again faced Max Hahn, this time in the struggle against Standard
Oil. At a meeting of the MWT held in late November, Hahn outlined the work
done to secure ready access to Yugoslav minerals, particularly copper, lead, zinc,
antimony, bauxite, and chrome, emphasizing the MWT's early recognition of
Yugoslavia's importance as a major source of raw materials for Germany. "The
Mitteleuropäischer Wirtschaftstag had the boldness for this initiative. We hope that
the German economy will follow our example and [share] the conviction that on
this path a large part of our raw material problems can be solved."[40] Hahn's efforts
on behalf of German expansionism earned him no thanks from Neuhausen and little support from his old colleagues in the Wilhelmstraße. After consulting with State
Secretary Keppler, Wiehl told the German legation to keep Neuhausen informed of
all details concerning the petroleum question and "[it] is to be recommended that
the Legation should only proceed in consultation with General Consul Neuhausen
on this matter."[41]

A draft agreement between Standard Oil and the Yugoslav government was waiting to be signed but Keppler and Wiehl decided not to exert official pressure
against it through the legation in Belgrade; instead Neuhausen was given official
sanction to pursue informal diplomacy with Stojadinović. Stojadinović fell from
power in February, 1939, and Neuhausen had not yet been able to persuade him to
exclude Standard Oil. Although Neuhausen's informal diplomacy had failed,
Göring gave his protégé an important role in the armaments credit negotiations,
making him responsible for the petroleum question.

It was apparently easier to circumvent the authority of the Wilhelmstraße than to
exclude big business pressure groups from an active role in the petroleum question.
After intercepting a private letter of Robert Smith, Standard Oil's general manager,
Hahn told Wiehl that no time should be lost in pressuring Yugoslavia to terminate
negotiations with Standard Oil.[42] Opinion was divided in Berlin. Keppler, for instance, was not convinced that the American concession would make the Hahn-Pašić
area worthless to Germany.[43] Hahn could not, however, be put off so easily. In late

---

[39] Heeren (DG Belgrad) to AA, November 28, 1938, PA, Gesandtschaft Belgrad, Fach 81,
G.2, Wirtschaftliches Geheim, Bd. 3.
[40] Max Hahn, 'Vortrag auf der Tagung des MWT', November 23, 1938, PA, Ha Pol, IVa,
Jugoslawien, Industrie 6, Bergbau, Bd. 1.
[41] Wiehl to DG Belgrad, November 28, 1938, Ha Pol, IVb, Jugoslawien, Rohstoffe und
Waren, Petroleum, Bd. 1.
[42] Hahn (Berlin) to Wiehl, December 4, 1938, ibid.
[43] Wiehl to DG Belgrad, December 15, 1938, ibid.

January, he again sounded the alarm; two cabinet ministers had threatened to resign over a proposed agreement with the German firm *Elwerath*, and the agreement with Standard Oil was ready to be signed. "There still remains, perhaps, twenty-four hours to prevent the worst . . ."[44] Hahn's second intervention provoked Neuhausen. "I have immediately informed Marotzke of the Four Year Plan, and Dr. Reinhardt [Economics Ministry] as well as Ministerial Director von Jagwitz [Four Year Plan] by telephone and requested that the *Mitteleuropäischer Wirtschaftstag* be seriously warned."[45] Accusing Hahn of trying merely to increase the profits of the MWT, Neuhausen threatened to bring Göring into the controversy if Hahn did not stop meddling. Neuhausen claimed that there was no resistance to German interests in the Cabinet and that the contract with Standard Oil had not yet reached the Cabinet for discussion.[46]

Neuhausen's threats effectively blocked the MWT, at least on the official level, from major participation in the struggle for petroleum rights in Yugoslavia. But it continued to play a significant part in German expansion toward southeastern Europe. His exclusion from the negotiations concerning the petroleum leases did not prevent Hahn from acquiring leases that were available to any private businessman; except for capital interests acquired via the Anschluß, the MWT projects became the largest block of German capital invested in the Yugoslav raw materials sector and were not eclipsed by new German investment until the defeat of France forced the *Mines de Bor* group to sell. Neuhausen depended upon his personal influence with Göring, whose own influence over economic policy declined after the outbreak of war and was virtually eliminated after Speer was appointed minister of armaments in 1942. The MWT had no party rivals to compare with Neuhausen. New documentation indicates that its partial eclipse in Yugoslavia during 1939 was only temporary[47], and its importance in German southeastern European policy increased after the outbreak of war. Neuhausen made his peace with the MWT after Max Hahn left as director and continued to function in Yugoslavia until he was summarily removed from office and jailed (temporarily) for corruption in 1943.[48]

---

[44] Hahn minute, January 24, 1939, ibid.

[45] 'Telephonische Mitteilung von Generalkonsul Neuhausen aus Belgrad', January 24, 1939, ibid.

[46] Ibid.

[47] Wolfgang SCHUMANN (ed.), Griff nach Südosteuropa: Neue Dokumente über die Politik des deutschen Imperialismus und Militarismus im Zweiten Weltkrieg, East Berlin 1973. Schumann provides an outline of MWT activity on pp. 51-53.

[48] Neuhausen was appointed plenipotentiary-general for economics in German-occupied Serbia, "who in addition held many important positions, such as the chairmanship of the boards of directors of the "*Bankverein für Serbien* und *Mines de Bor.*" RIIA, Survey of International Affairs, 1939-1945, Hitler's Europe, London, p. 182.

6. Oil and the Armaments Credit

Ribbentrop was sufficiently satisfied with Yugoslavia's political attitude during Cincar-Marković's visit to Berlin in April 1939 to authorize technical preparations for the negotiation of the armaments credit. Immediately after Cincar-Marković left, Ribbentrop approved a draft German proposal prepared by the Economic Policy Department.[49] Clodius summarized German progress in obtaining Yugoslav petroleum resources: four German firms had obtained exploration rights to the Pašić and Croatian Savings Bank concessions "in sharp competition with the Americans."[50] He then suggested a possible compromise with Standard Oil, giving Germany a monopoly in the north and Standard Oil control in southern Yugoslavia. This suggestion was never followed up, either by the Wilhelmstraße or by Göring.

After the fall of Stojadinović, Neuhausen had stopped trying to influence the Yugoslav government in a friendly fashion and went over to outright threats. He had already threatened the new Yugoslav Minister President, Cvetković, "with a radical re-structuring of all our orders from Yugoslavia" to other countries.[51] Cvetković assured Neuhausen that German firms would be given preferential treatment in the award of petroleum contracts.[52] According to Clodius, Neuhausen was told that drilling by German companies could begin as early as mid-June, 1939, with the cost of the German investment to be paid out of the dinar account of the Reichsbank at the Yugoslav National Bank in Belgrade. It is not clear where this German capital was to originate — Germany still ran a deficit on the current trade account.[53] Neuhausen agreed to contract conditions similar to those that Standard Oil had already negotiated; no Yugoslav capital would be permitted, but Yugoslavia would receive 12.5% of the profits when the oil came in, increasing to 15% at an unspecified later date.

In the wake of Neuhausen's optimistic reports, the Wilhelmstraße made the connection between the armaments credit and petroleum leases explicit for the first time. Clodius told the legation in Belgrade that the precondition for Germany to sign the armaments credit was the "final (and legally binding) guarantee of important petroleum concessions, either before or, at the latest, simultaneously with the signature of a secret protocol. . . . It will be better to avoid, if possible, the explicit

---

[49] Memorandum by Clodius, April 29, 1939, PA, Ha Pol, Handakten Clodius, Jugoslawien, Bd. 3.

[50] Ibid.

[51] Minute by Clodius, 'Deutsche Erdölkonzessionen in Jugoslawien', 'Vertraulich', April 29, 1939, ibid.

[52] While MWT and Germany first may have succeeded in obtaining exploration and drilling rights from private interests, such concessions were useless without government approval: "Crude petroleum has been made a state monopoly (along with sugar, salt, tobacco, matches, etc.)." Villaret (Belgrade) to the War Department, February 2, 1939, NA, RG 165, Military Attaché Report, File 2155-V-278.

[53] If Germany had had an export surplus, a surplus would have accrued in the German dinar account at the Yugoslav National Bank. This would have provided Germany with a capital sum available for investment within Yugoslavia.

linking of both questions in negotiation with Yugoslavia."[54] Considering the lengths to which Neuhausen had already gone, it is doubtful that such subtle distinctions had any impact on him. Rumors eventually reached even the American ambassador in Paris, Bullitt, about Neuhausen's struggle for petroleum leases.[55]

7. Trade Negotiations at Cologne: June, 1939

Despite the economic difficulties that followed the last meeting of the Mixed Commission and Neuhausen's open threats to divert German purchases to other markets, the difficult trade and armaments negotiations at Cologne went smoothly, at least with respect to advancing German interests. The hard bargaining on both sides over the trade protocol and arms credit did not precipitate a breakdown of economic relations, primarily because of Hitler's decision to conciliate Yugoslavia.

In the last quarter of 1938 German purchases of Yugoslav commodities had greatly exceeded German exports to Yugoslavia and there was an enormous increase in Yugoslav credits in Berlin. In the first quarter of 1939 drastic measures were taken to reduce this debt by cutting German purchases by 35% of earlier quotas, but the exports of the "old" Reich had declined from 134 million marks in 1937 to 118 million marks in 1938. According to the Yugoslav legation in Berlin this drop "resulted to a large extent from Germany's inability in her present situation of full employment to make satisfactory deliveries of machinery and other goods."[56] Absorbing Austria and the Sudetenland and annexing Czechoslovakia dramatically increased Greater Germany's share of Yugoslav trade but obtaining raw materials and foodstuffs for these areas (which had previously drawn upon the world market) worsened Germany's passive trade balance with Yugoslavia and reversed Czechoslovakia's export surplus into an import surplus in its bilateral trade with Yugoslavia. The exchange value of the clearing mark was fluctuating violently in Belgrade — generally in a downward direction. The Yugoslav National Bank quickly exhausted the limited funds committed to defend the clearing mark in a futile effort to support its exchange value. Yugoslavia reintroduced regulations governing the export of raw materials, requiring at least partial payment in free exchange in an

[54] Clodius to DG Belgrad, May 3, 1939, PA, Ha Pol, Handakten Wiehl, Jugoslawien, Bd. 3. At this time, the German government through the VOMI fostered the reorganization of the *Volksdeutsche* movement into a unified whole, reconciling the old moderate leadership around Dr. Kraft with the new Nazi *Erneuerer* led by Dr. Anwender. Both Kraft and Anwender were eased out and a new leadership was formed around the moderate *Erneuerer*, Dr. Sepp Janko. This move gave the Reich more effective control over the *Volksdeutsche* both to control demonstrations against the *status quo* and to utilize the ethnic Germans as a fifth column battering ram: see the detailed analysis of the May 18-19, 1939 meeting in Graz by BAGNELL, Influence, p. 145-146.

[55] Bullitt (Paris) to the secretary of state, July 21, 1939, NA, R 59, 760.H62/135.

[56] Kirk (Berlin) to the secretary of state, June 15, 1939, NA, RG 59, 66OH.6231/102.

attempt to divert raw material exports to hard-currency countries and away from Germany and Italy.[57]

The trade negotiations at Cologne dealt with the elimination of Germany's clearing passivity, the stabilization of the mark exchange rate, and achieving a mutually satisfactory regulation of the raw materials question. After several weeks, the Mixed Commission had not solved these last two questions. Germany wanted to stabilize the mark by having the Yugoslav National Bank sell the clearing mark at a fixed parity — to guarantee the mark no matter how large the Yugoslav credit balance in Berlin. Rumania had already agreed to this procedure, but as late as June, 1939, Yugoslavia was offering to increase its support of the clearing mark only from eight million to ten million marks.[58] If Germany's clearing debt went over ten million marks the Yugoslav National Bank would dispose of the excess in the free market. Paragraph 13 of the protocol records the opposing views of the two delegations on this question and on Yugoslavia's newly imposed regulations governing the export of raw materials.[59] Yugoslavia refused to budge on either position. The third question, that of Germany's trade passivity, was understood by both sides to depend upon the success or failure of the armaments credit negotiations and so was not subject to special agreement in the June trade protocol.

8. The Armaments Protocol: June-July, 1939

The negotiations for the German armaments credit began shortly before Prince Paul arrived in Germany and were concluded before he left. The German draft protocol underwent substantial revision in the Mixed Commission, greatly reducing Yugoslavia's immediate obligations to deliver raw materials in exchange for armaments. This revised draft protocol was informally approved by both delegations to the Mixed Commission but Göring withheld the German signature for another month.

There were, naturally, disagreements about such controversial provisions as when payments were to begin, a devaluation clause, and the extent of Yugoslavia's obligations to deliver raw materials rather than other commodities. On a number of important issues Germany made concessions to the Yugoslavia negotiation team.[60] Germany had originally proposed that Yugoslavia begin paying on the ten-year credit from the date the protocol was signed, while in the revised protocol payment

---

[57] As late as August, 1939, there were reports of strenuous Yugoslav efforts to increase the export of bauxite to hard-currency countries. 'Vertraulicher Sonderdienst', August 15, 1939, BA, R 7 VI/268/2.

[58] 'Achtes Vertrauliches Protokoll', June 7, 1939, Cologne, Anlage 16, Deutsche Verrechungskasse to the Jugoslawische Nationalbank, June 22, 1939, PA, Ha Pol, Handakten Wiehl, Jugoslawien, Bd. 3.

[59] Ibid., paragraph 13.

[60] The original German draft is in: PA, Ha Pol, Handakten Wiehl, Jugoslawien, Bd. 3. Two copies of the final signed version are found in ibid. and in PA, Ha Pol, Handakten Clodius, Jugoslawien, Bd. 3. The final version was signed in Belgrade on July 5, 1939, DGFP, D, Vol. 6, 620, pp. 860-862.

was to begin only after Yugoslavia had actually placed orders with German firms. Paragraph 6 of Germany's draft suggested payment in free currency or raw materials if the existing payments agreement was revised but in the final version Germany was given no special guarantees regarding future payments in raw materials or free currency. In paragraph 7, the German draft carried specific conditions regarding Yugoslavia's obligation to deliver raw materials — Yugoslavia was to assure that these raw materials exports would come from already exploited sources and rely upon German experts and German industry in exploring for new raw materials resources. German industry was to be treated on an equal basis with Yugoslav business. New raw materials resources coming into production were to be exported to Germany to cover at least one-third of the total credit. The final version of paragraph 7 gave no Yugoslav assurances on Germany's participation in the exploitation of Yugoslav raw materials resources; payment in raw materials was to be limited to only one-half of the annual amount due under the credit, with additional deliveries dependent upon Germany's requirements and Yugoslavia's ability to supply. Regarding Germany's participation in the Yugoslav raw materials sector, "as for surveying and exploitation of the raw material resources the Yugoslav Government shall favorably consider German requests and applications and grant them as far as possible."[61]

Germany's draft provision regarding devaluation was also revised in the final agreement (paragraph 4). Devaluation and/or appreciation of the mark or dinar had been the subject of considerable controversy within the German government.[62] The German Finance Ministry wanted to include a complex clause protecting German creditors from all eventualities[63], but the final protocol provided a resolution for only three eventualities, while the fourth possibility, that of the devaluation of the dinar, was covered only by a call for negotiations "with a view to giving the German creditors the same amount in *Reichsmark* which would have been due them had the dinar not been devalued."[64]

The terms of the Cologne Protocol were more liberal for the sale of military hardware than aircraft. Payment for military hardware was to be semiannual at 6% over ten years while payment for aircraft had the same interest rate but spread over a six-year period. Germany had compromised somewhat on the aeronautical material by extending the credit from five to six years.[65]

After the essential compromises had been made and Germany had, after the month's delay, signed the protocol, Yugoslavia could not pin the Germans down to

---

[61] DGFP, D, Vol. 6, 620, p. 862.

[62] 'Notiz über die Besprechung bei Herr Gesandten Clodius im Auswärtigen Amt am 25 Mai, 1939', June 6, 1939, signed by Nagel (RFM), BA, R 2/16476.

[63] 'Beste Lösung in unserem Sinne', June 6, 1939, signature illegible [Niemetz?], BA, R 2/16476.

[64] DGFP, D, Vol. 6, 620, p. 862. The compromise formulations were telephoned to Berlin by Reinhardt (RWM) on May 31, 1939. Unsigned minute, PA, Ha Pol, Handakten Clodius, Jugoslawien, Bd. 3. The Finance Ministry approved the final version, albeit without enthusiasm. Niemetz to Herrn Dirig 5U, Dir. 5, July 29, 1939, BA, R 2/16476.

[65] Telephone cables were also included in the credit over the opposition of the Finance Ministry.

specific assurances about types of equipment and delivery dates. Even the total amount of the credit was still undetermined. Göring had in fact reserved the right to veto the entire project even after it had been solemnly signed. This was nothing more than an extension of the stalling strategy used in the spring to extract the maximum in economic concessions from Yugoslavia.

Neuhausen and the legation in Belgrade recognized that Germany's procrastination was dissipating the political capital carefully nurtured since 1934. Schönebeck, the air attaché, reported that belief in German "good will" had been undermined when the negotiations dragged on from February to June.[66] Müller, an official of the Air Ministry, commented that coupling political questions with economic also had its bad side.[67] However, after Cvetković assured Neuhausen that Yugoslavia would sign an agreement granting the desired oil concessions simultaneously with the Armaments Protocol[68], the Wilhelmstraße moved swiftly. Wiehl concluded that the Armaments Protocol was "a matter of urgency" in view of the political dissatisfaction that Schönebeck had brought to Berlin's attention; the Wilhelmstraße was still concerned that a large British delivery (50 military aircraft) might still be available to Yugoslavia.[69] Even so, it required a personal démarche from Yugoslavia's minister in Berlin to Weizsäcker[70] and a telephone call from Neuhausen to State Secretary Keppler before the German legation was finally allowed to sign the draft agreement.[71] The protocol was signed in Belgrade on July 5, 1939.[72] The Yugoslav minister in Berlin told Woerman that the decision over the German oil concessions was already made, but no formal agreement concerning petroleum was signed together with the Armaments Protocol. Neuhausen and Heeren were, however, sufficiently convinced of Yugoslav sincerity that signing the Armaments Protocol was not delayed.[73] The first petroleum leases were granted by the end of July.[74]

From July to September, Göring's policy was determined by Germany's failure to achieve a one-to-one barter of Yugoslav raw materials for German armaments in the July 5 Protocol. The Wolhthat Treaty with Rumania and the Belgrade Protocol were similar in providing diplomatic means for German dominance of the raw materials without actually providing Germany with specific assurances for the

---

[66] Schönebeck (DG Belgrad) to RLM, June 15, 1939, enclosure in Müller (RLM) to Clodius, June 22, 1939, PA, Ha Pol, Handel mit Kriegsgerät, Jugoslawien, Bd. 1.

[67] Memorandum by Wiehl, June 27, 1939, DGFP, D, Vol. 6, p. 796.

[68] Memorandum by Wiehl, June 27, 1939, PA, Büro Staatssekretär, Jugoslawien, Bd. 1.

[69] Ibid. Heeren also reported that rumors were rife in Belgrade about a one-billion-franc French armament credit. In view of the possible Anglo-French competition, Heeren advised a swift signing of the draft protocol. Heeren (DG Belgrad) to AA, June 28, 1939, PA, Ha Pol, Handakten Clodius, Jugoslawien, Bd. 3.

[70] Memorandum by Wiehl, June 27, 1939, PA, Büro Staatssekretär, Jugoslawien, Bd. 1.

[71] Weizsäcker to DG Belgrad, July 1, 1939, PA, Ha Pol, Handakten Wiehl, Jugoslawien, Bd. 3.

[72] Heeren (DG Belgrad) to AA, July 5, 1939, DGFP, D, Vol. 6, p. 845, PA, Ha Pol, Handakten Wiehl, Jugoslawien, Bd. 3.

[73] Ibid.

[74] The Propaganda Ministry's confidential news service reported the signing of the first oil leases between the German firm Rudkop, A.G., and the Yugoslav company Pannoia on August 1. 'Vertraulicher Sonderdienst', 96, August 1, 1939, BA, R 7 VI 268/2.

export of raw materials. Yugoslavia, as had Rumania after the signing of the Wohlthat Treaty, put up strong rearguard resistance to further German encroachment upon its raw materials sector. However, Yugoslavia's vagueness about future raw materials deliveries and hesitancy in granting Germany monopoly privileges to explore petroleum reserves only provided Göring with an opportunity to delay "final" approval of the armaments credit. After Yugoslav resistance to Germany's petroleum demands collapsed and the protocol was signed, the arms were still withheld to force Yugoslavia to increase its deliveries of raw materials above the 50% quota agreed upon in the protocol. The outbreak of war not only provided Germany with good reasons to continue procrastinating, but put unbearable pressure upon Yugoslavia to capitulate to Göring's demands.

9. Arms and World War: The German Breakthrough in the Yugoslav Raw Materials Sector, July-October, 1939

The worsening international situation during the summer of 1939 prompted Yugoslavia to urgently request delivery of the promised armaments while allowing Berlin to tighten the conditions for delivery beyond those stipulated in the Belgrade Protocol. A domestic crisis over the Croat issue also contributed to the unenviable position of the Yugoslav government. Guaranteeing the oil concessions to Germany had lost Yugoslavia the friendship of Standard Oil and the goodwill of the U.S. government. Yugoslavia found itself facing a world war with woefully inadequate defenses and dependent upon Hitler's "word" for the delivery of modern arms. Yugoslavia vainly sought arms from the British, French, and even the Americans to counteract its dependence upon German sources; but the British and French needed their production and stocks for their own defense and the American, Belgian, and Swedish firms would sell only for cash. Faced with this impasse, Yugoslavia continued to pressure Berlin throughout the summer for immediate shipment of military and aeronautical hardware. Two weeks after the Armaments Protocol was signed, Andrić, the Yugoslav minister in Berlin, presented a list of Yugoslav requirements that had previously only been requests presented in a piecemeal fashion:[75]

1. 108 75mm antiaircraft guns and 200 antitank guns. (Order placed originally on June 27)
2. 50 Dornier 215 aircraft, 50 Messerschmidt 109 aircraft, 34 Fieseler aircraft (Order placed initially on April 5)
3. A further aircraft order: 50 Messerschmidt 109, 50 Dornier 215 (Tenders requested on June 23)

Yugoslavia wanted immediate delivery, out of German stocks if necessary. But even at this late date, over five months after Prince Paul's initial request, neither government knew exactly which armaments would come under the terms of the credit.

[75] Memorandum by Wiehl, July 17, 1939, DGFP, D, Vol. 6, p. 934. The same day Wiehl wrote the memorandum, the Yugoslav War Ministry told Heeren that a specific amount should be determined for the final credit so that orders could be expedited. Heeren (DG Belgrad) to AA, July 18, 1939, (at Bled), PA, Ha Pol, Handel mit Kriegsgerät, Jugoslawien, Bd. 1.

"When I [Wiehl] asked which of these deliveries were to be carried out under the provisions of the Protocol on an armaments credit last week in Belgrade, the Minister replied that he did not know; the details would have to be discussed by the experts."[76]

Andrić emphasized that Yugoslavia's neutrality was not "a passive but an active attitude" that might make obtaining arms in the West impossible. It was possible that Yugoslavia might "see herself stripped of arms" because of "her publicly declared attitude." Andrić also warned that "it would undoubtedly make a strange impression on world public opinion if the Yugoslav government had to place orders elsewhere, e.g., for artillery materiel in Sweden."[77] Wiehl merely promised to bring the matter to Ribbentrop's attention.

Wiehl's reticence stemmed from his awareness that German armaments deliveries to foreign countries had become the subject of consultations at the highest level of the Reich government. Hitler had ordered that no armament shipments would be made to enemy powers or to countries whose attitude could be characterized as "uncertain." He explicitly ordered that "weapons should be delivered to those areas where they would be useful to us or at least where they cannot hurt us, for example, to South America, the Baltic states, Norway, and Bulgaria."[78] Although Yugoslavia had excellent political relations with the Reich, Hitler decided to withhold certain weapons deliveries for a time and offer them to Italy.[79] Specifically, he ordered the allocation of 200 3.7cm antitank guns (Škoda) to the German army with a postponed delivery date to Yugoslavia of January, 1940, and the offer of 75mm antiaircraft guns to Italy. Rumania was clearly a greater political liability but Hitler allowed continued arms sales to Rumania, probably because of the importance of Rumanian petroleum in the German war economy.

Yugoslavia was not informed of Hitler's decision, so there the matter rested until Yugoslavia made more urgent inquiries in mid-August. Andrić was perturbed over information he received from the German Air Ministry that indicated that there were "political reasons" for German procrastination. In an interview with Weizsäcker, he emphasized that Cincar-Marković attached special importance to the question and wanted to be informed if any political reasons were causing the delay. Müller, of the Air Ministry, told the Wilhelmstraße the next day that "the signature of the contracts and thus the delivery of the total of 100 aircraft was dependent on a decision by the Field Marshal [Göring], who was waiting until certain questions were clarified."[80] Müller also passed on Göring's decision to grant a total credit of 200 million marks to be divided between aircraft (80 million marks) and military equipment and arms (120 million marks). "In any case the Yugoslav

---

[76] Ibid. Kaiser's brief comment on these complicated negotiations implies that Yugoslavia was excluded from the German arms market. KAISER, Economic Diplomacy, p. 270. German dilatoriness was aimed at achieving a one-to-one barter of arms for raw materials, not at shutting out the Yugoslavs.

[77] Ibid.

[78] OKW to Wiehl, July 22, 1939, PA, Ha Pol, Handel mit Kriegsgerät, Jugoslawien, Bd. 1.

[79] Ibid.

[80] Memorandum by Kalisch, August 17, 1939, ibid.

government were counting upon an armament credit of 200 million RM in all. This figure had already been mentioned to the Yugoslavs by Consul General Neuhausen."[81]

Göring had simply returned to his original intention to grant a credit of 200 million marks, without consulting Ribbentrop or subordinate Wilhelmstraße officials and ignoring Ribbentrop's attempt to interject Yugoslav adherence to the Anti-Comintern Pact as a condition for the second 100 million marks, although he had initially compromised with Ribbentrop's plan. Between the spring plan and the August plan, the share of the German aircraft industry had been cut by 20 million marks, partially due to the replacement of German war materiel with Czech. Göring, in his dual role as air minister and commandant of the *Luftwaffe*, had an interest in promoting exports of the aircraft industry, but he had a more direct interest in expanding Czech arms sales, since the Czech arms industry had been absorbed into the *Hermann Göring Werke*. Actually, since Germany was not committed to any specific figure or equipment in a formal agreement, both Göring and Neuhausen were using the 200 million marks as bait to draw the Yugoslav government into exclusive reliance upon German arms.

On August 24, the German legation in Belgrade was told that Neuhausen "has been authorized by the Field Marshal to inform the Yugoslav government that the contracts for the delivery of arms would now be signed."[82] Göring had decided to authorize all projects previously held up. State Secretary Keppler asked that Neuhausen "put through" the oil contracts and obtain permission to import duty free the machinery necessary for oil exploration and drilling. Germany was hoping to use a strike at the English owned Trepca mines to convince the Yugoslav government to take them over; once the mines were under Yugoslav administration the Wilhelmstraße hoped to increase German influence by providing technical assistance and personnel and thus secure the zinc and lead production for Germany via the clearing.

Germany's hand was being forced by the imminent outbreak of war. Göring was not interested in Ribbentrop's Anti-Comintern Pact — he authorized the delivery of war materiel subject to further Yugoslav concessions in the raw materials sector. Yugoslavia greeted Göring's decision with obvious relief, and Cincar-Marković promised a formal petroleum agreement between the two countries while the Yugoslav government permitted two trains of war materiel destined for Bulgaria to pass through on August 27.[83]

Göring's decision on August 24 contradicted Hitler's order of July and so created diplomatic difficulties with Italy, which had been promised the arms now given to Yugoslavia. Göring had also approved delivery of five more military aircraft to Yugoslavia before September 1 and eventual delivery of Škoda antiaircraft artillery. The German Air Ministry was put in an uncomfortable position when the Italians

[81] Ibid.
[82] Wiehl to DG Belgrad, August 24, 1939, DGFP, D, Vol. 7, p. 256.
[83] DG Belgrad to AA, August 26, 1939, PA, Ha Pol, Handakten Wiehl, Jugoslawien, Bd. 3. Heeren (DG Belgrad) to AA, August 27, 1939, ibid.

accepted Hitler's offer of the antiaircraft guns and Göring reversed the decision in favor of Yugoslavia.[84]

When war broke out, Yugoslavia, honoring its promise to remain actively neutral, continued normal exports to the Reich[85] and almost immediately went further. Andrić, Yugoslav minister in Berlin, spoke with Weizsäcker about the value of Yugoslav cooperation in the supplemental export of 30 tons of antimony and questioned the delay in delivering Czech weapons to Yugoslavia. Yugoslavia agreed to further supplemental exports of ten million marks during September[86] without demanding anything in return except that Germany fulfill its commitment to deliver armaments.

During the first week of September, 1939, Göring authorized shipping Czech artillery to Yugoslavia, but on September 7, Andrić complained to Wiehl that shipments intended for Yugoslavia had been stopped on the German-Yugoslav border and were being returned to the factories in Czechoslovakia. He warned Wiehl that Yugoslavia considered reneging on the credit agreement as "especially unfriendly", particularly considering Germany's continued shipment of armaments to Rumania and Bulgaria. Actually, this delivery delay was caused only by transport difficulties brought on by war mobilization, not by a high-level policy decision. Wiehl promised to quickly straighten out the situation.[87]

Although these delays were taken care of within a few days, Yugoslavia's long-simmering frustration over German procrastination finally surfaced. Heeren reported that the delays had created a most unfavorable impression in Belgrade[88] and that further delays could bring on Yugoslav intransigence over Germany's "many transport wishes", particularly with respect to Bulgaria. Neuhausen recommended that the armaments be released as well. The Yugoslav War Minister told Laurmen, the new German air attaché, that these continued delays in implementing already agreed upon transactions were creating a most unfavorable impression. Heeren, reporting this conversation, recommended swift compliance with Yugoslav wishes. "In view of the importance of the disposition of the Army for the line of Yugoslav foreign policy and of the danger that Yugoslavia could be swung to conclude treaties with enemy powers, [I] urgently recommend, in agreement with arms

---

[84] Memorandum by Kalisch, August 24, 1939, PA, Ha Pol, Handel mit Kriegsgerät, Jugoslawien, Bd. 1.

[85] Memorandum by Woerman, September 1, 1939, DGFP, D, Vol. 7, p. 508.

[86] Minute by Wiehl, September 6, 1939, PA, Ha Pol, Handakten Wiehl, Jugoslawien, Bd. 3.

[87] Memorandum by Wiehl, September 7, 1939, PA, Ha Pol, Handakten Wiehl, Jugoslawien, Bd. 3. Initial inquiries by Clodius demonstrated that neither the *Reichsbahn* nor the OKW had blocked the shipment. Although Heeren had reported that the problem was due to a mixup by Yugoslav customs officials, Wiehl subsequently discovered that local customs officials on the German side of the border had mistakenly intervened to stop the shipment. Clodius to DG Belgrad, September 7, 1939, Ibid.; Wiehl to DG Belgrad, September 9, 1939, ibid.; Koch (OKW) to RWM, September 12, 1939, PA, Ha Pol, Handel mit Kriegsgerät, Jugoslawien, Bd. 1.

[88] Heeren (DG Belgrad) to AA, September 7, 1939, PA, Ha Pol, Handakten Wiehl, Jugoslawien, Bd. 3.

attaché and General Consul Neuhausen, a far-reaching accommodation to Yugoslav armaments wishes, particularly as the desired conclusion of contracts would leave open the possibility of dilatory delivery."[89]

Arthur Bliss Lane, American minister in Belgrade, was aware of Yugoslavia's frustration over German delays. His reports clearly demonstrate that Yugoslavia, now desperate, was trying to find alternative sources of arms. ". . . the Prime Minister informed me verbally this evening that in view of the formation of a new government and in view of the fact that the Germans had not lived up to their promises to furnish Yugoslavia with war material requested, any commitments which the Yugoslav government may have conditionally made to Germany are now annulled. In reply to my direct question he assured me that the Standard Oil Company of New Jersey could count on the promise he had given me on June 17."[90] On September 16, War Minister Nedić asked Lane about the availability of arms.[91]

Göring, despite Yugoslav pressure and the advice of his subordinates, continued to withhold approval of complete compliance with Yugoslav wishes. On September 11, the Yugoslav air attaché was told that perhaps some training aircraft and Fieseler-Storch planes could be delivered, but "in no case will modern fighter aircraft be given."[92] Göring's stubbornness made Wiehl hesitant to raise the question again[93] and he left it up to Ribbentrop. The war with Poland made aircraft and antiaircraft artillery deliveries "extremely difficult."[94] However, an Air Ministry suggestion eventually overcame Göring's reluctance to part with Germany's most modern weaponry. "From the concerned bureau, mainly the Air Ministry, the idea has been suggested for discussion, whether we could, if necessary, perhaps obtain supplementary large amounts of goods especially of interest to us (copper, lead or hemp) by a train by train [barter of] aircraft and anti-aircraft artillery."[95]

Access to Yugoslav raw materials, the principal motive for German armaments sales to Yugoslavia, could not be put off after the outbreak of World War. The British blockade cut Germany off from her overseas raw materials sources and made southeastern Europe ever more vital to the German war economy. The British and French knew the fundamentals of political economy and began preemptive purchases for cash (in pounds, francs, dollars, and gold) wherever and whenever possible. They augmented this policy in Yugoslavia by deliberately reducing production at the French *Mines de Bor* and the English mines at Trepca. On September 14, Wiehl told Heeren to do what he could to hamper the Anglo-French preventive purchases.[96] On September 15, Yugoslavia suspended all German oil concessions

---

[89] Heeren (DG Belgrad) to AA, September 10, 1939, ibid.

[90] Lane (Belgrade) to the secretary of state, NA, RG 59, 760 H.62/140.

[91] Paraphrase of Lane telegram 236 of September 1, 1939, NA, RG 159, Military Attaché Report 329-T-7-15.

[92] Memorandum by Wiehl, September 11, 1939, PA, Ha Pol, Handakten Wiehl, Jugoslawien, Bd. 3.

[93] Ibid.

[94] Wiehl to DG Belgrad, September 14, 1939, ibid.

[95] Ibid.

[96] Ibid.

until Germany carried out the armaments agreement.[97] On September 16, Heeren reported that the prospects of a train-by-train barter of armaments for raw materials were good.[98] On September 18, the Yugoslav minister in Berlin told the Wilhelmstraße that the very stability of a regime friendly to Germany was threatened by its refusal to deliver the armaments. "Against strong military resistance [the government] prevailed politically, so that the orders were placed in Germany. . . . If the deliveries should really discontinue permanently, the Yugoslav government would naturally rather know it than to bring up the matter and then still not obtain the deliveries."[99]

In the midst of the successful Polish campaign and with a growing need for supplemental raw materials, Göring finally decided to release the aircraft and antiaircraft artillery if Yugoslavia made certain concessions. "The Field Marshal responds to this [Andrić's September 18 statement] [by saying] that Yugoslavia shall only receive the weapons in exchange for real, important, and tangible economic counter-concessions."[100] Göring had pressed Yugoslavia about the oil concessions in the spring and summer but he now considered petroleum a secondary issue in that it would not be quickly available in any case. Copper had become the price of arms. Göring had the far from original idea that Yugoslavia should make large quantities of *Mines de Bor* copper available for export to Germany because "the state of our copper supply" is "very blocked."[101] On September 25, Ribbentrop formally approved the exchange of antiaircraft and antitank artillery and Messerschmidt fighters for raw materials, particularly copper.[102] Prince Paul expressed his "lively satisfaction over the arrival of German armaments deliveries", and promised that every "available opportunity" would be used to bring the Bor and Trepca mines under state supervision. "The exchange of goods with Germany must be promoted in every way. Although wishing to always remain out of the war, Yugoslavia will always remain Germany's neighbor, and never be the neighbor of England."[103] Paul told the American minister the same day that he was "most anxious that the Germans shall not obtain direct evidence or information of his anti-Nazi sentiments."[104]

During September and early October, the Mixed Commission met in Belgrade to decide the details of the armaments/raw materials barter, leading to a Secret Protocol on October 5, 1939, which guaranteed the export to Yugoslavia of:[105]

I. Aircraft
    A. 100 Fighters — ME 109
    B. 13 Training — ME 108

---

[97] Heeren (DG Belgrad) to AA, September 15, 1939, ibid.

[98] Heeren (DG Belgrad) to AA, September 16, 1939, ibid.

[99] Minute by Woerman, September 18, 1939, ibid.

[100] Unsigned memorandum, September 19, 1939, ibid.

[101] Ibid.

[102] Wiehl to DG Belgrad, September 25, 1939, ibid.

[103] Heeren (DG Belgrad) to AA, September 28, 1939, ibid.

[104] Lane (Belgrade) to the secretary of state, September 28, 1939, NA, RG 59, 760 H.62/155.

[105] 'Geheimes Protokoll', October 5, 1939, BA, R 2/16476.

II. Artillery
  A. 28 Škoda Anti-Aircraft Artillery Pieces (7.5 cm)
  B. 80 Škoda Anti-Aircraft Artillery Pieces (7.65cm)
  C. 420 Škoda Anti-Tank Cannon (3.75cm) (including 1000 shells per artillery piece)

Yugoslavia promised to export various raw materials, including copper, copper ore, lead, lead ore, antimony, aluminum, bauxite, and lumber, as well as lard and hogs. The text of October's Secret Protocol did not go substantially beyond the Armaments Credit Protocol of July, 1939, but it was supplemented by an exchange of letters specifying monthly delivery dates for the armaments and raw materials. Yugoslavia guaranteed an initial quota of 3,000 tons of copper, 500 tons of lead, 1,000 tons of lead concentrate, 100 tons of aluminum, and 100 tons of antimony for October 1939. After November 1, 1939, they were to export 1,500-2,000 tons of copper, 500 tons of lead, 2,000 tons of lead concentrate, 100 tons of aluminum, and 100 tons of antimony.[106] Also included was an important price clause that specified that the price of the armaments and raw materials was to be the price prevailing in the world market in July, 1939. If the price of Yugoslav metals and ores rose 10% above the July, 1939, price, the price of the German armaments would be raised accordingly.[107] This provision protected Germany from price inflation induced by Anglo-French preemptive purchasing. The key feature of the agreement was, however, the "train-by-train" barter of armaments for raw materials, which guaranteed Germany direct and immediate access to the only source of copper, lead, and antimony other than the Soviet Union. Under the July Armaments Credit Protocol, Germany had been limited to 50% payment in raw materials of the total value of the Germany armaments and the payments were to have been spread over ten years.

German dilatory tactics had been initially a result of the compromise between Ribbentrop and Göring in which Ribbentrop hoped to use the armaments as a lever to force Yugoslavia to join the Anti-Comintern Pact. With Göring opposed to this project and Ribbentrop's influence with Hitler too weak to secure his intervention, procrastinating the negotiation of the credit and delivery of the armaments did not force Yugoslavia into the Anti-Comintern Pact but achieved a far more comprehensive end — obtaining hegemony over Yugoslavia's raw materials resources.

Postponing the delivery of the war materiel from July to October, 1939, qualitatively improved the terms of the agreement for Germany. Instead of a credit agreement payable in installments over ten years, half in raw materials and half in agricultural products, Yugoslavia had now accepted an agreement that specified immediate payment, primarily in raw materials. Hitler and Göring correctly assessed Germany's economic and political position and used the dilatory tactic as the most appropriate wedge to drive home a bid for hegemony. Although accepting the German credit offer, Yugoslavia did not simply wait hat in hand for Hitler and Göring to make up their minds to deliver, but neither the English nor French were able to compete with Germany in credit terms, amounts of equipment, or quality of mater-

---

[106] Pilja to Landfried, October 5, 1939, ibid.
[107] 'Geheimes Protokoll', paragraph 3, ibid.

ial.[108] The Swedes, Belgians, and Americans were willing to sell arms only for cash — not on credit or for barter. Also, in the October 5 Agreement, the price and exchange rate clause allowed Yugoslavia to profit from the war inflation of strategic raw materials up to a 10% increase over prices prevailing in July, 1939.

In setting particular quotas for raw materials, Yugoslavia pledged, for example, to deliver 1,500 to 2,000 tons of copper per month after November 1, 1939. However, the total production of the *Mines de Bor*, Yugoslavia's principal mine, annually produced 40,000 tons of copper and 7,000 tons of refined copper[109], so Yugoslavia was obligated to deliver from 38% to 51% of Bor production. This was a marked increase over Germany's 1938 share of Yugoslav copper (9,000 tons), requiring Yugoslavia to establish direct administrative control of the Bor mine if the new quotas were to be met.[110] An additional factor was that the barter of copper for armaments directly violated Yugoslav law and Yugoslav state agreements with Anglo-French mining interests that specified payment in free currency.[111]

The October 5 Protocol realized the goal pursued by Germany since 1934 — unlimited access to Yugoslav raw materials via the clearing mechanism. The stage was set for a direct confrontation between the Yugoslav government and Anglo-French blockade policy:[112] Yugoslavia proclaimed a state mineral monopoly by royal decree on November 11, 1939.[113]

---

[108] ". . . it is clear that none of the land armaments which the Yugoslav Government requires can be supplied from the British or very improbably from French sources." Draft paper for the War Cabinet, 'Yugoslav Mineral Monopoly and the Supply of Arms to Yugoslavia', no date [between November 29 and December 4, 1939], PRO, F.O. 371/23880.

[109] Lane (Belgrad) to the secretary of state, November 24, 1939, NA, RG, 660 H.6231/122. Lane's figures are based upon an interview with René Paix, manager of the Bor mines.

[110] Ibid.

[111] Campbell (Belgrade) to the F.O., telegram no. 75, December 20, 1938, PRO, F.O. 371, 23874.

[112] Paix told Lane that he was reducing production in order to prevent copper from being exported to Germany. op. cit., note 109. Apparently, the British were not fully informed of the extent of the Yugoslav capitulation. Until the end of 1939, Ronald Campbell continued to send optimistic reports on Yugoslav economic resistance to Germany. Campbell (Belgrade) to F.O., no. 66, September 5, 1939; no. 75, September 18, 1939; no. 75, September 20, 1939, all in PRO, F.O. 371/23874.

[113] Draft paper for the War Cabinet, op. cit., note 108.

CHAPTER IX

TRADE RELATIONS AFTER THE GRAIN CRISIS

1. The Rimma-Ferrostaal Credit

The Rimma-Ferrostaal project, a long-term credit for German construction of Rumanian heavy industry, ranked as the single most important transaction in the expanding German economy before the barter transaction of 1939. The Malaxa transaction and others similar to it had been designed to be repaid by a one-to-one barter of German commodities for Rumanian agricultural products. The Rimma credit, however, was to be repaid in installments over a period of years. It was unique in its scope, which eventually amounted to 25 million marks, and it involved not only the export of machines but on-site construction of a complete factory and an electric power station under German supervision. In 1933 Hitler had proposed proscribing the export of investment goods to underdeveloped countries, considering such exports to be partially responsible for worldwide industrial overproduction and thus for the Depression. But Germany's policy in southeast Europe was not hampered by such ideological considerations. Germany remained the only industrial power willing to deliver investment goods and construct plants in return for those raw materials and grains deemed by other industrial powers to be a glut on the world market. Such a policy greatly advanced German influence, draping Germany in the mantle of a fraternal ally of the underdeveloped nations in their drive to achieve industrial independence. The western powers, in contrast, appeared motivated by their conservatism: their need to protect existing capital investments while maintaining their flow of interest and profits. As long as the Depression continued, the economic policy of the western powers would stand opposed to the vital interests of agrarian eastern Europe. German policy did not fail to capitalize upon this.

While the treaty of 1935 was being negotiated, Paul Reusch of the *Gutehoffnungshütte* (GHH) approached Schacht with a proposal for a large-scale delivery of German investment goods to Rumania. Schacht, in turn, relayed these proposals to the Rumanian commerce minister, Manolescu-Strunga, in a personal letter written after the treaty was concluded. German business was eager and enthusiastic but nothing came of this preliminary initiative until the Munich negotiations in September, 1936, when a clause endorsing such projects (and armaments) was agreed upon. However, Ferrostaal, a subsidiary of GHH, was in the final negotiating stages with the Rumanian state corporation Rimma before the Munich protocol was signed. The Finance Ministry had previously approved Reich insurance for the project but the negotiations languished throughout the fall of 1936 and the winter of 1937, disappointing Berlin, which had been confident that the credit would be approved in November, 1936. "Ferrostaal-Rimma transaction, in which Rumania is supposed to deliver ore and petroleum, is ready to be signed. The initial payment is due in two years, so that the first delivery of mineral oil will take place at that time."[1]

The delay apparently prompted Germany to try renegotiating the terms[2], but the real cause of the delay was not a question of terms but of Rumania's fear that there would be an adverse domestic reaction to signing the credit. Ferrostaal refused to sign the contract without guaranteed payment by Rumania, which, under Rumanian law, would require an act of parliament; and King Carol was apprehensive that an open discussion of the credit in parliament would lead to a domestic political crisis. The agreement had to be postponed until a suitable alternative could be found, but it was months before King Carol suggested a compromise that he hoped would meet Ferrostaal's security demands. If Germany would agree to an extended payments schedule, he would publish a royal decree and the Cabinet would issue an irrevocable resolution, both of which would guarantee the transaction and so bypass the need for a parliamentary act. Fabricius quickly endorsed the compromise. "[I] recommend under all conditions to go forward on the King's proposal; otherwise, repercussions [are] to be feared in other areas of our activity in Rumania."[3] Under pressure from King Carol, last-minute negotiations expanded the credit from 14.86 million to over 18 million marks.[4]

The reluctant Finance Ministry was pressed by the Wilhelmstraße and Economics Ministry to extend state insurance coverage to the expanded credit. Under the terms of the new agreement, Rimma was to pay two million marks in cash when the contract was signed — under the old terms the entire payment was to have been deferred for two years. The original reasons for approving the treaty still held true and the terms for Ferrostaal were improved, so the Finance Ministry, although

---

[1] Wohlthat to Clodius, November 10, 1936, PA, Ha Pol, IVb, Rumänien, Rohstoffe und Waren, Petroleum, Bd. 1. For a brief survey of German policy in 1936, see KAISER, Economic Diplomacy, p. 145. In the view of Phillippe Marguerat, German foreign economic policy began to become interested in Rumanian petroleum in 1935, but a decisive turn did not result until 1938, so that "pétrole roumain devient un des soucis principaux de la diplomatie allemande." MARGUERAT, Le III Reich, p. 15. In fact, German interest in Rumanian petroleum was a constant throughout the period, with ever increasing emphasis after the inauguration of the Four Year Plan. Marguerat also passes over the strong German interest in Rumanian grains caused by the poor German harvest of 1936.

[2] King Carol told Fabricius that he did not want any changes in the contract. Fabricius (DG Bucharest) to AA, February 4, 1937, PA, Ha Pol, Handakten Clodius, Rumänien, Bd. 1. Fabricius mentioned the Ferrostaal project only in passing in his long survey of barter transactions. Minute by Fabricius, March 18, 1937, PA, Ha Pol, IVb, Rumänien, Handel 11 Nr.3A, Erdöl und Getreide, Bd. 1.

[3] Fabricius to AA, April 19, 1937, PA, Ha Pol, Handakten Clodius, Rumänien, Bd. 1. Carol was willing to accept simpler machines at the same price in exchange for an extended payments schedule.

[4] 'Bürgschaft Ferrostaal', May [?], 1937, BA, R 2/309936. According to the German Finance Ministry, the credit was initially approved at 16.95 million marks.

skeptical of the financial stability of Rimma and the Rumanian state, approved the insurance of the expanded credit.[5] "There are no objections to the extension of the already agreed upon surety obligation for the Reich of 2.2 million *Reichsmark*. The political and economic considerations which you regard as decisive are still in force today. Therefore, it does not seem reasonable to allow the Rimma transaction to fall through by refusing to increase the obligation, particularly as Ferrostaal has not extended the transaction on its initiative but rather as a consequence of pressure from political channels."[6]

Additional pressure was being exerted in Bucharest during the final stages of negotiation for another increase of 1.5 million marks in the total credit, bringing it to 19.5 million marks. Ferrostaal, naturally enough, refused to conclude the package without a Reich guarantee of the extra 1.5 million marks.[7] The Wilhelmstraße wanted written assurance from the Rumanian government and the National Bank that wheat and oil would be released for export and that the mark exchange rate would be stabilized before taking this last step. By using the Rimma credit as a lever to gain concessions on the still unresolved wheat question[8], the Wilhelmstraße received assurances "on the highest authority" from Valer Pop that German requests for oil and wheat would be met if the Reich government approved extending state insurance for the Rimma project.[9]

Despite such assurances other difficulties emerged during the final negotiations, not the least of which was King Carol's constant pressure to further extend the project. In May, the German Finance Ministry approved a guarantee for 12.6 million marks, which would be 70% of 18 million marks, but a later Economics Ministry document indicates that Germany agreed to a guarantee of 15 million marks, making it appear that the total credit reached 21.4 million marks. King Carol, however, wanted an even greater increase.[10] A second problem arose with Rumania's demand in the autumn of 1937 that the delivery period be shortened from 24 to 3 months.[11] The Wilhelmstraße brushed off the original request as impractical[12] but

[5] The original Reich insurance covered 70% of the 16.95 million marks; thus, the second stage of the negotiations did not require Finance Ministry intervention as the total credit was reduced. In the third stage of the negotiations, the extension of the credit to over 18 million marks required the formal intervention of the Finance Ministry, but since a cash down payment of 2 million marks was part of the new package, the total coverage of 16 million marks was less than in the original contract.

[6] 'Bürgschaft Ferrostaal', May [?], 1937, op. cit.

[7] Ibid.

[8] Ritter to DG Bukarest, May 20, 1937, ibid.

[9] Unsigned minute, 'Telephonat aus Bukarest', June 9, 1937, PA, Ha Pol, IVb, Rumänien, Handel 11 Nr.3, Austauschgeschäfte, Bd. 1.

[10] Warncke (RWM) to AA, October 31, 1937, PA, Ha Pol, IVb, Rumänien, Handel 11 Nr.3A, Erdöl und Getreide, Bd. 2. Fabricius (DG Bukarest) to AA, May 5, 1937, PA, Ha Pol, Rumänien, Handakten Clodius, Bd. 1.

[11] This demand was unusual. The Rumanians wanted a complete factory plus an electric power station delivered and constructed in less than six months, from shipment from Germany to the actual operation of the plant. Pochhammer (DG Bukarest) to AA, October 7, 1937, PA, Ha Pol, IVb, Rumänien, Handel 11 Nr.3A, Erdöl und Getreide, Bd. 2.

[12] Clodius to DG Bukarest, August 5, 1937, ibid.

saw an opportunity that could be turned to Germany's advantage. If Germany did deliver the entire factory in three months, then, by the same token, Rumanian payments in oil or wheat would have to be stepped up.

Although Ferrostaal refused to give written assurance of delivery in three months, a verbal statement to that effect was given to Valer Pop on the condition that the Reich guarantee the whole credit (21.4 million marks or 3.14 million marks over the May figures approved by the Finance Ministry), and provided that Rumania make additional on-site labor available for the job. In return for Rumania's guaranteed supplementary wheat and oil quotas, the Economics Ministry approved both the shortened delivery period and the expanded Reich guarantee. "I would be grateful for a particularly accelerated treatment of this matter, since in my opinion it is not reasonable that Ferrostaal A.G., which agreed to raise the volume of the transaction essentially on the basis of the political arguments placed in the foreground by the German Minister in Bucharest be delayed."[13]

Germany's compromise on the delivery question meant that the payments under the credit that were to begin after the original completion date of the factory, i.e., in October, 1939, would begin at least 18 months earlier. Thus Germany could purchase supplementary wheat or oil from the quarterly payments in lei that Rimma made into the clearing. These oil or wheat imports were in addition to normal and supplementary trade. Although the shortened delivery period involved considerable inconvenience for Ferrostaal and increased liability for the German state, the political benefits and the increased access to petroleum and wheat more than compensated.

The importance of the Ferrostaal-Rimma credit hardly needs to be emphasized. A delivery of more than 22 million marks of investment goods over a three-month period needs only to be put in the perspective of German exports to Rumania during 1932-34 to assess its significance. During these years German exports to Rumania had averaged only 53.3 million marks. This one barter transaction, delivered in a single three-month period, amounted to more than 40% of the 1932-34 average. Such barter arrangements not only provided German big business with guaranteed orders on a scale unthinkable during the doldrums of the Depression, but contributed to the solution of Germany's critical shortages of petroleum and grain imports. Under these conditions, German industrialists and policy makers inevitably concluded that the earlier enthusiastic prognoses of the *Mitteleuropäischer Wirtschaftstag* were justified.

---

[13] Warncke (RWM) to AA, October 14, 1937, ibid. Marguerat briefly mentions the Ferrostaal contract in the context of Rheinmetall-Borsig's relations with Malaxa. This, in fact, confuses two separate transactions and, also, fails to highlight the importance of the Rimma-Ferrostaal transaction in terms of its volume, and liquidation of Germany's clearing debt. It is also highly unlikely that the GHH, the parent company of Ferrostaal, would have permitted itself to be ensnared as junior partner with the rival Rheinmetall-Borsig combine. MARGUERAT, Le III Reich, p. 48-49.

2. *The First Armaments Orders from Rumania*

Rumanian enthusiasm for German armaments seemed unbounded in November and December of 1936. Malaxa's presence in Berlin as a sort of plenipotentiary general for Rumanian rearmament seemed to indicate that King Carol and the Cabinet had serious intentions. But the actual development of concrete projects lagged behind the wheat purchase, the Malaxa and related transactions, and the Rimma-Ferrostaal credit. Political considerations were involved in this mutual reluctance. Rumania's acceptance of German armaments was fraught with domestic and international political complications for the Rumanian government. In turn, the Reich government was concerned about Rumania's unclarified political attitude — in short, how Rumania would react in a crisis. If King Carol and Valer Pop had had to do everything possible to avoid a parliamentary discussion of the Rimma-Ferrostaal credit, how much more sensitive would domestic reaction be to an armaments deal with Germany? Göring's Air Ministry would not allow Yugoslavia to permit Rumanian air force officers to train on a German Dornier 17 bomber sold to Yugoslavia. "The release of the aircraft model Do 17 cannot follow. The release to Yugoslavia of the Do 17 model follows from reasons of political compromise and trust. A prerequisite for this was that Yugoslavia would keep the Do 17 secret from all other parties. The Yugoslav government must maintain its commitment to the secrecy obligation."[14]

Later, in September, 1937, when representatives of the German armaments industry reported a "pronounced productive turn" in Rumania and asked that the Wilhelmstraße allow them to begin negotiations on land and air armaments after concluding successful contracts on marine armaments, Weizsäcker reserved judgment. "The *Auswärtiges Amt* would like to mull over the political side of the question. . . . I refused approval of the latter, but promised a study of the matter as soon as it came to me officially."[15] But despite mutual misgivings, a modest breakthrough on naval hardware did occur and is significant because of the crucial role of armaments during 1938-39 in both trade and politics.

As early as 1934, German industry had been actively pursuing naval contracts in southeastern Europe in cooperation with Dutch firms. "Rumania plans the construction of warships and the renovation of the Galatz harbor. The composition of the plans is entrusted to the *Ingenieurskantoor voor Scheepsbau*, den Haag. The collaboration should proceed in such a way that the warships will be assembled in Dutch shipyards, while Germany should take over the harbor extension and the delivery of materials."[16] These early plans had fallen through, but the first breakthrough in the Rumanian naval armaments market did result from Dutch-German

---

[14] Hannesse (RLM) to AA, December 4, 1936, PA, Gesandtschaft Bukarest, Fach 48, IF 7, Rumänische Aufrüstung.

[15] Minute by Weizsäcker, September 21, 1937, PA, Ha Pol, IVb, Rumänien, Handel mit Kriegsgerät, Bd. 1.

[16] Memoradum by Willy Leese (Ferrostaal), 'Gemeingeschäfte Holland-Deutschland', enclosure in Reusch (Oberhausen) to Schacht (Berlin), January 12, 1934, HA-GHH 4001001290/33b. Projects for Bulgaria and Argentina were also under consideration.

cooperation. The preliminary orders called for torpedo boats, two submarines, a minesweeper, and a shipyard. "The ship construction material should be prefabricated in Holland or Germany. The machines and other facilities including the armaments come from Germany. The conclusion of the contract should be agreed upon with Herr Malaxa. Total cost: 14 million *Reichsmark*. 1/7 will be paid at contract signature, 6/7 in treasury bonds at seven per cent interest, over seven years."[17]

With stiff French competition and Rumanian complaints about exorbitant prices, the German firms were forced to submit new tenders for the contracts.[18] The price question was finally resolved, but the Dutch-German consortium found it difficult to pin the Rumanian government down to a payments agreement. Rumania rejected Germany's demand for a gold clause, proposing instead a currency clause based on the exchange rate of the mark in relation to the dollar and pound.[19] A subsequent plan to issue state bonds in lei, payable in marks or strong currencies, was discarded in favor of payment in Rumanian products selected by German firms.[20] This payment model was superseded in its turn by a revised Rumanian commitment to pay in strong currencies.[21] When agreement was once again reached on a payments mechanism, Germany would accept only free currency as payment. Fabricius was bewildered by Berlin's tactics. "In light of my efforts over the past months which were only directed at obtaining wheat or petroleum under the best possible conditions, it is incomprehensible to the government here why we now insist upon free currency."[22]

The Economics Ministry was willing to relent on its demand for payment in free currency only when Rumania agreed to discard the seven-year credit agreement and pay in petroleum or wheat before the end of 1938.[23] Unwilling to forgo the opportunity for credit, the Rumanian government accepted the original German proposal for the currency clause to be reckoned in terms of the gold/mark exchange rate at the official German rate. Concluding the agreement on this basis meant that Rumania accepted the officially administered mark exchange rate in terms of gold: a rate that had nothing to do with the mark's value on international exchanges or in Bucharest. Germany was thus able to buy either petroleum or wheat at the world market price without suffering the customary 40% cost increase caused by the mark's devaluation on the Bucharest bourse. Payment was to begin when the contract was signed and to continue in quarterly installments, so by the

---

[17] Minute by Fabricius (DG Bukarest), March 18, 1937, PA, Ha Pol, IVb, Rumänien, Handel 11 Nr. 3, Austauschgeschäfte, Bd. 1.

[18] Fabricius (DG Bukarest) to AA, April 15, 1937, PA, Ha Pol, Handakten Clodius, Rumänien, Bd. 1.

[19] Fabricius (DG Bukarest) to AA, July 7, 1937, PA, Ha Pol, IVb, Rumänien, Handel 11 Nr.3A, Erdöl und Getreide, Bd. 1.

[20] Minute by Clodius, July 8, 1937, ibid.

[21] Reinhardt (RWM) to AA, July 13, 1937, ibid. Benzler to DG Bukarest, July 14, 1937, PA, Ha Pol, Handakten Clodius, Rumänien, Bd. 1.

[22] Fabricius (DG Bukarest) to AA, July 19, 1937, PA, Ha Pol, IVb, Rumänien, Handel 11 Nr.3, Austauschgeschäfte, Bd. 1.

[23] Spitta (RWM) to AA, July [?], 1937, PA, Ha Pol, IVb, Rumänien Handel 11 Nr.3A, Erdöl und Getreide, Bd. 1.

time the submarines and minesweepers were actually delivered to Rumania in February, 1940, the Wilhelmstraße expected Germany to have already received 70% of the sale price in "vital raw materials."[24] If Germany were given a free hand to use the installments to purchase any Rumanian commodity and not merely oil or wheat, the Wilhelmstraße recommended approval of the contracts. The alliance of the Wilhelmstraße and Naval High Command (OKM) proved powerful enough to override the doubts of other ministries. "The *Auswärtiges Amt* and the Naval High Command have intervened vigorously for the transaction, which is to be regarded as the key transaction for other extensive deliveries to the Rumanian navy."[25]

The U-boat transaction was not large enough to transform trade relations or signal the final victory of German influence over Franco-Czech firms. The terms of the agreement did not have the approval of the Economics Ministry, but the Wilhelmstraße and Navy prevailed in their view that the transaction should be approved as an initial step in German penetration of the Rumanian armaments market. German political reserve postponed capitalizing in 1937 on the breakthrough represented by this transaction, but the groundwork had been laid for the intensive armament sales campaign of 1938. The *Anschluß* and the resulting shortfall of petroleum imports for the Greater Reich required increased supplies of Rumanian petroleum if both the armed forces and Austria were to be kept supplied.

3. The Protocol of December, 1937

The Reich had just cause for a certain amount of self-congratulation by the autumn of 1937. After having to deal with Rumania's procrastination during the first eight months of 1937, Germany was finally assured of virtually all Rumanian bread and fodder grains it wanted. As long as Rumania kept its word, Germany would never again face a grain crisis like that of the winter of 1936-37. Although German exports to Rumania had not kept pace with the increased cereals imports, the successful conclusion of the Malaxa barter, the Rimma-Ferrostaal credit, and the German-Dutch U-boat consortium transaction all boded well for German export interests. But there were still two problems: first, the Rumanian National Bank was unable or unwilling to live up to its promise to support the exchange rate of the mark, causing further devaluation of the mark and extreme exchange rate fluctuations even after the Schacht-Constantinescu *Aide-Memoire* of March 1937; and second, Germany's need for increased petroleum imports had to be subordinated to the grain crisis, so that the commodities exported under the nine-million-mark supplementary quota went to pay for wheat rather than petroleum. Although this problem stemmed from German mismanagement of the domestic agricultural sector, the mark exchange rate was not a purely German question and was amenable to a negotiated solution.

---

[24] Unsigned minute, August 4, 1937, PA, Ha Pol, IVb, Rumänien, Handel 11 Nr.3A, Erdöl und Getreide, Bd. 2.

[25] Unsigned minute, August 4, 1937; Clodius to DG Bukarest, August 10, 1937. Both in ibid.

During the first years of the 1935 treaty, the devaluation of the mark had been officially tolerated in order to promote German export interests in the Rumanian market by making German products competitive. However, this tactic was limited as a viable instrument of German policy and the limit was reached when aircraft gasoline imports became more important than German export promotion. The grain crisis of 1937 proved that Germany could not simultaneously secure large imports of wheat and oil and pile up large clearing debts. The massive mark clearing debts accumulated in Berlin during 1937 because of increased German cereal imports caused a situation in which there were simply no buyers for the mark in Rumania. "The Rumanian exporter, who had to utilize on the free Rumanian market the export proceeds in *Reichsmark* paid in through the clearing transaction, was forced because of the small demand to release the *Reichsmark* to Rumanian importers at a considerable discount (up to 38%). A special drawback was that the exchange rate of the Reichsmark in clearing transactions was subject to great fluctuations, so that neither the purchaser nor the seller had a sure basis for his calculations and had to include large risk premiums in them. In this way German imports from Rumania became so expensive that, except for grain, which had to be bought at excessive prices for reasons of domestic supply, Rumanian products — especially petroleum — could be bought only to a limited extent."[26] Wohlthat, chairman of the German delegation to the Mixed Commission, neglected to add that in the summer of 1937 the situation had become so serious that the Rumanian banks that had been advancing lei to the Rumanian oil exporters in exchange for clearing marks simply suspended trading in clearing marks. "Petroleum imports from Rumania have therefore come to a dead halt."[27]

Germany's problem with petroleum supply lay in the fact that, with the exception of Rumanian exports, aircraft gasoline was available only for cash on the world market. The stark realities of German trade policy and Four Year Plan economics were commented upon by Budezies of the Control Board for Oil: "The cash available to me is not sufficient in the long run to satisfy the ever rising needs of the *Luftwaffe.*"[28] The reserves of German oil import companies had fallen from 41,640 tons (March 31) to 22,104 tons (July 31)[29], while the requirements for August that

---

[26] Wohlthat to Göring, December 13, 1937, DGFP, D, Vol. 5, 154, pp. 205-206.

[27] Budezies (UB Öl) to Puhl (Reichsbank), August 13, 1937, PA, Ha Pol, IVb, Rumänien, Handel 11 Nr.3A, Erdöl und Getreide, Bd. 2. Marguerat's contention that Rumanian petroleum only became central to German foreign economic policy in 1938 is contradicted by this important document. Even in 1937, Germany was so dependent on the import of Rumanian aviation fuel that any interruption in the export of the fuel via the clearing mechanism threatened the build-up of the *Luftwaffe.* It was not that total percentage of petroleum products imported from Rumania compared to all other sources. It was not the price of Rumanian oil compared to free market or clearing partners. It was simply the unpalatable fact (to the Germans) that aviation fuel was only available on the world market for cash or through the clearing trade mechanism with Rumania. For Marguerat's view see, MARGUERAT, Le III Reich, p. 100.

[28] Ibid.

[29] The second figure included petroleum in a tanker which, as of July 31, 1937, had not arrived in port.

included military and air maneuvers were 32,000 tons. Although the extraordinary demands of August could be covered by drawing on reserves and the incoming imports of that month, Germany faced a total aircraft gasoline shortfall of at least 34,000 tons (September-December 1937).[30] As the reserves would be almost exhausted by the end of August, Budezies predicted a supply crisis to the *Luftwaffe* beginning in September, and saw only one possible solution. "In light of this embarrassing situation it is urgently recommended, without regard to normally recognized considerations, to do everything conceivable to get the supplies from Rumania."[31] The Rumanian oil export company, Rajinajul, was prepared to release 8,000 tons of aircraft gasoline for export to Germany if one million marks of its two-million-mark blocked clearing credit was released. Responding to German demands for stabilization of the mark, the Rumanian National Bank simply refused to release blocked marks for sale, leaving Rajinajul and other oil exporters with no way to obtain cash (lei) for their exports to Germany, i.e., they were extending interest-free commodity credits to Germany. Budezies asked the *Reichsbank* to intervene with the National Bank to press for the release of the blocked marks to Rajinajul. Quick action was necessary because Rajinajul had already sold elsewhere 3,000 tons of a shipment originally promised to Germany.

The crisis of August, 1937, over aircraft gasoline illustrates the resource constraints upon the German rearmament economy and the contradictions of the German trade drive in Rumania. Clearing balances accumulated in Berlin by the purchase of grain and raw materials served as an effective tool for forcing German exports on the Rumanians. This was, indeed, the original purpose of Schacht's whole trade policy. But blocked marks in Berlin that earned no interest were of little value to a Rumanian exporter who was unable to obtain the cash equivalent in lei. The policy eventually resulted, as demonstrated by the crisis of August, in the Rumanian oil exporters refusing to deliver to the German market. Germany had outsmarted itself. Germany, which had used a passive trade balance to exploit the import potential of the Rumanian market, was increasingly constrained by its growing need for Rumanian petroleum products. Thus, one of the major purposes of German policy at the Mixed Commission meeting in Bucharest (December 1937) was "to stabilize the rate of exchange [of the *Reichsmark*] at as high a level as possible."[32] The drive for secure and steady access to Rumanian petroleum, not for fiscal conservatism, was primary.

The negotiations at Bucharest revolved around two German aims other than the stabilization of the mark. "1. to reach an agreement on a further increase in reciprocal trade; 2. to ensure a settlement in trade and payments transactions with reduction of the payments balance. . . ."[33] The negotiations were long and difficult

---

[30] German needs were calculated to be: September 20,000 tons; October 17,000 tons; November 17,000 tons; December 16,000 tons. But Budezies could draw upon only convertible foreign exchange for 11,000 to 12,000 tons per month. The rest had to come either from Rumania or be imported at the expense of other strategic raw materials.

[31] Op. cit. note 27.

[32] Wohlthat to Göring, December 13, 1937, DGFP, D, Vol. 5, 154, p. 251.

[33] Ibid.

because Rumania ostensibly wanted to reduce bilateral trade to its 1936 volume, limit German imports from Rumania to the value of German exports to Rumania in the previous quarter, and change the composition of Rumanian agricultural deliveries at the expense of grains to the benefit of hogs, lard, bacon, and eggs. Rumania wanted to prevent Germany from buying up everything in sight by tying its exports to Germany's actual ability to pay quarterly while simultaneously increasing its exports of agricultural commodities that were difficult to market.

Wohlthat managed to reach an initial compromise acceptable to German interests by a series of concessions on the composition of Germany's agricultural imports and on the exchange rate of the mark. In return for Rumania's agreement to expand the volume of bilateral trade by one-third over 1937, Wohlthat proposed three major concessions to Berlin:

1. German guarantee of the mark at a fixed exchange rate. To this end a special 10-million-mark fund would be established to pay the difference between the fixed rate and fluctuations on the Rumanian market. Once Rumanian accounts in the clearing were reduced to 10 million marks, the fund would be paid back to Germany. This German guarantee was to be temporary, limited to the first eight months of 1938.[34]
2. German agreement to an exchange rate of 37-38 lei per mark, a substantial amount below the Reich goal of 44 lei.
3. Agreement to import hogs, lard, and geese at substantially higher prices than the prevailing world price.

Wohlthat was able to obtain Rumania's consent to a total program for the first nine months of 1938 that he felt justified the concessions. Total trade would be increased from 227.7 million marks (January-September 1937) by 100 million marks for the same period in 1938.[35] He estimated that this increase would mean the creation of up to 170 million marks in imports from Rumania, including over 40 million marks in cereals, nearly 40 million marks in petroleum and close to 12 million marks in lumber. To balance these increased German purchases, Rumania promised to issue import permits for one billion lei quarterly (75 million marks — January to September 1938), along with unlimited import permits for nonquota goods (primarily investment goods) and quota commodities (consumers' goods). Wohlthat forecast that special barter transactions would amount to some 90 million marks (January-September 1938) that would almost double total German exports to Rumania from the same period in 1937 (165 million marks versus 87.8 million marks). This package would lead, he promised, to liquidating the clearing debt and stabilizing the mark exchange rate.

Wohlthat was anxious to sell this compromise to Berlin and forecast dire consequences if his compromise formulae were not endorsed. If these concessions were not made, the "planned buildup" of trade relations from 1935-37 would receive a serious blow, at least according to Wohlthat. Rumania's improved financial condi-

---

[34] Wohlthat (DG Bukarest) to AA, November 18, 1937, PA, Ha Pol, IVb, Rumänien, Handel l3A, Regierungsausschüsse, Bd. 1. The Finance Ministry was particularly opposed to this proposal, fearing that implementing it would establish a precedent that all clearing countries could use against Germany. Unsigned minute, November 25, 1937, BA, R 2/14156.

[35] Wohlthat (DG Bukarest) to AA, November 18, 1937, PA, Ha Pol, IVb, Rumänien, Handel l3A, Regierungsausschüsse, Bd. 1.

tion and the improved situation of the world market gave Rumania sufficient latitude to throttle trade between the two countries if its vital interests were not met. If
Rumania refused to issue sufficient import permits, the mark could be further
depressed on the Bucharest exchange. "Grains and petroleum would then be
obtainable only through special barter transactions involving the delivery of commodities of foreign exchange value. It would then be an open question whether or
not Rumania would denounce the existing commodities agreement."[36] If Germany
refused the demand for an exchange rate guarantee, Wohlthat believed that the
Rumanian government would refuse to issue import permits for consumers' goods,
and "[t]hereby the structural composition of German exports to Rumania would be
shifted to the detriment of the German economy from the plentifully available consumers' goods to the capital and investment goods which are in worldwide
demand."[37] If Berlin rejected the excess prices for agricultural products, Rumania
could be expected to counteract by limiting grain exports.

Wohlthat particularly stressed Rumania's feeling of German discrimination as a
barrier to improved trade relations; German refusal to guarantee the mark would be
regarded in Bucharest as another example of its discriminatory tactics since Germany had already signed similar agreements with Yugoslavia and Turkey. "This
psychological factor plays a special role in the mentality of the Rumanians during
the negotiations."[38]

Wohlthat argued strongly for the payment of excess prices for hogs, lard, etc.
While he did not believe that Rumanian domestic prices were as high as those in
Hungary and Yugoslavia, and therefore the justification for the payment was not as
clear as in the case of those countries, he saw no way to avoid granting the concessions if Germany wanted the 40 million marks in cereals.[39] Rumania had made the
export of the cereals dependent on this concession. "I don't need to elaborate that a
relatively secure guarantee for the delivery of grain would be of greatest significance in the context of the program."[40] Wohlthat also argued that the explicit linking of the excess price to the grain exports would prevent Hungary and Yugoslavia
from using the concession to Rumania to extort further concessions from Germany.
Despite the excess prices, Wohlthat believed that the agricultural products could be
largely imported without resort to direct Reich subsidies.[41] He concluded his arguments for accepting the compromise package with a flourish. "After all our trade
and payments agreements with the other states of southeast Europe have been consolidated in a secure format, the proposed agreement with Rumania would form the
keystone of this development."[42]

---

[36] Ibid., p. 5.
[37] Ibid., p. 6.
[38] Ibid.
[39] Ibid.
[40] Ibid.
[41] The hogs and lard fell into this category. Wohlthat estimated that only 150,000 marks
would be required to market the geese.
[42] Wohlthat (DG Bukarest) to AA, November 18, 1937, op. cit., note 35.

Although it was strongly endorsed by Fabricius, Wohlthat's plea for compromise was not accepted in Berlin without substantial revision.[43] The interministerial committee did agree with Wohlthat that the package was of "great significance", but the Economic Policy Committee could not agree to a mark exchange rate guarantee because they feared that doing so would establish a precedent for other countries.[44] The Economic Policy Committee insisted on maintaining the position that stabilization of mark fluctuations must come through bilateral balancing of trade, by decreasing German purchases if necessary. The compromise mark exchange rate also proved unacceptable to Berlin, which maintained that Rumania "on its own" (einseitig) must guarantee the mark at a minimum of 39 to 40 lei per mark. The Economic Policy Committee did, however, agree to paying the excess price on condition that the mark exchange rate be set at 39-40 lei.

Clodius elaborated these decisions in his instructions to Bucharest.[45] The Reich government was even willing to limit its imports from Rumania over a period of time, rather than undertake to guarantee the mark. Naturally, Rumania had to continue to guarantee import quotas for German goods, or Germany's decrease in purchases from Rumania would not bring about the desired liquidation of the clearing debt. Clodius argued that the same policy had been applied successfully in Turkey, Greece, and Yugoslavia, proving that it did not necessarily mean a general decline in bilateral trade. If agreement on the exchange rate of the mark at 39-40 could not be reached, he indicated that the Wilhelmstraße was prepared to accept a de facto commitment of 37.5-38.5.[46]

The National Bank continued to resist supporting the mark without a German exchange rate guarantee, and negotiations broke down over Rumania's demand for the payment of excess prices on hogs. Wohlthat was authorized to go only as high as 80 marks per 100 kilos, although he attempted to persuade Berlin to meet Rumania's demand of 82 marks.[47] The Agricultural Ministry was absolutely opposed to this concession but did agree to Rumania's proposal to finance the excess prices out of wheat premiums.[48]

Although not all of Germany's demands were met[49], German compromises on the mark exchange rate were more than compensated for by Rumanian commit-

[43] Fabricius (DG Bukarest) to AA, November 18, 1937, DGFP, D, Vol. 5, 147, p. 198.

[44] Ha Pol Ausschuß, November 22, 1937, PA, Ha Pol, Handakten Wiehl, Ha Pol Ausschuß, unsigned minute, November 25, 1937, BA, R 2/14156.

[45] Clodius to DG Bukarest, November 22, 1937, PA, Ha Pol, IVb, Rumänien, Handel 13, Handelsvertragsverhältnisse zu Deutschland, Bd. 1.

[46] Ibid.

[47] Wohlthat, Fabricius (DG Bukarest) to AA, December 7, 1937, PA, Ha Pol, IVb, Rumänien, Handel 13A, Regierungsausschüsse, Bd. 1.

[48] Walter (RMEL) to Kalisch (AA), ibid. Walter was afraid that if Überpreise above 80 marks per 100 kilos were paid for Rumanian hogs there would be pressure from Hungary and Yugoslavia for the same concession.

[49] Two financial claims (the Gerlingkonzern and the Friedrich Wilhelm insurance companies) dating from before World War I remained outstanding. Friedrich Wilhelm was offered a settlement in December 1938 but the Gerlingkonzern grievance was not settled before the outbreak of war. Mackensen to DG Bukarest, November 3, 1937, PA, Ha Pol, Handakten Clodius, Rumänien, Bd. 1.

ments to expand trade, by specific commitments on the export of grains and by the issuance of import permits for German exports. Wohlthat characterized the negotiations as "long and difficult", but there were signs even during the talks of "promising business opportunities" that could be facilitated by Reich guarantees.[50] The negotiations confirmed Fabricius's earlier optimism. "If German-Rumanian relations develop within the framework of the present agreements, then we can count on the most favorable conditions obtaining for further economic cooperation when the present treaty period is at an end."[51] Wohlthat emphasized the conjunctional setting of the negotiations, i.e., the significance of a successful compromise during an election campaign where the Liberal government was criticized, not least for its policy towards Germany, and the visit of French Foreign Minister Delbos. This political setting and Wohlthat's audience with King Carol after the agreement was signed were "proof of the growth of German influence which has taken place in the years since the conclusion of the commercial treaty of 1935."[52] In future relations Wohlthat was particularly concerned that Rumania's feeling of discrimination by Germany be overcome. "Considering the importance of Rumania to Germany's balance of trade in Southeastern Europe because of the volume and character of her commerce, everything ought to be done to free our relations with this country, which has the greatest possibilities for the future in the Danube area, from the handicap which arises from a feeling of being discriminated against."[53]

The protocol and exchange of letters was the by-now familiar patchwork of compromises. While Germany was guaranteed "sufficient opportunities for importing grain" (150,000 tons of wheat, 500,000 tons of feed grains), and import permits for its shipments to Rumania, Rumania was guaranteed excess prices on a series of agricultural commodities (hogs, lard, bacon, eggs, geese) in return. Although Germany went a long way toward meeting the excess price demands of Rumania, a special proviso provided for the payment of export premiums by Rumania.[54] A schedule was set up establishing a proportion between Germany's import of grains and the excess price agricultural commodities.[55] "For petroleum and lumber imports, quotas of 37 and 10.8 million *Reichsmark* respectively have been provided for the period from January 1 to September 30. Should the quota for lumber be entirely filled, then further quotas for lumber should be made available from the other quotas [except grain] which are not filled."[56]

[50] Wohlthat to Göring (Berlin), November 14, 1937, DGFP, D, Vol. 5, 154, pp. 205-209.
[51] Fabricius (DG Bukarest) to AA, November 17, 1937, PA, Ha Pol, IVb, Rumänien, Handel 13A, Regierungsausschüsse, Bd. 1.
[52] Op. cit., note 50.
[53] Ibid.
[54] 'Vertrauliches Protokoll über das Ergebnis der zweiten Tagung des deutschen und des rumänischen Regierungsausschusses', December 9, 1937, PA, Ha Pol, IVb, Rumänien, Handel 13, Handelsvertragsverhältnisse mit Deutschland, Bd. 1. There was no agreement on hog prices, even though Germany raised its bid to 82 marks per 100 kilos. Rumania was so concerned to find markets for this commodity that it agreed to pay the difference between the final German offer and the Rumanian price by means of an export subsidy. Marion to Wohlthat (Schweinelieferungen), December 9, 1937, op. cit., note 50.
[55] Ibid.
[56] Wohlthat to Göring, December 13, 1937, op. cit., note 26.

The compromise solution reached on the clearing debt was similar to those reached with Yugoslavia and Turkey. Germany's refusal to establish a fund to guarantee the mark (which was the preferred Rumanian solution to the problem of Germany's clearing debts) was successfully maintained by Berlin. "The import and export plan is set up in such a way, by mutual agreement, that the existing balance in favor of the Rumanian National Bank will be covered within a few months. The balance of payments is to be assured by the regulation of German imports of goods. If, contrary to expectations, the balance should not decrease in the manner intended, or should again increase, German imports are to be correspondingly curtailed."[57]

The Mixed Commission also agreed upon a formula for the mark/lei rate. "Great efforts were necessary before the National Bank, influenced by the Rumanian government, gave up the guarantee and established a rate of exchange of 38/39. We have accepted the statement of the Rumanian government to this effect in substance, to be sure, but opposed it formally for reasons of currency policy."[58] Conditional free trading in marks was abolished and the Rumanian National Bank was made solely responsible for handling all transactions in mark foreign exchange. Fixing the mark rate above the prevailing market prices meant a price reduction of about 6% for Rumanian exports to Germany, while imports from Germany were 8% more expensive when compared to the average rate obtained under the earlier procedure.

The first actual quotas were set down in the agreement for armament deliveries that also specified the method of Rumania's payment. A general quota of 10 million marks to be paid in wheat was arranged for individual transactions up to 100,000 marks. The 10-million-mark wheat quota was, however, not linked to successful negotiation of individual transactions; Germany could use it at any time until the end of 1938 regardless of the condition of negotiations on individual transactions. When the 10-million mark quota was exhausted, the chairmen of the respective governmental committees would establish transitional rules for further orders up to the 100,000-mark limit. Each order over 100,000 marks would be regulated separately through individual negotiations, but the protocol specified particular interest in payment in petroleum or wheat.[59]

After the agreement was signed, Wohlthat met with King Carol and various ministers, which augured well for the future of German expansionist policy. "The reception by the King at the conclusion of the negotiations was intended to be a

---

[57] Ibid.; Protokoll, op. cit., note 54. German exports to Rumania were to conform to the following quotas: January 1938 — 1/9 of total quota (Jan. to Sept.); Feb./March — 2/9; April/May — 2/9; June/July — 2/9; Aug./Sept. — 2/9. If the Rumanian clearing credit did not drop to 17 million marks by January 15, 1938, German imports from Rumania were to be stopped until this figure was reached. A similar procedure was outlined for March 15, May 15 and July 15 if Rumania's clearing credit rose above 10 million marks.

[58] Wohlthat to Göring, December 13, 1937, op. cit., note 26.

[59] Wohlthat to Marian, December 9, 1937, 'Briefwechsel vom 9. Dezember 1937 betreffend Durchführung von Rüstungsgeschäften', Annex to Protocol, op. cit.; also, Protocol, paragraphs 20-21. The letter specified three transactions: a dry dock, a munitions factory, and a schooling ship for the navy.

special mark of consideration and gave a certain emphasis to the German position in Rumania."[60] As Carol was particularly interested in obtaining German cooperation for "a systematic development of the forest and lumber industry"[61], Wohlthat described three large projects under consideration at Czernowitz, Busau, and Closani. Carol also asked Wohlthat's views on "the state direction of foreign trade and domestic economy"[62] as well as the impact of rearmament on the foreign trade and raw materials requirements of Germany and England. "The King recognized that large economic projects to raise the standard of living of the people or to attain certain objectives in domestic or foreign policy force the state authority to intervene on the basis of multiple year plans." The impact of the German model, as exemplified in both the New and Four Year Plans, was patently obvious in this conversation. Although domestic political motives are sufficient to explain King Carol's drive for dictatorship, the direction of economic policy was heavily influenced by Germany's success in combating unemployment, in rearming, and in solving raw materials shortages. "At the conclusion of the audience, which went off in a notably friendly manner, the King stressed that he attached great value to economic cooperation with Germany and expressed the wish that the treaty just concluded might lead to a further favorable development, like that begun with the treaties of 1935."[63]

Wohlthat also met with Tartarescu, Commerce Minister Bujiou, and former Minister Manolescu-Strunga, and summarized these discussions under Tartarescu's rubric of an "economic community of relations" between Germany and Rumania. Tartarescu outlined far-reaching economic plans that he intended to initiate as soon as the new government was formed.[64]

1. Introduction of technology in agriculture, standardization, and storage of export goods, adoption of new crops, according to the example of Germany in soybean cultivation, such as flax, cotton, and rice.
2. Exploitation of raw material resources, expansion of the basic industries of coal and iron, modernization of gold production. Bauxite. Asbestos.
3. Exploitation of new petroleum fields, with alteration of the existing laws which discourage foreign capital.
4. Expansion of national industry (armaments).
5. Expansion of municipal enterprises (gas, electricity, meat packing houses, street-cleaning, etc.).

[60] Wohlthat to Göring (Berlin), December 14, 1937, DGFP, D, Vol. 5, 155, p. 209.
[61] Ibid.
[62] Ibid.
[63] Ibid.
[64] Ibid. The Liberals had lost the elections, despite an electoral system greatly favoring an incumbent government. These plans serve to indicate more the general ideas in circulation within King Carol's milieu than the mainstream of Liberal Party thought. Carol was, of course, surrounded by confidants with pro-Nazi or pro-fascist sympathies: "A frequent companion was his cousin, Prince Friedrich Wilhelm von Hohenzollern-Sigmaringen, an ardent Nazi, who tried to convice Carol of Hitler's benevolence. Carol's disreputable brother, Prince Nicolae, was intrumental in several proposed German-Rumanian commercial deals. Finally, Carol's fascination with things 'German' should be noted. He loved the uncomplicated order of fascism which contrasted so sharply with the disarray of Romanian politics. He had a taste for militaristic paraphernalia, plumes, uniforms, and decorations." BACON, Nicolae Titulescu, p.190.

6. Expansion of the transportation system, road-building, river regulation, expansion of the harbor of Constantza.

7. Legislative measures for increasing foreign credit. Payment of foreign debts, preferential treatment for foreign capital.[65]

Many of these ideas appear again in the Wohlthat Treaty of March, 1939. The notion of comprehensive cooperation on an economic basis was not simply a canard foisted on innocent and unwilling Rumania but an idea that had an independent origin in the soil of Rumania's economic and political crisis. King Carol's interest in Wohlthat's ideas on "state direction of foreign trade and domestic economy" was not academic, but motivated by a belief that German economic policy had solved the contradictions of capitalism through administrative techniques of authoritarian state control of the economy-techniques that were at odds with both the interests and policies of Great Britain, France, and the United States, and therefore attractive to Rumania, insofar as it freed Rumania from the onerous service of foreign capital. Thus, the idea of a comprehensive economic program supported by Germany was not merely a reflection of the growth of German influence but a reaction to the ongoing economic contradictions of the Depression that remained insoluble by means of British, French, or American policy.[66]

Although the German government could be well satisfied with the Bucharest Protocol of December, 1937, the subsequent growth of German influence in 1938 and 1939 was complicated by the political crisis in Rumania precipitated by the short-lived Goga government, appointed in late December 1937 by King Carol, and by the European crisis precipitated by the *Anschluß* and German demands on Czechoslovakia. By January, 1937, Schacht considered German economic expansion in Yugoslavia to have reached its natural limit. True, Germany was unable to import Yugoslav copper through clearing to any extent, but German policy until 1939 under both Schacht and Göring did not aim at forcing Yugoslavia unilaterally to abrogate its treaties with private companies guaranteeing them their right to payment in free currency. In the case of Rumania, German influence at the end of 1937 was not yet equal to its influence in Yugoslavia at the end of 1936. The critical solution to Germany's desperate petroleum supply problem was eased by the December, 1937 agreement, but was by no means solved.

[65] Ibid.

[66] The ideas of Professor Michail Manoilescu are the clearest expression of this tendency. Manoilescu and Virgil Madgearu (National Peasant Party supporter) were internationally known economists; before the negotiation of the Wohlthat Treaty Manoilescu had called for a "planned" national economy within east-central European *Großraumwirtschaft*. Mihail MANO-ILESCU, Ideea de plan economic national, in: Buletinul A.G. IR. 20, No.10, pp. 242-247; No.11, pp. 279-290, 1938, cited in Viorica MOISUIC, Diplomatia Romaniei si problema apararii suveranitatii si independentei nationale in perioada martie 1938 — mai 1940, Bucharest 1971, pp. 111-112. In spite of Manoilescu's erroneous assessment of German foreign economic policy, his ideas have found fertile soil in Rumania's post war economic emancipation from Soviet policy. Nicholas Burakow, formerly an American foreign service officer and economist, gives a very positive appraisal of Manoilescu's dynamic trade theory and impact upon economic planners in present day Rumania: Nicholas BURAKOW, The Dynamic Role of Trade in Development: Rumania's Strategy, U.Ph.D., University of Notre Dame 1980, pp. 42-63.

The economic and political chaos caused by the appointment of the Goga government did not directly facilitate the growth of German influence. Goga's anti-Semitic campaign exerted a staggering blow to the Rumanian economy that hurt Rumania as a market for German exports and disturbed the steady flow of grain and oil to the German market. Although Goga's rightwing politics were congenial to Berlin, the Wilhelmstraße had often rejected outright support for Goga because of legitimate fears that he could not hold power if he obtained it.[67] The clearest expression of German policy was the Wilhelmstraße's insistence that the German minority political organizations support the Liberal ticket, exactly paralleling Germany's policy in Yugoslavia where the minority was urged to support Stojadinović. Although German policy was geared to the support and conciliation of King Carol, the emergence of the royal dictatorship in February, 1938, interrupted Tartarescu's economic plans, while the appointment of new ministers and the general sorting-out process inevitably delayed German proposals, plans, and interests.

[67] The Wilhelmstraße also had legitimate fears that the German community would suffer under a Goga government.

CHAPTER X

ARMAMENTS AND WORLD WAR

1. The Ambiguity of German Policy: The Antitank Cannon Transaction December, 1938 - July, 1939

After successful negotiation of the December, 1938, Protocol, Germany paused in its drive to dominate the Rumanian petroleum sector. The existing figure of 250 million marks for trade in either direction gave Germany, under the 25% clause, access to 62.5 million marks of petroleum, not including payments for German armaments and other strategic materials that substantially increased the absolute amount of Rumanian petroleum Germany could import.[1] The large volume of petroleum available under the Protocol, with the payments in petroleum coming due for earlier armaments deliveries, allowed German policy makers a respite. Although Germany certainly had an eye on Rumanian petroleum from a strategic perspective, policy in early 1938 was not directly affected.[2]

---

[1] Phillipe Marguerat's thesis of a great economic offensive by Germany after Munich unfortunately ignores the key role which armaments exports played in opening up the Rumanian oil to Germany. By and large, the results of the December, 1938, protocol were considered so favorable to Germany by the most informed opinion in Germany (in contrast to Marguerat's view that Germany's preponderance was "faible et fragile, sans cesse menacée par le jeu des arrières de clearing et par le pouvoir d'attraction de la livre sterling"), that leading government officials, such as Clodius, did not believe further economic expansion could be obtained except through the armaments barter. Thus, the relative pause in the German drive for armaments sales after Munich fundamentally contradicts Marguerat's thesis. Marguerat also leaves out of discussion the rearguard reistance of the RMEL which limited Germany's access to Rumanian petroleum: For a differing view see: MARGUERAT, Le III Reich, pp. 100, 124, 138, and 150. Sixty percent of Rheinmetall's 8.6-million-mark antiaircraft gun transaction was to be paid in petroleum, with the first payment (20%) due before the end of 1938 and the second due in the first quarter of 1939. Payments for other projects, such as the Krupp Germaniawerft U-boat transaction, fell due during 1939. In early 1939, the Rumanian Economic Ministry permitted 1.25 million marks of petroleum to be exported in payment for Siemens deliveries to the Rumanian Armaments Ministry. The German legation reckoned that the 20% down payment and the 30% first payment would make 50% of the petroleum due from total transaction available by March 31, 1939. Fabricius (DG Bukarest) to AA, January 4, 1939; Malzar (DG Bukarest) to AA, January 24, 1939, PA, Ha Pol, IVb, Rumänien, Rohstoffe und Waren, Petroleum, Bd. 1.

[2] Although petroleum supply was a strategic problem, the limitations of German economic resources, particularly evident in the strained steel industry and the shortage of capital, would not permit the problem to be solved by a planned German economic penetration of east-central Europe with such projects as expanded tank capacity on the Danube, construction of an oil pipeline, or acquisition of Rumanian oil companies or exploration rights.

However, total trade did not live up to expectations, endangering the supply of petroleum due under the 25% clause, while the political tensions of the spring and summer meant that once again Germany had to try to dramatically increase its share of Rumanian petroleum production.

That Germany had been initially satisfied with the December Protocol is shown by several incidents: in late 1938, the OKH declared that export of 4.7cm infantry howitzers to Rumania was "out of the question."[3] Also during this period, Clodius told the German legation in Bucharest that there was no pressing reason for Malaxa, the Rumanian industrialist, to make a trip to Berlin.[4] Although other policy questions were involved in the howitzer question, the curt denial of these two Rumanian overtures indicates that the Germans were not on the prowl for new armaments contracts.

In a similar vein, German interest in an antitank gun transaction was motivated more by a desire to stop Italian, Czech, and Polish competition in the Rumanian market than by strategic considerations. In late January, the German legation in Bucharest reported that Rheinmetall was in danger of losing its contract for anti-tank guns because the Italian firm Breda was ready to deliver 400 4.7cm guns immediately while Rheinmetall was offering only 150 in 42 months plus 250 manu-factured under license in 16 months.[5] General Thomas (Wi Rü Amt) replied that because this particular model had not yet been introduced in Germany, there was obviously no way Rheinmetall could meet the foreign competition with respect to delivery time, which was, in any case, not as long as the legation claimed.[6] Von Lupin (*Reichsgruppe Industrie*) clarified matters further. It was not the Italians but Škoda who was competing with Rheinmetall. Škoda offered immediate delivery of 400 4.7cm. guns that Lupin claimed were outdated and heavy.[7] In addition, the German firm Bohler offered a smaller number of guns (recent model, but not as advanced as Rheinmetall's) with license arrangement. Thus, Rumanian procure-

---

[3] OKH (Berlin) to AA, December 2, 1938, PA, Ha Pol, IVb, Rumänien, Handel mit Kriegsgerät, Bd. 1. The OKH and OKW were more reluctant to approve heavy field artillery than modern aircraft or antiaircraft guns, an attitude that apparently stemmed from military reluctance to strengthen land forces and from economic considerations — German production was particularly strained in this area. The acquisition of Škoda and Brunn armaments factories made the OKH and OKW more willing to consider the export of heavy field artillery to Rumania.

[4] Malaxa was King Carol's chief advisor on the armaments question. While Malaxa's presence in Berlin was not necessary for increased armaments sales, if Germany had been interested in such sales at that particular time, his visit would certainly not have been rebuffed. According to the research of Bacon, Malaxa was an early financial supporter of the Iron Guard. BACON, Nicholae Titulescu, p.152

[5] Stelzer (DG Bukarest) to AA, January 25, 1939, PA, Ha Pol, Handakten Clodius, Rumänien, Bd. 1.

[6] Thomas (OKW) to AA, January 31, 1939, PA, Ha Pol, IVb, Rumänien, Handel mit Kriegsgerät, Bd. 1. Thomas indicated that Malaxa's Astra firm was working closely with Rheinmetall on the licensed construction of the weapon in Rumania.

[7] Von Lupin (*Reichsgruppe Industrie*) to AA, February 2, 1939, ibid. This was summarized in a later dispatch to Bucharest: Kalisch (Berlin) to DG Bukarest, February 20, 1939, PA, Ha Pol, IVb, Rumänien, Handel mit Kriegsgerät, Bd. 1.

ment officials had a choice between three weapons models (outdated, recent, and newly developed) at three delivery dates (immediate, delayed, or long-term). Their choice would depend upon how desperately Rumania needed the weapons.

Apparently, the Rumanians were unable to make up their minds, at least not before the German destruction of Czechoslovakia resolved the issue of Czech "competition." German interest in the question waned without foreign competition, reviving only when the Polish evinced interest in the antitank transaction. In late May, a worried Lupin told the Wilhelmstraße that the German firms involved could lose the contract entirely, because a Polish firm had offered immediate delivery of 200 weapons.[8] He suggested that the German firms be allowed to ship either from stock or directly from the production line. General Thomas made his approval of this concession contingent upon the Wilhelmstraße declaring that the "implementation of the antitank cannon transaction and the exclusion of Polish competition was an urgent German interest and the failure to carry out [the transaction] would constitute a heavy burden to total war material deliveries and thereby the whole economic program."[9]

Although Germany would eventually be in a position to win the contracts, the Secret Protocol on Armaments and the Aeronautical Protocol of July 8 would then have been signed, both of which qualitatively lessened German accommodation on the antitank gun question. In mid-July, Bohler was ordered not to immediately conclude a contract for 400 4.7cm antitank cannon but to handle the negotiations in a dilatory fashion, and finally to try to obtain Rumania's agreement to a two-year extension of the delivery period — until July, 1941. However, negotiations were not to be abruptly broken off.[10] Under such conditions it is highly unlikely that any antitank cannon were delivered to Rumania until well after the outbreak of the war. Germany's rebuff of Rumania's feeler for artillery, Germany's lack of interest in Malaxa's trip, and Germany's dilatory treatment of the antitank cannon transaction all indicate that there was not a concerted armaments sales campaign in early 1939. Even later in the year, when there *was* an armaments sales campaign, Germany was reluctant to provide certain types of war materiel. German efforts and Rumanian interest both centered on aeronautical, not military or marine, war materiel.

[8] W[iehl] Aufzeichnung, May 25, 1939, ibid.

[9] Ibid. It is interesting that Rumania also approached England for 3.7cm cannon. Because of commitments to Portugal and inquiries from Belgium and Turkey, the best offer the War Office could come up with was three cannon per month beginning in 1940. Ross noted: "This is not very much but it is at least an offer which will, I hope, serve to show that we do take some interest." Ross minute (March 16) to Harding (War Office) to ADM Ross (Foreign Office), London, March 14, 1939, P.R.O., F.O. 371/23879.

[10] *Reichsgruppe Industrie* (Berlin) to Bohler & Co., A.G. (Wien), July 20, 1939, PA, Ha Pol, IVb, Rumänien, Handel mit Kriegsgerät, Bd. 1. Rheinmetall's license agreement with Malaxa continued along lines parallel to the other German initiatives. It is notable because most interpretations of German armaments sales policy emphasize that Germany was willing to deliver only obsolete equipment to Yugoslavia and Rumania.

2. *The Aeronautical Protocol of July 8, 1939 — The Rumanian Initiative*

The key to German trade policy in Rumania in the months before the outbreak of war can be found in the negotiations over aircraft and related war materiel that began in February, 1939. Although there are clear indications that the export interests of the German aircraft industry played a role in German policy, export considerations were subordinated to a virtually single-minded quest for greater access to petroleum resources. This turn in German policy from the relative lassitude of January and February came after the dismemberment of Czechoslovakia. Two factors are important in the renewed drive for armaments sales cum oil imports: first, the international tensions resulting from the establishment of the Protectorate prompted even greater German interest in securing adequate petroleum supplies from Rumania, and second, the failure of German purchases to conform to the Protocol of December, 1938, threatened "normal" petroleum imports. Armament sales in conjunction with increased grain purchases were intended to secure the Rumanin petroleum sector for Germany.

As in the case of the Wohlthat Treaty, it was King Carol who initiated negotiations for the purchase of aircraft on the same day (January 30) that Prince Paul made a similar request to von Schönebeck, the German air attaché in Belgrade.[11] In his interview with Gerstenberg, German air attaché in Bucharest, King Carol not only proposed a "new German-Rumanian raw materials agreement" — the proposal that eventually led to the Wohlthat Treaty — but also indicated Rumania's desire to order German military aircraft, i.e., 50 BMW VI, 10 Wecke, 56 Arado 79 or 60 Arado 104, and approximately 50 Messerschmidt or Heinkel 112s.[12] As a sign of good faith, King Carol promised to immediately authorize orders for the 50 BMW VI. A few days later Fabricius reported Air Minister Teoderescu's intention to place orders with Germany totaling from 13 to 50 million marks.[13] Later in the month Fabricius learned that the Rumanian government was especially interested in obtaining 72 Heinkel fighters, the He 112 model equipped with the Junkers Jumo 211 motor.[14]

Although Wohlthat was attentive to the proposed aircraft transaction and other armaments projects during his two negotiating sojourns in Bucharest, nothing concrete was decided in either the Treaty or Confidential Protocol of Signature.[15] The Wilhelmstraße agreed in principle to supply Czech armaments and gave formal

---

[11] Heeren (DG Belgrad) to AA, February 17, 1939, DGFP, D, Vol. 6, p. 397.

[12] Fabricius (DG Bukarest) to AA, February 1, 1939, PA, Ha Pol, Handakten Clodius, Rumänien, Bd. 1. Memorandum by Gerstenberg, Bukarest, February 3, 1939, PA, Ha Pol, IVb, Rumänien, Handel mit Kriegsgerät, Bd. 1. Prince Paul wanted 200 bombers, 100 fighters, 70 150mm howitzers, 120 antiaircraft guns, and a 200 million mark credit to finance the transaction.

[13] Fabricius (DG Bukarest) to AA, February 6, 1939, DGFP, D, Vol. 6, p. 385.

[14] Auriel Stefanescu (DG Bukarest) to Heinkel, February 24, 1939, enclosure in Fabricius (DG Bukarest) to AA, February 24, 1939, PA, Ha Pol, IVb, Rumänien. Handel mit Kriegsgerät, Bd. 1.

[15] Formally, war materiel was regulated by Article 1, paragraph 7 of the Wohlthat Treaty.

approval to the Ferrostaal powder factory after the Treaty was concluded, but no further specific commitments were undertaken concerning delivery of warplanes or other requests.[16]

The first Rumanian orders for military aircraft arrived in early April. Fabricius reported Rumanian orders for 30 Junkers 112 fighters with 15 extra motors for a value of 5.1 million marks. The Rumanian Air Ministry wanted Germany to dispatch an economic commission to work out a 40-million-mark air rearmament program.[17] It is sometimes difficult to differentiate in the sources among Rumanian intention to place orders, written orders from the respective Rumanian ministries to German industry, and the signing of binding contracts between Rumania and German firms; in this particular case it appears likely that the second case prevailed. The problem in interpretation arises because the Rumanians did not always place the orders they initially intended, or, having ordered, did not always sign contracts. The war materiel commodities under negotiation changed over time in response to the vagaries of Rumanian policy and the political-economic priorities of the German government. It cannot be determined with certainty whether the Junkers transaction was actually carried through. It was not part of the war materiel package signed July 8, 1939.

3. The Crisis of German Petroleum Supply

By mid-April, the German government had become seriously concerned by the failure of trade relations with Rumania to develop as projected in the December 1938 Protocol. Here the situation is briefly related to the armaments question. The Wilhelmstraße and the Economics Ministry had both realized by this time that German petroleum imports from Rumania were endangered by the failure of German agricultural purchases to live up to the December Protocol projections, a failure primarily the result of rearguard resistance from the Agricultural Ministry which considered Rumanian grain prices to be far too high. To remedy the deteriorating situation, the Wilhelmstraße and the Economics Ministry pressed for a variety of measures:

1. Substantial raising of the mark/lei rate: this would automatically cheapen Rumanian imports for Germany.[18]
2. Overcoming the Agricultural Ministry's opposition to increased grain imports, i.e., meet-

---

[16] In late March, Armaments Minister Slavescu asked if the Ferrostaal powder factory fell within the Wohlthat Treaty and had received German approval. Clodius informed the legation of Reich approval a few days later. Clodius to DG Bukarest, April 3, 1939, PA, Ha Pol, Handakten Clodius, Rumänien, Bd. 1.

[17] Fabricius (DG Bukarest) to AA, April 4, 1939, PA, Ha Pol, Handakten Wiehl, Rumänien, Bd. 1.

[18] Memorandum by Clodius, April 12, 1939, PA, Ha Pol, IVb, Rumänien, Handel 11, Handelsbeziehungen zu Deutschland, Bd. 1.

ing Rumanian price demands. The first step in this direction was taken April 13 with German offer to purchase 200,000 tons of wheat.[19]

3. German government sponsorship of private German efforts to corner the Rumanian-owned petroleum market through marketing agreements and capital penetration.

Although the Economics Ministry specified that "all means must be utilized to increase imports in peacetime"[20], surprisingly, no mention was made of using armaments barter in this context. The subsequent character of negotiations indicates that the German government wished to first remedy the faltering trade relationship by implementing the grain purchases projected in the December Protocol. Also, the increasing political tensions of the spring and early summer of 1939 prompted Germany to use dilatory tactics in negotiating armaments transactions with both Yugoslavia and Rumania in order to obtain the best possible deals. Despite Germany's acute need for Rumanian oil, a greater need than for any other single raw material, Berlin kept a cool head and was willing to bluff the Rumanians almost to the edge of the abyss.

Studied nonchalance began with Göring's decision in early May to offer Czech, rather than German, aircraft to Rumania. The Wilhelmstraße instructed the representatives of the *Wirtschaftsgruppe Luftfahrtindustrie* (representing Heinkel and Junkers) to negotiate only over the smaller Heinkel fighter, drawing out the negotiations if necessary.[21] In addition to the strategic reason for a tactic of delay, two other motives prompted Göring's decision. The Rumanians had been pressing Germany to resume armaments deliveries under contracts negotiated with Czechoslovakia before March 15, 1939, and for access to the windfall of Czech military stores that had fallen into German hands after March 15.[22] Göring may have hoped to deflect Rumania from this course by offering Czech aircraft. Secondly, Czech industry came to play an increasingly important role in the emerging German-dominated *Großraumwirtschaft* in east-central Europe. An important portion of Czech industry was directly assimilated into Göring's empire through the *Reichswerke Hermann Göring*; exploiting Czech industry was readily seen as a means of supplementing German heavy industry strained by the double burden of rearmament and Four Year Plan economics.[23]

The German commission was unable to fob off the Rumanians with Czech air-

[19] Clodius (Berlin) to DG Bukarest, April 13, 1939, PA, Ha Pol, Handakten Clodius, Rumänien, Bd. 1. Unsigned memorandum of the RWM, April 21, 1939, PA, Ha Pol, IVb, Rumänien, Rohstoffe und Waren, Petroleum, Bd. 2. Darré's Ministry put up considerable resistance even at this date. The RWM asked the Wi Rü Amt (OKW) to intervene in order to increase grain imports from Rumania. Wochenmeldung Chef W Wi vom 6.-12.5. 1939, May 11, 1939, BA-Mi, Wi VI, 322.

[20] Unsigned memorandum of the RWM, April 21, 1939, ibid.

[21] Moraht to DG Bukarest, May 6, 1939, PA, Ha Pol, Handakten Clodius, Rumänien, Bd. 1.

[22] Quartermaster General Wagner commented on the "einfach erschütternde Zahlen" of the Czech stores in a letter to his wife, March 30, 1939. Eduard WAGNER, Der Generalquartiermeister, Munich/Vienna 1963, p. 87.

[23] This was particularly important in the negotiations with Yugoslavia.

craft[24], but German delaying tactics did begin to make the Rumanian government
uneasy. By May 6, King Carol had expressed his concern over Germany's possibly
reneging on the Wohlthat Treaty. "If we left Rumania in the lurch now with deliveries of armaments he [King Carol] would have to provide himself from elsewhere
and that would shift the whole foundation of the Economic Treaty, which his
government wanted to carry out loyally."[25] King Carol received Fabricius again less
than two weeks later, informing him that the "chief thing was that the Reich should
carry out the Economic Treaty in respect of the delivery of armaments; he, the
King, was resolved to carry through Rumania's great air rearmament programme in
conjunction with Germany."[26] As always, Fabricius was more impressed by King
Carol's sincerity than was Berlin. Fabricius was convinced that if Germany were
"forthcoming in the armaments question, it is quite possible that Rumania would
adopt an attitude similar to that which Yugoslavia obviously intends to take up."[27]
After the Rumanians rejected the offer of Czech aircraft, Fabricius complained to
Berlin that failing to grant Rumanian wishes could easily endanger the success of
the Wohlthat Treaty.[28] He again reiterated his belief that a "particularly skillful and
generous handling of Rumania's wishes in the field of [armaments]" would result in
closer Rumanian ties with Germany, similar to those of Yugoslavia, as well as bring
great economic advantages.[29] Berlin quickly relented from insisting upon Czech aircraft for Rumania[30] but continued to allow negotiations to drag on. The failure of
the fifth meeting of the Mixed Commission to achieve concrete gains for Germany
was an added reason not to be very forthcoming with Rumania on the armaments
question. Rumanian intransigence dashed German hopes of cheapening Rumanian
agricultural produce by substantially increasing the mark/lei rate. Incorporating the
Protectorate (Bohemia-Moravia) into the clearing system was the only major result
of the negotiations.[31]

Although the mark/lei rate and the German stalling tactics resulted in friction,

[24] Fabricius (DG Bukarest) to AA, May 13, 1939, PA, Ha Pol, Handakten Clodius,
Rumänien, Bd. 2.

[25] Fabricius (DG Bukarest) to AA, May 6, 1939, DGFP, D, Vol. 6, p. 439.

[26] Fabricius (DG Bukarest) to AA, May 17, 1939, DGFP, D, Vol. 6, p. 521. See also Fabri-
cius (DG Bukarest) to AA, May 18, 1939, Telegram 229, PA, Ha Pol, Handakten Clodius,
Rumänien, Bd. 2. Rumanian complaints over Czech armaments continued. Fabricius (DG
Bukarest) to AA, May 19, 1939, Telegram 235, PA, Ha Pol, IVb, Rumänien, Handel mit
Kriegsgerät, Bd. 1.

[27] Fabricius (DG Bukarest) to AA, May 6, 1939, op. cit., note 25.

[28] Fabricius (DG Bukarest) to AA, May 13, 1939, Telegram 224, PA, Ha Pol, Handakten
Clodius, Rumänien, Bd. 2.

[29] Fabricius (DG Bukarest) to AA, May 13, 1939, Telegram 226, DGFP, D, Vol. 6, p. 487.

[30] Clodius to DG Bukarest, May 16, 1939, ibid. Permission to go ahead on the basis of the
Rumanian program came from Göring via the RLM, minute by Wiehl, May 19, 1939, ibid.

[31] The agreements of May 20, 1939, consisted of a Protocol, an agreement on the clearing
and payments regulations between the Protectorate and Rumania, an agreement on tariff
questions between the Protectorate and Rumania, and a German letter on the mark rate. PA,
Ha Pol, Handakten Wiehl, Rumänien, Bd. 11.

neither side was prepared to let the negotiations fail — quite the contrary.[32] This prompted Berlin to permit the aeronautical commission to make the first small concession and deliver most German aeronautical war materiel.[33] By mid-June, Berlin was concerned enough over the possible loss of the Rumanian arms market to take practical steps to conclude a large-scale transaction and the Mixed Commission approved a credit of unspecified duration and amount for the aircraft transaction. Berlin aimed at securing 100% of the payment for the aircraft in petroleum, but if this were not possible a 50/50 split between grains and petroleum would be acceptable. A minimum of 10 million marks in petroleum was to be made available to Germany before the end of 1939 in either case, and was to be subtracted from the total before the 50/50 division. Additional war materiel deliveries to Rumania were to be determined on the basis of German needs and the claims of other Balkan countries, while payment was to be secured in vital raw materials. Clodius was authorized to go to Bucharest at the end of June to negotiate the individual projects into a coherent program for the next period.[34]

The authorization of the aircraft transaction was followed by a committee decision in favor of increased wheat imports, amplified a few days later by a joint decision of the Agricultural Ministry and the Four Year Plan to raise Germany's grain reserve "as quickly as possible" from 6.2 million to 9 million tons. This decision was, of course, prompted by the increasing prospect of world war. Naturally, Rumania came first to mind as the appropriate supply source. According to Wiehl, Clodius was required to be personally in Bucharest to ensure that the benefits of this "great concession", that of raising Rumanian grain exports to Germany to 1.5 million tons, be properly reaped.[35] Obviously not motivated by an outpouring of sympathy for Rumania's agricultural problems, this "great concession" came about through a simple fear of wartime starvation if a British blockade were again imposed. Wiehl's insistence on Clodius's presence implies using the guarantee of increased grain purchases as a lever to pry both greater access to petroleum and structural guarantees from the Rumanians.

By the end of May, the German aeronautical commission had reached agreement on a substantial list of military aircraft and materiel totaling some 15.3 million marks:[36]

---

[32] Fabricius reported Rumania's frustration and anger over Germany's lack of generosity. The Rumanian government wanted quick supply of military hardware from Czech stocks; after these were exhausted they wanted to be supplied with German, not Austrian, weapons. Fabricius (DG Bukarest) to AA, June 2, 1939, PA, Ha Pol, IVb, Rumänien, Handel mit Kriegsgerät, Bd. 1. Another copy in PA, Gesandtschaft Bukarest, Fach 48, Rumänische Aufrüstung. David Kaiser presents a somewhat too optimistic appraisal of Rumania's receipt of armaments under these old contracts: KAISER, Economic Diplomacy, p. 268-270.

[33] Schönlein (*Wirtschaftsgruppe Luftfahrtindustrie*) to Junker (AA), May 31, 1939, PA, Ha Pol, IVb, Rumänien, Handel mit Kriegsgerät, Bd. 1.

[34] Minute by Clodius, June 17, 1939, ibid.

[35] Minute by Wiehl, June 22, 1939, PA, Ha Pol, Handakten Wiehl, Rumänien, Bd. 11.

[36] Schönlein (*Wirtschaftsgruppe Luftfahrtindustrie*) to Ripke (AA), May 30, 1939, PA, Ha Pol, IVb, Rumänien, Handel mit Kriegsgerät, Bd. 1. Schönlein (*Wirtschaftsgruppe Luftfahrtin-dustrie*) to Junker (AA), May 31, 1939, ibid. None of the aircraft had been delivered. Rumania

1.   Heinkel — 30 He 112 with Jumo 210 motors
2.   Focke-Wulff — 10 FW 58
3.   Gotha — 15 60 145
4.   Junkers — 15 Jumo 211 aircraft engines
5.   BMW — 110 BMW l32A aircraft engines
6.   Additional ground support equipment

1-5 =   9.9 million marks
  6 =   5.4   "   "
Total   15.3 million marks

Neither deliveries nor payment schedules were worked out until after the negotiation of the Armaments Protocol of July 8, 1939. Probably prepared to take what they could get, the Rumanians delayed making arrangements for payments in the hope of obtaining Germany's agreement to credit at low interest rates.[37]

A series of friendly gestures smoothed the way for Clodius's visit to Bucharest and reflected Germany's determination to reach agreement. The Wilhelmstraße influenced the OKW to give permission for negotiations between Czech firms and Rumania on long-term delivery of heavy artillery and to scotch Renault's bid to supply Rumania with armored cars.[38] General Thomas, Wi Rü Amt (OKW), went along with the Wilhelmstraße on this issue, but made it clear that the Czech firms were authorized to conclude only contracts not prejudicial to the interests of the *Wehrmacht.* In other words, delivery of heavy artillery could run from 1 1/2 to three years.[39] Thomas did refuse to permit deliveries of weapons from the stocks of

---

had made only a down payment on the BMW motors. However, the Dresdner Bank backed the Focke-Wulff transaction. The RLM approved these six transactions but withheld approval on Rumania's request for 30-50 fighters (ME 109s or He 112Ks). Minute by Wiehl, June 3, 1939, PA, Ha Pol, Handakten Wiehl, Rumänien, Bd. 11.

[37] The Rumanians wanted a seven-year credit at 4.5% interest; the Germans started negotiating at 6% and were willing to go as low as 5%. Fabricius (DG Bukarest) to AA, June 16, 1939, PA, Ha Pol, Handakten Clodius, Rumänien, Bd. 2. Unsigned telegram (Berlin) to DG Bukarest, June 20, 1939, ibid. On June 22, the German Mixed Commission decided to offer Rumania a revolving credit of 20 million marks (total liability: 65 million marks) for German (not Czech) war materiel other than military aircraft and equipment. Minute by Wiehl, July 7, 1939, PA, Ha Pol, Handakten Wiehl, Rumänien, Bd. 11.

[38] Fabricius (DG Bukarest) to AA, June 13, 1939. Junker (AA) to Radtke (Wi Rü Amt — OKW), June 21, 1939, PA, Ha Pol, IVb, Rumänien, Handel mit Kriegsgerät, Bd. 1. In General Thomas's letter of June 24, [see note 39 below] Thomas approved this transaction. The Rumanians were also interested in Czech tanks. Kalisch (AA) to DG Bukarest, June 27, 1939, ibid.

[39] Unsigned minute, 'Rumänischer K.G.-Bedarf', initialed by Wiehl, June 25, 1939, ibid. The delivery period for British heavy artillery was 12 to 18 months. Representatives of Škoda arrived in Bucharest the third week in June to discuss orders for heavy artillery, offering 63 10cm howitzers (total cost: 141 million crowns), the first to be delivered in 10 months, the remainder spread over the following 23 months. Brünner offered 200,000 rifles and 2,000 machine guns (total cost: 229 million crowns) with delivery of 25,000 rifles a month beginning in September 1939, part of the machine guns in July 1939 and the remainder in February 1940. Credit: 20% upon signing the contracts, 30% upon first deliveries, the remainder spread over the following four years with 15% the first year, 8% the second, 12% the third and 14% the fourth. Fabricius (DG Bukarest) to AA, June 22, 1939, ibid.

the Czech army, although uniforms, harness, and similar items in which the Rumanians expressed interest were released for sale.[40]

Proceeding swiftly, negotiations over the armaments protocol were completed barely a week after Clodius's arrival in Bucharest. The usual pattern of marathon negotiations was avoided as both governments by now were interested in a quick agreement. It helped that the terms of credit proposed by both governments were very close even before the negotiations began.[41] On July 8, the armaments negotiations concluded with the signing of a Secret Protocol on Armaments, the deliveries of war materials[42], Exchange of Letters[43], and an Aeronautical Protocol.[44] The first two were agreements between the Rumanian and German states, signed by Clodius and Bujoiu, while the latter was signed by representatives of German industry and Air Force General Negresco for the Rumanian state. The Secret Protocol, which laid down general conditions for the extension of credit, and the Exchange of Letters were both very brief. Credit was to depend upon the type of equipment delivered and the delivery period, which could range from three to seven years from the date of signing of the contract. Upon signing of individual contracts, a down payment of 20% was due, with the remainder of the sale price to be financed through Rumanian Treasury Bonds, yielding 5% interest, guaranteed by the Rumanian state. In the Exchange of Letters, Bujoiu agreed to prepayment, exclusively in oil, of installments on the aeronautical credit before the end of 1939.[45]

> ... the Rumanian Government have agreed to make advance deliveries of 12 million in the second half of 1939 and 6 million in the first quarter of 1940. Therefore taken together with a payment of an installment of 12 million we can obtain an additional 30 million of petroleum up to January 1940. [All amounts are in values of RM.][46]

Providing for prepayment of installments by supplementary deliveries of petroleum allowed Germany to secure a 50% increase in petroleum over and above the 60 million marks foreseen in December, 1938.

[40] Thomas (Wi Rü Amt — OKW) to AA, June 24, 1939, PA, Ha Pol, IVb, Rumänien, Handel mit Kriegsgerät, Bd. 1. The Rumanian government had sent a military commission to Germany in May without consulting the Wilhelmstraße. This miffed the Germans and the commission cooled its heels in Berlin without achieving anything concrete. Clodius to DG Bukarest, May 10, 1939, DGFP, D, Vol. 6, p. 464. Clodius also details the original German refusal to deliver harness and uniforms. In late May, the *Wi Rü Amt* reversed its position on harness, uniforms, canteens, helmets, packs, and the like. Genscher (Wi Rü Amt — OKW) to AA, May 25, 1939, PA, Ha Pol, IVb, Rumänien, Handel mit Kriegsgerät, Bd. 1.

[41] Berlin decided to go as low as 5% interest on June 20. Two days later, Bujoiu spontaneously offered 5% and seven years as Rumania's terms for the aircraft transaction. Unsigned telegram to DG Bukarest, June 20, 1939, PA, Ha Pol, Handakten Clodius, Rumänien, Bd. 2. Fabricius (DG Bukarest) to AA, June 22, 1939, ibid.

[42] 'Geheimes Protokoll', signed by Carl Clodius and I. Bujoiu, Bucharest, July 8, 1939, PA, Ha Pol, Handakten Wiehl, Rumänien, Bd. 11.

[43] Clodius to Bujoiu and Bujoiu to Clodius, Bucharest, July 8, 1939, ibid.

[44] 'Protocole: pour le matériel aeronautique à commander en Allemagne dans le cadre de la convention Roumaino-Allemande du 23 Mars 1939', Bucharest, July 8, 1939, signed by General Negresco, Carl Soenning, et al., PA, Ha Pol, IVb, Rumänien, Handel mit Kriegsgerät, Bd. 1.

[45] Bujoiu to Clodius, July 8, 1939, PA, Ha Pol, Handakten Wiehl, Rumänien Bd. 11.

[46] Memorandum by Wiehl, July 7, 1939, ibid.

With the exception of the Focke-Wulff and Gotha aircraft that were to be paid for in cash, virtually all the aircraft and aeronautical war materiel under negotiation was included in the Protocol[47]; in other words, all Rumanian military aeronautical purchases were made on credit.[48] Included in the Protocol were:

Type	Value (million marks)	Delivery
1. 32 Heinkel He 111 H Bombers equipped with Jumo engines and accessories	13.0	November 1939 – May 1940[49]
2. 200 Junkers Jumo 211 engines with parts	8.0	July 1939 – January 1940
3. License, Machine Tools, Semi-Manufactures, and Raw Materials for the construction of Jumo 211 engines	3.7	?
4. 30 Dornier Do 215 Reconnaissance Aircraft with Jumo 211 engines	?	?
5. 15 Fieseler Storch, Argus 240 Aircraft with CV As 10c Engines	0.6	immediately
6. 30 Heinkel He 112 Ea	4.7	July – September 1939
7. Aeronautical War Material — Ground Equipment	5.4	?
8. 50 BMW Aircraft Engines	1.7	Sept. 1939 – Jan. 1940
9. Eventually: 30 – 50 Messerschmidt 109s (with Daimler-Benz P.B. 601 motors) or Heinkel 112K (with Jumo 211 motors)	4.6 (for 30)	January – May 1940

The war materiels protocols of July 8, 1939, mark the consummation of German expansionist trade policy in the interwar period. These agreements, even more than the Wohlthat Treaty, provided Nazi Germany with the levers necessary to turn Rumania into a semicolonial satellite. In contrast to the Wohlthat Treaty, these

[47] This was simply deduced from the fact that negotiations continued on these transactions, but they were not mentioned in the aeronautical protocol of July 8.
[48] 'Protocole', July 8, 1939, op. cit., note 44.
[49] For Göring's second thoughts on the delivery of these aircraft see note 52.

armaments protocols provided for increasing bilateral trade beyond the levels set in the December, 1938, Protocol and gave Germany specific guarantees on the raw material most necessary for waging modern warfare: petroleum. Without access to Rumanian petroleum, Germany's ability to wage war for any extended period of time was highly questionable.

As the list of military aircraft set out above indicates, Germany was willing to supply the most modern armaments in massive quantities, a fact that has not been recognized in the historical literature. It is generally assumed that the Balkan countries were placated with outdated Austrian and Czech equipment, while in actuality Rumanian petroleum was so critical to the German war economy that Berlin simply dared not risk offering second rate equipment.

German policy makers emphasized the crucial nature of these negotiations; Weizsäcker noted specifically that the program for substantially increased petroleum and grain imports hung in the balance.[50] After learning that there was basic agreement on a draft protocol, Wiehl wrote: "Because the counter deliveries are extraordinarily important to us, and on the other hand, the delivery periods for the middle and heavy artillery are relatively long, permission for signature is recommended, assuming the Field Marshal [Göring] agrees in spite of the uncertain political attitude of Rumania."[51] The Armaments Protocol of July, 1939, with Rumania was, without doubt, the single most important economic agreement negotiated by Nazi Germany in 1939 (apart from the economic provisions of the nonaggression pact with the Soviet Union). But even though the agreements with Rumania constituted the essential element in German military economic planning, Clodius was not successful on all fronts. The Rumanians successfully warded off German pressure to substantially increase the mark/lei rate and make specific commitments on the export of grain.

4. Implementation of the Protocol — July-September 1939

As the tense international atmosphere of July and August, 1939, would indicate, the armaments barter did not proceed smoothly, although the Economic Policy Department of the Wilhelmstraße, while recognizing the uncertainty of Rumania's political intentions, continued to recommend it. Göring, however, set his own course. He allowed Clodius to sign the agreements but reserved judgment on the type and delivery period of the military hardware.[52] In this respect, Göring showed

---

[50] Weizsäcker to DG Bukarest, July 11, 1939, DGFP, D, Vol. 6, pp. 899-900.

[51] Memorandum by Wiehl, July 7, 1939, op. cit., note 46.

[52] Göring's position did not become clear until July 14, when *Ministerialrat* Müller (RLM) telephoned the Wilhelmstraße. Unsigned minute, July 14, 1939. The author of this minute (probably Clodius) commented: "Ich habe darauf hingewiesen, daß damit unser zusätzliches Erdölbezugsprogramm erneut ins Wanken geriete." The same day Masur (*Wirtschaftsgruppe Luftfahrtindustrie*) informed the AA, that for the time being, the Heinkel He 111, Dornier Do 215, Messerschmidt Me 109, and Heinkel He 112K were not to be delivered. Masur (*Wirtschaftsgruppe Luftfahrtindustrie*) to Junker; AA, July 14, 1939, PA, Ha Pol, IVb, Rumänien, Handel mit Kriegsgerät, Bd. 1. However, Göring did approve the shipment of the Fiesler-Storch reconnaissance planes and the aircraft engines.

himself to be more distrustful of King Carol than was Hitler, who had given permission for the export of military aircraft, stipulating only that land armaments should not be delivered before the winter of 1940-41.[53] There is no reason to doubt the sincerity of Göring's distrust of Rumania, but he may also have been motivated by the hope that a slow implementation of the accord would increase Rumanian pliability.

Before the signing of the Non-Aggression Pact with Soviet Russia, the prospect of a general European war against a grand coalition put Germany policy makers in a quandary. Germany, although well armed and with ample stocks on hand as a result of the Czech coup, had no margin for error in the export of armaments. A single false step could mean disaster on the battlefield. But, without crucial raw materials, particularly the petroleum available only from southeastern Europe in the event of an effective British blockade, the German military machine would quickly grind to a halt. These same considerations remained in force even after the conclusion of the Hitler-Stalin Pact in August, 1939, albeit to a lesser extent. Apparently, Hitler expected France to sit out the Polish campaign, while Germany, by the terms of the Pact, was assured of substantial supplies of Russian raw materials, including petroleum. So, while southeastern Europe did remain crucial to Germany's raw materials supply, some pressure was relieved. However, Göring still had to make a decision. Even assuming Soviet cooperation, Rumanian oil was needed for the war economy so, despite any doubts of Rumania's political reliability, Rumania had to be supplied with armaments in order to obtain increased petroleum imports. The only other alternative, never seriously contemplated in Berlin, was outright military aggression to secure Rumanian petroleum production at the source.

The Rumanians were apparently unaware of Göring's decision to delay shipment. Because the bulk of the shipments were to begin on a piecemeal basis after September, the Germans had some room to maneuver. In the weeks following the conclusion of the armaments protocols, the Rumanian government seemed convinced of Germany's good intentions. Calinescu, the prime minister, even requested a supplementary revolving credit for further armament orders.[54] It was in August that a barrage of protest was lanched against Fabricius (the earliest deliveries of critical military aircraft had been scheduled for July and August). Berlin did not respond to Calinescu's request for a supplementary credit, but negotiations continued on a broad range of war materiel and related projects. In the third week of July the Rumanian government gave permission for a Krupp director (Weiske) to visit a chromium ore site in the Banat[55], and Škoda reported virtual agreement on a 370-

---

[53] This decision was made on July 11. Hitler wanted to concentrate armaments sales where they would do the most good (South America, the Balkans, and Norway) and avoid delivering weapons to hostile or uncertain states. Keitel (OKW) to Wiehl (AA), July 22, 1939, PA, Ha Pol, IVb, Yugoslawien, Handel mit Kriegsgerät, Bd. 1.

[54] Fabricius (DG Bukarest) to AA, July 14, 1939, PA, Ha Pol, IVb, Rumänien, Handel mit Kriegsgerät, Bd. 1.

[55] Although the documents are not explicit, this amounts to the first concrete initiative for joint exploitation of Rumania's mineral resources as projected in the Wohlthat Treaty. Stelzer (DG Bukarest) to AA, July 20, 1939, PA, Ha Pol, Handakten Wiehl, Rumänien, Bd. 11.

million-crown contract for heavy artillery.[56] Ferrostaal, one week later, concluded a
78-million-mark contract to construct a powder factory in Rumania over a two-
and-a-half-year period.[57] Also in July, Fabricius began pressuring the Rumanian
government to award a military contract to German industry for motorcycles and
staff cars.[58] German activity in Rumania was at a fever pitch — although they failed
to obtain structural guarantees, the Germans were pressing the offensive on all
fronts: finance and banks[59], agriculture[60], and transport and communications.[61] The
impact of all this activity on the German position in Rumania can scarcely be over-
estimated.

By the end of July, Göring relented on his earlier refusal to approve the aeronautical package and German companies were finally authorized to sign individual
contracts with the Rumanian Air Ministry.[62] Authorization to supply the most modern fighters (Me 109s and He 112s) followed a week later.[63] Despite Göring's shipment delay, Rumania demonstrated its good faith by beginning petroleum deliveries
to pay for the aircraft as early as July 21.[64]

By mid-August, however, Germany's situation had become desperate. Having
exhausted its normal petroleum quotas, the Greater Reich could look only to the

[56] Malzar (DG Bukarest) to AA, July 22, 1939, PA, Ha Pol, IVb, Rumänien, Handel mit
Kriegsgerät, Bd. 1.

[57] Ferrostaal A.G., Essen (signatures illegible) to AA, August 3, 1939, PA, Ha Pol, IVb,
Rumänien, Handel mit Kriegsgerät, Bd. 2.

[58] Fabricius (DG Bukarest) to AA, July 14, 1939, op. cit., note 54. Stelzer (DG Bukarest) to
AA, August 5, 1939, PA, Ha Pol, Handakten Wiehl, Rumänien, Bd. 12. The British firm Nor-
ton and the American firm Ford were the competitors for the motorcycles and staff cars, respectively.

[59] In early June, Clodius urged the quick conclusion of the "credit action" of the Deutsche
Bank, i.e., infiltration of the Banque de Crédit for political reasons. Clodius to DG Bukarest,
July 8, 1939, PA, Ha Pol, Handakten Clodius, Rumänien, Bd. 2. The Germans were also
pressuring private Rumanian banks to advance lei for the purchase of oil and grain. German
agents would approach bank officials and simply ask "how large an advance are you going to
make us?" This was reported to Playfair (British Treasury) by M. Mandel of the Mandel
Bankers (Bucharest). "The banks as a whole wanted to resist this tactic but M. Mandel
thought many of the weaker brethren would fall through sheer fright." Playfair (British Treasury) to Nichols (Foreign Office), August 2, 1939, PRO, F.O. 371/23847.

[60] The Rumanians also wanted a one-million-lei credit for agricultural machinery. Stelzer
(DG Bukarest) to AA, July 20, 1939, PA, Ha Pol, Handakten Wiehl, Rumänien, Bd. 11.

[61] Communications and Transport: As part of the armaments package, the Rumanians
awarded Germany the teleprinter contract in preference to British interests. The Rumanian
Transport Minister, Ghelmegeanu, visited Berlin in early July and had extensive interviews
with Fritz Todt (*Generalinspekteur für das deutsche Straßenwesen*) and with officials of the
Reichspost. Ghelmegeanu returned to Bucharest enthusiastic over Todt's willingness to assist in
the development of the Rumanian road network and Todt's promise of German credit
(financed through Rumanian treasury notes) for 30% of the construction costs, Fabricius (DG
Bukarest) to AA, PA, Ha Pol, Handakten Clodius, Rumänien, Bd. 2. The German firm Joseph
Voegele A.G. (Mannheim) had been negotiating with the Rumanian state railway for a large
contract but was not successful before the outbreak of war intervened.

[62] Clodius to DG Bukarest, July 30, 1939, DGFP, D, Vol. 6, pp. 1021-1022.

[63] Clodius to DG Bukarest, August 6, 1939, ibid.

[64] Stelzer (DG Bukarest) to AA, August 1, 1939, PA, Ha Pol, Handakten Clodius,
Rumänien, Bd. 1.

aircraft barter for an uninterrupted flow of oil to Germany and the Protectorate.[65] But despite the unquestioned importance of Rumanian petroleum to Germany, representatives of German firms did not travel to Bucharest until Rumania held up a Germany-bound steamer laden with petroleum. This German neglect could have been either simple mismanagement or a deliberate tactic to see how far the Rumanians could be pushed. In any case, Rumanian pressure brought a Junkers representative to Bucharest by plane and a promise to immediately deliver the Heinkel 112 fighters in exchange for the release of the steamer.[66] The German government was even prepared to pay in convertible currency, an extraordinary concession, if petroleum could not be obtained in any other way.[67]

By this time, it was very clear that Germany intended to implement armaments deliveries under the July protocols as quickly as possible to obtain the needed petroleum. Calinescu assured Stelzer, the German chargé, that Rumania was resolved to carry out the treaties with Germany.[68] Events moved quickly and on August 19 Calinescu authorized the release of four million marks worth of petroleum in exchange for German war material. Petroleum loading began the same day at Constantza. As a further conciliatory gesture Bujoiu announced that he was prepared to release an additional 1.5 million marks in petroleum when the Junkers aircraft engine contract was completed and the Heinkel aircraft were ready for delivery.[69]

Also on August 19th, Wiehl telegraphed permission for the release of Czech machine guns in exchange for the release of further supplies of petroleum.[70] Convinced of Rumanian goodwill, the German government began sending the Heinkel fighters; by August 21st, ten Heinkel fighters had already left Germany while nineteen more were being prepared for departure.[71]

Despite this auspicious beginning, the last days of August were marked by confusion and delay. The Wilhelmstraße and the Economics Ministry wanted to carry out the deliveries as smoothly and quickly as possible but there was opposition from the German Air Ministry, and this, together with other factors, postponed deliveries of air materiel until the beginning of September. Concerned over the example set by Turkey, Müller (RLM) wanted the Wilhelmstraße to obtain an unequivocal declaration of Rumania's neutrality, which was almost assured by this time, before deliveries were resumed.[72] Furthermore, once mobilization was declared in late August,

---

[65] Stelzer (DG Bukarest) to AA, August 16, 1939, DGFP, D, Vol. 7, p. 85.

[66] Wiehl to DG Bukarest, August 17, 1939, PA, Ha Pol, Handakten Clodius, Rumänien, Bd. 2. Stelzer telegraphed on Wednesday, August 16, informing Berlin that Bujoiu wanted the contract to be signed by Friday the 19th. The Junkers representative was supposed to arrive in Bucharest on August 19, but neither the Junkers nor Heinkel representatives had arrived as late as August 24.

[67] Ibid.

[68] Stelzer (DG Bukarest) to AA, August 17, 1939, DGFP, D, Vol. 7, 97, pp. 105-106.

[69] Stelzer (DG Bukarest) to AA, August 19, 1939, DGFP, D, Vol. 7, 127, p. 136.

[70] Wiehl to DG Bukarest, August 19, 1939, ibid., p. 131.

[71] Wiehl to DG Bukarest, August 21, 1939, ibid., p. 170.

[72] Müller (RLM) to Junker (AA), August 22, 1939, PA, Ha Pol, IVb, Rumänien Handel mit Kriegsgerät, Bd. 2. It is not clear whether Müller was acting on his own initiative or was being prompted by Göring.

all existing export permits became invalid and had to be reissued.[73] Not until September 1 was the situation sorted out. By this time, the Rumanian government had made its neutrality clear, allowing the Wilhelmstraße to reassert its earlier position.

> 1. Antiaircraft and machine guns have been released and are already in transit by rail to Yugoslavia.
> 2. Delivery of the second series of Heinkel fighters will be made as soon as the Rumanian pilots have arrived by air, probably at the beginning of next week.
> 3. The contract for engines has been signed by Junkers and submitted to the Foreign Ministry for forwarding to Bucharest by the next courier.
> All departments are agreed that armaments deliveries to Rumania are to be carried out in all circumstances.
> For guidance on language to be held: Delivery is at present made extremely difficult by the other demands on the railways. We are trying to fit the transport trains into the military timetable.[74]

The Czech machine guns had been initially delayed by an administrative mix-up, then by the need to reissue export permits, and finally by the disruption of transport caused by mobilization. Gerstenberg, seconded by Fabricius, was quite disturbed at the repeated delays. The German air attaché felt that Rumania had already clearly indicated its military and political attitudes by delivering petroleum over the negotiated quantities. "Rumania", he stated, "would in all circumstances adhere to this attitude in future and would continue all deliveries to Germany. Nevertheless, it seems to me necessary for further supplies of petroleum that we should quickly fulfill the obligations we have undertaken and thus remedy the grievances brought forward."[75] In fact, Rumanian approval of German requests for further supplementary petroleum deliveries hinged upon "our releasing the supplies which we do in fact owe. I consider the continuation without friction of supplies of petroleum from Rumania to be more important than the military value of the armaments held back."[76] A letter from General Thomas the following day attributed the delay in shipping machine guns to unfavorable circumstances, not policy.[77] It does, however, seem apparent that Air Ministry opposition to the delivery of aircraft and antiaircraft guns was largely responsible for the other delays at the end of August. Nevertheless, the Wilhelmstraße was able to carry the day with the other ministries in Berlin, so that by September 1 the armaments were once again being delivered, assuring Germany access to Rumanian petroleum.

At the end of August, Germany was urgently pressing for increased grain

---

[73] Clodius to DG Bukarest, August 28, 1939, PA, Ha Pol, Handakten Clodius, Rumänien, Bd. 2.

[74] Clodius to DG Bukarest, September 1, 1939, DGFP, D, Vol. 7, 497, p. 481.

[75] Gerstenberg/Fabricius (DG Bukarest) to AA, August 30, 1939, DGFP, D, Vol. 7, 454, p. 444.

[76] Ibid.

[77] Thomas (Wi Rü Amt — OKW) to Garbea (Rumanian military attaché in Berlin), August 31, 1939, PA, Ha Pol, IVb, Rumänien, Handel mit Kriegsgerät, Bd. 2. Repeated delays over the export of these machine guns was a constant source of irritation to the Rumanian government.

exports[78] while simultaneously trying to transfer the value of 100,000 tons of wheat (approximately 10 million marks) to the normal petroleum quota, offering in exchange the immediate purchase of 400,000 tons of wheat.[79] Two days after this offer, Rumania agreed to export 300,000 tons of wheat with an option to Germany for another 100,000 tons.[80] The same day, Fabricius chartered 220 Danube barges for September to carry the wheat.[81]

Also during August, in addition to frantically negotiating the armaments barter, Germany attempted to secure its supply lines through the Danube.[82] The Wilhelmsstraße had previously asked the *Reichsbahn* for railway tank cars to carry Rumanian oil[83], finding to its chagrin that the *Reichsbahn* was simply incapable of supplying them.[84] In late August, Clodius sent an urgent telegram — everything possible must be done to increase petroleum transport to Germany — instructing the legation to sound out the Rumanians if (and how many) railway tank cars could be made available for transport to Germany. In addition, Bavarian Lloyd was commissioned to lease oil barges from both Rumanian and Hungarian companies.[85]

Rumania was actually quite forthcoming about transporting oil by railway. Only four days after Clodius's initial enquiry, and despite its usual reluctance to send tank cars outside the country, the Rumanian state railway authorized 5 to 10 trains per day (with 25 tank cars) to carry petroleum to Germany.[86] However, the number of tank cars available was inadequate, making it necessary for Germany to lease more from private companies. Fortunately for Germany, the firm Auxiliana owned 2,000 tank cars and was controlled by German interests.[87] The prompt Rumanian response to the German enquiry, warmly appreciated in Berlin, indicates the servility that would become increasingly characteristic of Rumanian policy in economic and political relations with Nazi Germany.

5. Rumanian Oil and the German War Machine

Just as the Wohlthat Treaty is the most appropriate symbol of German economic expansionism, expressing the extent of German ambitions, the armaments protocols

[78] The Rumanians had sidestepped any commitments regarding grain during Clodius's stay in Bucharest in early July.

[79] Clodius to DG Bukarest, August 26, 1939, PA, Ha Pol, Handakten Clodius, Rumänien, Bd. 2.

[80] Fabricius (DG Bukarest) to AA, August 28, 1939, Telegram No.370, ibid.

[81] Ibid.

[82] "Da Erdöltransport mit allen Mitteln gefördert werden muß, erbitte Nachprüfung, ob und wieviel Kesselwagen Rumänien für Pendelverkehr nach Deutschland zur Verfügung stellen kann." Clodius to DG Bukarest, August 26, 1939, ibid.

[83] Junker (AA) to Ministerialrat Sommerlatte (*Reichsverkehrsministerium*), August 9, 1939, PA, Ha Pol, IVb, Rumänien, Handel mit Kriegsgerät, Bd. 2.

[84] Sommerlatte to AA, September 1, 1939, ibid.

[85] Clodius to DG Bukarest, August 26, 1939, PA, Ha Pol, Handakten Clodius, Rumänien, Bd. 2.

[86] Fabricius (DG Bukarest) to AA, August 29, 1939, Telegram No. 385, PA, Ha Pol, IVb, Rumänien, Handel mit Kriegsgerät, Bd. 2.

[87] Ibid.

of July 8, 1939, and their realization in subsequent months express most accurately the substance of German policy, particularly the inherent tendencies of Nazi imperialism. By its example and influence, the German model of a state-controlled economic system, whose linchpin lay in armaments production, was exported to Rumania with the Heinkels and Messerschmidts. Certainly King Carol and his entourage were not motivated by a desire to reduce their country to colonial servitude, but the failure of either Great Britain or France to come up with substantial armaments aid made King Carol's turn to Germany virtually inevitable, and with it an imitation of German economic policy. Carol was convinced of the certainty of war by the beginning of 1939, and the Rumanian state, surrounded by hostile neighbors, naturally sought armaments where available. It was unfortunate for Rumania that only Germany was willing to provide substantial amounts of war materiel.

Successful until the outbreak of war in neutralizing the more obnoxious portions of the Wohlthat Treaty, Rumania's eagerness for German arms and willingless to provide petroleum in payment completely negated Rumanian efforts in other areas. Having once acquiesced to German demands for supplementary petroleum exports during the political crisis of August, 1939, Rumania was hardly in a position to rebuff similar demands after war began. Despite protests and countermeasures such as the delay of petroleum shipments in response to German dilatory deliveries, Rumania's overall policy during August and September was active cooperation with Germany in the supply of petroleum. For Germany, it scarcely needs emphasizing, this was a matter of life or death. When, in the first three weeks of August, the Germans exhausted their petroleum quota for the entire third quarter of the year, the Rumanians made a supplementary quota of 8 million marks available almost immediately[88], releasing the petroleum as a prepayment of payments coming due in 1940 for earlier credit transactions and for war materiel *that had not yet been delivered.* Through the armaments barter, Germany and the Protectorate were able to secure approximately 40 percent of Rumania's petroleum exports for the first six months of 1939, which, in turn, served to give Germany a de facto claim on an equivalent amount for the remainder of 1939, i.e., some 600,000 tons. This was the limit that Germany could either pay for or transport via the Danube.[89]

The extent to which the armaments barter provided the lever to break down remaining Rumanian resistance to German economic hegemony is revealed by the Seventh Protocol negotiated in Bucharest during middle and late September, 1939.[90] By its terms, Germany achieved victory both on the grain and currency questions, while substantially increasing the German share of Rumanian trade. German demands for increased grain imports were satisfied through a 120 million-mark

[88] Stelzer (DG Bukarest) to AA, August 25, 1939, PA, Ha Pol, IVb, Rumänien, Rohstoffe und Waren, Petroleum, Bd. 1.

[89] Fabricius (DG Bukarest) to AA, September 3, 1939, DGFP, D, Vol. 7, 566, p. 540. The RWM allocated a quota of 18.9 million marks for the import of Rumanian petroleum for the final quarter of 1939. Anlage zu D.St/151/39 R.St., BA, R 7, XIV/254.

[90] Protocol and attached documents, September 21, 1939, BA, R 2/1544.

quota for wheat, barley, and corn (October 1, 1939 to September 30, 1940). No
specific figures for petroleum are given, but the sum of the other quotas amounts to
234 million marks.[91] Under the 25% clause, Germany was then entitled to import
petroleum up to 25% of total trade (discounting armaments and special barters), so
estimating 234 million marks as 3/4 of the total German imports from Rumania,
Germany thus acquired rights to import a further 80 million marks in petroleum
under its "normal" quota. Total German imports from Rumania would then
amount to some 314 million marks, or 62% of Rumania's total 1938 trade
(reckoned in marks at the old rate). The physical amount of commodities imported
was actually greater since Rumania agreed to raise the exchange rate of the mark
from 41.40/40.50 Lei to 50/49 as of January 1, 1940.[92] The armaments barter thus
provided the means for obtaining the Rumanian guarantees for delivery of petroleum and grains absent from the Wohlthat Treaty. Although Germany faced other
difficulties in exercising its suzerainty, particularly in transporting commodities via
the Danube and in countering British economic warfare, the armaments barter deal
of 1939 forged the final links in the chain that would bind Rumania to Germany
until 1944.

---

[91] Anlage A to Protocol, ibid.

[92] 'Vertrauliches Protokoll', September 21, 1939, signed by Carl Clodius and E. Marian,
ibid., paragraph 6, pp. 3-4. This clause was moderated to some extent by the following provision: until March 31, 1940, Rumania could pay its debts on contracts signed before September
20, 1939, at the old rate. Economists of IG Farben estimated that Rumanian prices rose from
60 (1929 = 100) to over 80 by November, 1939. They attributed this inflation to commodity
scarcity, speculation and British preemptory purchasing. IG Farben, Volkswirtschaftliche
Abteilung, 'Die Reichsmark in Rumänien', August 5, 1940, BA, R 63/216. Germany was unable in the long run to increase its terms of trade through this maneuver because Rumanian
inflation was so severe. This became a serious problem for the German war economy. Dr.
Schultze-Schlutius (RWM) to Walter (RMEL), August 27, 1942, in BA, R 2/21460. Rumanian inflation reached such proportions that peasants began to hold their products back, which
became a concern even in the *Reichskanzlei*, Willuhn (Reichskanzlei) to Lammers (Reichsminister), December 13, 1941, BA, R 43 II/1486.

CHAPTER XI

GERMAN EXPLOITATION OF DANUBIAN EUROPE: A TENTATIVE BALANCE SHEET

1. The Singer-Prebisch Controversy and the Problem of Measuring "Terms of Trade"

Since the end of World War II, there has been a growing interest in the problem of trade relations between primary producing and industrial countries. As terms of trade have been used since classical economics to assess the real income accruing to a country from its international trade relations, changes in the terms of trade have been used as indicators of trends in benefits from trade. Economists in the postwar period have argued over the actual behavior of the terms of trade of developing countries over the long run, i.e., secular changes. One group has maintained that the attempts of developing countries to achieve self-sustaining growth is constrained by the trend of the terms of trade to turn against them.[1] Classical economic theory, on the other hand, holds that the terms of trade for primary producers would improve over time because of diminishing returns combined with economics of scale in the industrialized nations.[2] The deterioration hypothesis, originally suggested by statistical studies that seemed to show that industrial countries, Great Britain in particular, have improved their terms of trade over the last 50 to 100

[1] The first studies to emphasize the secular deterioration in terms of trade were published by the League of Nations and United Nations: League of Nations, Industrialization and Foreign Trade, Geneva 1945, pp. 16, 18; United Nations, Relative Prices of Exports and Imports of Underdeveloped Countries, Lake Success/N.Y. 1949; United Nations, Economic Commission for Latin America, The Economic Development of Latin America and Its Principal Problems, Lake Success/N.Y. 1949, pp. 8-9 (written by Raul Prebisch); H. W. SINGER, The Distribution of Gains between Investing and Borrowing Countries, in: American Economic Review, Papers and Proceedings XL, No.2 (May 1950), pp. 473-485; Raul PREBISCH, Commercial Policy in the Underdeveloped Countries, in: American Economic Review, Papers and Proceedings XLIX, No.2 (May 1959), pp. 252, 261; Towards a New Trade Policy for Development, Report by the Secretary General of the United Nations Conference on Trade and Development New York, 1964, pp. 14, 18-19, 79 (written by Raul Prebisch).

[2] This was the view of, for example, Mill. John Stuart MILL, Principles of Political Economy, 5th ed., New York 1909, Vol. II, p. 113. "... the richer countries ... gain the least by a given amount of foreign commerce since, having a greater demand for commodities generally, they are likely to have a greater demand for foreign commodities and thus modify the terms of interchange to their own disadvantage ..." Mill believed, however, that the aggregate gains of industrial countries were greater because they carried on more trade.

years, has been challenged theoretically by several orthodox economists[3] and statistically by detailed studies made by American economists.[4]

The relation of this question to the question of the short-term problem of Germany's economic relations with Danubian Europe during the Depression years lies in the increasing terminological and statistical clarity resulting from the critique of the Singer-Prebisch (deterioration) hypothesis. Primarily, the concept of commodity or net barter terms of trade, defined as the ratio of import prices to export prices, has gained acceptance as the most useful definition in measuring gain from international trade. However, the attempt by Frank Taussig to introduce "gross barter terms of trade" to account for invisible exports and imports (interest and amortization payments, insurance, capital export, freight revenue, etc.) to arrive at a more accurate picture of trade relations has not found wide acceptance.[5]

> The gross barter terms of trade of any year are made better by the income of that year from investments. This example shows what a confusing concept the gross barter terms of trade are. Loading unfavorably the terms of trade of countries when they send it abroad, they load it favorably when borrowers proceed to pay back. In fact, the concept takes invisible exports and imports into consideration but in such a crude way that no clearcut indication can be derived from it.[6]

Consequently, the net commodity terms of trade used in the studies under consideration exclude items such as freight revenues — a lacuna noted by critics.

---

[3] Robert E. BALDWIN, Secular Movements in Terms of Trade, in: American Economic Review, Papers and Proceedings XVL, No.2 (May 1955), pp. 259-269; P. T. ELLSWORTH, The Terms of Trade between Primary Producing and Industrial Countries, in: Interamerican Economic Affairs X, No.1 (Summer 1956), pp. 47-65; Gottfried HABERLER, Terms of Trade and Economic Development, in: Howard S. ELLIS (ed.), International Economic Association, Economic Development for Latin America, New York 1961, pp. 275-297; Gerald M. MEIER, International Trade and Development, New York 1963, pp. 58-61; Theodore MORGAN, The Long Run Terms of Trade between Agriculture and Manufacturing, in: Economic Development and Cultural Change VIII, No.1 (October 1959), pp. 1-23, and idem, Trends in Terms of Trade and Their Repercussions on Primary Producers, in: R. F. HARROD and Douglas HARROD (eds.), International Economic Association, International Trade in a Developing World, London 1963, pp. 52-95.

[4] The following are all unpublished doctoral dissertations: Dennis APPLEYARD, Terms of Trade and Economic Development: A Case Study of India, Univ. of Michigan 1966, 67-1704; Edward BALDWIN, Trade between Mexico and the United States: The Prebisch Hypothesis, Univ. of Houston 1970, 70-24259; Sarah MONTGOMERY, The Terms of Trade of Primary Products and Manufactured Goods in International Trade, 1872-1952, Univ. of Wisconsin 1960, 60-3241; Emile QUERVIN, Terms of Trade and Economic Development, Princeton 1958; Robert S. RIPPEY, Jr., Terms of Trade of Underdeveloped Countries, Syracuse 1966, 66-9860; Joel W. SAILORS, Secular Terms of Trade: Theory and Measurement, University of Texas at Austin 1956. In addition to the above, there are two purely theoretical investigations of the problem in terms of trade: Raveendra BATRA, Economic Growth and the Terms of Trade, Southern Illinois Univ. 1969, 70-422; James A. HANSON, The Terms of Trade and Economic Growth, Yale 1968, 68-11, 189. The most systematic critique of the Singer-Prebisch hypothesis is by an Indian economist: Kishwar Shabbir KHAN, Gains from International Trade: Their Distribution between Investing and Borrowing Countries, Bombay 1971.

[5] Taussig defines gross barter terms of trade as ratios of the physical quantity of exports to the physical quantity of imports, constructed by valuing the exports and imports of each year in the prices of a given year. F. W. TAUSSIG, International Trade, New York 1927, Chs. 20, 21.

[6] QUERVIN, Terms of Trade, p. 44.

On the elementary level, the United Nations economists have been criticized for inadequately covering industrial countries and for their choice of an end point for their studies. Specifically, it has been charged that too great a reliance has been placed upon the evidence of the British case, which cannot be taken to represent the trends of all industrial countries.[7] The choice of 1947 as the terminal date of the first United Nations study has been questioned on the basis of the ongoing disruptions resulting from World War II. "It does not seem too jaundiced to propose that perhaps the authors of *Relative Prices . . .* were so impressed with the pattern they found from 1876-1880 to the Second World War that they were kept from taking as seriously as they should have the possibility that the price relationships might have considerably altered after the war."[8]

Although these problems were easily solved by extending the coverage in time and to other major industrial countries, the critics also noted other problems inherent in constructing an index series: price indices cannot take into account changes in the quality of goods, and it is generally accepted that manufactured goods have improved to a greater extent than raw materials and foodstuffs. Thus, the developing countries, while paying more for their imports, may have been receiving higher-quality products, making their terms of trade less unfavorable than the original research indicated.[9] To construct a long-term series, the commodities covered must be traded throughout the time under consideration to avoid distortion — no allowance can be made for the introduction of new commodities, a phenomenon more frequent from industrial than primary producing countries. If, as neoclassical economists contend, the price history of a new product involved rapid decrease in the early years, this omission weights the export price of industrial countries at a level higher than the import price index[10], thus skewing the index in favor of the industrial countries. A third problem is that all indices suffer to some extent from the lack of accurate and comprehensive data, in this case the problem of adequate commodity coverage. This overlaps to some extent with the inherent elimination of new commodities but also involves the statisticians' tendency to omit capital goods exports because price per unit of weight has been challenged as a measure of economic benefit derived from capital and investment goods.

[7] The most detailed discussion of the British bias may be found in MONTGOMERY, Terms of Trade, pp. 38-39, p. 60, pp. 94-95; also, ELLSWORTH, Terms of Trade, pp. 51-57; C. P. KINDLEBERGER, Industrial Europe's Terms of Trade on Current Account, 1870-1953, in: Economic Journal LXV, No. 257 (March 1953), pp. 32-33; MORGAN, Long Run; idem, Trends; C. M. WRIGHT, Convertibility and Triangular Trade as Safeguards Against Depression, in: Economic Journal LXV, No. 259 (September 1955), pp. 424-426.

[8] MONTGOMERY, Terms of Trade , p. 37.

[9] APPLEYARD, Terms of Trade, p. 5; QUERVIN, Terms of Trade, p. 62; BALDWIN, Secular Movements, p. 268; ELLSWORTH, Terms of Trade, p. 48; MEIER, International Trade, pp. 59-60; MORGAN, Long Run, pp. 4-5; and POBRECITO, Development, Scientific Pretension and the Need for a Policy of the Informed Neighbor, in: Inter-American Economic Affairs X, No. 3 (1969), p. 55.

[10] BALDWIN, Trade, and HABERLER, Terms of Trade, p. 280. MONTGOMERY, Terms of Trade, p. 11.

Further difficulties will be encountered if the smaller classes of manufactured exports to a given area are averaged over an extended period of time, because in reality there are large fluctuations in the commodity composition of this group and they are nonhomogeneous "which makes it difficult to estimate meaningful unit value and volume indices for them."[11] If, however, commodities such as machinery, vehicles and ships, precision instruments and electrical apparatus, which have a usually qualitatively higher price per unit of weight, are left out of the index, it would be biased in favor of the primary producer. To omit capital goods would seem to understate the real fall in purchasing power of primary producers, particularly in periods such as the Depression when the industrialization programs of the primary producers required increased imports of capital equipment. Further, unless the series is weighted according to the relative importance of each commodity selected for inclusion, it results in the equal weighting of all components throughout the period. If there has been a significant change in the structure of trade during such a period, a trend might result from the change in structure alone.[12] In evaluating German trade policy in the 1930s, when a conscious effort was made to improve the terms of trade by reducing imports of finished products and semimanufactures while promoting exports of finished commodities, this is particularly important.

The assault on the Singer-Prebisch hypothesis brought to light the significant role of transport and insurance charges in biasing downward the terms of trade of primary producers. The original research, finding that the terms of trade had improved for industrial countries, and Britain in particular, was subject to a simple inversion leading to the conclusion that the developing countries had suffered deterioration. The UN economists failed to note that the industrial nations of Europe record the value of their imports inclusive of freight charges (c.i.f.) but exclude such charges in valuing their exports (f.o.b.). Declining transport costs could have significantly influenced the upward trend of British terms of trade. Quervin and Montgomery corrected for the freight rate factor, discovering a net improvement in the terms of trade of the primary producers as opposed to a secular decline over the period 1870-1952.

Even taking these factors into account, certain other problems render calculation of German terms of trade in the 1930s difficult, if not impossible. From 1931, the German mark was maintained at official parity by a variety of administrative maneuvers, making its "real" exchange rate in terms of the leading currencies of world trade and finance difficult to calculate. Also, together with the official *Reichsmark* maintained at gold parity, there was a series of other marks sold abroad at a discount as part of the program of export stimulation and debt liquidation. The

---

[11] C. P. KINDLEBERGER, German Terms of Trade by Commodity Classes and Areas, in: Review of Economics and Statistics XXXVI (1954), p. 167.

[12] QUERVIN, Terms of Trade, p. 196. After noting that certain primary products fared considerably better in the last 50 years than did others, and that certain countries benefited from this trend, Rippey points out that the terms of trade would not necessarily be favorable for these countries because the terms were also dependent upon what they chose to import. RIPPEY, Terms of Trade, p. 124.

clearing mark was usually sold at a discount in terms of the clearing partner's currency, while that clearing partner's currency was discounted in relation to dollars or pounds.

> . . . in many European countries, differential exchange rates are used for imports from or exports to other countries, the rates varying, not only as between countries, but also as between different classes of commodities. The total of imports and exports are given as equal to a certain amount in national currency, but it is uncertain at what average rate of exchange these totals should be reckoned. The relationship between imports and exports, or between import and export prices, and calculations of the barter terms of trade are therefore subject to an unknown margin of error.[13]

To arrive at a true picture of the terms of trade under a multiple exchange system, each transaction would have to be converted at the exchange rate in convertible currency prevailing at the time of the transaction. If, in addition, the multiple exchange rate system is reinforced with subsidies, private compensation, export promotion via script, blocked marks, or bond repatriation, it is very difficult indeed to tell what the declared values published in German statistical handbooks really mean. To calculate the actual prices at which a country trades abroad, declared values should include export taxes and import subsidies, and exclude import taxes and export subsidies.[14] It is uncertain if subsidies were included in the declaration of value of exports (for transactions conducted in marks) or at what exchange rate between marks and convertible currency individual export transactions took place. Charles Kindleberger concludes that it is unlikely that "German export valuations consistently exclude subsidies."

It does appear that German trade values with clearing partners could be reconstructed by converting German import and export values into the clearing partners' currencies at the average rates of exchange prevailing, and then converting the domestic currency values into constant dollars. This would take into account the double depreciation of the mark — in terms of the Danubian clearing partner's currency and of that currency in terms of hard currency. Because the mark's depreciation in terms of the domestic currency and the domestic currency's depreciation in terms of hard currency fluctuated throughout the 1930s, such a reconstruction would differ markedly from calculations made in constant marks or dollars. The average "value" of the mark in terms of constant dollars, for example, would differ from country to country and from year to year within any country.

2. The Classical Critique of the German Trade Drive: An Evaluation

Historical scholarship concerning Nazi Germany's relations with Danubian Europe has been dominated by an image first propagated by the popular anti-Fascist polemics of the 1930s and later given scientific legitimacy by such prominent

---

[13] League of Nations, Economic Intelligence Service, World Economic Survey — Fifth Year 1935/36, Geneva 1936, p. 300.

[14] KINDLEBERGER, German Terms of Trade, pp. 167-174, I am relying particularly on Kindleberger's discussion on pp. 171-172.

economists as Howard Ellis and Antonin Basch.[15] Germany was presented as a "vampire" country sucking its victims of their valuable raw materials and giving in return only useless junk — aspirin, cameras, and musical instruments. "The Greeks have to accept payment in mouth organs or radio sets, and in such large quantities that their demand for these articles could be satisfied for many years to come. Optical instruments which the Nazi Reich could not export elsewhere were offered to the Bulgarian peasants."[16] What is the substance of this critique and how far is it justified by a documented study of German commercial policy?

One of the first critical studies of German policy, written by Paul Einzig in the aftermath of the May Crisis in 1938, offers a convenient point of departure to present the classic critique — both for its brevity and systematic presentation and because of Einzig's subsequent controversy with Frederic Benham.[17]

In Einzig's view Nazi Germany intended from the beginning to obtain more than its "natural" share of the markets of southeastern Europe by means of "clever, too clever, tricks."[18] Einzig also contends that more than trade was at stake in the question of German trade dominance in Danubian Europe — the strategic question. "By acquiring political control over these countries as a result of economic penetration, Germany would increase her economic strength and military striking power to a considerable degree."[19] What then were the characteristics of Germany's policy of deception and trickery?

[15] The most important scholarly works were: BASCH, Danubian Basin; Howard S. ELLIS, Exchange Control in Central Europe, Cambridge/Massachusetts 1941. Basch/Ellis's work has already been superseded by postwar scholarship: Frank CHILD, The Theory and Practice of Exchange Control in Germany: A Study of Monopolistic Exploitation in International Markets, The Hague 1958; BEREND and RANKI, Economic Development. Except for the study by Frederic Benham issued under the auspices of the RIIA, the following works generally follow the classic critique: Paul EINZIG, Bloodless Invasion, London 1938; A. G. B. FISHER, The German Trade Drive in Southeastern Europe, in: International Affairs 18 (1939), pp. 143-170; F. HILGERDT, The Approach to Bilateralism: A Change in the Structure of World Trade, in: Index 10 (1935), pp. 175-188; Albert HIRSCHMAN, National Power and the Structure of Foreign Trade, Berkeley 1945; Graham HUTTON, Danubian Destiny: A Survey after Munich, London 1939; Lagos JOCSIK, German Economic Influences in the Danube Valley, Budapest 1946; Frederick Elwyn JONES, Hitler's Drive to the East, New York 1937; Cleona LEWIS, Nazi Europe and World Trade, New York 1941; M. MITNITZKY, Germany's Trade Monopoly in Eastern Europe, in: Social Research 6 (February 1939), pp. 22-39; Maurice PERNOT, German Trade Policy: Dr. Funk's System, Paris 1938; Wilhelm ROEPKE, German Commercial Policy, London 1934; Gunter REIMANN, The Vampire Economy, New York 1939; RIIA, The Balkan States, London 1936; RIIA (Frederic Benham), Southeastern Europe, London 1939; RIIA, Southeastern Europe: A Brief Survey, London 1940; Gerhard SCHACHER, Germany Pushes Southeast, London 1937; R. SCHUELLER, Commercial Policy between the Two Wars, in: Social Research 10 (1943), pp. 152-174; Hans STAUDINGER, The Future of Totalitarian Barter Trade, in: Social Research 7 (1940), pp. 410-433.

[16] REIMANN, Vampire Economy, p. 227.

[17] Paul EINZIG, Why Defend Nazi Trade Methods? in: The Banker, London (May 1941), pp. 108-113. Frederic BENHAM, A Reply to Dr. Einzig, ibid. (June 1941), pp. 182-186. And two rejoinders by Einzig and Benham, ibid., pp. 186-193.

[18] EINZIG, Bloodless Invasion, pp. 8-9.

[19] Ibid., pp. 10-11.

Contraction of Large-Scale Indebtedness

In order to gain predominance over the Danubian countries, Germany ran up a large debt in clearing trade, violating the spirit, if not the letter, of its trade agreements.[20] With malice aforethought, Germany did not exert itself to deliver exports to pay debts, causing heavy losses among the Danubian exporters who were forced to dump their clearing marks at a substantial loss. In order to prevent such losses, the central banks of Germany's clearing partners were forced to take over the clearing marks at parity, thus in effect assuming responsibility for Germany's trade debt:

> Since the mechanism of the clearing system still made it essential that trade should balance between the countries concerned and Germany, and since the receivers of the credits did not have to pay for their imports at once, insufficient money accumulated in the South-Eastern countries' central banks on account of purchases from Germany to pay their exporters for sales to that country, and the central banks had again to provide more credit, thus assuming the burden of lending nominally taken on by Germany.[21]

Thus the Danubian central banks were obliged to increase their rediscounts and note circulation in order to finance interest-free commodity credits to Germany. In this way, the capital poor countries unwillingly helped finance German rearmament, because the blocked clearing marks deposited in Berlin were not withdrawn from circulation, as were earmarked gold deposits, but were reloaned to finance the program of internal economic expansion.[22]

German Dumping

Germany not only did not pay for the commodities purchased but dumped Danubian agricultural products on the world market in order to obtain sorely needed foreign exchange. "A less obvious consequence is that the market for the commodities concerned is spoiled for the countries producing the commodities."[23]

> Huge quantities of Central and South-East European grain, tobacco, attar of roses, and numerous other agricultural produce, which at the moment were less urgently required than foreign exchange bills, with which it was possible to purchase certain special raw materials overseas, were sold by Germany on the world exchanges. . . . As a result of exchanges the market prices of Hungarian wheat, Yugoslavian maize, Greek tobacco and Balkan grain of all kinds were naturally kept at a low level, so that the South-Eastern states' possibilities of selling their agricultural produce for their own account were reduced still further.[24]

Einzig contends that by dumping, Germany was able to come "to the rescue" and take over the entire unsalable surplus of a particular country on favorable terms.

---

[20] Ibid., pp. 18-19.

[21] RIIA, Southeastern Europe: A Brief Survey, London 1940, p. 117. See also pp. 3 and 126. See also Godfrey BRIEFS, Shifting Patterns in Eastern Europe's Foreign Trade, 1928-1948, U.Ph.D., Harvard University 1950, pp. 167-168.

[22] One of the first scholars to note this was by Kenyon POOLE, German Financial Policies, 1933-1939, Cambridge/Massachusetts 1939. Also see BEREND and RANKI, Economic Development.

[23] SCHACHER, Germany Pushes Southeast.

[24] Ibid., pp. 155-156. BRIEFS, Shifting Patterns, pp. 170-171.

Export of Secondhand Armaments and Unwanted Merchandise

At a certain point the existence of the blocked balances in Berlin began to exert considerable pressure upon the governments of the Danubian countries, making them willing to accept almost any German export in order to liquidate the credits — from secondhand armaments to harmonicas.[25]

> The Nazis calculate that Dr. Schacht's technique of forced sale of arms to the small countries of South-East Europe will have important political and military results. Greece and Bulgaria, armed by Germany, will be dependent on further supplies of arms from there in the event of war. Having bought Nazi cannon, they will be dependent on Nazi goodwill for spare parts from Germany, and the four submarines and destroyers which Greece is contemplating buying from Germany will depend on Nazi training to man them.[26]

Germany was thus able to liquidate the clearing debt by disposing of commodities that had no real market value and promote its military/political interests at the same time.

The Long-Term Credit Trick

Germany's competitors were astounded to find German exporters offering long-term credit for consumer goods (12 months to 2 years), popularizing installment buying to an unprecedented extent in the Danubian states. Similarly, "German manufacturers reverted to the pre-war practice of outbidding their rivals regarding the terms of credit."[27] How could Germany, with such low foreign exchange and gold reserves, extend such credit and outbid its capital-rich commercial rivals? According to Einzig, it was actually the borrowing countries that eventually extended the credit. German ingenuity had found a loophole in the clearing agreements that did not specify when the Rumanians, for example, should pay for the German goods they purchased.

> While Roumanian exporters sold their goods on a cash basis, Roumanian importers bought their goods mainly on a credit basis. This means that, owing to the delay in payment by Roumanian importers, there were no funds available for the settlement of the claims of the Roumanian exporters. The latter would have to wait until the credits granted by Germany to Roumanian importers had matured and the importers actually paid for the goods received.
> Germany could well afford to grant long-term credits to Roumanian imports, since she received payment, in the form of goods exported from Roumania, long before the credits matured.[28]

In effect, the governments of the Danubian countries unwillingly financed the credits contracted by their own nationals.

---

[25] EINZIG, Bloodless Invasion, pp. 30-32.
[26] JONES, Hitler's, pp. 45-46.
[27] EINZIG, Bloodless Invasion, p. 37.
[28] Ibid., pp. 39-40.

Bettering Germany's Terms of Trade

By forcing the Danubian governments to increase the value of the clearing mark in terms of the domestic currency, Germany was able to pay much higher prices for Danubian products than those prevailing on the world market. For this reason, Balkan exporters were anxious to sell to the Germans. "The price of Roumanian oil, for instance, is at the time of writing something like 20 per cent above the world market price, and it is difficult to induce Roumanian producers to sell their oil elsewhere than in Germany."[29] It was alleged by former *Reichsbank* official Emil Puhl, as well as Frank Child, an American economist, that Germany was successful in improving its terms of trade by exploiting its monopsonist/monopolist position in the Danubian markets. "[Schacht] cleverly exploited Germany's bartering power in driving down import prices and raising export prices and, in some instances, securing credits from weaker countries which were subsequently used for imports from Germany.[30] Child devotes much of his study to demonstrating the theoretical possibility of Germany's implementing such a policy on the basis of the pure theory of international trade.[31] Thus, while Germany paid higher than world market prices for Danubian products, it was still the net gainer by charging yet higher prices for its industrial products.[32]

The only contemporary challenge to the dominance of this thesis was made by the British economist Frederic Benham, in a study issued under the auspices of RIIA, and in an article in *Economica*.[33] Briefly, Benham concluded (on the basis of the statistics of the Danubian countries) that while Germany paid higher prices for Danubian products, it sold competitively in these markets (contra — page 217 above). He further challenged the popular view that Germany forced "unwanted goods" on the Balkan countries, noting that statistics showed that "aspirin and harmonicas" constituted only a tiny fraction of German exports (contra — page 216 above). He noted that German sales of Messerschmidt 109 aircraft in 1939 were highly welcome in southeastern Europe and hardly conform to Einzig's image of secondhand, useless arms dating from intervention in the Spanish Civil War. Benham also thought that the issue of Germany's frozen balances had been highly exaggerated (contra — page 215 above).

> It is usual for an agricultural country to acquire a considerable foreign balance when she is paid for her exported crops. The "frozen" mark balances were seldom, except for Turkey, more than 10 per cent or so of the annual value of the country's exports. Although, as I pointed out, they did represent a "real problem", the "huge indebtedness" was just a myth.[34]

---

[29] Ibid., p. 48. See also, RIIA, Southeastern Europe, op. cit., pp. 121-122.

[30] 'Affidavit of Emil Puhl', November 7, 1945, ND, ED-436, NCA, Vol. VII, p. 498.

[31] CHILD, Theory and Practice.

[32] RIIA, Southeastern Europe, op. cit., p. 116. See also JONES, Hitler's, p. 90.

[33] RIIA, Southeastern Europe, a Brief Survey, op. cit. See also F. BENHAM, The Terms of Trade, in: Economica 1940.

[34] BENHAM, Reply to Dr. Einzig, p. 184.

Benham concluded that, on the whole, southeastern Europe had made fairly good bargains with Germany on an economic plane. He recognized, however, the potential danger presented by German policy to labor-intensive agriculture and industrialization as well as important political considerations.

Einzig answered Benham with the accusation that the British economist was a virtual tool of Nazi propaganda. Shorn of polemical exaggeration and appeals to war hysteria, Einzig's argument amounts to a critique of Benham's methodology and a reiteration of the thesis of German "trickery." With respect to Benham's statistics on the competitive position of German sales in southeastern Europe, Einzig claimed that the index numbers "did not, of course, allow for the deterioration of the quality of German manufactures imported by the South-Eastern European countries."[35] He further claimed that the revaluation of the mark in terms of the various domestic currencies made the higher prices previously paid in lei, for example, illusory. In Einzig's view, the policy of forced mark revaluation was aimed at improving Germany's terms of trade and not, as Benham contended, aimed at increasing Germany's share of the particular country's exports. For some reason, Einzig did not attack Benham's critique (creation of excessive debts, see page 215 above) but merely remarked that the amounts were "very substantial from the point of view of the impecunious South-Eastern European countries."[36]

Thus the debate between Einzig and Benham focused on the terms of trade issue more than on the other alleged Nazi trade methods, and specifically, whether Germany promoted its larger aims by granting favorable terms of trade or by cunning devices of economic exploitation.

To what extent can the popular conception of the German trade drive be reconciled with the actual course of German policy found in the formerly secret files of the German government?

3. The German Trade Drive: A Reappraisal

Contraction of Large-Scale Indebtedness

During the course of trade negotiations, Germany made it quite clear that it was able to pay for increased imports only by means of exports. While the treaties with Yugoslavia and Rumania contained secret German purchase guarantees for agricultural products, no such equivalent obligations were undertaken by Germany's trading partners. Under these circumstances, an increase in Danubian credits in Berlin was a foregone conclusion unless there was a spontaneous increase in demand for German products in the Danubian countries.[37] For various reasons this did not occur. From 1934 to 1937 in both Yugoslavia and Rumania there is no question that

---

[35] EINZIG, Why Defend, p. 110.

[36] EINZIG, Rejoinder, p. 188.

[37] Overvaluation of the mark was not responsible for this increase, as alleged by League of Nations economists. League of Nations, Inquiry into Clearing Agreements, Geneva 1935.

Germany exerted itself to increase exports, although Einzig maintains that Germany refused to export. The German efforts were part of a general program of export promotion, and *during the first period* of German expansion, the clearing credits were consciously used by Schacht as a means to increase exports.[38] The slow liquidation of these debts was primarily due to Yugoslav and Rumanian resistance to the introduction of a discriminatory import policy in favor of Germany. They resisted because of domestic political fears of German expansionism, the orthodox economic qualms of the respective central banks and pressure from Great Britain, France, Czechoslovakia, and the United States. Although the moneys paid into the clearing accounts were not lost to Germany and were reloaned to help finance the rearmament (and *Arbeitsbeschaffung*) drives, the weight of the evidence clearly indicates that from 1934 to 1937 Germany would have preferred to promote exports rather than accumulate bad debts. Benham did, however, underestimate the impact of the clearing credits upon the Danubian governments. Twenty to thirty million marks was a very large sum indeed for Danubian countries to risk.

In the second period of German expansion, 1937 to 1939, clearing balances were significantly reduced, primarily because discriminatory import policies favoring Germany were introduced. The clearing debts still reappeared episodically and pressure was put on Berlin to prevent them. By and large, equilibrium was reached by cutting back German purchases rather than expanding German exports. This concession was made reluctantly by Germany. During the 1937 to 1939 period, the phenomenon of *Exportmüdigkeit* (German concentration on the home market because of large armaments orders) clearly emerges as the principal cause of the periodic accumulation of German debts. By 1937, it was widely held in German government circles that further increases in German imports of raw materials could be paid for only through armaments exports.

German Dumping

The extent of German dumping of Danubian products on the world market is difficult to gauge from the German archives. In the cases of Rumania and Yugoslavia, however, Einzig surely exaggerated. The 1934 treaty with Yugoslavia, for example, provided for the dumping of Yugoslav grain purchased by Germany on the world market. This was explicit and was fully understood by the Yugoslav government. Whether "hoodwinked" or not, the Yugoslavs were glad to accept German assistance despite the fact that the dumping could eventually result in "spoiling" the world market for Yugoslav grains. This indicates that Danubian policy makers were convinced that no market other than Germany existed for their products. Insofar as dumping existed without the consent of the trading partner, it was more extensively done in the case of commercial agricultural products such as Bulgarian or Greek tobacco than in perishable foods or raw materials.

[38] Schwerin von Krosigk to Schacht, February 11, 1937, PA, Ha Pol, IVa, Yugoslawien, Handel 11, 3, Austauschgeschäfte, Bd. 1.

Export of Unwanted Merchandise and Secondhand Armaments

The harmonica/aspirin/camera thesis has exerted a fascination for virtually all classic analysis of the German trade drive. It is peculiar that no one has recognized the obvious interest German heavy industry had in an export promotion program. There has been no attempt by any critic of German policy to detail the alleged forcing of unwanted commodities by comparing the commodity structure of German exports to Danubian Europe in 1925-29 to that in 1934-37. The two limited empirical attempts to subject this theory to statistical verification have concluded that there is little basis in fact to the notion that Germany forced aspirins and harmonicas on unwilling trading partners.

Germany tried and succeeded in promoting a commodity far more critical than the superfluous goods alleged by Einzig — the export of capital and investment goods. Schacht's real genius lay in his conception of matching the peculiar structure of German industry with the industrialization programs of the primary producers. This program was given explicit theoretical justification by IG Farben's leading economist, Max Ilgner.[39] Far from sponsoring a policy of deindustrialization of Danubian Europe, Germany actually provided valuable capital equipment in return for unmarketable agricultural commodities — either overabundant on the world market or of inferior quality. It is highly unlikely that any industrial competitor of Germany would have been willing to barter integrated factories (Zenica in Yugoslavia and Rimma in Rumania) for plums, cattle, or lightweight grains. An understanding of this aspect of German policy makes the success of the trade drive explicable, while the aspirin/harmonica thesis makes the whole episode appear to be medicine-show chicanery.

It appears that the more industrialized primary producers, Hungary and Poland, had more trouble in finding acceptable German commodities to import than did Yugoslavia and Rumania. It is clear that countries already suffering from industrial overcapacity or stagnation would not be eager for new plant capacity. For Hungary, in particular, the early appearance of armaments barter indicates that this was the means used to solve the problem. Here the complaints over secondhand, outmoded military equipment may be completely justified. However, armaments barter in 1939 of Messerschmidt 109s, antiaircraft artillery and Czech military equipment demonstrates that Germany would barter high-quality merchandise to obtain needed raw materials.

The Long-Term Credit Trick

If it were as easy to finance credits at the expense of its trading partners as Einzig contends, it is inexplicable why the German Economics Ministry, the Wilhelmstraße, and the Finance Ministry opposed granting such credits as a general principle and agreed to such requests only when special political or military conditions were

---

[39] Max ILGNER, Exportsteigerung durch Einschaltung in die Industrialisierung der Welt, Jena 1938.

obtained. Einzig's theory of the credit trick is based upon simple ignorance. When, for example, German exports crossed the Rumanian frontier, the lei value of the commodity was recorded, but lei available for German purchase of Rumanian commodities became available only when the Rumanian importer paid his debt into the *Reichsbank* account at the Rumanian National Bank in Bucharest. The granting of credit therefore reduced the total value, and volume, of Rumanian products available to be imported into Germany during any given year. This is why Germany tried to barter capital equipment and armaments outside the normal regular clearing agreement on a one-to-one basis for strategic raw materials such as copper or petroleum. Einzig's analysis does not fit the facts.

Terms of Trade

Germany's alleged ability to extort better terms of trade out of its trading partners in Danubian Europe was the most important issue in the Einzig/Benham debate. This question was also put in the center of discussion by Frank Child's substantial monograph on the New Plan. Unfortunately for the classic critique, the only attempts at empirical verification of the theory (by Benham and Kindleberger) have shown quite the opposite. Germany sold competitively while paying higher prices and therefore Germany's terms of trade with Danubian Europe deteriorated. None of the classical critiques of German policy has attempted to subject the exploitation via bettered terms of trade hypothesis to statistical analysis. The limited studies which have been made do indicate that Germany pursued a differential price policy, but the implications of this policy for the total terms of trade remain unknown.

The surviving available files of the German government do not provide much insight into the terms of trade question. Nevertheless, the existing published foreign trade statistics of Germany and the Danubian countries could yield new insight if subjected to the careful statistical scrutiny that has been the result of the critique of the Singer-Prebisch hypothesis. The files of the *Reichsbank* and big Berlin banks in East Berlin, as well as the files of the National Banks of the Danubian countries, could provide the evidence needed to determine the average rate of the clearing mark in terms of any particular Danubian currency, Germany's average net trade debt for calendar or fiscal year, and the approximate devaluation of each Danubian currency in terms of the leading "hard currencies." With this information, some determination of the total value of foreign exchanges between the two countries in a standard monetary unit could be made; the aggregate amount of "lost interest" on the clearing credits calculated and balanced against the higher prices paid for agricultural goods; and the comparative pricing of similar commodities by Germany in the various Danubian markets. Close inspection of German statistics along the lines laid out by Kindleberger should yield insights into the trends of prices of different categories of German exports, while elimination of nonhomogeneous categories should lead to a better picture of the trend in Germany's terms of trade throughout 1925-39.

Even if this arduous statistical work were carried out, there would remain certain qualitative considerations that would have to be taken into account, no matter what the outcome of the empirical work. First, all calculations of German terms of trade generally show a favorable trend in 1933-39 despite rising world market prices and the shift to high-cost producers of primary products. In these calculations, no account can be taken of German export subsidies in their manifold forms. Thus the most careful study, that of Kindleberger, shows the least deterioration in Germany's terms of trade throughout the period in the face of rising world market prices. However, the real cost to the German economy is hardly reflected in these figures — the actual cost of Germany's imports should aggregate the import and subsidy price. It can scarcely be doubted that the actual cost of imports to the German economy increased substantially throughout the period and, if the total subsidies were known, the actual course of the terms of trade would show deterioration. By and large, the cost of the subsidy program was borne by the German consumer, the wage and salaried classes, who suffered from a regressive tax system, deterioration of food quality and consumer goods, and so forth. On the whole, industry fared very well, as statistics on profits and evidence concerning shares of the national income testify.

Even if it could be conclusively shown that Germany had improved its terms of trade at the expense of its Danubian trading partners, the classical case would still face an insurmountable obstacle. This case for superexploitation rests explicitly on a comparison of the ratio of prices offered by Germany for its exports as compared with the prices paid for imports to a similar ratio offered by Germany's competitors. This static comparison, however, overlooks the essential fact that the commodities that Germany bought would not have been exported had Germany not initiated a discriminatory trade policy. If Germany improved its terms of trade at the expense of its Danubian trading partners, it is the obvious implication that these countries would have done better to trade elsewhere. But the "elsewheres" did not exist. Only a coordinated international effort such as the ones that failed at Lausanne and Stresa could have provided credit assistance and markets for the countries of east-central Europe. The inward looking policies of Britain and France, the commitment of the United States to liberal economic policies, and the absence of the Soviet Union from the European scene all contributed to the isolation and economic weakness of the east Euroepan countries. Under these circumstances, comparing German and British price ratios is questionable.

In recent years Alan Milward, Larry Neal, and Philippe Marguerat have proposed revisionist critiques of the classic school of Ellis and Basch without, however, going much beyond re-examining the terms of trade issue.[40] In several reviews of recent scholarly works, Milward, in particular, takes David Kaiser to task for using a diplomatic historical method in analysing the trade drive, ignoring the published

---

[40] Larry NEAL, The Economics and Finance of Bilateral Clearing Agreements: Germany, 1934-1938, in: Economic History Review, 2nd series, XXXII (1979); MARGUERAT, Le III Reich; idem, Le Protectionisme financier allemande et le bassin danubien a la veille de la seconde guerre monidale: L'Exemple de la Roumanie, in: Relations Internationales 16 (1978).

work on the terms of trade issue, and finally floundering indecisively between a point of view stressing the intentional and exploitative character of these relationships and a later emphasis on the relative unimportance of the Danubian countries for Nazi Germany.[41] Milward treats with distain the argument "because the contribution of southeastern Europe was so small, Germany was driven inexorably to a war of expansion to solve its economic policies. There is no proof at all from this [Kaiser's] book that Germany's contemporary economic difficulties had any impact on Hitler's foreign aims."[42] In reviewing the work of Philippe Marguerat, Milward characterizes the work as another well aimed blow "at the persistent historical myth that German international economic policy before 1940 exploited the economies of central and southeastern Europe."[43] Milward alleges that Germany accumulated persistent clearing debts because her exports were too dear, that the German government could not release suffcient raw materials or armaments to pay for such needed raw materials as Rumanian oil, and that German foreign economic policy was hampered by the relative weakness of the *Reichsmark* in relation to the British pound. "It can only be hoped in the face of the constant accumulation of evidence, historians will at last give up the myth of a positive, aggressive National Socialist foreign economic policy and see it for what it was, the desparate and unsatisfactory last resort of a government which had accorded domestic economic reconstruction an absolute priority."[44] Echoing Milward, Larry Neal finds it "curious, then, to find that the only cases where the German share of trade with an East European country was clearly higher in 1938 than in 1928 were Yugoslavia, and Hungary. Both the British and French had higher shares with Austria (1937), Czechoslovakia, Poland, and Lithuania; the British had, in addition, higher shares with Latvia, Estonia, Yugoslavia, Rumania, and Hungary. All three European powers expanded at the expenses of the United States, and to a much lesser extent, the Soviet Union."[45]

In a paper presented to the Cologne conference of historians in December, 1979, Milward expanded this line of argumentation in a spirit reminiscent of A.J.P. Taylor's habit of turning traditional historical interpretations on their head.[46] Milward's main target is the interpretation of Howard Ellis (also criticized above), which alleged that German policy used its monopsonistic powers against the small countries of Danubian Europe to turn the terms of trade against these countries. In the

---

[41] Alan MILWARD, review, KAISER, Economic Diplomacy, in: American Historical Review (December 1981), pp. 1066-1067.

[42] Ibid., p. 1066.

[43] Alan MILWARD, review of MARGUERAT, Le III Reich, in: English Historical Review (April 1979), pp. 472-473.

[44] Ibid.

[45] Larry NEAL, review of KAISER, Economic Diplomacy, in: Journal of Economic History (December 1981), pp.920-921.

[46] Alan MILWARD, The Reichsmark Bloc and the International Economy, Paper presented at the Cologne conference of historians, December 1979. In Milward's definition the *Reichsmark* bloc consists of Bulgaria, Greece, Hungary, Rumania, Turkey, and Yugoslavia. I shall limit the discussion to examples from German policy in Yugoslavia and Rumania.

traditional interpretation, then, the increasing trade with central and southeastern Europe is always presented as a first stage in the building of an autarchic *Großraum-wirtschaft* which would be relatively isolated from external forces. For Milward, this traditional interpretation is unsatisfactory insofar as it ignores the potential econo-mic benefit which the less developed countries of Europe may have garnered through Schacht's foreign trade policy. Milward makes three caveat's to this argu-ment, in effect concessions to the traditional point of view, which have little impact on the balance of his thesis. Firstly, even if the less developed countries derived some economic benefit from association with Germany, "this would in no way weaken the fearful threat to which the economic revival of national Socialist Ger-many implied nor diminish the strong liklihood that Hitler would indeed seek to reshape the countries, with little regard for governments or peoples, as part of an intended war against the Soviet Union."[47] Secondly, Milward alleges that it was important from the propaganda point of view for the Nazi government to demon-strate to its citizens that Germany was deriving great benefit from the *Reichsmark* bloc.[48] Thirdly, even if it can be conclusively demonstrated that Germany did not succeed in exploiting the *Reichsmark* bloc, this does not necessarily mean that the policy was not intended to be exploitative.

Relying on the research of Neal, Milward shows that the blocked mark balances in Berlin could have an expansive effect on the economies of southeastern Europe if the country in question chose to treat the credit as a reserve which could serve the expansion of the domestic credit base. (This was done in Hungary but resisted in Yugoslavia and Rumania.) Even if the clearing balances in Berlin gave Germany the option of postponing payment, there is no evidence that the countries of the *Reichs-mark* bloc "before 1939 were forced to accumulate such debts."[49] In fact, the emphasis on the clearing balances which pervades the work of Einzig, Ellis, and Basch, is, in Milward's view, a perception which emphasizes the similiarity of Ger-many with other advanced industrial countries, whereas conditions in the 1930's argue for the comparison of developed with less devloped countries across a broad range. From this point of view, the six countries of the *Reichsmark* bloc were among the few primary producers "whose share of international trade increased in the thir-ties."[50] While foodstuffs were being destroyed elsewhere, Milward argues that there is a "lack of proportion" in alleging Danubian countries forfeited economic advan-tages by accumulating *Reichsmark* balances in Berlin. Here Milward repeats the argument first made by J.B. Condliffe in the 1930's that the acummulation of export

[47] Ibid.
[48] On the contrary: see the comments of the Propaganda Ministry upon the conclusion of the German-Yugoslava treaty of 1934: "In the light of the enormous importance of the treaty for German trade policy the Reich government attaches great importance to an unsensational treatment of the treaty before the German public." 'Der deutsch-jugoslawische Handelsver-trag', Streng Vertraulich , by Bertinger, May 4, 1934, BA, ZSg 101/27.
[49] MILWARD, Reichsmark Bloc, p.11.
[50] Ibid., p.12.

balances in London occurred in the case of other primary exporting countries.[51] These balances were far larger than the equivalent *Reichsmark* balances in Berlin.

Secondly, while Milward admits that the statistics on price information are not entirely satisfactory, the prices paid by Germany appear to be higher than those in the international markets of Britain and Holland, "thus giving the European less developed countries the best of both worlds."[52] Rather than stressing the economic cost of extending interest free commodity credits to Germany, Milward argues that the penalty of the system involved rather the restriction on the choice of supplier, given the fact that Germany could not abritarily raise export prices. While some economists have argued that this could create a costly misallocation of resources if German prices were so high as to shift domestic resources away from activities more in line with the long term development of the economy, Milward retorts that only Britain showed a similiar rise in food consumption in the 1930's which could have served as a rival to the German market.[53] Only a momentous political decision on the part of the British government would have enabled Britain to be an effective competitor to Germany. Even if there was a shift in resources to the export trade destined for Germany and the creation of economic pressure groups favorable to the Schacht trade system, Milward argues that it would be impossible to factor out this element as so many other domestic trends in the Danubian countries favored this development.

In terms of periodization and in relation to different countries, Milward sees quite a variation in the impact of German policy in the Danubian region. In the case of Bulgaria, which had 52% of its import trade and 59% of its export trade with Germany by 1938, Milward admits it would be absurd to deny that Germany would seek to obtain every advantage from such a disportion. Nevertheless, Milward sees the Bulgarian case as exceptional. In Rumanian-German relations, for example, Milward follows Marguerat in emphasizing that Rumanian oil only became important after the revision of the synthetic oil production plans in July, 1938 (the *Wehrwirtschaftliche neue Erzeugungsplan* which embodied Hitler's realization that Ger-

---

[51] J.B. CONDLIFFE, International Trade, in: The Political Quarterly, London 1938, pp.99-105. Condliffe was, of course, an economic liberal and author of many League of Nations publications, including the important World Economic Survey reports. Condliffe was extremely critical of German foreign economic policy, albeit in a muted fashion as required by the objective tone of the League reports.

[52] MILWARD, Reichsmark Bloc, p.12.

[53] N. MOMTCHILOFF, Ten Years of Controlled Trade in South-East Europe, N.I.E.S.R. Occasional Papers VI, Cambridge 1944. Milward never addresses the argument of Mihail Maniolescu that the export of primary products in exchange for manufactured goods involves the less developed country in a vicious cycle of dependence from which it cannot escape. Similiarly, W.A. Lewis has argued that the fluctuations in the terms of trade which so concerned Prebisch and Singer conceal a structure which is disadvantageous to the developing country: Mihail MANIOLESCU, The Theory of Protection and International Trade, London 1931. A detailed survey of the neglected theories of Maniolescu and the impact of his ideas upon post war Rumanian economic policy may be found in: Nicholas BURAKOW, The Dynamic Role of Trade in Development: Rumania's Strategy, U.Ph.D., University of Notre Dame 1980, pp.26-63.

many might be at war with both France and Britain at the same time). Thus, the recovery of German trade with Rumania represented a great increase, but no more than a revival of trade to levels similiar to the late 1920's. Therefore, in spite of the striking German success in reviving trade with the Danubian countries, Milward argues that "until the Munich argreements it would be impossible to claim that, setting aside foreign trade, German economic 'penetration' was a matter of any significance."[54] Therefore, evidence of any sort of preparation for economic exploitation is confined to the period after Munich and, in particular, is identified in Milward's eyes with the Wohlthat Treaty of March 23, 1939. At this point then, Milward is willing to admit that evidence of exploitation exists by remarking in a negative sense that "at least in the case of Romania evidence of 'exploitation' is lacking until the final collapse of Czechoslovakia."[55]

Some would argue that while the Danubian countries could not supply all of Germany's needs, they nevertheless offered commodities in exchange for *Reichsmark*, saved the expenditure of hard currency, permitted the German government to use these raw materials to pursue an aggressive foreign policy, and finally provided a fallback region of secure raw materials in case of a British blockade. Milward simply retorts that "this argument exaggerates the strategic significance of the *Reichsmark* bloc to the German economy."[56] First and foremost, Milward sets aside food supply and then conveniently ignores the substantial labor reserves which the 100 million people of the region would supply to the German war economy. In terms of strategic raw materials, Milward sees the area as only supplying significant quantities of chromite, bauxite, and petroleum. Commodities which the German government and business regarded as important, such as copper, lead, and antimony, are not mentioned.[57]

---

[54] MILWARD, Reichsmark Bloc, p. 18. If we set aside foreign trade, we might as well move on to another subject. The failure of Germany to export capital to the *Reichsmark* bloc had been recognized by virtually all scholars in this field, regardless of political persuasion. In fact, the British Foreign Office commented in 1938: "Germany will, no doubt, take all steps open to her to stimulate the capacity of these markets to absorb larger quantities of her exports in the future, and will in fact seek to develop them as 'colonial' markets have always been developed by capitalist countries. But for the time being she appears to be weak in the chief requisites for colonial development — capital to export." Unsigned Foreign Office Memorandum, 'German Economic Penetration in Central and Southeast Europe', London, May 6, 1938, PRO, F.O. 371/21705. The lack of export capital motivated the German government to put pressure on the Danubian countries to create special administrative measures aimed at fostering joint development of raw materials resources.

[55] MILWARD, Reichsmark Bloc, p. 18.

[56] Ibid., p. 23.

[57] See, for example, the efforts of Max Hahn, the business manager of the MWT, to secure the "antimony monopoly in Europe" through mineral concessions in Yugoslavia: Max Hahn to Clodius, October 30, 1936, PA, Ha Pol, IVa, Jugoslawien, Industrie 6, Bergbau, Bd. 1. The shortage of copper supply in September, 1939, prompted Göring to release large quantities of German armaments to Yugoslavia: Unsigned memorandum, September 18, 1939, PA, Handakten Wiehl, Jugoslawien, Bd. 3. The author of this memonandum commented upon the "blocked" state of German copper supply.

In terms of chromite supply, small quantities were of decisive importance to German armaments manufacture because high quality steel could not be manufactured without chromite. In the region, Turkey was the world's second largest producer while Greece and Yugoslavia also produced significant amounts for export. However, Germany obtained no more than 30 percent of the total output of Greek, Yugoslavian, and Turkish chromite in the period 1935 to 1938. Although there was a steep rise in the exports of Turkish chromite in 1938, both Yugoslav and Greek exports actually fell from 1937 to 1938. In contrast to chromite, which was freely traded on international markets and which offered the exporting countries the opportunity to resist German policy by selecting other export markets, the production of bauxite in Hungary and Yugoslavia grew in direct proportion to the increasing use of aluminum in Germany for rearmament purposes. Therefore, selection of alternative markets was difficult for the Danubian countries, at best. However, Milward emphasizes the economic benefit to the countries involved as German policy resulted in the creation of a new industry in Hungary. In terms of petroleum, Milward repeats the arguments of Marguerat: German share of Rumanian exports never exceeded 15.7 percent of total Rumanian exports. The largest proportion of these exports were vulnerable to blockade, as they were shipped via the Mediterrean and not up the Danube or via railroad.

In terms of the food economy, Milward admits that the proportion of foodstuffs coming from the *Reichsmark* bloc rose from 11.1 percent in 1930 to 28.2 percent in 1939. However, Milward immediately undercuts the seeming significance of this jump by observing that the volume and value of foodstuff imports as a proportion of total consumption fell as a consequence of Darré's autarchic agricultural policy and other import saving policies pursued under the New Plan. Nevertheless, the significance of this development is again minimized by the observation that in real constant prices imports of foodstuffs from the *Reichsmark* bloc did not surpass the previous high point of the period 1925-1929. Milward recognizes, however, that the increase in the trade in agriculutural commodities was the foundation of the economic expansion under the New Plan: "It was the shift in the origins of German foodstuff imports in the 1930's which constituted the biggest part of the altered pattern of trade in the decade and it was the exchange of food against manufactured goods which held together the *Reichsmark* bloc as a trading area."[58]

Nevertheless, Milward seems puzzled by the fact that traditional stable exports did not increase as fast as other types of exports, which reflected both the price stablization scruples of Darré and the terms of trade considerations of Schacht in the period up to the end of 1936. Milward seems unaware of the grain crisis of the winter of 1936-1937 which forced the Reich to turn in desperation to its clearing trade partners in the Danubian basin.[59] In the face of the worldwide collapse of

---

[58] MILWARD, Reichsmark Bloc, p. 27.
[59] See the aftermath of this crisis in chapter 8 above. The full story of the economic diplomacy of this episode is treated in detail in: William S. GRENZEBACH, Germany's Informal Empire in East-Central Europe, U.Ph.D., Brandeis University 1978, chapter 11 (Yugoslavia); chapter 16 (Rumania).

grain prices in the summer of 1937, Milward remarks Pollyannishly that "few of these trades were so dependent on the sole German market as to leave no hope at all of adjustment should there be a threat to withdraw that market."[60] Nevertheless, in the face of the decline of capital inflow associated with the Great Depression the significance of export trade for the Danubian countries "had come to have a greater importance for development."

In terms of Germany's own foreign trade, Milward regards the orientation to the low income markets, characteristic of the 1930's, as an aberration from Germany's long term trends, as exemplfied in the period before 1929 and after 1953. In the thirties, the growth of the domestic economy was so rapid that foreign trade as a percentage of GNP actually declined which indicated that foreign trade was not a factor for growth in the German economy in the 1930's. In an interesting counter thesis which finds no support in the exisiting literature, Milward contends that the New Plan of 1934 was merely a systematization of economic regulations introduced under *Reichsbank* President Luther in order to prevent the flight of foreign exchange. Under Luther, certain blocked mark accounts were created with the approval of the international banking community and the Bank of International Settlements to help ease the liquidity crisis within Germany. Blocked marks could be used within Germany, used for the purchase of German commodities, or sold at a discount abroad. These accounts were the origin of the *Zusatzexport* program under Economics Minister Schmidt which proceeded the New Plan. In contrast, Milward sees Schacht's New Plan as merely the "systematization into a deliberate policy a set of trading devices which were already widespread and also extended into a deliberate policy a geographical pattern of trade which had in any case begun to emerge as a response to Germany's alarming external situation in the Depression."[61] In other words, there was no German policy, but merely a Pavlovian reflex to the severity of the Depression.

The single difference between late Weimar and the Nazi policy was the fact that the Nazi promotion of domestic economic revival threatened a foreign exchange deficit similiar to the one which occurred in 1928. There is no mention of the fact that the New Plan contradicted the basic priniciple of the most-favored-nation system which hitherto had been the foundation of German foreign economic policy. The pursuit of a discriminatory foreign economic policy led to a direct economic and political confrontation with the United States.[62] Even if one takes National

---

[60] One perceptive contemporary observer, William Chase (the American Consulate in Hamburg), noted: "In some quarters, it was rumored that, despite the much smaller 1937 corn crop, the export embargo of July 23rd [1937] was decreed in order to prevent Germany from cornering the exportable surplus of corn in Rumania at the then prevailing prices, Rumania desiring to force Germany to buy later at the day's market price. If that were the case Rumania was the dupe, for world corn prices collapsed at the end of the summer of 1937 and between the end of June and the end of October 1937 had dropped more than 50 per cent." William M. Chase, U.S. Consulate Hamburg, 'Recent German-Rumanian Trade Relations', March 1, 1938, NA, RG 59, 662.7131/110.

[61] MILWARD, Reichsmark Bloc, p. 32.

[62] See SCHRÖDER, Deutschland und die Vereinigten Staaten.

Socialist propanganda about *Großraumwirtschaft* seriously there was little geographic congruence between the *Reichsmark* bloc and the proposed Large Space Economy. Both Poland and Czechoslovakia stood outside the *Reichsmark* bloc, a point which seemingly would lead Milward to conclude that both countries were earmarked for aggression, but he does not. Even after the victories in 1939 and 1940 when *Großraumwirtschaft* became a reality, the statistical contribution of the *Reichsmark* bloc declined to "relative insignificance" compared to the great increase in both foodstuffs and manufactured goods from western Europe. "From 1940 onwards foodstuff imports from occupied western Europe far eclipsed imports from central and southeastern Europe."[63]

In terms of a systematic interpretation of the trading experience under the New Plan, Milward advances the proposition that Germany was relatively helpless in its choice of foreign economic policy. Given the facts of a discouraging economic reality in which the National Socialist government gave "overwhelming priority" to domestic and social policies, these policies made "Germany's economic situation even weaker, untenable, indeed without assuming permanent trade and exchange controls and a very wide and possible permanent discrepancy between German prices and those of the other major traders."[64] Therefore, once Hitler became Chancellor all chances for reintegrating Germany into the international payments system disappeared: "The *Reichsmark* bloc, far from being a positive policy, was a desperately unsatisfactory attempt to maintain at high international costs to the German economy, the absolute primacy of domestic economic policy."[65]

The evidence which Kindleberger, Benham, and Neal discovered on terms of trade should come as no surprise in the view of Milward because it was part and parcel of the price for defending other priorities. In the case of Rumania, for example, Milward suggests that Germany was not able to maintain a satisfactory Reichsmark/lei rate because Anglo-French competition made it difficult for Germany to raise prices on manufactured exports. The recurrent blocked mark balances were, therefore, not a cunning device of economic exploitation but reflected the genuine difficulties which the German economy faced in paying for the imports of cereal and oil. Both in the long and short term the *Reichsmark* bloc reflected Germany's weaknesses far more than her strengths.

In terms of the National Socialist *Weltanschauung* Milward sees the propaganda of the period as reflecting the ingenious ablity of the Nazis to "explain all events, however unwelcome, as being in accord with the new *Weltanschauung*."[66] Although Milward admits the *Reichsmark* bloc did save foreign exchange and gold, he downgrades the significance of this policy as merely permitting the German government to puruse its program of domestic economic expansion. If the *Reichsmark* bloc enabled Germany to manipulate its terms of trade in such a way as to prevent deterioration of the terms of trade caused by rising world market prices, Milward is willing

---

[63] MILWARD, Reichsmark Bloc, p. 33, citing MILWARD, The New Order and the French Economy, Oxford 1970, pp. 257-258.
[64] MILWARD, Reichsmark Bloc, p. 34.
[65] Ibid.
[66] Ibid., p.41.

to admit only in this case there may be a cause for using the term "exploitation." But, in his view, no one presented the case in this light and furthermore, there is no evidence to support this point of view. Therefore, rather than harping on the old theme of German exploitation, Milward recommends that historians turn their attention to "the successful exploitation of Germany's economic weakness before 1939 by the small economies of central and eastern Europe."[67]

Apart from a few statistical illustrations, Milward's argument resolves itself into the simple proposition that Germany did not have a well conceived and carried out foreign economic policy. All the evidence of the research carried out by Bernd-Jürgen Wendt, Hans-Jürgen Schröder, David Kaiser, and others suggests the exact opposite to Milward's position. That Germany was not able to arbitrarily raise the prices of its exports, and therefore not able to raise its terms of trade, was already demonstrated by Frederic Benham in the late 1930's. However, he did not suggest that Germany did not have a consistent foreign economic policy nor that the resources of Danubian Europe could not increase the striking power of the Greater German Reich. Indeed, the aims and intentions of German policy cannot be determined by statistical analysis alone, however sophisticated, but must be based upon study and anlysis of the policy itself. However much Milward and economic historians may treat with disdain the method of diplomatic history for dealing with international economic problems, Milward's contribution to this field demonstrates that statistics are no substitute for solid archival work.

Milward does not address the central propositions which motivated Ellis's critique of German policy. Ellis was an economic liberal who conceived the international economic order in terms of the allocative efficiency of the competitive market mechanism. Although this mechanism had broken down in the Depression, Ellis and many other liberal economists saw Germany as the chief villain in maintaining the policy of economic regionalism. Ellis' notion of the economic exploitation of German policy is based squarely upon access to open, free competetive markets which would presumably maximize income for both the importing and exporting nations. Secondly, Milward makes no reference to the extensive discussion and statistical clarification in the concept of terms of trade in the postwar period which has been analyzed in previous paragraphs. No doubt further work in this field would yield new insight, but not on the basis of Milward's simple inversion of Ellis' work.

The evidence of the German archives gives a far different picture of the nature of German foreign economic policy than Milward would allow. From 1931 onward, a significant group of German industrialists advocated a forward economic policy in the Danubain basin to substitute for markets lost in high income countries.[68] In 1932, Schacht made it his personal task to reconcile the conflicting economic goals

---

[67] Ibid., p. 42.

[68] The way for the German trade drive was prepared as early as 1931 and 1932 both by the formation of the MWT and exploratory trips by the representatives of important Ruhr industry pressure groups to southeastern Europe. In spite of the urging by these groups for a forward, energetic trade policy in Danubian Europe, the late Weimar governments were unable to make any breakthroughs because of continued adherence to the most favored nation treaty system. See the references in chapter VI, footnote 55 above.

of a National Socialist movement led by Hitler with Ruhr industry led by Paul Reusch. The outcome of this concentrated and highly intellectual effort was Schacht's "Import Monopoly" memorandum, produced in December, 1932, which foreshadows the abandonment of the most-favored-nation treaty system, the introduction of a discriminatory trade policy aimed at Danubian Europe and Latin America.[69] In contrast to Milward's portrayal of the New Plan as merely a visceral response to a situation of economic weakness, Schacht had not only anticipated the problem but planned for it at least eighteen months before the event.

National Socialist foreign economic policy was not run by Nazi ideologues such as Gottfried Feder, Alfred Rosenberg, or Werner Daitz, but by bureaucrats of the respective ministries who had served Weimar, and some, like Karl Ritter, dated from the Wilhelmine period. Once the decision was made in September, 1934, to pursue a discriminatory economic policy on a worldwide basis (Schacht's New Plan), the stage was set for a worldwide confrontation with the United States, a policy which reflected the direct economic interest which German industry had in seeking markets in Latin America and Danubian Europe. Milward does not discuss the success of German policy in Latin America, which in economic terms (cheapness of raw materials and primary products) was of equal or greater interest than Danubian Europe. In terms of German exports and imports, despite declining percentages in terms of GNP, both areas doubled their relative percentages in the total trade of Germany. Without these new markets for German industry and the raw materials and foodstuffs which came with the exports, the scope of the German economic recovery is scarcely conceivable. The use of the percentage of exports or imports to gauge the importance of foreign economic policy in the 1930's is a deceptive practice. One could not buy copper, bauxite, grain, or petroleum with percentages of GNP: either one had to possess hard currency (pounds, dollars, francs) or be willing to trade with those countries with raw material surpluses.

In terms of German goals in east-central Europe, Milward is apparently unaware of the published evidence of German goals reflected in the 'Documents on German Foreign Policy', let alone the detailed research by Hans-Jürgen Schröder, and the Hungarian team of I. Berend and G. Ranki. In terms of the archival work upon which this work is based, it is clear that the political aspiration of unlocking the Danubian basin to both economic and political exploitation was never far from German policymakers' consciousness, whether the figure in question was Hitler, Schacht, Neurath, Weizsäcker, or the bureaucrats which manned the Danubian desks at the various ministries. Initially, both the Hungarian and Yugoslav treaties of 1934 were justified on the grounds of politics: the one aimed at securing a foothold in the Italian sphere of influence, and the other directed at unlocking the French alliance system. If we take Overy's critique of the *Blitzkrieg* strategy seriously, the 1934 treaties can be seen as the first step in the planned consolidation of Fortress *Mitteleuropa*. In terms of the question of access to the raw materials resources of Danubian Europe, Milward completely misses the mark. If Germany

---

[69] Schacht 'Einfuhrmonopol' Memorandum, contained in the cover letter, Schacht to Reusch, December 20, 1932, HA-GHH, 400101290/33a.

failed before 1939 to gain a complete monopoly over the raw materials of the region it was not for want of trying. Furthermore, certain raw materials, such as aviation gasoline, were critical even before the summer of 1938. In 1937 the head of the Control Board for Petroleum was desperately advocating increased access to Rumanian oil resources.[70]

In essence, Milward has repeated some of the very same arguments which both Schacht and Stojadinović used to justify their policies. Schacht, an international banker of distinction and some reputation in the United States (before 1933), always pleaded the German case in terms of relative German weakness and aversion to the clearing agreements as such: "At any rate, it is a false assumption that the bilateral trade system, with which Germany is today supporting her economy, arose from our deliberate judgement. Oh no. It is the natural and necessary result of the war tributes and the clearings which are forced on us."[71] In Yugoslavia, where some 76 percent of the population lived on the land, national income rose from 37.7 billion dinars in 1934 to 47.5 billion dinars in 1938. The rural population garnered some 48 percent of this increased national income. Although the balance of payments in 1935 showed a deficit of 164 million dinars, by 1937 it showed a surplus of 1200 million dinars. By September, 1938, deposits in banks and savings accounts rose to a new high, 11.8 billion dinars.[72] Agriculutural production rose from an estimated 18.6 billion dinars in 1934, to 23.9 billion dinars in 1938. According to the memoirs of the pro-German prime minister Stojadinović, this progress was brought about "by the favorable economic treaties, especially with Germany, which offered us preferential prices (for agricultural products), which were 20 per cent higher than market prices, while at the same time we could buy industrial products from Germany at a forty per cent discount."[73]

Even if it could be shown conclusively that Yugoslavia did benefit to the extent that Stojadinović claimed, the question still remains whether the game was worth the gamble. The economic rapprochement with Germany brought rising exports and increased national income but at the cost of adapting the national economy to German needs and opening up the whole of east-central Europe to the depredations of German imperialism, a type of Darwinian struggle for raw materials and market shares which was already evident in Yugoslavia in 1937.[74] Milward remarks, "if an economic argument is to be made in favour of Germany's 'exploitation' of the

---

[70] In the summer of 1937, Budzies (Control Board for Petroleum) complained that "petroleum imports from Rumania have therefore come to a dead halt." He demanded immmediate action to increase aviation fuel imports from Rumania: "In light of this embarassing situation it is urgently recommended, without regard to normally recognized considerations to do everything conceivable to get the supplies from Rumania." Budzies (UeB Öl) to Puhl (Reichsbank), August 13, 1937, PA, Ha Pol, Rumänien, Handel 11 Nr. 3A, Erdöl und Getreide, Bd. 2.

[71] Schacht, 'Miracle of Finance and the New Plan', Speech before the Economic Council of the German Academy at Berlin, Novemeber 29, 1938. ND,ED-611, NCA, VI, p. 600.

[72] BAGNELL, Influence, p. 81.

[73] Milan STOJADINOIVĆ, Ni Rat Ni Pakt, Buenos Aires 1963, p. 48-49.

[74] See Chapter VII above.

Reichsmark bloc the precise element of the 'exploitation' has to be identified."[75] The economic exploitation in the application of the New Plan to the *Reichsmark* bloc involved the conscious sacrifice of short term terms of trade (even with subsidies for the marketing of Danubian imports within Germany or dumped on the world market) in favor of long term benefits of increased export markets for German industry and access to the raw materials without the expenditure of foreign exchange. This was indeed an "especially vicious stage of late imperialism."[76] The fact that the resources of Danubian Europe did not measure up to German expectations and played less of a role in the war economy after 1940 is a good argument against the reactionary utopianism of the policy, but in no way should cloud our understanding of German intentions. In any case, after 1939 the policy of the German government did not even bother with classic forms of imperialist domination but simply resorted to plunder.

One aspect of Milward's argument which has cogency and substance is his emphasis on the reorientation of German trade towards low income countries versus the longer term historic trend for German export trade to seek high income markets. The failure of German exports to keep pace with imports from the *Reichsmark* bloc was one of the most puzzling aspects of the German trade drive, which was intended to be an export drive but turned out to be an import drive. This contradiction was resolved in the Ellis-Basch thesis by positing a German desire to accumulate clearing balances in order to obtain interest free commodity credits. When the trade drive policy was initiated in 1934, German industry still had considerable slackness; indeed the justification for the discriminatory trade policy was to promote exports so that the German economic recovery could continue.

In fact, German exports were not hampered by the overvalued *Reichsmark* as Milward alleges because there were many methods for discounting the *Reichsmark* in the interest of export promotion. It can only be argued that Germany lacked the resources to pay for increased imports after the time at which full employment was reached. In terms of the previous period of high exports (1925-1929), David Kaiser has pointed out the remarkable drop in German textile exports to the region in the later period (1934-1938).[77] This was caused by the intertwining of two factors: firstly, Schacht refused to permit light industry in order to secure the needed foreign exchange to return to high levels of production. Heavy industry and the finishing industry were given discrimatory treatment in the allocation of raw materials within the context of the New Plan. This led in turn to the extraordinary expansion of the German artifical fibers industry (*Zellwolle*). Secondly, the industrialization policies of the Danubian countries focused upon import substitution, which hurt Austrian and Hungarian industry even more than German. If German exports

---

[75] MILWARD, Reichsmark Bloc, p. 8.

[76] Ibid. This is Milward's formulation which is not intended to express agreement with the concept, particularly in view of his comments on the work of Dörte DÖRING, Deutsch-österreichische Außenhandelsverflechtung während der Weltwirtschaftskrise, in: Hans MOMMSEN, Dietmar PETZINA, Bernd WEISBROD (eds.), Industrielles System und Politische Entwicklung in der Weimarer Republik, Düsseldorf 1974.

[77] KAISER, Economic Diplomacy, p. 141.

did not rise spontanenously, the low income countries of the *Reichsmark* bloc were increasingly forced to resort to discrimatory policies in the award of state contracts and other large scale projects (the Zenica rolling mill in Yugoslavia and the Rimma-Ferrostaal project in Rumania.) Paradoxically, Milward hit upon the resolution of the contradiction in German policy without pursuing the argument to its logical conclusions. Deprived of high income markets in the West because of the continuing Depression, imperial preference, national protectionism, and the anti-German boycott (which the Germans brought on themselves), Germany turned to the Danubian governments as the only high income "consumer" of the exports which German industry was capable of delivering.

Initially, this seemed a positive development to some policy makers in the Danube because it fit in with the industrialization plans which were widely supported. In the long run, however, the greater the share of German trade with the Danubian countries, the more threatened industrialization became because while Germany could deliver capital goods and integrated factories, Germany was unable to supply the raw materials to keep these factories going. Unlike the London merchant bankers who engaged in the self-liquidating acceptance trade in supplying raw materials to the German economy, Germany simply did not possess sufficient capital reserves to engage in the same type of policy with respect to Danubian Europe. Again, these economic facts pointed toward ever increasing pressure upon the *Reichsmark* bloc to deliver raw materials by whatever means necessary.

In sum, then, the Einzig-Basch-Ellis thesis is not substantiated by the statistical work that has been done to date and is unlikely to be supported by the kind of intensive statistical investigation suggested by criticism of the Singer-Prebisch hypothesis. Even less cogent is the simple inversion of the thesis suggested by the statistical history of Alan Milward.

To a great extent, research on the purely economic aspects of German trade under the New Plan remains to be done. The qualitative evidence based on the record of the German archives suggests the following conclusions regarding the German trade drive:

1. The single most important factor for the success of German policy was the agriculture purchase guarantees. These guarantees proved to be an irresistible attraction for Yugoslavia and Rumania, despite their recognition of the deficiencies of German policy under the New Plan. Available evidence indicates that Germany paid higher prices for such agricultural commodities than those prevailing on the world market despite the devaluation of the clearing mark in terms of the domestic currency.

2. Until 1938, at least, Nazi Germany pursued a trade policy that was complementary to the industrialization programs of the less-developed Danubian countries, by delivering capital goods.

3. The structural inadequacies of the German economy were increasingly papered over by armaments barter for strategic raw materials. The barter of high-quality armaments in 1939 proved to be the decisive lever in opening up the raw materials resources of the Danube to German domination.

4. Tendencies toward deindustrialization of the Danubian countries were less a

consequence of Hitler's ideological predisposition or conscious policy decision than
of Germany's inroads into Danubian exports that had previously been exported to
the world market and provided free exchange to buy industrial raw materials. The
greater Germany's share in Danubian exports, the more threatened became Danubian industrialization.[78]

5. Neither the economic benefits of the German trading system (guaranteed markets) nor the economic benefits of world trade (cheap imports) offered a solution to
the problems posed by the demographic crisis in east-central Europe. Insofar as
both economic systems were premised upon the export of agricultural foodstuffs
actually needed for home consumption, neither offered a way of escape. While the
Nazi system discouraged the increase in labor productivity, the world market system encouraged high labor productivity in "enclave" areas — raw materials extrac-
tion, commercial crops, and large-scale farms. Neither system offered the slightest
hint of how the countries of east-central Europe could utilize their most abundant
resource — labor — for a comprehensive strategy of economic development.

4. Political and Economic Aspects of German Expansionism Toward Southeastern Europe

The term "political", as variously used by German policy makers in the 1930's
and by postwar historians, cannot be limited to mean the quest of one state to dominate another. The nuances involved get lost in such a broad concept. Germany
could, and did, disclaim any interest in the purely "political" relations among the
Balkan states. Nazi policy was initially neutral in the clash between revisionist and
antirevisionist countries, although Germany would later make an informal commitment to antirevisionist Yugoslavia guaranteeing the Yugoslav-Hungarian border
and pressure Hungary to stop plans to annex Transylvania from Rumania. Germany did have a "political" strategy toward Danubian Europe that can be defined
by Germany's vigorous attempts to isolate Czechoslovakia and restrain Hungary's
appetites. This use of "political" strategy is tactical and narrows to the bilateral
relations between Germany and Hungary, Germany and Yugoslavia, and Germany
and Rumania.

Germany's generals, industrialists, bankers, and bureaucrats shared a perspective
concerning Germany's legitimate role in east-central Europe. They assumed that
German hegemony in east-central Europe was natural, right, and necessary, an
assumption, central to German history between 1890 and 1945, which made German business rally to Brüning's customs union plan, despite any misgivings over the

---

[78] British Commercial Counselor Adam (Bucharest) divided Rumania's raw materials
imports into two categories, calculated the share supplied by free currency and clearing trade
partners, and concluded that "should Rumania increase her exports to United Germany above
the present figures she will not be able to maintain her industrial system at its present level."
'Rumanian Industry and Raw Materials', memorandum by Commercial Counselor Adam
(Bucharest), April 22, 1939, PRO, F.0. 371/23830, p. 7.

economic rationality of the project. Similarly, Germany's traditional political elite was gratified by the success of Hitler's Austrian and Sudeten coups and gave little thought to the tensions that would result from German hegemony in east-central Europe.

Hitler's program delineates another nuance of "political." Hitler's opportunism in selecting means to an end has long been recognized, but the historical emphasis has been on his single-minded devotion to alleged long term goals.

> The erroneous assessment of Great Britain turned out to be the decisive error in Hitler's equation and it continued to remain so. Because of this mistake, Hitler was forced to modify his grand design repeatedly, especially in the case of the Soviet-German Pact of 1939. But the grand design remained the lodestar of all his decisions in the field of foreign policy just the same. Few statesmen have ever pursued their goals with greater obstinacy or tenacity. One may continue to call his innumerable breaches of promises and treaties along the way opportunist, but two things should be kept clearly in mind. This opportunism of cunning and lies was, first of all, one of principle. For Hitler, politics, as he repeatedly stated and as we shall see below, was a natural struggle for power fought according to the laws of the jungle. And secondly, this opportunism had clearly defined goals which did not at all arise from the opportunities offered by any given moment. They remained unflinchingly the goals and means which had been developed in the 1920's and which had been unified into a coherent conception of foreign policy by 1926 at the latest.[79]

The ultimate goal of Hitler's policy was the search for *Lebensraum* at the expense of Soviet Russia. Insofar as this goal depended upon dominating east-central Europe, there was an obvious structural identity between Hitler's program and the more conventional views of German conservatives — at least in the initial phases of expansionism.[80]

The virtual unanimity of German opinion concerning the desirability of expanding eastward makes identification and analysis of independent economic factors behind the expansionist policy seem almost superfluous. Historians and economists have characterized the German trade drive as politically motivated and an instrument of Hitler's bid for world power, leading to almost exclusive concentration

---

[79] JÄCKEL, Hitler's Weltanschauung, p. 46. Jäckel's formulation of the relation between Hitler's goals and opportunistic tactics follows Alan BULLOCK, Hitler and the Origins of the Second World War, London 1967.

[80] Hitler's views on eastward expansion were hardly unique, but the distillation and synthesis of at least 30 years of Pan-German propaganda. Both Ludendorff and Seeckt expressed similar views during World War I. Even the most barbarous Nazi policies, as directed against the Soviet Union (*Generalplan Ost*), for massive popuation shifts, colonization, and Germanization had appeared in Pan-German propaganda before the outbreak of World War I. See, on the *Volk ohne Raum* and the need for new land to expand (surplus population): Anonymous, Deutschland bei Beginn des 2Osten Jahrhunderts, von einem Deutschen, 1900, p. 115; Ernst HAASE, Die Besiedlung des deutschen Volksbodens, 1905, p. 126; HAASE, Deutsche Grenzpolitik, 1906, p. 168. On the question of forced migration of "inferior peoples" and expropriation of land for German proprietors, see Friedrich LANGE, Reines Deutschtum, 5th ed., 1906, p. 206; Klaus WAGNER, Krieg, 1904, p. 170. On the Germanization of subject peoples, see Joseph Ludwig REIMER, Ein Pangermanisches Deutschland, 1905, p. 137. Seeckt's views in 1915: "Separate peace with France and Belgium, on the basis of status quo. Then all land forces against Russia. Conquest [of] ten thousand [square] miles expelling the population, except, of course, Germans", in Gustav HILGER and Alfred MEYER, Incompatible Allies, New York 1953, pp.191-192.

upon Hitler's crisis diplomacy during 1938 and 1939 or the political structure of German foreign policy to the neglect of German foreign economic policy. Such neglect of economic factors in the politics of the Great Powers is not confined to German historiography but characterizes scholarship concerning the Great Depression.[81]

This study has attempted to show that simply characterizing German foreign economic policy as an instrument of political expansion is misleading — if not entirely false. Looking at the total pattern of world trade in the aftermath of the Depression from the viewpoint of German trade policy, the commercial treaties with Hungary and Yugoslavia in 1934 anticipate the New Plan of discriminatory trade policy, an answer to the pervasive economic regionalism created by the Depression. Pushed out of northern European and Baltic markets by Britain's devaluation and aggressive trade policy (the "coal clauses"), facing high tariffs in the United States, a tariff wall in Great Britain, and protectionism in western Europe, German exports were given the *coup de grace* by the increasing trade of European mother countries with colonial empires. Cut off from markets and so unable to earn foreign exchange to pay for raw materials, Schacht developed Germany's own version of preferential colonial trade by reducing imports costing hard currency and promoting trade with Danubian Europe and Latin America. Economically, this policy was reasonable and had the added benefit of solidarizing business with the Nazi regime; the new export markets and state contracts at home were ample compensation for the lost traditional markets.[82] The economic advantages of Schacht's foreign trade policy depended upon a certain context — that of the battle against unemployment and the rearmament drive, both of which were motivated by a complex nexus of political, economic, and social causes.

During the first phase of German economic expansion into Danubian Europe, the accent was upon export promotion even though the Hungarian and Yugoslavian treaties, dependent upon subsidies, were being justified within the government on political grounds. It was expected to take several years to "soften up" Rumania and Yugoslavia, and, meanwhile, Germany wanted to regain its former position in these markets so that heavy industry could be stimulated by large-scale contracts from Danubian governments. Raw materials were a secondary priority, in that the governments of southeastern Europe would allow a marked increase in raw materials export only *after* foodstuff exports were increased. Also, the raw materials avail-

[81] With the exception of the works by Lloyd Gardner on United States policy, Bernd-Jürgen Wendt on English-German relations, and Hans-Jürgen Schröder on American-German competition, the economic factor in the foreign policy of the Great Powers has been sadly neglected. Folke Hilgerdt did ample work on the statistics of the regionalization of international trade, but research on commercial policy has lagged far behind.

[82] "Economic" is understood here in its broadest sense. It is traditional to define Nazi commercial policy as "uneconomic" because it imported commodities at prices above world market prices. This technical definition, establishing world market prices as the final arbitrator of economic rationality, denies an economic motivation to Schacht's export promotion policy. Schacht and big business clearly expected benefits to be derived from the export drive via clearing agreements; to maintain otherwise would fly in the face of reality.

able were owned by French or British firms that would export to Germany only in exchange for hard currency. These two factors combined to cause imports, consisting primarily of foodstuffs, from Danubian Europe to rise faster than German exports to Danubian markets. The German monopoly marketing organizations virtually assured import of the specific volumes of foodstuffs agreed upon by the treaty negotiators or Mixed Commissions. These monopoly marketing organizations, under the Agricultural Ministry/*Reichsnährstand*, negotiated binding contracts with Danubian exporters after the treaty negotiations were concluded, making a sharp rise in German imports from Danubian Europe inevitable. Any immediate and corresponding increase in German exports was highly unlikely. During cyclical economic crises, exports to primary producers normally lag behind imports from them: The Danubian governments, and particularly Rumania and Yugoslavia, were reluctant to impose discriminatory trade measures to promote German imports — old fears lingered and hampered economic rapprochement with Germany, the National Banks were vigorously opposed to discriminatory trade measures, and there was strong opposition from France, Britain, and the United States.

With ever-increasing clearing credits blocked in Berlin, however, it was inevitable that the Danubian governments would have to chance the ire of creditor powers and increase imports from Germany. Slowly but surely came the award of state contracts to German firms, later followed by discriminatory import policies favoring Germany. Germany deliberately ran up a clearing deficit, not to get free commodity credits but to promote exports.

The economic assumptions underlying Schacht's initial *Einfuhrmonopol* proposal and his New Plan became ever more irrelevant as the economic boom and the export offensive raised production to 1929 levels. In 1934, the Ruhr steel barons had talked of "going under" if the situation did not improve[83]; in 1936, investment and capital goods production were about 15 percent above the boom level of 1929. The New Plan had sought to export capital investment goods to the industrializing primary producers, but both the Zenica project in Yugoslavia and the Rimma credit in Rumania, the two most significant successes, were not implemented until 1937, well after the crisis conditions in heavy industry had already been overcome.

Schacht, no longer faced with finding markets to promote industrial production, had to find a way to maintain and increase German exports when industry was finding it increasingly convenient to sell in a now-booming domestic market — the phenomenon of *Exportmüdigkeit*. The rearmament and Four Year Plan economics exacerbated this problem, so that, while from 1934 to 1936 Germany's passive trade balance with Danubian Europe had resulted from reluctance to take German exports, from 1937 to 1939 the episodic passive balances reflected German industry's increasing difficulty in meeting the demands of both home and export markets. In German priorities, also, Danubian countries took third place to the Four Year Plan and armaments drive or exports to hard currency countries. This priority list

---

[83] Peter Klöckner (Director of Klöckner Steel Works) on the export situation: "Wenn wir nicht exportieren, gehen wir in ein paar Monaten zugrunde." May 5, 1934. In Sitzung A-Produkte Verband, Stahlhof Düsseldorf, HA-GHH, 40000010/46.

did, however, suffer the constant violations required to conciliate southeastern trading partners.

The erratic pattern of trade relations with southeastern Europe does not contradict the conclusion that the Four Year Plan signaled a decision to turn from export promotion to increasing supplies of raw materials. After 1936, Germany was able to use its strong economic position to run up clearing debts, but when the situation threatened to develop into a crisis, Germany was quick to allow "normal" German exports to liquidate the debt or to take special measures to bring it down. The priority list had to be disregarded frequently to maintain stability in Germany's informal empire.

By 1938, the initial political justification for the treaties with Hungary and Yugoslavia was no longer operative — the "softening-up" process had isolated Czechoslovakia and created not one but two positions of influence within the Little Entente. The economic sacrifices that had been necessary to pay subsidies were justified and now control of the raw materials of the Danube was critically important to the Reich's political expansion. After 1937, the possibility of war played an increasingly important role in Germany's foreign economic policy toward the Danube, which was the only reliable area for raw materials and foodstuffs supply in the event of a British blockade.

Thus the discussion of the political attitudes of German conservatives and Hitler's program comes full circle. The struggle of German foreign policy from mid-1930 for hegemony in east-central Europe allows no sharp separation of economic and political factors. The resurgence of *Mitteleuropa* propaganda developed in inverse proportion to the plunging world economy. Obviously, there were options open to German business other than labor repression at home and export promotion abroad, but the political attitudes of German business leadership militated against expanding the domestic market through reform and a Social Democratic work creation policy. Excluding this option made abandoning the multilateral trading system a foregone conclusion. To Schacht goes the credit for showing how economic domination of Danubian Europe could be reconciled with a general strategy of export promotion. By late 1937, Germany was rearmed, employment and production were at 1929 levels or above, and the economic domination of southeastern Europe was virtually assured.

The question of the relationship between Hitler's program and the causes of World War II can probably not be answered by searching for a direct link between his conceptions and his tactics in 1938-39, although there is a clear line of development between his early foreign policy and his attack on the Soviet Union in 1941. By and large, however, the documentation of Hitler's attitudes and ideas during the crucial crisis period of 1938 to 1939 is already in and it does not provide sufficient evidence to precisely characterize his motives during this period.[84] This study has

---

[84.] The controversy between Hugh Trevor-Roper and A. J. P. Taylor rests on the interpretation of a few well-known documents: the Hossbach Memorandum, Hitler's speeches to his generals in April and August 1939, etc. Much has been written to define Hitler's attitude toward the general course of German policy in these documents. T. W. Mason has introduced

attempted to view German policy from the perspective of its expansion toward the key antirevisionist countries of the Danube: Yugoslavia and Rumania.

The structure of German economic policy in these countries clearly demonstrates that Germany intended to control their raw materials, peacefully, if possible, but through direct military appropriation if necessary. Through political renunciation and economic expansion, Germany had isolated Czechoslovakia and created an informal empire in the Danube but found it increasingly difficult to service the demands of the Four Year Plan and the export market it had created. Resources were strained, with little margin existing to conciliate trading partners. German economic expansion depended upon imposing an economic subservience very like colonial servitude — and Poland was the one country in east-central Europe that resisted. No matter how ridiculous Poland's posturing as a "great power" may seem in retrospect, its refusal to act like a small power provided the country with the indispensable moral resources to resist Germany's "peaceful" expansion. It is obvious that any country that was determined to defend its independence at all costs would find unacceptable the German economic program as exemplified by Rumania and Yugoslavia.

To the extent that Poland remained committed to trading with several trading partners and protecting the interests of foreign owners of Polish resources, collision with German foreign policy was inevitable. Although actively cooperating with Germany throughout the 1930's, Poland had no intention of becoming a junior partner in an eastern European empire. Neither the Danzig nor autobahn issue was intrinsically important for Hitler, but Poland's acquiescence on these issues was critical to the consolidation of Germany's informal empire. Hitler did not shrink from war as a means of providing Germany with an economic alternative to the world market or as a means of promoting expansion.

the domestic pressures for expansion into the discussion, which is the only new material that has been brought to light. That the traditional approach of diplomatic history is of little help here can be seen by the lack of works comparable to those of Sidney Fay, Bernadotte Schmidt and Luigi Albertini on World War I. The literature on the Taylor thesis is collected in E. M. ROBERTSON (ed.), The Origins of the Second World War, London 1971. The magisterial archival research of Gerhard Weinberg encompassed in his two volume history of German foreign policy in the 1930's suffers from inattention to economic diplomacy and resolves itself into an indirect polemic against A. J. P. Taylor's revisionist views. Weinberg, like Walther Hofer, argues the "war premeditated" thesis which results in an uncritical assessment of Chamberlain and British appeasement policy: Gerhard WEINBERG, The Foreign Policy of Hitler's Germany: Diplomatic Revolution in Europe, 1933-1936, Chicago 1970; idem, The Foreign Policy of Hitler's Germany: Starting World War II, Chicago 1981. For a balanced critique of Weinberg see: Paul KENNEDY, Aggressors and Appeasers, in: Times Literary Supplement, June 26, 1981, p. 737. Other recent political studies do not break out of the framework of traditional diplomatic history: Anthony ADAMWAITE, France and the Coming of the Second World War, London 1977; Sidney ASTER, 1939: The Making of the Second World War, London 1973; Williamson MURRAY, The Change in the European Balance of Power, 1938-1939: The Path to Ruin, Princeton 1981; Simon NEWMAN, March, 1939: The British Guarantee to Poland: A Study in the Continuity of British Foreign Policy, Oxford 1976; Telford TAYLOR, Munich: The Price of Peace, New York 1979.

Germany's trade drive was an aggressive response to the deprivation of its traditional markets created by the Depression. Constructing an economic *Mitteleuropa* went hand in hand with political domination of east-central Europe, which had been left by the trade policies of Great Britain, France, Belgium, and Holland to face the Depression on its own. The initial bilateral conflict with Poland became a World War because neither Great Britain nor France could permit Nazi empire building to continue without irreparable damage to their own political and economic positions in the world. It is ironic that Germany's "need" for a secure source of raw materials and foodstuffs became actualized by the war provoked by that need — a truly self-fulfilling prophecy.[85]

While Hitler and traditional conservatives agreed that it was only morally right that Germany should dominate east-central Europe and thus have its own sphere of influence, Hitler, at least, was well aware that the resources of this area were not sufficient for German *Lebensraum*. His eyes were focused on the riches of the Ukraine and beyond.

[85] For a similiar point see KAISER, Economic Diplomacy, p. 282.

KEY TO ABBREVIATIONS

AA	Auswärtiges Amt
AKG	Ausfuhrgemeinschaft für Kriegsgerät
AO	Auslandsorganisation, NSDAP
APA	Außenpolitisches Amt, NSDAP
BA	Bundesarchiv, Koblenz
BA-Mi	Bundesarchiv — Militärarchiv, Freiburg im Breisgau
DBFP	Documents on British Foreign Policy, 1919-1939 (Second and Third Series)
DDF	Documents Diplomatiques Français, 1932-1939 (First Series, 1932-1935; Second Series, 1936-1939)
DG	Deutsche Gesandtschaft
DGFP	Documents on German Foreign Policy (Series C, 1933-1937; Series D, 1937-1939)
DVK	Deutsche Verrechnungskasse
FRUS	Foreign Relations of the United States
GHH	Gutehoffnungshütte
HA-GHH	Historisches Archiv der Gutehoffnungshütte, Oberhausen
Ha Pol	Handelspolitische Abteilung, Auswärtiges Amt
IG	Interessengemeinschaft [Farben] (IG Farben)
MWT	Mitteleuropäischer Wirtschaftstag
NA	National Archives, Washington, D.C.
NCA	Nazi Conspiracy and Aggression
ND	Nürnberg Document — Documents presented at the International Military Tribunal at Nürnberg
NI	Nazi Industrialist — National Archives Microfilm Publication
NSDAP	Nationalsozialistische Deutsche Arbeiterpartei
OKH	Oberkommando des Heeres
OKM	Oberkommando der Kriegsmarine
OKW	Oberkommando der Wehrmacht
PA	Political Archives of the Auswärtiges Amt, Bonn
PRO	Public Records Office, London
RFM	Reichsfinanzministerium
RGBL	Reichsgesetzblatt
RIIA	Royal Institute of International Affairs, London
RKM	Reichskriegsministerium
RLM	Reichsluftfahrtministerium
RMEL	Reichsministerium für Ernährung und Landwirtschaft

RSDB   Reichstelle für Devisenbewirtschaftung
RWM   Reichswirtschaftsministerium
UB   Überwachungsstelle(n)
Wi Rü Amt Wehrwirtschafts- und Rüstungsamt, OKW

BIBLIOGRAPHY

I. PRIMARY SOURCES

Political Archives of Auswärtiges Amt, Bonn

A full listing of the files consulted would make this bibliography far too cumbersome, so listed here are only the document groups. Individual footnotes give complete references to the files consulted. The Political Archives uses the catalog of George O. Kent for all files except the *Botschaft* and *Gesandtschaft* records. Although the fourth volume of Kent's index has appeared, I have listed the files consulted from the Legations in Belgrade and Bucharest according to the manuscript index in use at Bonn: George O. KENT, A catalog of Files and Microfilms of the German Foreign Ministry Archives, 1920-1945, 3 volumes, Stanford 1962-1966.

Kent I

Büro des Reichsministers
Büro des Staatsekretärs
Politische Abteilung II
Abteilung II, Wirtschaft
Geheimakten

Kent II

Politische Abteilung III
Sonderreferat Wirtschaft
Handakten Ritter

Kent III

Büro des Reichsaußenministers
Büro des Staatsekretärs
Büro des Unterstaatsekretärs
Politische Abteilung I
Politische Abteilung I M
Politische Abteilung IV
Handelspolitische Abteilung (Ha Pol)
Handakten Wiehl
Handakten Clodius
Handakten Hausschild
Handakten Benzler
Handakten Hudeczek
Inland Abteilung II AB
Büro des Chefs der Auslandsorganisation
Außenpolitisches Amt

Gesandtschaft Belgrad

Fach 40/41, IA 28, Balkan-Gemeinschaftliches Bd. 1-3, 1932-1940
Fach 43/44, IA 38, Nationalsozialismus, Bd. 1-6, 1932-1940
Fach 43/44, IA 38a, Verbot Nationalsozialismus Zeitungen, Bd. 1-2
Fach 70, Po 2, Politik Deutschland — Jugoslawien, Besuch Göring, Neurath, Stojadinović, 1935-1939
Fach 72, Po 3, Balkan Pakt, 1938-1939
Fach 76, Po 6, Nationalitätenfrage, Bd. 1- 6, 1921-1939
Fach 79, Po 18, Vorkriegsanleihen, 1927-1930
Fach 81, G 2, Wirtschaftliches — Geheim, Bd. 1-4, 1920-1939
Fach 83, Pol. 12e, Politische Beziehungen Jugoslawiens zu Deutschland und Balkanblock, Bd. 1-2, 1934-1943
Fach 83, Politisches — Geheim, Jugoslawiens Haltung zu Deutschland und Balkanblock, Bd. 1-2, 1939-1943
Fach 83, Pol. 2, Deutscher Handelsattaché, Nr.2 f., 1940
Fach 84, Pol. 39, Kroatische Frage, 1940

Gesandtschaft Bukarest

Fach 34, II A 2, Adolph Konradi, 1936-1940
Fach 36, II A 1B, Mitgliedschaft der Beamten und Angestellten bei der NSDAP 1984. NSDAP Parteiangelegenheiten — Geheim, 1937-1940
Fach 36, II A 6, Personalien — Geheim, 1938-1943
Fach 40/41, IA 32, Römisches Protokoll, 1936-1937
Fach 45, IB 6, Minderheiten — Geheim, 1936-1940
Fach 45, IB 6, Handelsattaché Konradi — Geheim, 1938-1939
Fach 45, IB 6, Militärisches — Geheim, 1938-1942
Fach 45, IB 6, Krisenmaßnahmen — Geheim, 1938-1939
Fach 45/46, IC 4, Handelsvertragsverhältnisse Deutschland mit Rumänien, Bd. 1-8, 1932-1939
Fach 48, IF 7, Rumänische Aufrüstung, 1936-1939
Fach 48, IH 3, Spionage Abwehr, 1932-1939
Fach 50, IJ 36, (Deutscher) Presse Attaché, 1936-1939
Fach 58, R 19, N 1, Beschlagnahme deutschen Eigentums in Rumänien, 1922-1925
Fach 59, V 4, Rumänien — Deutschland, Wirtschaftlich, Bd. 1-3, 5-7, 1932-1937
Fach 60, V 26, Handelsreklamation gegen die rumänischen Eisenbahnen, Bd. 1-11
Fach 61, V 27, Handelsreklamation gegen sonstg. rumänische staatliche Stellen, Bd. 1-6, 1931-1938
Fach 80, WJ 10, Rüstung, Bd. 1-4, 1939-1940
Fach 83, Geheim 23, Verschiedenes Geheim, 1937-1942

Bundesarchiv, Koblenz

R2   Reichsfinanzminsterium
R7/V — R7/XIII Reichswirtschaftsministerium
R11   Reichswirtschaftskammer
R13/VI — R13/XII Reichsstellen
R16   Reichsbauernführer
R43/II Reichskanzlei
R58   Reichssicherheitshauptamt (RSHA)
R63   Südosteuropa Gesellschaft
NS8 — NS19 Nationalsozialistische Mischbänder

Sammlung Brammer (Zsg 101), Mitschriften von "Bestellungen" und "Vertraulichen Informationen" der Pressekonferenz des Reichsministeriums für Volksaufklärung und Propaganda.

Sammlung Sänger (Zsg 102), Mitschriften aus der Pressekonferenz des Reichsministeriums für Volksaufklärung und Propaganda.

Sammlung Oberheitmann (Zsg 109), "Vertrauliche Informationen" des Reichsministeriums für Volksaufklärung und Propaganda für die Presse.

Sammlung Traub (Zsg 110), Mitschriften von "Vertraulichen Informationen" der Pressekonferenz des Reichsministeriums für Volksaufklärung und Propaganda.

Bundesarchiv-Militärarchiv, Freiburg im Breisgau

Wehrwirtschafts- und Rüstungsamt (Wi Rü Amt)

National Archives, Washington, D.C.

General Files of the Department of State, RG 59
War Department, General Staff Military Attaché Reports, RG 165

National Archives Microfilm Publications

Nazi Industrialists (NI), T-301

Public Record Office, London

Foreign Office F.O. 371/...

II. DOCUMENTARY PUBLICATIONS

France

Documents diplomatiques français 1932-1939. 1st series, 1932-1933, Vol. 2; 2nd series, 1936-1939, Vols. 1-3, Paris 1963-67. Les Evénements survenues en France de 1933 a 1945, temoignages et documents recueilles par la commission d'enquête parlementaire, 9 vols., Paris 1947.

Germany

Documents secrets du ministère des affaires étrangère de l'Allemagne. 2. Hongrie, La politique allemande 1937-1943. 3. La politique allemande en Espagne 1936-1943, trans. by Madeleine and Michel Eristov, Paris 1946.

Documents on German Foreign Policy 1918-1945. German edition: Akten zur Deutschen Auswärtigen Politik 1918-1945, Series B, 1925-1933, is cited from the German edition, Göttingen 1966-; Series C, 1933-1937, is cited from the English language edition, Washington 1957-; Series D, 1937-1945, is cited from the German edition, Baden-Baden 1950-.

Great Britain

Documents on British Foreign Policy 1919-1939. 2nd series, 1930-1937. Vols. 4-6, 1933-1934, London 1950-57.
Parliamentary (Command Papers): Cmd. 5143. Correspondence showing the course of certain Diplomatic Discussions directed towards securing an European Settlement, June 1934 to March 1936. Miscellaneous No. 3 (1936), London 1936.

Hungary

Diplomaciai iratok magyaroszag kulpolitikajahaz 1936-1945, Vols. 1-2, Budapest 1962-66. These volumes contain German-language summaries of each document.
Allianz Hitler-Horthy-Mussolini, Dokumente zur ungarischen Außenpolitik (1933-1944), Budapest 1966.
The Confidential Papers of Admiral Horthy, Budapest 1965.

Italy

I Documenti diplomatici italiani. 7th series, 1922-1935; 8th series, 1935-1939, Rome 1952-.
Ciano, Galeazzo. Ciano's Diplomatic Papers, Malcolm MUGGERIDGE (ed.), trans. by Stuart Hood, Lond 1948.

United States

Foreign Relations of the United States. Washington 1861-. The volumes all include the title of the main series in their respective titles, with the exception of:
Peace and War, United States Foreign Policy 1931-1941, Washington 1943.
F.D.R.: His Personal Letters, 1928-1945, Elliot ROOSEVELT (ed.), 2 vols. New York 1950.
Franklin D. Roosevelt and Foreign Affairs, January 1933 January 1937, Edgar B. NIXON (ed.), 3 vols, Cambridge/Massachusetts 1969.

III. OTHER OFFICIAL AND SEMI-OFFICIAL PUBLICATIONS

League of Nations. Commercial Policy in the Inter-War Period, Geneva 1942.
—, Enquiry into Clearing Agreements, Geneva 1935.
—, Europe's Trade, Geneva 1941.
—, Network of World Trade, Geneva 1942.
—, Report on Exchange Control, Geneva 1938.
—, World Economic Survey, 1931-1939, Geneva 1932-1939.
Mitteleuropäische Wirtschaftstagung. Bericht über die Mitteleuropäische Wirtschaftstagung am 8. und 9. September 1925 (Auszug), Vienna 1925(?).
—. Bericht über die Verhandlungen der V. Mitteleuropäischen Wirtschaftstagung in Breslau am 28. Februar und 1. März 1930, Berlin-Grunewald 1930.
Nationalsozialistische Deutsche Arbeiterpartei. Reichorganisationsamt. ...Wirtschaftliches Sofortprogramm der N.S.D.A.P., Munich 1932.
Nationalsozialistisches Denken und Wirtschaft, von Rudolf Heindel..., Stuttgart 1932.
Royal Institute of International Affairs, London. The Balkan States, London 1936.
—. Europe under Hitler, London 1941.
—. The Problem of International Investments, London 1937.
—. Raw Materials, London 1939.
—. South-Eastern Europe: a Political and Economic Survey, London 1939.
—. Survey of International Affairs, 1930-1938, London 1931-1939.

IV. DIARIES, MEMOIRS, COLLECTED WORKS

BECK, Joseph, Dernier Rapport, Neuchatel 1951.

COOPER, Alfred Duff, Old Men Forget, New York 1954.
CURTIUS, Julius, Sechs Jahre Minister der deutschen Republik, Heidelberg 1948.

DIRKSEN, Herbert von, Moskau-Tokyo-London, Stuttgart 1949.
DODD, William E., Jr., Ambassador Dodd's Diary, New York 1941.

EDEN, Anthony, The Memoirs of Anthony Eden: Facing the Dictators, Boston 1962.
EINZIG, Paul, In the Centre of Things, London 1960.

HELFFERICH, Emil, 1932 bis 1946 Tatsachen, Ein Beitrag zur Wahrheitsfindung, Jever 1969.
HOSSBACH, Friederich, Zwischen Wehrmacht und Hitler, 1934-1938, Wolfenbüttel 1958.

JONES, Thomas, A Diary with Letters, London 1954.

KORDT, Erich, Nicht aus den Akten, Stuttgart 1950.
KROLL, Hans, Lebenserinnerungen eines Botschafters, Köln/Berlin 1967.

LANGE, Serge, and SCHENCK, Ernst von (eds.), Memoirs of Alfred Rosenberg, Chicago 1949.
LAROCHE, Jules, La Pologne de Pilsudski, 1926-1935, Paris 1953.
LUTHER, Hans, Vor dem Abgrund, Reichsbankpräsident in Krisenzeiten, Berlin 1964.

NADOLNY, Rudolf, Mein Beitrag, Wiesbaden 1955.
NEUBACHER, H., Sonderauftrag Südost, Göttingen/Berlin/Frankfurt 1957.

ROBBINS, Lionel, Autobiography of an Economist, London 1971.
RIBBENTROP, Annelies von (ed.), Joachim von Ribbentrop, Zwischen London und Moskau, Leoni 1953.

SCHMIDT, Paul, Statist auf diplomatischer Bühne, 1923-1945, Bonn 1950.
SCHWERIN VON KROSIGK, Lutz Graf, Es geschah in Deutschland, Tübingen & Stuttgart 1951.
SERAPHIM, Hans-Gunther, (ed.). Das Politische Tagebuch Alfred Rosenbergs aus den Jahren 1934/1935 und 1939/1940, Berlin 1956.
SZEMBEK, Jean, Journal, 1933-1939, Paris 1952.

TEMPLEWOOD, Viscount (Sir Samuel Hoare), Nine Troubled Years, London 1954.
TREVIRANIS, Gottfried R., Das Ende von Weimar, Heinrich Brüning und seine Zeit, Düsseldorf 1968.

VANSITTART, Robert, The Mist Procession, London 1958.

WEIZSÄCKER, Ernst von, Erinnerungen, Munich, 1950.

V. UNPUBLISHED U.S. DOCTORAL DISSERTATIONS

AGRANAT, Leon, Price Control in Germany, New School for Social Research 1954.
ALEXANDER, Jules, Hungaro-German Economic Relations, 1919-1939, McGill University 1970.
ALTERAS, Issac, The Geneva Disarmament Conference: The German Case, City University of New York 1971.

APPLEYARD, Dennis, Terms of Trade and Economic Development: A Case Study of India, Michigan 1966.

BATRA, Raveendra, Economic Growth and the Terms of Trade, Southern Illinois 1969.
BECKER, Peter, The Basis of the German War Economy Under Albert Speer, 1942-1944, Stanford 1971.
BRIEFS, Godfrey, Shifting Patterns in Eastern Europe's Foreign Trade, 1928-1948, Harvard 1951.
BRIGHT, Charles, Britain's Search for Security, 1930-1936: The Diplomacy of Naval Disarmament and Imperial Defense, Yale 1970.

CALDERWOOD, James, The International Implications of British Foreign Economic Policy, 1931-1939, Ohio State 1943.
CAMPBELL, Fenton, Jr., Czech-German Relations During the Weimar Republic, Yale University 1967.
CHALK, Frank, The U.S. and the International Struggle for Rubber, 1914-1941, Wisconsin 1970.
CLOE, Carl, The German Coal Industry, 1935-1946, Iowa 1947.
COLLADO, Emilio, Japanese Competition in International Trade, Harvard 1936.
COOPER, Charles, Agriculture, Labor Surplus, and Foreign Trade, Bulgaria, 1925-1960, MIT 1961.
COSTIGLIOLA, Frank, The Politics of Financial Stabilization: American Reconstruction Policy in Europe, 1924-1930, Cornell 1973.
CRONENBERG, Allen T., The Volksbund fuer das Deutschtum im Ausland: Voelkisch Ideology and German Foreign Policy, 1881-1939, Stanford 1970.

GASTONY, Endre, Revisionist Hungarian Foreign Policy and the Third Reich's Advance to the East, 1933-1937, University of Oregon 1970.
GILLINGHAM, John R., The New Economic Order in Belgium, University of California — Berkeley 1973.

HANNAFORD, John W., French Interwar Monetary Problems, Harvard 1951.
HANSON, James A., The Terms of Trade and Economic Growth, Yale 1968.
HARPER, Glenn, German Economic Policy in Spain During the Spanish Civil War, 1936-1939, Duke 1963.
HARRIMAN, Helga, The German Minority in Yugoslavia, 1941-1945, Oklahoma State 1973.
HILTON, Stanley, Brazil and the Great Power Trade Rivalry in South America, 1934-1939, University of Texas at Austin 1969.

JOHNSON, Norman, The Austro-German Customs Union Project in German Diplomacy, University of North Carolina at Chapel Hill 1974.

KLEIN, John J., German Monetary Development, 1932-1945, Chicago 1955.

LITTLEFIELD, Frank., Yugoslav Relations with Germany and Italy and the Nationality Problem, 1933-1941, New York University 1973.

MONTGOMERY, Sarah, The Terms of Trade of Primary Products and Manufactured Goods in International Trade, 1872-1952, Wisconsin 1960.

MOORE, James, A History of the World Economic Conference, London 1933, State University of New York (Stoneybrook) 1972.

PAPP, Nicholas, The Anglo-German Naval Agreement of 1935, Connecticut 1969.
PERKINS, Maurice, Long Term Trends and Intermediate Fluctuations in Raw Materials Prices and Production, 1900-1950, Harvard 1952.

POWELSON, John P., French Exports and Commercial Policy, 1919-1949, Harvard 1949.
PROCHAZKA, Zora, Foreign Trade and Economic Development of Czechoslovakia, 1919-1937, Radcliffe 1960.

QUEVRIN, Emile, Terms of Trade and Economic Development, Princeton 1958.
QUINLAN, Paul, British and American Policies Toward Romania, 1938-1947, Boston College 1974.

REPKO, Allen, New Deal Commercial Policy and Germany, 1933-1939, University of Missouri — Columbia 1973.
RIPPEY, Robert S., Jr., Terms of Trade of Underdeveloped Countries, Syracuse 1966.
RITTER, Harry, Herman Neubacher and the German Occupation of the Balkans 1940-1945, Virginia 1969.
RUPIEPER, Hermann-Josef, Politics and Economics: The Cuno Government, 1922-1923, Stanford 1974.

SAILORS, Joel W., Secular Terms of Trade: Theory and Measurement, Texas 1956.
SAKMYSTER, Thomas, Hungary and the Coming of the European Crisis, 1937-1938, Indiana 1971.
SHARPE, Williard D., The Economic Policies of the Popular Front Governments of France, 1936-1938, Harvard 1956.
SIDDIQUE, Abil, The International Monetary and Economic Conferences of the Inter-War Period, Yale 1970.
SMELSER, Ronald, Volkstumpolitik and the Formation of Nazi Foreign Policy: The Sudeten Problem, 1933-1938, University of Wisconsin 1970.
SMILEY, Ralph A, The Lausanne Conference, 1932, State University of New Jersey 1971.
SOPER, Michael, The Lausanne Conference of 1932, Wisconsin 1971.

TOTEFF, Anastas, Prices in Bulgaria, Cornell 1938.

VAN METER, Robert Jr., The United States and European Recovery, 1918-1923: A Study of Public Policy and Private Finance, Wisconsin 1971.

WANG, Yuan Chao, German Exchange Control, 1931-1936, Harvard 1937.
WINCHESTER, Betty Jo, Hungarian Relations with Germany, 1936-1939, Indiana 1970.

VI. CONTEMPORARY BOOKS (to 1945)

BASCH, Antonin, The Danube Basin and the German Economic Sphere, New York 1943.
—, Germany's Economic Conquest of Czechoslovakia, Chicago 1941.
BEHREND, Hans, The Real Rulers of Germany, London 1939.
BEYER, Günter, Umsichtung und Umlenkung der Einfuhr durch handelspolitische Mittel, Diss. Basel 1934.
BOBCHEV, C., Reglementation du commerce et politique commerciale en Bulgarie, Sofia 1939.
BONNELL, Alan T., German Control over International Economic Relations, Urbana/Illinois 1940.
BRANDT, Karl, The German Fat Plan and Its Economic Setting, Stanford 1938.
BREZA, Robert, Wirtschaftliche Bestimmungsgründe der Außenhandelsstruktur Südosteuropas, Vienna 1942.
BRÜCHMANN, Heinz L., Zwischenstaatliche Wirtschaftsprobleme im Donauraum, Ludwigshafen 1936.

CRNÍC, Ivan, Die jugoslawische Eisenindustrie, Diss. Cologne 1938.

EGGERS, Hans Peter, Die Tendenzen des zwischenstaatlichen Warenverkehrs im südöstlich-
    mitteleuropäischen Wirtschaftsraum, Diss. Rostock 1935.
EINZIG, Paul, The Exchange Clearing System, London 1935.
—, German's Default; The Economics of Hitlerism, London 1934.
—, Bloodless Invasion, London 1938.
ELLIS, Howard S., Exchange Control in Central Europe, Cambridge/Massachusetts 1941.
ERBSLAND, Kurt, Die Umgestaltung der deutschen Handelspolitik durch den "Neuen Plan"
    und die Möglichkeiten ihrer künftigen Ausgestaltung, Diss. Heidelberg 1937.

FIMMEN, Hans-Onno. Die Bedeutung Nord- und Südosteuropas für die deutsche Volkswirt-
    schaft. Ein Vergleich, Diss. Munich 1936.
FISCHER, Werner August, Devisenclearing, die Entwicklung der Zahlungs- und
    Verrechnungsabkommen in Deutschland, mit einem Vorwort von Karl Blessing, Berlin
    1937.
FLAIGG, Herbert, Untersuchung über den Einfluß des "Neuen Planes" auf den deutschen
    Außenhandel und die Außenhandelspolitik, Diss. Freiburg im Breisgau 1941.

GERSCHENKRON, A., Bread and Democracy in Germany, Berkeley/California 1943.
GROSS, Hermann, Deutsch-rumänische Wirtschaftsbeziehungen, Berlin 1929.
—, Die Wirtschaftliche Bedeutung Südosteuropas für das Deutsche Reich, Stuttgart 1938.

HAIGHT, F. A., French Import Quotas, London 1935.
—, A History of French Commercial Policies, New York 1941.
HANTOS, Elemer, Denkschrift über die wirtschaftlichen Probleme Mitteleuropas im Auftrage
    der Mitteleuropäischen Wirtschaftstagung..., Vienna 1927.
—, Memorandum on the Economic Problems of the Danube States, London 1933.
—, Le regionalisme économique en Europe, Paris 1939.
HARRIS, C. R. S., Germany's Foreign Indebtedness, London 1935.
HODŽA, M., Federation in Central Europe, London 1942.
HOLT, John Bradshaw, German Agricultural Policy, 1918-1934, Chapel Hill/North Carolina
    1936.
HORVATH, Jenoe, Die Kleine Entente. Beitrag zur Geschichte der Diplomatie, Budapest/
    Leipzig/Mailand, no date [1940's].

ILGNER, Max, Exportsteigerung durch Einschaltung in die Industrialisierung der Welt, Jena
    1938.

JURKOVIĆ, B., Das ausländische Kapital in Jugoslawien, Stuttgart 1941.

KERNER, Robert Joseph and Harry Nicholas HOWARD, The Balkan Conferences and the Bal-
    kan Entente 1930-1935. A Study in the Recent History of the Balkan & Near East Peo-
    ples, Berkeley, California 1936.
KRUGMANN, Robert Werner, Südosteuropa und Großdeutschland; Entwicklung und
    Zukunftsmöglichkeiten der Wirtschaftsbeziehungen, Breslau 1939.

LOSSOS, Harald, Bilanz der deutschen Devisenbewirtschaftung, Jena 1940.
LUCKAS, Hans, Theorie der Devisenzwangswirtschaft auf Grund der deutschen und auslän-
    dischen Erfahrungen in der Zeit von 1914 bis 1940, Jena 1940.

MACARTNEY, C. A,. Hungary and Her Successors. The Treaty of Trianon and Its Conse-
    quences, 1919-1937, London/New York/Toronto 1937.
MACHRAY, Robert, The Little Entente, London 1929.
—, The Struggle for the Danube and The Little Entente 1929-1938, London 1938.
MADGEARU, Virgil, Rumania's New Economic Policy, London 1930.
—, Le contrôle des changes en Roumanie, Bucharest 1939.

—, Evoluţia economiei româneşti după razboiul mondial, Bucharest 1940.
—, La politique économique éxterieure de la Romanie, 1927-1938, Paris 1939.
MAJOR, Emil Endre, Die Handelspolitik der Donaustaaten von 1919 bis 1935, Diss. Bern
      1936.
MANIOLESCU, Mihail, L'Imperatif de la crise, Bucharest 1933.
—, La methode dans l'économie politique, Bucharest 1931.
—, Une nouvelle conception du protectionnisme industriel, Bucharest 1931.
—, The Theory of Protection and International Trade, London 1931.
MARCZEWSKI, Jean, Politique monetaire et financière de III Reich, Paris 1941.
MOORE, Wilbert, Economic Demography of Eastern and Southern Europe, Geneva 1945.

NATHAN, Otto, The Nazi Economic System, Durham, N.C., 1944.

OBRADOVIĆ, Sava, La politique commerciale de la Yugoslavie, Belgrade 1939.
—, Zwischen Clearing und Devise, Leipzig 1939.

PASVOLSKY, Leo, Economic Nationalism of the Danubian States, New York 1928.
PLUMMER, A., Raw Materials or War Materials? London 1937.
POOLE, Kenyon, German Financial Policies, 1932-1939, Cambridge, Mass., 1939.

REIMANN, G., Patents for Hitler, New York 1942.
REINHARDT, Fritz, Finanz und Steuerpolitik im nationalsozialistischen Staat, Berlin 1934.
REITHINGER, Anton, Stand und Ursachen der Arbeitslosigkeit in Deutschland, Berlin 1932.
—, Why France Lost the War; a Biologic and Economic Survey, New York 1940.
—, Das wirtschaftliche Gesicht Europas, Stuttgart/Berlin 1936.
ROBBINS, Lionel, The Great Depression, London 1934.
ROEPKE, Wilhelm, Weltwirtschaft. Eine Notwendigkeit der deutschen Wirtschaft, Tübingen
      1932.
-, What's Wrong With the World, Philadelphia 1932.

SAINT-JEAN, Maurice, La politique économique et financière du docteur Schacht, Paris 1936.
SALEWSKI, Wilhelm, Das ausländische Kapital in der deutschen Wirtschaft, Essen 1930.
SCHMIDT, Carl, German Business Cycles, 1924-1933, New York 1934.
SCHULMEISTER, Otto, Werdende Großraumwirtschaft — die Phasen ihrer Entwicklung in
      Südosteuropa, Berlin 1943.
SERING, Max, Germany Under the Dawes Plan, London 1929.
SUVHA, A., Economic Problems of Eastern Europe and Federalism, Cambridge 1941.
SWEEZY, Maxine, The Structure of the Nazi Economy, Cambridge, Mass., 1941.

THOELKE, Erich, Das Kontingentierungssystem als Mittel der Außenhandelspolitik, Diss.
      Halle-Wittenberg 1936.
TISCHLER, Ludwig, Der tschechoslowakische Außenhandel mit besonderer Berücksichtigung
      der Handelsbeziehungen zum Deutschen Reich..., Diss. Vienna 1938.
TRIVANOVICH, Vaso, Economic development of Germany under National Socialism, New
      York 1937.

WAGEMANN, Ernst, Der Neue Balkan: Altes Land - Junge Wirtschaft, Hamburg 1939.
WARRINER, Doreen, Eastern Europe After Hitler, London 1940.
—, Economics of Peasant Farming, London 1939.
WEINBRENNER, Karl, Voraussetzungen, Möglichkeiten und Grenzen der landwirtschaftlichen
      Selbstversorgung Deutschlands, Diss. Gießen 1938.

VII. CONTEMPORARY ARTICLES (signed to 1945)

BALOGH, Thomas, Some Theoretical Aspects of the Central European Credit and Transfer Crisis, in: International Affairs, XI, No. 1, 1932, pp. 346-369.

-, National Economy of Germany, in: Economic Journal, Vol. 48, pp. 461-497, Sept. 1938.

BASCH, Antonin, European Economic Regionalism, in: American Economic Review, XXXIII, 1943 (supplement), pp. 408-419.

—, Probleme der Devisenkontrolle, in: Mitteilungen des Verbandes Österreichischer Banken und Bankiers, Vienna, XIV, No. 9-10.

BENNING, Bernhard. Der "Neue Plan" und die Notwendigkeit der deutschen Außenwirtschaft, in: Jahrbücher für Nationalökonomie und Statistik, vol. 142, 1935, pp. 35-62.

BRANDT, Karl, The Crisis in German Agriculture, in: Foreign Affairs, vol. 10, July, 1932, pp. 632-646.

—, Farm Relief in Germany, in: Social Research, vol.1, Feb. 1934, pp. 185-198.

—, German Agriculture Policy — Some Selected Lessons, in: Journal of Farm Economics, vol. 19, Feb. 1937, pp. 287-299.

—, The German Fat Plan and its Economic Setting, in: Fats and Oils Studies No. 6, Food Research Institute, Stanford University, 1938.

—, Junkers to the Fore Again, in: Foreign Affairs, vol. 14, Oct. 1935, pp. 120-134.

—, Recent Agrarian Policies in Germany, Great Britain and the United States, in: Social Research, vol. 3, May 1936, pp. 167-201.

BRINKMANN, Carl, Gruppenautarkie und Freihandel im südosteuropäischen Raum, in: Weltwirtschaftliches Archiv, vol. 36l, No. 2/1, 1932, pp. 476ff.

de BUDAY, K., Foreign Loans in Central Europe, in: Annals of the American Academy of Political Science, CLXXIV, 1934, pp. 22-30.

CHALMERS, H., The Depression and Foreign Trade Barriers, in: Annals of the American Academy of Political Science, CLXXIV, 1934, pp. 88-106.

CHRISTY, Donald, The German Animal Fat Protection Program, in: Foreign Crops and Markets, vol. 27, July 31, 1933, pp. 103-111.

—, The German Food Situation, in: Foreign Crops and Markets, vol. 31, Oct. 14, 1935, pp. 528-532.

COLE, G. D. H., Nazi Economics: How Do They Manage It? in: Political Quarterly, vol. 10, Jan. 1939 pp. 55-68.

CRUMP, N., Economics of the Third Reich, in: Journal of the Royal Statistical Society, vol. 102, No. 2, 1939, pp. 167-212.

"Danas" Fall of the Dinar: From Stabilization by Law to Transfer Moratorium, in: Slavonic Review, Vol. 11, 1933, pp. 304-313.

DAVENPORT, N., Oil and the Dictatorships, in: New Statesman and Nation, vol. 15, Feb. 12, 1938, pp. 239-240.

deWILDE, John C., Germany's Controlled Economy, in: Foreign Policy Reports, 14, March 1, 1939, pp. 280-304.

—, Germany's Trend Toward Economic Isolation, in: Foreign Policy Reports, vol. 10, 1934/35, pp. 226-236.

—, Europe's Economic War Potential, in: Foreign Policy Reports, vol. 15, Oct. 15, 1939, pp. 185-189.

—, German Economic Dilemma, in: Foreign Policy Reports, vol. 13, March 1932, pp. 2-16.

—, Raw Materials in World Politics, in: Foreign Policy Reports, vol. 12, 1936, pp. 162-176.

—, The Secret Debts and Other Aspects of German Government Financing, in: The Annalist, Jan. 18, 1939, vol. 53, No. 1357. pp. 68, 94.

—, Unfavorable Trade Balance: Most Vulnerable Spot in German Economic Armor, in: The Annalist, vol. 53, No. 1362, Feb. 22, 1939, pp. 292, 294.

DIETZE, Constantin von, Agrarpolitik im Deutschen Reich Anfang 1933 bis Mitte 1934, in: Jahrbücher für Nationalökonomie und Statistik, CXL, 1940, pp. 427-459.

—, Measures for Combatting the Agricultural Crisis in Germany, in: Proceedings of the Third International Conference of Agricultural Economists, Oxford 1935.

DRUCKER, Peter, Underwriting Central Europe, in: Virginia Quarterly Review, vol. 12, Jan. 1936, pp. 15-28.

EINZIG, Paul, German Trade and British Policy, in: Spectator, vol. 161, July 1, 1938, pp. 10-11.

ELLIS, H. S., Exchange Control and Discrimination, in: American Economic Review, XXXVI, 1947, pp. 877-888.

FISCHER, L., Economic Crisis in Germany, in: New Statesman and Nation, vol. 11, March 21, 1936, pp. 446-447.

FRANGES, Otto von, Die Donaustaaten Südosteuropas und der deutsche Großwirtschaftsraum, in: Weltwirtschaftliches Archiv, LIII, 1941, pp. 284-328.

—, Fighting the Crisis in the Peasant Countries of the Danube Basin, in: Proceedings of the Third International Conference of Agricultural Economics, London 1935, pp. 97-107.

—, Die treibenden Kräfte der wirtschaftlichen Strukturwandlungen in Jugoslavien, in: Weltwirtschaftliches Archiv, XLVIII, 1938, pp. 309-333.

FREUND, R., Germany Faces the Winter, in: Spectator, vol. 158, Jan. 1, 1937, p. 7, and Feb 12, 1937, p. 270.

GREBLER, L., Work Creation Policy in Germany, in: International Labour Review, vol. 35, March/April, 1937, pp. 329-351, 505-527.

GREENWOOD, H. P., Germany and Europe: The Four Year Plan, in: Spectator, vol. 160, May 6, 1938, pp. 796-797.

GUILLABAUD, C. W., How Germany Finances the War, in: Spectator, vol. 163, Dec. 29, 1939, pp. 924-925.

HABERLER, G., The Political Economy of Regional or Continental Blocs, in: S. E. HARRIS (ed.), Postwar Economic Problems, New York 1943, pp. 325-344.

HAHN, Max, Agrarpolitische Produktionslenkung zwischen Deutschland und dem Südosten, in: Der Wirtschafts-Ring, vol. 11, No. 1, Jan. 7, 1938.

—, Der Donauraum in der Europäischen Wirtschaft, in: E. WUNDERLICH (ed.), Der Donauraum und seine Probleme, vol. 7, Stuttgart, 1933.

—, Importverlagerung als vordringliche Aufgabe der deutschen Handelspolitik, in: Der Deutsche Volkswirt, No. 12/13, Dec. 22, 1933, pp. 510ff.

—, Mitteleuropa als Ziel deutscher Politik, in: Volk und Reich, No. 10/11, 1931, pp. 563-572.

HEUSER, H. K., The German Method of Combined Debt Liquidation and Export Stimulation, in: Review of Economic Studies, vol. 1, 1934, pp. 210-217.

HIGGINS, Benjamin, Germany's Bid for Agricultural Self-Sufficiency, in: Journal of Farm Economics, vol. 22, May 1939, pp. 435-461.

HILDEBRAND, Walter, The Austrian Contribution to German Autarchy, in: Foreign Affairs, July 1938, pp. 587-600, 601-611, 719-722.

HILLMAN, H. C., Analysis of Germany's Foreign Trade and the War, in: Economica, vol. 7, new series, 1940, pp. 166-188.

HUBER, J. R., Effects of German Clearing Agreements and Import Restriction on Cotton, in: Southern Economic Journal. vol. 6, 1939-1940, pp. 419-439.

JASNY, Naum, Germany's Capacity to Produce Agricultural Products, in: Foreign Agriculture, vol. 1, May 1937, pp. 217-256.

—, Wheat Problems and Policies in Germany, in: Wheat Studies of the Food Research Institute, 13, Nov. 1936, pp. 65-140.

KEYNES, J. M., National Self-Sufficiency, in: Yale Review. vol. 22, June 1933, pp. 755-769.

LAMER, Miko, Die Wandlungen der ausländischen Kapitalanlagen auf dem Balkan, in: Weltwirtschaftliches Archiv, 1938, pp. 470-524.

MANDELBAUM, K., An Experiment in Full Employment controls in the German Economy, 1933-1938, in: Oxford Institute of Statistics, The Economics of Full Employment, Oxford 1944.

MILLER, James W., Pre-War Nazi Agrarian Policy, in: Agricultural History, 15, Oct. 1941, pp. 175-181.

PALYI, Melchior, Economic Foundations of the German Totalitarian State, in: American Journal of Sociology, vol. 46, 1941, pp. 469-486.

PAVLOVSKY, George, The Course of the Agricultural Depression in 1931-1932, in: Monthly Bulletin of Agricultural Economics and Sociology, vol. 24, Jan. 1933, pp. 1-41.

PERTOT, Vladimir, Die Weizenregulierung in Jugoslavien, in: Weltwirtschaftliches Archiv, vol. XLV, 1937.

POSSE, Hans Ernst, Deutschland und der Südosten Europas, in: Deutscher Außenhandel, vol. 36, No. 12, pp. 89-91.

—, Deutsche Außenhandelspolitik, in: Weltwirtschaft, vol. 22, 1934, pp. 44-45.

—, Die Hauptlinien der deutschen Handelspolitik, in: Probleme des deutschen Wirtschaftslebens, Berlin 1937, pp. 481-513.

—, Die Ziele der deutschen Außenwirtschaftspolitik, in: Jahrbuch der nationalsozialistischen Wirtschaft, Munich 1937, pp. 372-381.

—, Die deutsche Wirtschaft. Grundlagen, Aufbau, und Wirtschaftsgründung des nationalsozialistischen Staates, Bd. III, Beitrag 44, Berlin [mid. 1937].

PREDOEHL, A., Die sogenannten Handelshemmisse und der Preisaufbau der Weltwirtschaft, in: Weltwirtschaftliches Archiv III, 1941, pp. 193-222.

RINGER, Alfred, Die deutsche Außenwirtschaft im Jahre 1934, in: Jahrbuch für nationalsozialistische Wirtschaft, Stuttgart 1935, pp. 183ff.

—, Die Entwicklung der deutschen Außenwirtschaft, in: Jahrbuch der nationalsozialistischen Wirtschaft, Munich 1937, pp. 382ff.

RITTER, Karl, Germany's Experience with Clearing Agreements, in: Foreign Affairs, XIV, April 1936, pp. 465-475.

RITTER, Kurt, Les buts de la politique agraire nationale-socialiste, in: Revue Economique International 261, Feb. 1934, pp. 239-254.

ROSENSTEIN-RODAN, P. N., Problems of Industrialization of Eastern and Southeastern Europe, in: Economic Journal Vol. VIII, 1943, pp. 202-211.

SARNOW, Otto, Die Aufgaben der deutschen Handelspolitik im Jahre 1934, in: Deutsche Wirtschafts-Zeitung, vol. 31, 1934, pp. 73-75.

—, Deutschland-Südosteuropa, in: Der Wirtschafts-Ring, vol. 11, No. 1, Jan. 7, 1938.

—, Ziele der Deutschen Handelspolitik und die Deutschen Handelskammern, in: Deutsche Wirtschafts-Zeitung, vol. 31, 1934, pp. 620-622.

SCHILLER, Karl, Meistbegünstigung, Multilateralität und Gegenseitigkeit, in: Weltwirtschaftliches Archiv, vol. 53, 1941, pp. 370-402.

SCHLOTTERER, Gustav, Das Auslandsdeutschtum als Pionier der deutschen Außenwirtschaft, in: Nationale Wirtschaft, vol. 3, 1935, pp. 172-173.

—, Deutscher Außenhandel, in: Westermanns Monatsheft, vol. 160, 1936, pp. 149-152.

SCHNITZLER, Georg von, Germany and World Trade After the War, in: Atlantic Monthly, vol. 165, 1940, pp. 817-821.

SETON-WATSON, Hugh, Jugoslavia and the Axis, in: Spectator, Vol. 162, June 16, 1939, pp. 1027-28.

—, Rumania and the Crisis, in: Spectator, Vol. 163, August 25, 1939, pp. 284-285.

SCHWEITZER, A., The Role of Foreign Trade in the Nazi War Economy, in: Journal of Political Economy, vol. LI, 1943, pp. 322-337.

SOLLHUB, W. A., Conversion of Agricultural Debts in Roumania, in: Economic Journal Vol. 42, Dec. 1932, pp. 588-94.

SPENDER, M., Guns and Carbohydrates, in: Spectator, vol. 158, April 9, 1937, pp. 657-8; April 30, 1937, p. 810.

STEERE, Lloyd, German Agriculture in the Four Year Plan, in: Foreign Agriculture, I, March 1937, pp. 103-118.

STRAUSS, Frederick, The Food Problem in the German War Economy, in: Quarterly Journal of Economics, vol. LV, May 1941, pp. 364-412.

WAGEMANN, Ernst, Das Devolationsproblem, in: Wochenbericht des Instituts für Konjunkturforschung, vol. 4, 1931, pp. 145-150.

WARRINER, Doreen, The Population Question in Eastern Europe, in: Slavonic Review, vol. 16, 1937-38, pp. 628-637.

WASLEY, K. T., Germany Agriculture: The Drive For Self-Sufficiency, in: The Contemporary Review, CLVII, March 1940, pp. 334-340.

WISKEMANN, Elizabeth, Yugoslavia and the Anschluß, in: Contemporary Review, 1935, pp 46-54.

—, Yugoslavia and the Axis, in: Spectator, Vol. 162, April 18, 1939, pp. 701-702.

—, Yugoslavia Since Marseilles, in: Political Quarterly, Vol. 6, July 1935, pp. 369-378.

WOHLTHAT, Helmuth, Deutschlands Zahlungsverkehr mit den Staaten Südosteuropas, in: Der Wirtschafts-Ring, vol. 11, No. 1, Jan. 7, 1938.

—, Devisenbewirtschaftung und zwischenstaatlicher Zahlungsverkehr, in: Grundlagen, Aufbau, und Wirtschaftsordnung des nationalsozialistischen Staates, Bd. III, Beitrag 54, Berlin [1937].

—, Der neue deutsch-rumänische Wirtschaftsvertrag, in: Vierjahresplan, vol. 3, 1939, pp. 560-563.

—, Großräume und Meistbegünstigung, in: Deutsche Volkswirtschaft, 1938/39.

WYNN, A., Notes on German Agriculture, in: Economic Journal, Vol. 43, Sept. 1933, pp. 518-24.

YATES, P. L., The German Food Problem, in: Political Quarterly, vol. 7, Jan. 1936, pp. 33-48.

VIII. POST WORLD WAR II (Books)

ADAMTHWAITE, Anthony, France and the Coming of the Second World War, London 1977.

ASTER, Sidney, 1939: The Making of the Second World War, London 1973.

AVRAMOVSKII, Zivko, Balkanske zemlje i velike sile 1935-1937. Od Italijanske Agresije Na Etiopiju do Jugoslovensko-Italijanskog Paktu, Belgrad 1968.

BAAR, Stefan, Die Jugoslawienpolitik des faschistischen deutschen Imperialismus in der Zeit von 1935 bis zum 6. April 1941, Diss. Leipzig 1968.

BANDERA, V. M., Foreign Capital as an Instrument of National Economic Policy, The Hague 1964.

BAY, Achim, Der nationalsozialistische Gedanke der Großraumwirtschaft und seine ideologischen Grundlagen, Diss. Erlangen-Nürnberg 1962.

BECHTEL, Heinrich, Wirtschaftsgeschichte Deutschlands im 19. und 20. Jahrhundert, Munich 1956.

BENNET, Edward W., Germany and the Diplomacy of the Financial Crisis, 1931, Cambridge/Massachusetts 1962.

BEREND, Ivan. T, and György RANKI, Economic Development in East-Central Europe in the 19th and 20th Centuries, New York 1974.

—, Hungary: A Century of Economic Development, New York 1974.

—, Magyarrorszag a Fasiszta Nemetorszag "Elettereben" 1933-1939, Budapest 1960.

BERNHARDT, Walter, Die deutsche Aufrüstung 1934-1939. Militärische und politische Konzeptionen und ihre Einschätzung durch die Alliierten, Frankfurt/Main 1969.

BIBER, Dusan Nacizem in Nemci v Jugoslaviji 1933-1941, Ljubljana 1966.

BIRKENFELD, Wolfgang, Der synthetische Treibstoff 1933-1945, Göttingen 1964.

BORN, Karl Erich, Die deutsche Bankenkrise 1931, Munich 1967.

BRAUSCHE, Gerd, Deutschland-Ungarn. Die diplomatischen Beziehungen vom Herbst 1937 bis Frühjahr 1939, Diss. Göttingen 1956.

BREYER, Richard, Das Deutsche Reich und Polen 1932-1937, Außenpolitik und Volksgruppenfragen, Würzburg 1955.

BROOK, Shepard Gordon, Anschluss; The Rape of Austria, London 1963.

BROSZAT, Martin, Zweihundert Jahre deutsche Polenpolitik, Munich 1963.

BRUEGEL, Johann W., Tschechen und Deutsche, 1918-1938, Munich 1967.

BRY, Gerhard, Wages in Germany 1871-1945, Princeton 1960.

BUDUROWYEZ, B. B., Polish-Soviet Relations, 1932-1939, New York 1962.

CAMERON, Norman and R. H. STEVENS (eds.), Hitler's Secret Conversations, New York 1961.

CAMPUS, Eliza, Mica Intelegere, Bucharest 1968.

CARMI, Ozer, La Grande-Bretagne et la Petite Entente, Geneva 1972.

CARR, William, Arms, Autarchy, and Agression, London 1972.

CARROLL, Bernice A., Design for Total War: Arms and Economics in the Third Reich, The Hague 1968.

CELOVSKY, Boris, Das Münchener Abkommen, 1938, Berlin 1958.

CHILD, Frank C,. The Theory and Practice of Exchange Control in Germany. A Study of Monopolistic Exploitation in International Markets, Den Haag 1958.

CIENCIALA, Anna, Poland and the Western Powers, Toronto 1968.

CONSTANTINESCU, N. N., Contribuţii la istoria capitalului străin în Romania, Bucharest 1960.

—, Studii privind istoria economică a Romaniei, Bucharest 1961.

—, and V. AXENCIUE. Capitalismul monopolist în Romania, Bucharest 1962.

—, and O. CONSTANTINESCU, Cu privire la problema revoluţiei iin Romania, Bucharest 1957.

CRAIG, Gordon and Felix GILBERT (eds.), The Diplomats, 1919-1939, Princeton 1953.

DEBICKI, Roman, Foreign Policy of Poland, 1919-1939, New York 1962.

DENNE, Ludwig, Das Danzig Problem in der deutschen Außenpolitik, 1934-1939, Bonn 1959.

DIMITRIJEVIĆ, Sergije, Das ausländische Kapital in Jugoslavien vor dem Zweiten Weltkrieg, Berlin 1963.

DIMITROFF, Dimiter, Der Außenhandel als Faktor zur Förderung der Wirtschaft in kapitalarmen Ländern, mit besonderer Berücksichtigung der Balkanländer, besonders Bulgariens, Diss. Wien 1946.

DOERING, Dörte, Deutsche Außenwirtschaftspolitik, 1933-1935, Diss. Free University of Berlin 1969.

DUBAIL, René, Une experience d'économie dirigée, Paris 1962.

DUBOIS, J. E., The Devils' Chemists, 24 Conspirators of the International Farben Cartel who Manufactured Wars, Boston 1952.

EBEL, Arnold, Das Dritte Reich und Argentinien. Die diplomatischen Beziehungen unter besonderer Berücksichtigung der Handelspolitik, Köln 1971.

EICHHOLTZ, Dietrich, Geschichte der deutschen Kriegswirtschaft, 1939-1945, vol. I, Berlin 1969.

EMESSEN, T. R. (ed.), Aus Görings Schreibtisch: Ein Dokumentenfund, Berlin 1947.

ERBE, René, Die nationalsozialistische Wirtschaftspolitik 1933-1939 im Lichte der moderne Theorie, Zürich 1958.

FATU, Mihai, Garda de Fier, organizaţie teroristă de tip fascist, Bucharest 1971.

FISCHER, Peter, Wirtschaftsprobleme des Donauraums in der Zwischenkriegszeit, Diss. Graz 1955.

FISCHER, Wolfram, Deutsche Wirtschaftspolitik 1918-1945, Opladen 1968.

GEHL, Jürgen, Austria, Germany and the Anschluss, 1931-1938, Oxford 1963.

GHEORGHE, Jon, Rumäniens Weg zum Satellitenstaat, Heidelberg 1952.

GREER, Johann Sebastian, Der Markt der geschlossenen Nachfrage: Eine morphologische Studie über die Eisenkontingentierung in Deutschland, Berlin 1961.

GROTKROP, W., Die große Krise, Düsseldorf 1954.

GRUCHMANN, Lothar, Nationalsozialistische Großraumordnung, Stuttgart 1962.

HELBICH, Wolfgang J., Die Reparationen in der Ära Brüning, Berlin 1962.

HENKE, Josef, England in Hitlers politischem Kakül, 1935-1939, Boppard am Rhein 1973.

HILDEBRAND, Klaus, Deutschlands Rolle in der Vorgeschichte der beiden Weltkriege, Göttingen 1967.

HILLGRUBER, Andreas, Hitler, König Carol und Marschall Antonescu. Die deutsch-rumänischen Beziehungen, 1938-1944, Wiesbaden 1954.

—, Probleme des Zweiten Weltkrieges, Cologne 1967.

HOEFT, Klaus, Zur Agrarpolitik des deutschen Imperialismus von 1933 bis zur Gegenwart, Berlin 1960.

HOENSCH, Jörg, Die Slowakei und Hitlers Ostpolitik, Cologne 1965.

HOPTNER, Jacob, Yugoslavia in Crisis 1934-1941, New York 1962.

HORAK, Stephan, Poland's International Affairs, 1919-1960, Bloomington/Indiana 1964.

JAEGER, Jörg-Johannes, Die wirtschaftliche Abhangigkeit des Dritten Reiches vom Ausland dargestellt am Beispiel der Stahlindustrie, Berlin 1969.

KIMMICH, Christoph M., The Free City: Danzig and German Foreign Policy, 1919-1934, New Haven/Connecticut 1968.

KISZLING, Rudolf, Die militärischen Vereinbarungen der Kleinen Entente, 1929-1937, Munich 1959.

KLEIN, Burton H., Germany's Economic Preparations for War, Cambridge/Massachusetts 1959.

KOEBEL, Josef, Poland Between East and West: Soviet and German Diplomacy Toward Poland, 1919-1933, Princeton/New Jersey 1963.

KOMJATHY, Anthony, The Crises of France's East Central European Diplomacy, 1933-1938, East European Monograph No. XXI, Boulder/Colorado 1976.

KRISCHAN, Alexander, Österreichs Außenhandel mit den Südostländern von der Weltwirtschaftskrise bis zum Umbruch, Diss. Vienna 1950.

KUEHL, Joachim, Föderationspläne im Donauraum und in Ostmitteleuropa, Munich 1958.

KUHN, Axel, Hitlers außenpolitisches Programm. Ensthehung und Entwicklung, 1919-1939, Stuttgart 1970.

LANDAU, Zbigniew und Jerzy TOMASZEWSKI, Kapitaly obc w Polsce 1918-1939, Warsaw 1964.

LAPP, Klaus, Die Finanzierung der Weltkriege 1914-1918 und 1939-1945 in Deutschland, Diss. Nürnberg 1957.

LEXKES, Rolf, Die äußere Wirtschaftspolitik Rumäniens von 1919-1938, Diss. Vienna 1952.

LOCHNER, Louis, Herbert Hoover and Germany, New York 1960.

—, Tyrants and Tycoons: German Industry From Hitler to Adenauer, Chicago 1954.

LUEKE, Rolf, Von der Stabilisierung zur Krise, Zürich 1958.

LUETGE, Friedrich, Deutsche Sozial- und Wirtschaftsgeschichte, Berlin 1952.

MACARTNEY, C. A., October Fifteenth. A History of Modern Hungary, 1929-1945, 2 vols., Edinburgh 1956-1959.

— and A. W. PALMER, Independent Eastern Europe. A History, London 1962.

MCSHERRY, James, Stalin, Hitler and Europe: Vol. I, The Origins of World War II, Cleveland 1968.

MADAJCZYK, Czeslaw, Die deutsche Besatzungspolitik in Polen (1939-1945), Wiesbaden 1967.

MALENBAUM, Wilfred, The World Wheat Economy, 1885-1939, Cambridge/Massachusetts 1953.

MAMATEY, Victor S., The United States and East Central Europe, 1914-1918, Cambridge 1957.

MASCHKE, Erich, Es entsteht ein Konzern, Paul Reusch und die GHH, Tübingen 1969.

MARGUERAT, Philippe, Le IIIème Reich et le pétrole roumain, Leiden 1977.

MEINCK, G., Hitler und die deutsche Aufrüstung, 1933-37, Wiesbaden 1959.

MEISS, Klaus-Dietrich, Die deutsch-jugoslawischen Beziehungen von Hitlers Regierungsantritt bis zum Ausbruch des 2. Weltkriegs, Diss. Göttingen 1955.

MENZE, Otto, Deutsch-österreichische Anschlußversuche vor 1933, Diss. Freiburg i. Br. 1957.

MIEGE, Wolfgang, Das Dritte Reich und die deutsche Volksgruppe in Rumänien, 1933-1938. Ein Beitrag zur national-sozialistischen Volkstumspolitik, Frankfurt/Main 1972.

MIELCKE, Karl, Nationalsozialistische Außenpolitik 1933-1939, Alfeld 1961.

MILWARD, Alan S., The German Economy at War, London 1965.

MIRKOVIĆ, M., Ekonomska Historija Jugoslavije, Zagreb 1958.

MOISIUC, Viorica, Diplomaţia României şi problema apărării suveranităţii şi independenţei naţionale în perioada martie 1938 — mai 1940, Bucharest 1971.

NEWMAN, William, The Balance of Power in the Interwar Years, 1919-1939, New York 1968.

OBERMANN, Karl and Josef POLISENSKY (eds.). Die Hintergründe des Münchener Abkommens von 1938, Berlin 1959.

OFFNER, Arnold, American Appeasement. United States Foreign Policy and Germany, 1933-1938, Cambridge/Massachusetts 1969.

OLSHAUSEN, Klaus, Zwischenspiel auf dem Balkan. Die deutsche Politik gegenüber Jugoslawien und Griechenland von März bis Juli 1941, Stuttgart 1973.

OPREA. I. M., Nicolae Titulescu's Diplomatic Activity, Bucharest 1968.

ORLOW, Dietrich, The Nazis in the Balkans, Pittsburgh 1968.

PAIKERT, G. C., The Danube Swabians: German Populations in Hungary, Rumania, and Yugoslavia and Hitler's Impact on Their Patterns, The Hague 1967.

PETERSON, Edward N., Hjalmar Schacht, For and Against Hitler. A Political Economic Study of Germany 1923-1945, Boston 1954.

PETZINA, Dietmar, Autarkiepolitik im Dritten Reich, Stuttgart 1968.

PIETTRE, André, L'économie allemande contemporaine, Paris 1952.

PIPER, Wolfgang, Grundprobleme des wirtschaftlichen Wachstums in einigen südosteuropäischen Ländern in der Zwischenkriegszeit, Berlin 1961.

POPIŞTEANU, Cristian, România şi Antanta Balcanică, Bucharest 1968.

PREBISCH, R., The Economic Development of Latin America and its Principal Problems, New York 1950.

PREDOEHL, Andreas, Das Ende der Weltwirtschaftskrise, Reinbek bei Hamburg 1962.

PRITZKOLEIT, Kurt, Auf einer Woge von Gold, Munich 1961.

—, Gott erhält die Mächtigen, Düsseldorf 1963.

—, Männer, Mächte, Monopole, Düsseldorf 1953.

—, Wem gehört Deutschland? Vienna/Munich/Basel 1957.

PUCHERT, Berthold, Der Wirtschaftskrieg des deutschen Imperialismus gegen Polen 1925-1934, Berlin 1963.

RADICE, Lisanne, Prelude to Appeasement: East Central European Diplomacy in the Early 1930's, East European Monograph No. LXXX, Boulder/Colorado 1981.

RAUPACH, H., Wirtschaft und Politik in Ost-Europa, Berlin 1968.

REICHERT, Günter, Das Scheitern der Kleine Entente, 1933-1938, Munich 1971.

RICHARDSON, H. W., Economic Recovery in Britain 1932-1939, London 1967.

RIEDEL, Mathias, Eisen und Kohle für das Dritte Reich. Paul Pleigers Stellung in der nationalsozialistischen Wirtschaft, Göttingen 1973.

RIEKHOFF, Harald von, German-Polish Relations, 1918-1933, Baltimore 1971.

ROBERTS, Henry L., Rumania: Political Problems of an Agrarian State, New Haven, Conn., 1951.

ROBERTSON, E.M., Hitler's Pre-War Policy and Military Plans: 1933-1939, London 1963.
ROBERTSON, E. M. (ed.), The Origins of the Second World War, London 1971.
ROCK, William R., Appeasement on Trial, 1938-1939, Hamden, Conn., 1966.
ROENNEFAHRT, Helmut, Die Sudetenkrise in der internationalen Politik, Wiesbaden 1961.
ROOS, Hans, Polen und Europa, Studien zur polnischen Außenpolitik, 1931-1939, Tübingen 1967.
ROOSE, K. D., The Economics of Recession and Revival 1937-38, London 1954.
ROSS, Dieter, Hitler und Dollfuß, Hamburg 1966.

SALVEMINI, Gaetano, Prelude to World War II, Garden City 1954.
SARKOTIC, Erwin, Die wirtschaftlichen Annäherungsversuche in Mitteleuropa zwischen den beiden Weltkriegen, Diss. Innsbruck 1953.
SASULY, Richard, I. G. Farben, New York 1947.
SAVU, Alexandru, Dictatura Regală 1938-1940, Bucharest 1970.
SCHELER, Eberhard, Die politischen Beziehungen zwischen Deutschland und Frankreich Ende 1937 bis zum Kriegsausbruch, Frankfurt 1962.
SCHMELZER, Janis, Unternehmen Südost: Südosteuropa-Pläne der I. G. Farben, Wolfen 1966.
SCHRÖDER, Hans-Jürgen, Deutschland und die Vereinigten Staaten, 1933-1939. Wirtschaft und Politik in der Entwicklung des deutsch-amerikanischen Gegensatzes, Wiesbaden 1970.
SCHUMANN, Wolfgang (ed.), Griff nach Südosteuropa: Neue Dokumente über die Politik des deutschen Imperialismus und Militarismus gegenüber Südosteuropa im Zweiten Weltkrieg, Berlin 1973.
SCHÜRMANN, Hermann, Grundzüge südosteuropäischer Außenwirtschaftspolitik, 1929-1934, Diss. Cologne 1947.
SCHWABE, G., Der deutsch-rumänische Wirtschaftsvertrag vom 23. März 1939, Diss. Humboldt Univ. Berlin 1968.
SCHWEITZER, Arthur, Big Business in the Third Reich, Bloomington 1964.
SCOTT, William E., Alliance against Hitler: The Origin of the Franco-Soviet Pact, Durham/North Carolina 1962.
SEABURY, Paul, The Wilhelmstrasse, Berkeley 1954.
SETON-WATSON, Hugh, Eastern Europe Between the Wars, 1918-1941, Cambridge 1945.
SIEMENS, Georg, Geschichte des Hauses Siemens, Bd. 3 — Die Dämonie des Staates, Munich 1952.
STEVANOVIĆ, Radomir, Der Außenhandel der Balkanländer zwischen den beiden Weltkriegen, Diss. Cologne 1952.
STOLPER, Gustav, Deutsche Wirtschaft, 1870-1914, Stuttgart 1950.
STRANG, Lord, The Moscow Negotiations — 1939, Leeds 1968.
STÜCKEN, R., Deutsche Geld- und Kreditpolitik 1914 bis 1953, Tübingen 1953.
SVENNILSON, Ingvar, Growth and Stagnation in the European Economy, Geneva 1954.

TAYLOR, A. J. P., Origins of the Second World War, London 1961.
TEICHOVA, Alice, An Economic Background to Munich: International Business and Czechoslovakia, 1918-1938, Cambridge 1974.
THOMAS, Georg, Geschichte der deutschen Wehr- und Rüstungswirtschaft (1918-1943/45), Boppard/Rhein 1966.
THORBECKE, Erik, The Tendency towards Regionalization in International Trade, 1928-1956, The Hague 1960.
TREUE, Wilhelm, Deutschland in der Weltwirtschaftskrise — in Augenzeugenberichten, Düsseldorf 1967.
—, Die Feuer verlöschen nie, Düsseldorf 1966.
—, Die Geschichte der Ilseder Hütte, Peine 1960.
—, Gummi in Deutschland. Die deutsche Kautschukversorgung und Gummi-Industrie im Rahmen weltwirtschaftlicher Entwicklungen, Munich 1955.
—, Georg von Giesche's Erben, 1704-1964, Hamburg 1964.

—, Ilseder Hütte, 1858-1958; ein Unternehmen der eisenschaffenden Industrie, Peine 1958.
—, Konzentration und Expansion als Kennzeichen der politischen und wirtschaftlichen Ge-
schichte Deutschlands im 19. und 20. Jahrhundert, Dortmund 1966.
—, Wirtschaft und Politik 1933-1945, Braunschweig 1955.
TURNER, Henry Ashby, Jr., Stresemann and the Politics of the Weimar Republic, Princeton/
New Jersey 1963.

VANDER ESCH, Priscilla, Prelude to War, The Hague 1951.

WAGENFÜHR, Rolf, Die deutsche Industrie im Krieg 1939-1945, Berlin 1963.
WANDYCZ, Piotr, France and Her Eastern Allies 1919-1925: French-Czechoslovak-Polish
Relations from the Paris Peace Conference to Locarno, Minneapolis/Minnesota 1962.
WATKINS, K. W., Britain Divided, London 1963.
WATT, D. C., Personalities and Policies; Studies in the Formulation of British Foreign Policy,
London 1965.
WEINBERG, Gerhard, The Foreign Policy of Hitler's Germany: Diplomatic Revolution in
Europe, 1933-1936, Chicago 1970.
—, The Foreign Policy of Hitler's Germany: Starting World War II, Chicago 1981.
WENDT, Bernd-Jürgen, Appeasement 1938. Wirtschaftliche Rezession und Mitteleuropa,
Frankfurt/Main 1966.
—, Economic Appeasement. Handel und Finanz in der britischen Deutschland-Politik 1933-
1939, Düsseldorf 1971.
—, München 1938, Frankfurt/Main 1965.
WHEELER-BENNET, John W., Munich: Prologue to Tragedy, London 1948.
WOJCIECHOWSKI, Marian, Die polnisch-deutschen Beziehungen, 1933-1938, Leiden 1971.
WOLFE, M., The French Franc Between the Wars, 1919-1939, New York 1951.
WOLFERS, Arnold, Britain and France Between Two Wars, London 1940.
WÜSCHT, Johannes, Jugoslawien und das Dritte Reich, Stuttgart 1968.

ZAGOROFF, S. D., J. BEGH, and A. D. BILLIMOVICH, The Agricultural Economy of the Danu-
bian Countries, 1935-1945, Stamford 1955.
ZAMBONI, Giovanni, Mussolinis Expansionspolitik auf dem Balkan, Hamburg 1970.
ZAUBERMAN, Alfred, Economic Imperialism: The Lesson of Eastern Europe, London 1955.
ZIMMERMANN, Ludwig, Deutsche Außenpolitik in der Ära der Weimarer Republik, Göttingen
1958.

IX. POST WORLD WAR II (Articles)

ADAM, Magda, Les pays danubiens et Hitler (1933-1936), in: Revue d'histoire de la deuxième
guerre mondiale, No. 98, 1975, pp. 11-25.
—, Confederation Danubienne ou Petite Entente. in: Acta Historica (Budapest), vol. 25,
1979, pp. 61-113.
ASENDORF, Manfred, Ulrich von Hassells Europakonzeption und der Mitteleuropäische Wirtschaftstag, in: Jahrbuch des Instituts für deutsche Geschichte, vol. 7, 1978, pp. 387-419.
AXENCIUC, W., La place occupée par la Roumanie dans la division mondiale capitaliste a la
veille de la seconde guerre mondiale, in: Revue Roumaine d'Histoire, 1966.

BARRACLOUGH, Geoffrey, Hitler's Master Builder, in: The New York Review of Books, January 7, 1971, pp. l6-14.
—, Mandarins and Nazis: Part I, in: The New York Review of Books, Oct. 19, 1972, pp.
37-43.
—, The Liberals and German History: Part II, in: The New York Review of Books, Nov. 2,
1972, pp. 32-40.

—, A New View of German History: Part III, in: The New York Review of Books, Nov. 16, 1972, pp. 25-31.

BAUMGART, Winfried, Zur Ansprache Hitlers vor den Führern der Wehrmacht am 22. August 1939, in: Vierteljahreshefte für Zeitgeschichte, vol. 16, 1968, pp.120-149.

BELL, P. M. H., Hitler et les origines de la Seconde Guerre Mondiale, in: Revue d'histoire de la deuxième guerre mondiale, No. 67, July 1967, pp. 1-13.

BENHAM, F., The Muddle of the Thirties, in: Economica, Vol. XIII, new series, 1946, pp. 1-9.

BEREND, Ivan, Contribution to the History of Hungarian Economic Policy in the Two Decades Following WW II, in: Acta Historica (Budapest), vol. 13, No.1-2, 1967, pp. 3-47.

BEREND, Ivan and György RANKI, Capital Accumulation and the Participation of Foreign Capital After the First World War, in: Domel CSARTARI and Laszlo KATUS (eds.), Nouvelles études historique publiées a l'occasion du XIIème Congrès International des Sciences Historiques, Budapest 1966, pp. 269-292.

—, Die deutsche wirtschaftliche Expansion und das ungarische Wirtschaftsleben zur Zeit des Zweiten Weltkrieges, in: Acta Historica, vol. 5, pp. 313-359.

—, German-Hungarian Relations Following Hitler's Rise to Power, in: Acta Historica, vol. 8, 1961, pp. 313-346.

—, The Hungarian Manufacturing Industry 1900-1945, in: Gyula EMBER et al. (eds.), Etudes Historiques Publiées par la Commission Nationale des Historiens Hongrois, vol. 2, Budapest 1960, pp. 421-457.

BEROV, L., Le capital financier occidental et les pays balkaniques dans les années vingt, in: Etudes balkaniques (Sofia) T. II-III (separatum), 1965.

BISHOP, Larry V., England, France and the Rhineland Crisis of 1936, in: Research Studies vol. 34, No. 4, 1966, pp. 219-249.

BLOCH, Charles, La Grande Bretagne face au réarmement allemand et l'accord naval de 1935, in: Revue d'histoire de la deuxième guerre mondiale, No. 63, 1968, pp. 41-68.

—, L'influence reciproque entre la politique interieure et la politique exterieure nationale-socialiste, in: Relations Internationales, No. 4, 1975, pp. 91-109.

BOEHM, Eric, Hitler's Decision to Attack the Soviet Union: The End of the Grand Design, in: Essays in Russian History, Presented to George Vernadsky, Hamden/Connecticut 1964.

BOEHME, K. R., Die deutsch-polnischen Handelsbeziehungen 1923-1933, in: Zeitschrift für Ostforschung, vol. 12, 1963-64, pp. 500-578.

BOELCKE, Willi, Die Waffengeschäfte des Dritten Reiches mit Brasilien, in: Tradition, vol. 16, No. 3/4, pp. 177-200; No. 5/6, pp. 280-288.

BORCHARDT, Knut, Ein neues Urteil über die deutsche Währungs- und Finanzpolitik von 1931 bis 1938, in: Vierteljahrschrift für Sozial- und Wirtschaftsgeschichte, vol. 26, 1959, pp. 526-540.

BOTSAS, E., The Big Powers and Interbalkan Economic Relations, in: East European Quarterly, vol. 12, 1978, pp. 257-282.

BROSZAT, Martin, Deutschland-Ungarn-Rumänien: Entwicklung und Grundfaktoren nationalsozialistischer Hegemonial- und Bündnispolitik, 1938-1941, in: Historische Zeitschrift, vol. 206, No. 1, 1968, pp. 45-96.

—, Faschismus und Kollaboration in Ostmitteleuropa zwischen den Weltkriegen, in: Vierteljahreshefte für Zeitgeschichte, vol. 14, No. 3, 1968, pp. 25-51.

BRUEGEL, J.W., Czechoslovakia Before Munich: The German Minority Problem and British Appeasement, in: Central European History, vol 8., 1975, pp. 73-77.

—, German Diplomacy and the Sudeten Question before 1938, in: International Affairs, vol. 37, No. 3, 1961, pp. 323-331.

BURENS, Peter-Claus, Kontinuität und Wandel der deutschen Ostpolitik seit 1919, in: Zeitgeschichte im Unterricht, vol. 6, 1978-1979, pp. 25-31.

CALAFETANU, I., The Last Conference of the Balkan Entente and the Problem of the Territorial Status Quo in Southeast Europe, in: Revue Roumaine d'Histoire, vol. 19, 1980, pp. 215-227.

CARLSON, Vernon, The Hossbach Memorandum, in: Military Review, vol. 63, August 1983, pp. 14-30.

FEJES-SCHULMANN, Judith Alternativen der ungarischen Außenpolitik während der Weltwirt-schaftskrise, Paper presented at the Mainz Symposium on east-central Europe between the Wars, Mainz, West Germany, December, 1979.
—, On the Question of Hungarian-German Economic and Political Relations at the End of the 1920's and the Beginning of the 1930's (in Hungarian), in: Tortenelmi Szemle, vol. 4, 1976, pp. 769-774.
FLEISSIG, Heywood, War Debts and the Great Depression, in: American Economic Review, vol. 66, No. 2, 1976, pp. 52-58.

GILBERT, Felix, Mitteleuropa — The Final Stage, in: Journal Of Central European Affairs, vol. 7, 1947-48, pp. 58-73.
GROSS, Hermann, Mitteleuropäische Handelspolitik 1890-1938 und der Donauraum, in: Der Donauraum, vol. 7, No. 2/3, 1962, p. 100ff.
GRUENER, Erich, Europa als Schöpfer und Zerstörer des Weltwirtschaftskreislaufes, in: Schweizer Monatshefte für Politik, vol. 48, 1968-69, pp. 258-272.
GROMADA, Thaddeus, Joseph Beck in Light of Recent Polish Historiography, in: Polish Review, vol. 26, No. 3, 1981, pp. 65-73.
GUELICH, Wilhelm, Wirtschaftliche Entwicklung und völkische Eigenständigkeit in Südosteu-ropa, in: Südosteuropa Jahrbuch, vol. 3, 1959, pp. 1-15.

HABERLER, G., Integration and Growth of the World Economy in Historical Perspective, in: American Economic Review, vol. 54, No. 2, 1964, pp. 1-22.
HALLGARTEN, George W. F., Adolf Hitler and German Heavy Industry, 1931-1933, in: Jour-nal of Economic History, vol. 12, No. 3, 1952, p. 22-246.
HEINEMANN, S. L., Constantin von Neurath and German Policy at the London Economic Conference, 1933, in: Journal of Modern History, vol. 41, 1969, pp. 160-88.
HELBICH, Wolfgang J., Between Stresemann and Hitler: The Foreign Policy of the Bruening Government, in: World Politics, vol. 12, 1959, pp. 24-44.
HERZFELD, Hans, Zur Problematik der Appeasement Politik, in: Waldemar BESSON and Friedrich HELLER VON GAETUNGEN (eds.), Geschichte und Gegenwartsbewußtsein. Festschrift für Hans Rothfels, 1963.
HILL, Leonidas, Three Crises, in: Journal of Contemporary History, vol. 3, 1968, pp. 113-144.
HILDEBRAND, Klaus, Hitler's War Aims, in: Journal of Modern History, vol. 48, 1976, pp. 522-543.
HILLGRUBER, Andreas, Quellen und Quellenkritik zur Vorgeschichte des Zweiten Welt-krieges, in: Wehrwissenschaftliche Rundschau, vol. 14, 1964, pp. 110-126.
—, Die Sudetenkrise in der internationalen Politik, in: Wehrwissenschaftliche Rundschau, vol. 11, 1961, pp. 409-414.
HINSLEY, F. H., Review of A. J. P. Taylor, in: Historical Journal, vol. 4, 1961, pp. 222-229.
HOISINGTON, Jr., William A., The Struggle for Economic Influence in Southeastern Europe: the French Failure in Romania, 1940, in: Journal of Modern History, vol. 43, No. 3, Sept. 1971, pp. 468-483.
HOLBORN, Hajo, Origins and Political Character of Nazi Ideology, in: Political Science Quarterly, vol. 79, No. 4, 1964, pp. 542-555.
d'HOOP, Jean Marie, André MEYER, and Oswald HAUSER, Frankreichs Reaktion auf Hitlers Außenpolitik, 1933-1939, in: Geschichte in Wissenschaft und Unterricht, vol.15, No. 4, 1964, pp. 211-223.
HORTHY, Miklos, Horthy's Secret Correspondence with Hitler, in: New Hungarian Quart-erly, vol. 11, 1963, pp. 174-191.
HUGHES, Thomas P., Technological Momentum in History: Hydrogenation in Germany, 1898-1933, in: Past and Present, No. 44, August 1969, pp. 106-132.

JACOBSEN, Hans-Adolf, Les buts et la politique de guerre de Hitler de 1939 a 1943, in: Revue
  d'histoire de la deuxième guerre mondiale, No. 63, 1966, pp. 23-40.
—, Das "Halder-Tagebuch" als historische Quelle, in: Festschrift für Percy Ernst Schramm,
  Wiesbaden 1964, vol. 2, pp. 251-268.
—, The Second World War as a Problem in Historical Research, in: World Politics, vol. 16,
  July 1964, pp. 620-641.
JARAUSCH, Konrad, From Second to Third Reich: The Problem of Continuity in German For-
  eign Policy, in: Central European History, vol. 12, 1979, pp. 68-82.
JAUERNIG, Eduard, Neue tschechoslowakische Quellen und marxistische Forschungen über
  München 1938, in: Zeitschrift für Geschichtswissenschaft, vol. 9, 1961, pp. 668-674.

KALBE, E., Zu den Etappen der Balkanpolitik des faschistischen deutschen Imperialismus, in:
  Revue des études sud-est européenes, vol. 13, No. 3, 1975, pp. 347-351.
KASPAR, H., Das Erdöl in den Raubplänen des deutschen Faschismus in der Vorbereitung und
  bei der Durchführung des Zweiten Weltkrieges, in: Jahrbuch für Wirtschaftsgeschichte,
  vol. 17, No. 3, 1976, pp. 55-77.
KARSAI, Elek (ed.) The Meeting of Goemboes and Hitler in 1933, in: The New Hungarian
  Quarterly, vol. 3, No. 5, 1962, pp. 170-196.
KINDLEBERGER, Charles, German Terms of Trade by Commodity Classes and Areas, in:
  Review of Economics and Statistics, vol. 36, 1954, pp. 167-174.
—, Germany's Overtaking of England, 1806-1914, Parts I and II, in: Weltwirtschaftliches
  Archiv, vol. III, No. 2 and 3, 1975, pp. 253-282, and pp. 477-505.
—, Industrial Europe's Terms of Trade, 1870-1953, in: Economica, vol. 65, 1955, pp. 19-35.
KLEIN, Burton, Germany's Preparation for War: A Reexamination, in: American Economic
  Review, vol. 38, 1948, pp. 56-77.
KLEIN, Fritz, Neue Dokumente zur Rolle Schachts bei der Vorbereitung der Hitlerdiktatur,
  in: Zeitschrift für Geschichtswissenschaft, vol. 5, No. 2, 1957, pp. 818-823.
KLUKE, Paul, Nationalsozialistische Europaideologie, in: Vierteljahreshefte für Zeitge-
  schichte, vol. 3, 1955, pp. 240-275.
—, Politische Form und Außenpolitik des Nationalsozialismus, in: Waldemar BESSON (ed.),
  Geschichte und Gegenwartsbewußtsein, Göttingen 1963, pp. 428-462.
KNAPP, W. F., The Rhineland Crisis of March 1936, St. Anthony's Papers, No. 5, London
  1957.
KOMJATHY, Anthony, The First Vienna Award (November 2, 1938), in: Austrian History
  Yearbook, 15-16, 1979-80, pp. 131-156.
KOZENSKI, Jerzy, Southeastern Europe in Nazi Expansionist Plans, in: Polish Western Affairs,
  vol. 21, 1980, pp. 47-57.
KUHN, Axel, Die Unterredung zwischen Hitler und Papen im Hause des Barons von
  Schröder, in: Geschichte in Wissenschaft und Unterricht, vol. 24, 1973, pp. 709-722.
KUZMANOVA, A., La Roumanie face aux actes agressifs de l'Allemagne et d'Italie (Octobre
  1935-Mars 1936), in: Etudes Balkaniques, No. 2, 1977, pp. 5-19.

LAMPE, John, and Marvin JACKSON, An Appraisal of Recent Balkan Economic Historiography, in: Eastern European Quarterly, vol. 9, No. 2, 1975, pp. 197-240.

MACDONALD, C. A., Economic Appeasement and the German Moderates, 1937-1939, in: Past
  and Present, No. 56, 1972, pp. 103-135.
McKIBBIN, R. I., The Myth of the Unemployed: Who Did Vote for the Nazis? in: Australian
  Journal of Politics and History, August 1969.
MADAJCZYK, Czeslaw, War Economic Preparations of the Third Reich, in: Acta Polonica His-
  torica, vol. 10, 1964, pp.81-92.
MAIER, Charles, The Truth About the Treaties, in: Journal of Modern History, vol. 51, No. 1,
  March 1979, pp. 56-67.

MARGUERAT, Philippe, Le protectionisme financier allemand et le Bassin Danubien à la veille de la Seconde Guerre Mondiale: L'Exemple de la Roumanie, in: Relations Internationales, No. 16, 1978, pp. 351-364.

MASON, Timothy W., Innere Krise und Angriffskrieg 1938/1939, in: Friedrich FORSTMEIER and Hans-Erich VOLKMANN, Wirtschaft und Rüstung am Vorabend des Zweiten Weltkrieges, Düsseldorf 1975, pp. 158-189.

—, Some Origins of the Second World War, in: Past and Present, No. 29, 1964.

MARCZEWSKI, Jerzy, The Nazi Concept of "Drang nach Osten" and the Basic Premises of the Occupation Policy in the "Polish Question", in: Polish Western Affairs, No. 2, 1967.

MARZARI, Frank, Projects for an Italian and Balkan Bloc of Neutrals. Sept.-Dec. 1939, in: Historical Journal, vol. XIII, 4, 1970, pp. 767-788.

MITROVIĆ, Andreij, "Ergänzungswirtschaft. Eine Theorie über den gemeinsamen Wirtschaftsraum des Dritten Reiches und Südosteuropa", in: Jugoslov. ist. casopis, vol. 13, No. 3-4, 1974, pp. 5-42.

MILWARD, Alan S., Der Einfluß ökonomischer und nicht-ökonomischer Faktoren auf die Strategie des Blitzkrieges, in: Friedrich FORSTMEIER and Hans-Erich VOLKMANN (eds.), Wirtschaft und Rüstung am Vorabend des Zweiten Weltkrieges, Düsseldorf 1975, pp. 189-202.

—, The End of the Blitzkrieg, in: Economic History Review, 2nd ser., vol. 16, 1963, pp. 499-518.

—, Fritz Todt als Minister für Bewaffnung und Munition, in: Vierteljahreshefte für Zeitgeschichte vol. 14, No. 1, 1966, pp. 40-58.

MOISIUC, Viorica, Actiuni diplomatice desfăsurate după Anschluss împotriva expansiunii Germanie hitleriste spre sud-estul Europei, in: Studii, vol. XIX, 1966, pp. 707-722.

—, Unele date noi cu privire la situaţia maselor populare in perioada, 1938-1940, in: Studii, vol. XVII, 1964, pp. 1325-1339.

—, Orientations dans la politique exterieure de la Roumanie après le pacte de Munich, in: Revue Roumaine d'histoire, vol. V, 1966, pp. 327-340.

—, Tratatul economic Romano-German din 23 Martie şi semnificaţia sa, in: Analele Institutului de Studii Istorice si Social-Politice de pe Cînga C.C. al P.C.R., vol. XIII, 1967, pp. 130-146.

MOLTMANN, Günther, Weltherrschaftsideen Hitlers, in: Otto BRÜNER and Dietrich GERHARD (eds.), Europa und Übersee, Hamburg 1961, pp. 197-241.

MONTIAS, John M., Rumania's Foreign Trade in the Post-War Period, in: Slavic Review, vol. 25, 1966, p. 421ff.

NEWMAN, Michael, The Origins of Munich: British Policy in Danubian Europe 1933-1937, in: Historical Journal, vol. 21, 1978, pp. 371-386.

NOETEL, R., International Capital Movements and Finance in Eastern Europe 1919-1949, in: Vierteljahrschrift für Sozial- unnd Wirtschaftsgeschichte, vol. 61, 1974.

NOLTE, Ernst, Big Business and German Politics, in: American Historical Review, vol.75, No. 1, Oct. 1969, pp. 71-79.

ORMOS, M. Sz., Sur les causes de l'échec du pacte danubien (1934-1935), in: Acta Historica, vol. 14, 1968, pp. 21-81.

OLDSON, William, Romania and the Munich Crisis August-September 1938, in: East European Quarterly, vol. 11, No. 2, 1977, pp. 177-190.

OVERY, R. J., Transportation and Rearmament in the Third Reich. Historical Journal vol. XVI, 2, 1973, pp. 389-409.

—, Hitler's War and the German Economy: A Reinterpretation, in: Economic History Review, series 2, vol. 35, 1982, pp. 272-291.

—, Goering's "Multi-National Empire", in: Alice TEICHOVA and P.L. COTTRELL (eds.), International Business and Central Europe, 1918-1939, New York 1983, pp. 269-308.

PETZINA, Dietmar, Germany and the Great Depression, in: Journal of Contemporary History, vol. 4, October 1969, pp. 59-74.

—, I. G. Farben und nationalsozialistische Autarkiepolitik, in: Tradition, 1968.

—, Vierjahresplan und Rüstungspolitik, in: Friedrich FORSTMEIER and Hans-Erich VOLK-MANN (eds.), Wirtschaft und Rüstung am Vorabend des Zweiten Weltkrieges, Düsseldorf 1975, pp. 65-81.

PETZOLD, Joachim, Zur Kontinuität der Balkanpolitik des deutschen Imperialismus in der Zeit der Weimarer Republik, in: Geschichte der sozialistischen Länder Europas, vol. 19, 1975, pp. 173-182.

POULAIN, Marc, Deutschlands Drang Nach Osten contra Mussolinis Hinterlandpolitik, in: Der Donauraum, vol. 22, 1977, pp. 129-153.

PERTOT, Vladimir, Die langfristigen Tendenzen in der regionalen Orientierung des Außenhandels Jugoslawiens, in: Rudolf VOGEL (ed.), Südosteuropa: Gedenkschrift für Wilhelm Gülich, Munich 1961, pp. 492-543.

PUCHERT, Berthold, Die deutsch-polnische Nichtangriffserklärung und die Außenwirtschaftspolitik des deutschen Imperialismus gegenüber Polen bis 1939, in: Jahrbuch für die Geschichte der UdSSR und der volksdemokratischen Länder Europas, vol. 12, 1968, pp.339-354.

—, Die Handelsbeziehungen des Deutschen Reiches zu Rumänien zwischen den beiden Weltkriegen, in: Jahrbuch für Wirstschaftsgeschichte, No. 3, 1983, pp. 51-76.

QUINLAN, Paul, The Tilea Affair: a Further Inquiry, in: Balkan Studies, vol. 19, 1978, pp. 147-157.

RANKI, György, Die Forschungsarbeit der ungarischen Historiker auf dem Gebiet der Neuen Geschichte Ungarns, in: Österreichische Osthefte, vol. 8, 1966, pp. 392-402.

—, The German Occupation of Hungary, in: Acta Historica, vol. 11, 1965, pp. 261-283.

—, The Great Powers and the Economic Reorganziation of the Danube Valley after World War I, in: Acta Historica, vol. 27, No. 1/2, 1981, pp. 63-97.

—, L'Occupation de la Hongrie par les Allemands 1943-1944, in: Revue d'histoire de la deuxième guerre mondiale, vol. 16, No. 62, 1966, pp. 37-52.

—, Orientamento per una valutazione del Fascismo in Ungheria e nei paesi dell'Europa Orientale, in: Revista Storica del Socialismo, vol. 7, No. 21, 1964, pp. 143-161.

—, Il Patto Tripartito de Roma e la Politica Estera della Germania (1934), in: Studi Storici, vol. 3, No. 2, 1962, pp. 343-375.

—, Problems of the Development of Hungarian Industry, in: Journal of Economic History, vol. 24, No. 2, 1964, pp. 204-228.

—, Surmounting the Economic Crisis in Southeast Europe in the 1930's, in: Acta Historica, vol. 27, 1981, pp. 499-523.

RAUPACH, Hans, The Impact of the Great Depression in Eastern Europe, in: Journal of Contemporary History, vol. 4, No. 4, 1969.

REYNOLDS, P. A., Hitler's War. History, vol. 46, 1961, pp. 212-217.

SAUER, Wolfgang, National Socialism: Totalitarianism or Fascism, in: American Historical Review, vol. LXXIII, 1967.

SCHMELZER, Janis, Europapatent — Ein I. G. Farben Projekt zur Neuordnung Europas (1939-1945), in: Studia Historiae Oeconomicae, vol. 6, 1971.

SCHMITT, Bernadette E., After Munich, in: The Fashion and Future of History (Cleveland/Ohio), 1960, pp. 151-154.

SCHOENFELD, Roland, Deutsche Rohstoffsicherungspolitik in Jugoslawien, 1934-1944, in: Vierteljahrshefte für Zeitgeschichte, vol. 24, 1976, pp. 215-258.

—, Die Balkanländer in der Weltwirtschaftskrise, in: Vierteljahrschrift für Sozial- und Wirtschaftsgeschichte, vol. 62, 1972, pp. 179-214.

—, Exportförderung und Verrechnungsprobleme im deutsch-ungarischen Handel während der

Weltwirtschaftskrise, in: Südost-Forschungen, vol. 42, 1983, pp. 231-280.

SCHRÖDER, Hans-Jürgen, Deutsche Südosteuropapolitik 1926-1936. Zur Kontinuität deutscher Außenpolitik in der Weltwirtschaftskrise, in: Geschichte und Gesellschaft. vol. 2, 1976, pp. 5-32.

—, Südosteuropa als Informal Empire. Das Beispiel Jugoslawiens, in: Jahrbücher für die Geschichte Osteuropas, Bd. 23, 1975, pp. 70-97.

—, Die neue deutsche Südamerikapolitik, in: Jahrbuch für die Geschichte ... Lateinamerikas, vol. 6, 1969, pp. 337-452.

—, Economic Appeasement: Zur britischen und amerikanischen Deutschlandpolitik vor dem zweiten Weltkrieg, in: Vierteljahrshefte für Zeitgeschichte, vol. 30, 1982, pp. 82-97.

—, German Southeast European Policy and the Reaction of the Anglo-Saxon Powers 1929-1933/34 (in Serbo-Croat with German summary), in: Jugoslov. ist. casopis, No. 3/4, 1980, pp. 289-307.

SCHWEITZER, Arthur, Business Power under the Nazi Regime, in: Zeitschrift für Nationalökonomie, vol. 20, pp.414-42.

—, Business Policy in a Dictatorship, in: Business History Review, 38, pp. 413-438.

—, Die wirtschaftliche Wiederaufrüstung Deutschlands, in: Zeitschrift für die gesamte Staatswissenschaft, vol. 114, 1948, p. 599ff.

—, Der ursprüngliche Vierjahresplan, in: Jahrbücher für Nationaloekonomie und Statistik, vol. 114, No. 4, 1958, pp. 594-637.

—, Foreign Exchange Crisis of 1936, in: Zeitschrift für die gesamte Staatswissenschaft, vol. 118, 1962, pp. 243-277.

SCHUMANN, Wolfgang, Die "Neuordnungs"-Pläne des faschistischen deutschen Imperialismus in Europa, in: Bulletin — Arbeitskreis Zweiter Weltkrieg, DA Wiss., Zentralinstitut für Geschichte, No. 3/4, 1971, pp. 7-41.

SILBERSCHMIDT, Max, Die Weltwirtschaftskrise, 1929-1931, Festschrift Hans von Greyerz, Bern 1967, pp. 651-669.

SINGER, H. W., The Distribution of Gains Between Investing and Borrowing Countries, in: The American Economic Review, May 1950.

SOHN-RETHEL, Alfred, Die politischen Büros der deutschen Großindustrie, in: Blick in die Welt, No. 15, 1948 (ed. J. S. C. Branch Control Commission for Germany, British Forces, Hamburg).

SONTAG, R. J., The Last Months of Peace, 1939, in: Foreign Affairs, vol. 35, April 1954, pp. 508-524.

—, The Origins of the Second World War, in: American Historical Review, vol. 67, No. 4, 1962, pp. 992-994.

-, The Origins of the Second World War, in: Review of Politics, vol. 25, 1963.

SPENCER, Frank, The publication of material from the British and German diplomatic archives for the period of the inter-war years, in: History, vol. 47, No. 161, 1962, pp. 254-286.

SPIRA, Thomas, Hungary and the Little Entente: The Failed Rapprochement of 1937, in: Südostforschungen, vol. 40, 1981, pp. 144-163.

STEGMANN, Dirk, Zum Verhältnis von Großindustrie und Nationalsozialismus 1930-1933, in: Archiv für Sozialgeschichte, vol. 13, 1973, pp. 399-482.

—, "Mitteleuropa" 1925-1934. Zum Problem der Kontinuität deutscher Außenpolitik von Stresemann bis Hitler, in: Schriftenreihe des Forschungsinstituts der Friedrich Ebert Stiftung, No. 137, 1979, pp. 203-221.

STOKES, Geoffrey, "More Unfinished Business?" Some Comments on the Evolution of the Nazi Foreign Policy Programme, 1919-1924, in: European Studies Review, vol. 8, pp. 425-442.

SUNDHAUSSEN, Holm, Politisches und wirtschaftliches Kalkül in den Auseinandersetzungen über die deutsch-rumänischen Präferenzvereinbarungen von 1931, in: Revue des Etudes Sud-Est Européennes, vol. XIV. No. 3, 1976, pp. 1-20.

—, Die Weltwirtschaftskrise im Donau-Balkan-Raum und ihre Bedeutung für den Wandel der deutschen Außenpolitik unter Brüning, in: Aspekte deutscher Außenpolitik im 20. Jahrhundert: Aufsätze Hans Rothfels zum Gedächtnis, Stuttgart 1976, pp. 121-165.

TEICHOVA, Alice, Die deutsch-britischen Wirtschaftsinteressen in Mittelost- und Südosteu-
ropa am Vorabend des Zweiten Weltkrieges, in: Friedrich FORSTMEIER and Hans-Erich
VOLKMANN (eds.), Wirtschaft und Rüstung am Vorabend des Zweiten Weltkrieges,
Düsseldorf 1975, pp. 275-296.

TREVOR-ROPER, Hugh R., Hitlers Kriegsziele, in: Vierteljahrshefte für Zeitgeschichte, vol. 8,
1960.

TREUE, Wilhelm, Das Dritte Reich und die Westmächte auf dem Balkan, in: Vierteljahrshefte
für Zeitgeschichte, vol. 1, 1953, pp. 45-64.

TURNER, Henry Ashby, Jr., Big Business and the Rise of Hitler, in: American Historical
Review, vol.75, No. 1, Oct. 1969, pp. 56-71.

—, Großunternehmertum und Nationalsozialismus, in: Historische Zeitschrift, vol. 221, 1975,
pp. 18-69.

—, Hitler's Secret Pamphlet for Industrialists, 1927, in: Journal of Modern History, Sept.
1968.

—, Hitler's Einstellung zu Wirtschaft und Gesellschaft vor 1933, in: Geschichte und Gesellschaft, vol. 2, 1976, pp. 89-117.

VANKU, Milan, La lutte de la Petite Entente contre le revisionisme et le revanchisme, 1920-
1938, in: Revue des études sud-est européene, vol. 14, No. 3, 1976, pp. 425-438.

VUCO, Nikola, La crise agricole en Yougoslavie, 1930-1934, in: Studia Historiae Oeconomicae (Posnan), vol. 7, 1972, pp. 159-169.

WATT, D. C., Diplomatic History, 1930-1939, in: New Cambridge Modern History, vol. 12,
rev. ed. 1968, pp. 684-735.

—, The German Diplomats and Nazi Leaders, 1933-1939, in: Journal of Central European
Affairs, vol.15, No. 2, 1955, pp. 148-160.

WEBSTER, Charles, Munich Reconsidered, in: International Affairs, vol. 37, No. 2, 1961, pp.
137-153.

WEHLER, Hans-Ulrich. Reichsfestung Belgrad: Nationalsozialistische Raumordnung in
Südosteuropa, in: Vierteljahreshefte für Zeitgeschichte, vol.11, 1963, pp. 72-84.

WEINBERG, Gerald L., The Defeat of Germany in 1918 and the European Balance of Power,
in: Central European History, Sept. 1969.

—, The May Crisis, 1938, in: Journal of Modern History vol. 24, Sept. 1957.

—, German Foreign Policy and Poland, 1937-1938, in: Polish Review, vol. 20, No. 1, 1975,
pp. 5-29.

—, German Colonial Plans and Policies 1938-1942, in: Waldemar BESSON (ed.), Geschichte
und Gegenwartsbewußtsein, Göttingen 1963, pp. 462-492.

—, Hitler's Image of the United States, in: American Historical Review, vol. 69, No. 4, 1964,
pp. 1006-1021.

WENDT, Berndt-Jürgen, Der blockierte Dialog: Neuere Literatur zu den deutsch-englischen
Beziehungen in den 30er Jahren, in: Militärische Mitteilungen, vol. 17, No. 1, 1975, pp.
201-211.

—, England und der deutsche "Drang nach Südosten". Kapitalbeziehungen und Warenverkehr in Südosteuropa zwischen den Weltkriegen, in: Imanuel GEIS and Bernd-Jürgen
WENDT (eds.), Deutschland in der Weltpolitik des 19. und 20. Jahrhunderts, Fritz Fischer
zum 65. Geburtstag, Düsseldorf 1973, pp. 483-512.

—, Strukturbedingungen der britischen Südosteuropapolitik am Vorabend des Zweiten Weltkrieges. in: Friedrich FORSTMEIER and Hans-Erich VOLKMANN, (eds.), Wirtschaft und
Rüstung am Vorabend des Zweiten Weltkrieges, Düsseldorf 1975, pp. 296-308.

WENGST, Udo, Der Reichsverband der Deutschen Industrie in den ersten Monaten des Dritten Reiches, in: Vierteljahrshefte für Zeitschichte, vol. 28, 1980, pp. 94-110.

WILLIAMS, T. Desmond, The Historiography of World War II, in: Historical Studies I: Papers
read before the Second Irish Conference of Historians, 1958.

—, Negotiations Leading to the Anglo-Polish Agreement of 31 March 1939, in: Irish Historical Studies, vol. 10, 1957, pp. 59-93, 156-192.

WINCHESTER, Betty Jo, Hungary and the Austrian Anschluss, in: East European Quareterly, vol. 10, No. 4, 1976, pp. 407-425.

ZAHARIA, G. and I. CALAFENTEANU, The International Situation and Romania's Foreign Policy between 1938 and 1940, in: Revue Roumaine d'Histoire, vol. 18, No. 1, 1979, pp. 83-105.

ZIEBURA, Gilbert, Die Krise des internationalen Systems 1935, in: Historische Zeitschrift, vol.203, No. 1, 1966, pp. 90-98.